SPACES, JOURNEYS AND NEW HORIZONS
FOR POSTGRADUATE SUPERVISION

EDITORS

ELI BITZER
LIEZEL FRICK
MAGDA FOURIE-MALHERBE
KIRSI PYHÄLTÖ

Spaces, journeys and new horizons for postgraduate supervision

Published by AFRICAN SUN MeDIA under the SUN PReSS imprint.

All rights reserved

Copyright © 2018 AFRICAN SUN MeDIA and the contributing authors

This publication was subjected to an independent double-blind peer evaluation by the Publisher.

The authors and the publisher have made every effort to obtain permission for and acknowledge the use of copyrighted material. Please refer enquiries to the publisher.

No part of this book may be reproduced or transmitted in any form or by any electronic, photographic or mechanical means, including photocopying and recording on record, tape or laser disk, on microfilm, via the Internet, by e-mail, or by any other information storage and retrieval system, without prior written permission by the publisher.

Views expressed in this publication do not necessarily reflect those of the publisher.

First edition 2018

ISBN 978-1-928357-80-3
ISBN 978-1-928357-81-0 (e-book)
DOI: 10.18820/9781928357810

Set in Futura Lt BT 10.25/14.5 pt

Cover design and typesetting by **AFRICAN SUN MeDIA**

SUN PReSS is an imprint of AFRICAN SUN MeDIA. Scholarly, professional and reference works are published under this imprint in print and electronic format. This publication may be ordered directly from www.sun-e-shop.co.za.

Produced by AFRICAN SUN MeDIA

www.africansunmedia.co.za
africansunmedia.snapplify.com (e-books)
www.sun-e-shop.co.za

ACKNOWLEDGEMENTS

The volume editors are pleased to acknowledge the different authors who contributed to this book and made its publication possible. Those colleagues who acted as reviewers of chapters as well as those who reviewed the completed manuscript are also sincerely thanked for their contributions and valuable comments. As always, Ella Belcher deserves an editor's Golden Globe for the meticulous language editing of the manuscript and we also want to thank the publisher, AFRICAN SUN MeDIA and Emily Vosloo, for her highly appreciated support in making this contributed book possible. Last, but not least, we acknowledge all research degree candidates and study supervisors across disciplines and nationalities for availing their work and experience to make inquiry into this important field of research possible.

THE EDITORS
JUNE 2018

DEDICATION

This book is dedicated to the memory of Professor Brenda Leibowitz, who sadly passed away during the first half of 2018. Brenda co-authored one of the chapters in this volume and was a long-standing contributor and dear colleague in the field of higher education teaching and learning. To quote from a tribute by one of her closest colleagues, Professor Chrissie Boughey: "Although Brenda's capacity to conceptualise and lead teaching and learning projects was enormous, her real interest was in research. She read widely, wrote extensively and, best of all, loved leading groups of people on big projects. Her ability to bring on board novice researchers, particularly as writers, was unparalleled and is seen in the number of collections she edited. Although this tribute to Brenda pays homage to her enormous intellectual and leadership achievements, for many she will always be remembered first and foremost as a dear friend and colleague because her support for those she cared for (and there were many) was truly boundless" (http://heltasa.org.za/a-tribute-to-brenda-leibowitz/). We, as editors of this volume, salute Brenda for her sterling work and contributions over many decades.

CONTENTS

Overview i

Introductory chapter

1 Practice, theory and doctoral education research 9
   Nick Hopwood

SECTION A • Supervisory spaces

2 'Success' and 'failure' in two postgraduate research learning spaces:
   An Activity Theory analysis 29
   Carolyn (Callie) Grant

3 Supervising up - A (fictionalised) report from the research training trenches 45
   Nick Mansfield & Sally Purcell

4 I am a postgraduate research supervisor: Who am I? 59
   Nonnie Botha

5 Fibonacci power in a descriptive equation for postgraduate throughput 79
   Sanchen Henning

6 'More than writing a thesis': Reflections on cohort research supervision 93
   Christine Winberg & Simon Winberg

7 Reconceptualising the supervisory role: Border crossings and bounded spaces 109
   Rebekah Smith-McGloin

SECTION B • Supervisory journeys

8 PhD employability in corporate South Africa 133
   Amaleya Goneos-Malka

9 'Crossing over' into research on teaching and learning 149
   Brenda Leibowitz, Gina Wisker & Pia Lamberti

10 Writing the Introduction chapter of PhD theses:
   Comparative international perspectives 163
   Shosh Leshem, Eli Bitzer & Vernon Trafford

11 Factors affecting time to completion of master's mini-dissertations 177
   Sumari O'Neil & Carla dos Santos

12 Mentoring for student success: Three stages in the PhD journey 193
   Suzanne T Ortega & Julia D Kent

13 Function of supervisory and researcher community support in PhD
   and post-PhD trajectories 205
   Kirsi Pyhältö

14 "I have learnt but am still developing": Master's students' evolving concepts of research 223
Peter Rule & Jaqueline Naidoo

15 Employability and graduate attributes of doctoral graduates 233
Rachel Spronken-Smith, Kim Brown & Romain Mirosa

SECTION C • New horizons for postgraduate supervision

16 Doctoral education for successful examination in the education discipline: An analysis of examiners' critiques 257
Petro du Preez and Shan Simmonds

17 The original contribution: Myth or reality in doctoral work? 273
Liezel Frick

18 Cohort-wide research education 287
Wendy Bastalich

19 In sickness and health, and a 'duty of care': PhD student health, stress and wellbeing issues and supervisory experiences 301
Gina Wisker & Gillian Robinson

20 Research as transformation and transformation as research 315
Anisa Vahed, Ashley Ross, Suzanne Francis, Bernie Millar, Oliver Mtapuri & Ruth Searle

CODA

Spaces, journeys, new horizons – where are we now and where do we want to go? 333
Cally Guerin

Notes on Contributors 339

LIST OF TABLES

TABLE 1.1	Selected education-focused theories in use	12
TABLE 4.1	Target population and sample	64
TABLE 4.2	A framework for postgraduate supervision identity	73
TABLE 6.1	Participants and their roles	98
TABLE 6.2	Coding the data	99
TABLE 8.1	Relationship between select countries' full-time researchers and knowledge economy readiness	134
TABLE 11.1	A summary of studies focusing on coursework master's students	185
TABLE 14.1	Students' responses to the question 'What is research?'	224
TABLE 14.2	Students' evolving conceptions of 'approach' and 'paradigm'	225
TABLE 14.3	Students' evolving conceptions of 'truth'	226
TABLE 14.4	Students' evolving conceptions of being a researcher	227
TABLE 15.1	Characteristics of survey respondents (n=136)	240
TABLE 16.1	Shortcomings identified by examiners in terms of the research design	261
TABLE 16.2	Shortcomings identified by examiners in terms of the technical aspects	262
TABLE 16.3	Shortcomings identified by examiners in terms of the scholarly review	263
TABLE 16.4	Shortcomings identified by examiners in terms of the contributions claimed	264
TABLE 16.5	Shortcomings identified by examiners in terms of the background	264
TABLE 16.6	Shortcomings identified by examiners in terms of the validity, reliability and trustworthiness	265

TABLE 16.7	Shortcomings identified by examiners in terms of the ethical considerations	265
TABLE 18.1	Foci in cohort-wide research education	289
TABLE 19.1	Advice themes and data/evidence from our research with specific comments for supervisors	312

LIST OF FIGURES

FIGURE 1.1	Rough map of theories referenced in selected literature 1980–2017	11
FIGURE 2.1	Parallel curriculum processes necessary in the accomplishment of the objective of community research learning	40
FIGURE 5.1	Fibonacci patterns in nature	83
FIGURE 6.1	Cohort supervision showing the scaffolding of projects and researcher roles at different research levels	94
FIGURE 7.1	UK professional standards dimensions of the Framework for Doctoral Supervisors (2016): Summary elements	122
FIGURE 8.1	Distribution of 21 399 PhDs in South Africa by sector of employment	143
FIGURE 11.1	Nested contexts influencing retention and completion	178
FIGURE 11.2	The model of factors influencing degree completion and creative performance	180
FIGURE 11.3	Bitzer's conceptual framework for exploring doctoral success	181
FIGURE 11.4	Carroll et al's (2009:200) framework	182
FIGURE 13.1	Anatomy of the Researcher Community and Supervisory Support Model	209
FIGURE 15.1	Employment outcomes (n=133) vs expectations (n=112)	241
FIGURE 15.2	Development and application of graduate attributes – all doctoral graduates (n=108 to 133; the number varies because of differing response rates to the questions)	241
FIGURE 15.3	Difference between application and development of graduate attributes for all PhD respondents (n=108 to133)	243
FIGURE 15.4	Development and application of graduate attributes in commerce graduates (n=10 to 13)	244

FIGURE 15.5	Development and application of graduate attributes in the humanities graduates (n=20 to 27)	244
FIGURE 15.6	Development and application of graduate attributes in health science graduates (n=48 to 52)	245
FIGURE 15.7	Development and application of graduate attributes in science graduates (n=31 to 41)	245
FIGURE 15.8	Perceived development of graduate attributes by career type (n=89 to 104)	247
FIGURE 15.9	Perceived application of graduate attributes by career type (n=89 to 104)	248
FIGURE 16.1	An illustration of the development of a conceptual framework	268
FIGURE 17.1	Overview of the data (Level 1 analysis)	277
FIGURE 19.1	Interrelation between dimensions of personal, emotional, health and wellbeing, with those of intellectual development	303
FIGURE 20.1	Individual projects	317
FIGURE 20.2	Activity Theory	318
FIGURE 20.3	Activity systems of the TAU projects	321
FIGURE 20.4	Sub-activity triangle of the dialectic relationship between the subject and object of activity mediated by tools	322
FIGURE 20.5	Sub-activity triangle of the dialectic relationship between the subject and community of activity mediated by rules	325
FIGURE 20.6	Sub-activity triangle of the dialectic relationship between the object and community of activity mediated by division of labour	326
FIGURE 20.7	'Schizodemics' – the transformed beings	328

OVERVIEW

Following four books on postgraduate studies and supervision in the *'Studies into Higher Education'* series, the title for this fifth volume is: 'Spaces, journeys and new horizons for postgraduate supervision'.

The idea of 'spaces' refers to the variety of spaces where supervision and postgraduate work take place: personal, individual, disciplinary, collective, institutional, material, physical, virtual, and other spaces. The 'journey' metaphor has been debated as useful but probably insufficient to capture all the complexities and intricacies of supervision and postgraduate work. The term 'journey' is thus used here to indicate beginnings, movements, challenges, obstacles, assistance, support and other dynamic features of the supervision–study interface. The notion of 'horizon' associates with concepts such as transitions, changes, ranges of experience, outlook, perspective, vista, among others. The chosen volume title was thus sufficiently comprehensive and open to theorise, report, discuss and debate particular aspects of research on postgraduate supervision in its current variety and complexity.

The Introductory chapter, which is of a more theoretical nature, was contributed by Nick Hopwood from Sydney University of Technology, who is also a research associate at Stellenbosch University. He pursues the argument that practice, theory and doctoral education research are entangled through embodied actions, empirical access to the world and subjective experiences of it, and the conceptual tools at our disposal. Nick argues that theory enables us to pose new questions, engage in debates through particular vocabulary, work differently with data, and re-imagine what is possible in doctoral education. This position becomes useful when embroiled in educational practices or in acts of generating and analysing appropriate data, and when reflecting on theory, Nick rightfully asks what it permits us to do within the sphere of research into and supervising doctoral education.

Section A contains six chapters under the rubric of *'supervisory spaces'*. In the first chapter of Section A, Cally Grant from Rhodes University, outlines her experiential investigation into teaching and supervising several cohorts of postgraduate students in Educational Leadership and Management over a number of years. She reports on evidence of how postgraduate research learning took place within community spaces and how such learning might be best supported.

In the second chapter, Nick Mansfield and Sally Purcell from Macquarie University, Australia, exhibit the tangle that some postgraduate candidates can get into during the course of their research. They claim that although it is possible to put in place specific remedies for specific issues, doctoral candidature is experienced as a uniquely complex whole where multiple issues intersect and cross-multiply to place the candidate in an unprecedented situation. In describing a number of real cases, they address questions such as how candidates navigate their way in such a unique space, and how possible it is to provide them with skills that will empower them for their own academic destiny – given the multi-faceted connections between candidates, supervisors and the university.

The third chapter in Section A, contributed by Nonnie Botha from Nelson Mandela University, outlines a framework for postgraduate research supervisor identity. She explains how this framework was developed by considering data that emanated from empirical research and applying a theoretical model for identity development to the data. The significance of her chapter lies in its potential to enhance insights into the supervisory space of identity development, capacity building and the quality of postgraduate supervision.

In the next chapter of Section A, Sanchen Henning from the University of South Africa, explores the constrained spaces for research that master's students experience. Students often interpret research requirements as working in spaces of solitary confinement, thereby contributing to their agony and isolation during their research. Student feedback reveals postgraduate students' anxieties about failure and in this chapter Sanchen advocates for a compelling reason to assist master's students to conduct research that creates a sense of meaning and to inspire them to complete a quality dissertation.

Christine Winberg (Cape Peninsula University of Technology) and Simon Winberg (University of Cape Town) use an activity systems approach in the following chapter of Section A to show how the supervision space at two research sites expanded to include project-based cohort supervision – a practice that involves more supervisors, more peer learning and a larger research community. They claim that while project-based cohort supervision is a model more common in engineering and the applied sciences than in the social sciences, it embodies a form of collaboration consistent with the view that research supervision is an inherently social practice extending beyond the relationship between candidate and supervisor, and having implications for individual and group transformation.

The last chapter of Section A belongs to Rebekah Smith McGloin from Coventry University. She suggests that the spaces that supervisors inhabit are increasingly prescribed and circumscribed by frameworks and regulations. Yet the borders, boundaries and hierarchies that frame the 'traditional' supervisory domain are increasingly tested and made more permeable and contingent by the complexities, challenges and opportunities of negotiating collaborative, cross-cultural and cross-sectoral work. The chapter considers a range of external forces – from the macro to the individual – that are reshaping supervisory spaces and re-examines the changing roles and developmental needs of supervisors set against the skills, competencies and training that currently predominate.

Section B comprises eight chapters under the subtitle: *'Supervisory journeys'*. With the first contribution, Amaleya Goneos-Malka from Pretoria University, highlights details of an independent study she conducted on PhD employability in corporate South Africa. The findings from a nationwide cross-industry study on the distribution of South Africa's PhD graduates in leading companies confirm the problem of low PhD employability across all industrial sectors. She holds that the resulting low penetration of PhDs across the private sector might be detrimental to the South African economy and she concludes by asking questions about the difficulty of contemplating whether the low representation of top talent is due to deliberate discrimination, as a result of inadequate understanding about the value contributing potential of PhDs, or a failure to market such qualifications and graduates effectively.

The second chapter in this section was co-authored by Brenda Leibowitz (University of Johannesburg), Gina Wisker (University of Brighton) and Pia Lamberti (University of Johannesburg). Their chapter focuses on academics teaching in higher education institutions who choose interdisciplinary projects for their own postgraduate studies, linking their basic discipline with that of education or with teaching and learning. These candidates that are on 'crossing over' journeys face opportunities and challenges that are similar to those of other part-time postgraduate students, but they also experience specific opportunities and achievements related to academic identity in their research journeys. Some difficult questions which remain to be untangled include whether colleagues who come from fields other than education are being done a disservice by uncritically promoting higher degree studies in teaching and learning and, also, what would work for this group of academics to support and recognise their work in researching teaching and learning?

In chapter three of Section B, co-authors Shosh Leshem (Oranim Academic College of Education and Kibbutzim Academic College, Israel), Eli Bitzer (emeritus Professor from Stellenbosch University, South Africa) and Vernon Trafford (emeritus Professor from Anglia Ruskin University, UK) propose that in doctoral journeys in general, and thesis writing in particular, the introductory chapter is often considered difficult. It is often also difficult to provide students with clear guidance on this issue. This is because candidates are forced to grapple with decisions ranging from selecting an organisational framework to making adequate word choices. In scrutinising a total of nine doctoral theses – three from each country – the chapter reports a versatility of styles and scope of chapters among theses and nationalities. They suggest possible explanations for these differences among contexts, which include cultural, regulatory, disciplinary, style, convention and relational factors.

The next chapter in Section B, written by Sumari O'Neil and Carla Dos Santos, both from the University of Pretoria, highlights the problem of completion time for students on their master's coursework journeys. These students are mostly not interested in becoming researchers or proceeding to doctoral study which distinguishes them from other levels of study regarding student experiences, student expectations and supervision effort. The authors consider it important for the education of coursework master's students to include clear requirements and expectations for the 'mini-dissertation', and for the roles of the supervisors and students to be clarified before any supervision takes place. They also suggest that the standards for coursework master's research dissertations should be more uniform to ensure the alignment of student, supervisor and examiner expectations.

In the next chapter, from a North American perspective, Suzanne Ortega and Juli Kent, who are both from the US Council of Graduate Schools, address the question of why postgraduate mentoring (supervision) needs to change. Three stages of development during the doctoral journey seem crucial, namely when students enter graduate school, during their pathways through graduate school, and during the transition to early career scholar or scientist. They highlight three major Council of Graduate Schools' projects that represent these three stages, addressing the implications of each stage for both mentors (supervisors) and mentees (candidates). They suggest, in the final analysis, that graduate students need mentors, but they also need a community of fellow students and academics who can provide different types of feedback and support which is also an excellent preparation for professional life.

Adding to the quest for a most productive doctoral journey, Kirsi Pyhältö from the University of Helsinki, contributed a chapter to Section B on the function of supervisory and researcher community support in PhD and post-PhD trajectories. With this chapter she adds to bridging the literature gap by proposing a theoretical model which explains an understanding of supervisory and researcher community support. The model specifies forms, sources, support dynamics and fit as complementary components of support. Kirsi provides empirical evidence for key components of the framework and emphasises the importance of social support for doctoral and post-doctoral researchers. Finally, she proposes possible future directions for research in this area and points to implications for developing doctoral and post-doctoral trajectories.

The next chapter in Section B was co-authored by Peter Rule from Stellenbosch University and Jaqueline Naidoo from the University of KwaZulu-Natal. They report on tracking the journeys of master's students' understandings of research from the beginning to the end of an academic semester. The importance of students' 'mid-conceptions' of research, which are students' ideas about research that have developed from their initial conceptions, but are still evolving in their journeys as 'becoming-researchers', are emphasised and the authors highlight the problem of how master's students often battle with threshold concepts in educational research such as 'paradigm', 'method', 'approach', 'evidence' and 'truth'. Recognising and valuing students' mid-conceptions of research can help supervisors to contribute to students' learning identities in their research journeys.

The final chapter in Section B, contributed by Rachel Spronken-Smith, Kim Brown and Romain Mirosa – all from the University of Otago – does not only address the lack of knowledge regarding the graduate attributes of PhD graduates, but also their employment pathways after graduation. The sparse research that has been conducted is mainly from Europe, North America and Australia; little has been conducted in New Zealand. In their chapter they report on a study that was aimed at ascertaining initial employment destinations for New Zealand PhD graduates as part of their study and career journeys and soon after completing their PhDs. They also indicate how doctoral studies helped prepared doctoral graduates for these jobs.

Section C, which links to the sub-topic *'Postgraduate supervisory horizons'*, contains five chapters. The first chapter, which is co-authored by Petro du Preez and Shan Simmonds from North-West University, reports on an analysis of examiners' critiques on doctoral theses in the discipline of education. Their findings reveal that candidates often fail to demonstrate their contribution to new knowledge and existing bodies of scholarship, mainly because they fail to develop sound conceptual frameworks. In contributing to new horizons for doctoral assessment, the authors suggest a theoretical view of how supervisors and candidates could use critical questions to interrogate theses before submission for examination.

In the second chapter of Section C, Liezel Frick from Stellenbosch University, challenges views on how 'originality' is explicated and viewed in doctoral work. Her work is based on an analysis of 1 566 theses produced across nine faculties at one research-intensive university over period of nine years. This analysis shows that originality is more often an implicit rather than an explicit feature of doctoral written outputs, despite the prominence given to this aspect of doctoral work in national and international rhetoric on the doctorate. New horizons for doctoral assessment are opened up as claims to originality remain a nebulous aspect of doctoral theses, lacking 'golden rules' for making originality explicit in thesis construction and providing evidence of the multi-faceted nature of originality.

Wendy Bastalich, from the University of South Australia, wrote the third chapter of Section C on cohort-wide research education. She points towards new horizons for supervision practices and provides an outline of cognitive learning theory that broadly informs three salient foci, namely 'cognitive processing', 'situated learning' and 'research writing'. She emphasises that educational theory and academic literacies are notable contributors to research and practice about pedagogy and curriculum in cohort research education. This thinking opens up new horizons for learning beyond current supervision spaces, thus bringing insights that offer radical and progressive transformations in research education.

The fourth chapter in Section C was contributed by Gina Wisker (University of Brighton) and Gillian Robinson (emeritus Reader from Anglia Ruskin University). They point out that ill health (mental and physical) of candidates during PhD studies is becoming increasingly recognised but is still under-researched. Their illustrative cases indicate a close connection between success in doctoral learning and sensitive, informed management of and support for physical and mental health issues as experienced by doctoral students. Their study opens up new horizons for research in the area of doctoral health and supervisor sensitivity and support. The authors conclude that health issues need to be recognised as part of doctoral education and that the supervisor's role in relation to this issue needs much more clarification.

The multi-authored final chapter in Section C was contributed by Anisa Vahed (Durban University of Technology), Ashley Ross (Durban University of Technology), Suzanne Francis (University of KwaZulu-Natal), Bernie Millar (Cape Peninsula University of Technology), Oliver Mtapuri (University of KwaZulu-Natal) and Ruth Searle, a private higher education consultant. The authors suggest that the processes of research engagement are profoundly transformative and that through personal engagement in the research process student researchers are understood to be 'remodelled' in terms of their identity, thinking and agency. Supervisors are equally challenged to stretch their own experiences and identities according to the needs of those they supervise, as well as in relation to the emergent academic demands.

This volume closes with a summative coda written by Cally Guerin from the University of Adelaide.

ELI BITZER, LIEZEL FRICK, MAGDA FOURIE-MALHERBE
AND KIRSI PYHÄLTÖ
EDITORS

PRACTICE, THEORY AND DOCTORAL EDUCATION RESEARCH

Nick Hopwood

INTRODUCTION

Kurt Lewin's maxim 'There is nothing as practical as a good theory' disrupts notions of theory and practice being separated by a chasm that requires bridging. I argue practice, theory and doctoral education research are entangled through embodied actions, empirical access to the world and subjective experiences of it, and the conceptual tools at our disposal. Theory enables us to pose new questions, engage in debates through particular vocabulary, work differently with data, and re-imagine what is possible in doctoral education. It becomes useful to us when embroiled in educational practices or in acts of generating and analysing data. When reflecting on theory, I am asking what it permits us to *do*.

Humility is called for when embarking on a chapter such as this. It is not an account of the doctoral education field *as a whole*. Partialities of multiple sources – historical, geographical, linguistic, and theoretical – frame the analysis. Nonetheless, in the spirit of Evans's (2011) mapping of the terrain, I suggest we find ourselves in a particular historical moment where empirical work, international exchange, and educational practices have reached a point where taking stock seems worthwhile, however partial this may be.

The chapter proceeds with a rough and incomplete map of the field. This points to particular theoretical spaces and the horizons they bring into focus. I then consider practice theories and the new horizons appearing through them. I conclude with a reflection on promising glimpses of possible futures with roots in different traditions of thought, histories, geographies and cultures.

INTRODUCTORY CHAPTER

I write this in an institution built on land of the Gadigal People of the Eora Nation in what is now called Australia. Our work as researchers involves collisions between cultures, historical and spatial trajectories, language practices, and politics reminding us that horizons and the spaces we view them from are not neutral. A researcher not embodied as white, male, historically privileged, schooled in an Anglo tradition and now working in a still-colonised setting (all of which shaped and mis-shaped what I have written) would produce a different account.

THEORIES IN USE: A ROUGH AND INCOMPLETE MAP OF THE FIELD

The theoretical map I construct below is based on over 200 articles, chapters, and books referring explicitly to theory in discussion of doctoral education. They were published between 1980 and 2017, in English. Therein lies the first source of partiality. Relevant references were found by reading abstracts and searching for 'theory' and 'theoretical' in within-journal search fields in a range of titles in higher education and academic development. Formal databases and Google Scholar broadened the search. In October 2016 I asked members of the International Doctoral Education Research Network (IDERN) listserv to refer me to theoretical work they were familiar with. Responses from generous colleagues expanded the pool of references considerably. If readers find their work or theoretical reference points missing in what follows, the fault is mine. Not all identified publications are cited below, but they did all contribute to the analysis.

My analysis groups different theoretical approaches together. These groups are more awkward collage than reflection of homogeneity. Figure 1.1 arranges them in a rough and incomplete map. I have tried to use proximity to indicate connections I see between theories, but the arrangement necessarily undermined this at times. Nonetheless I maintain it guides and prompts helpful reflection on theory use in our field and practice.

CHAPTER 1 • **PRACTICE, THEORY AND DOCTORAL EDUCATION RESEARCH**

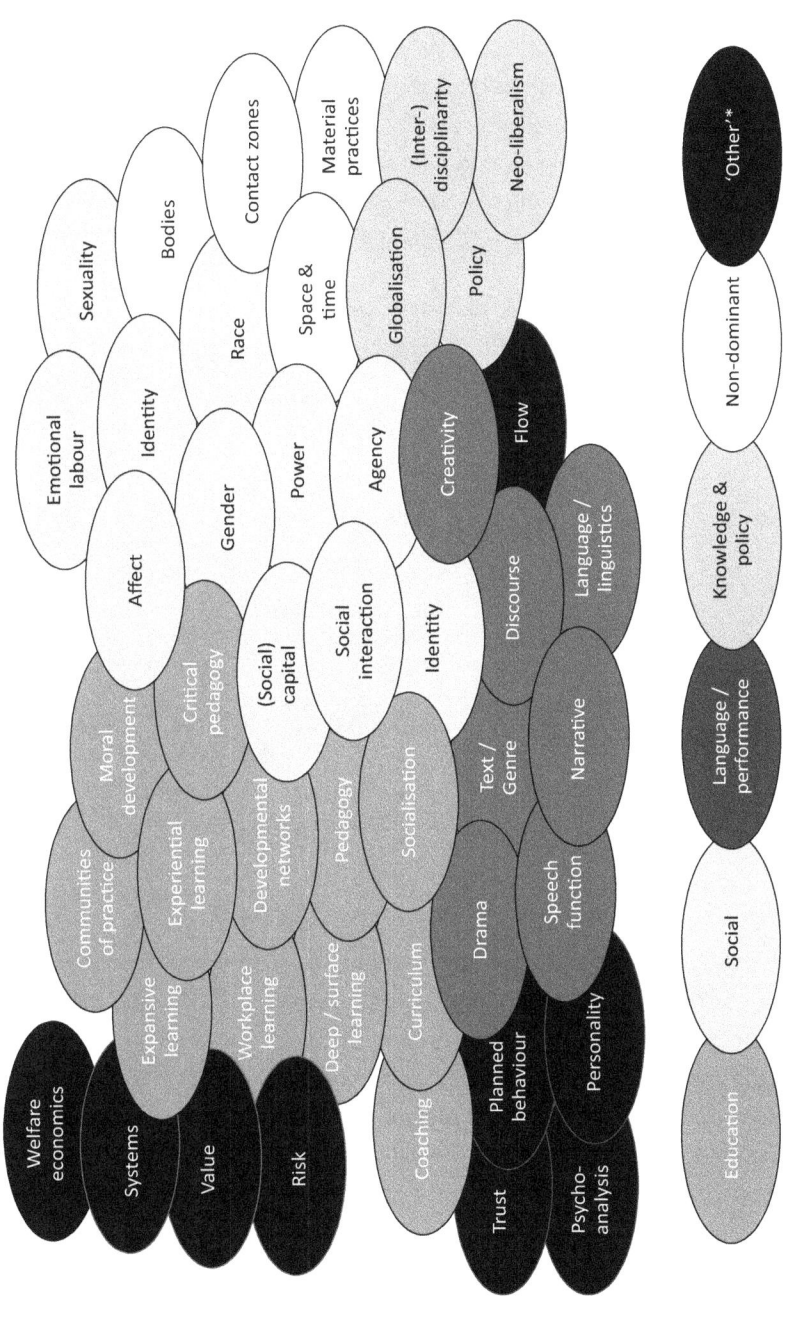

FIGURE 1.1 Rough map of theories referenced in selected literature 1980–2017

* 'Other' only in respect to their fit in this way of grouping theories together

INTRODUCTORY CHAPTER

Various theories explicitly addressing education have been used, centred on questions of learning, pedagogy, curriculum and concepts adjunct to these, such as developmental networks, which are seen to support learning. Education-focused theories reflect diverse theoretical traditions and schools of thought. Each orients our gaze at a particular analytical distance and in a specific direction, as Table 1.1 outlines. They have provoked questions of relationships between what students and those supporting them do, and what and how they learn. They have also drawn our attention to the role of doctoral education in (re)producing the values and practices associated with scholarly disciplines, and potential problems with this.

TABLE 1.1 Selected education-focused theories in use

Theory	Example of source theorists	Example of application	Horizon features
Socialisation	Tinto, Van Maanen & Shien; Wiedman	Austin 2002	Disciplinary norms and practices as doctoral curriculum
Communities of practice	Lave & Wenger	Botha 2014	Changing participation in social practices
Expansive learning	Engeström	Hopwood & Stocks 2008	Contradictions between system features as driving force of learning
Workplace learning	Eraut; Billett	Hopwood 2010	Doctoral learning as work activity
Deep/surface learning	Marton	Zuber-Skerritt & Cendon 2014	Individual approaches to learning
Critical pedagogy	Freire; Rancière	Van Schalkwyk 2012	Links between pedagogy and justice

Doctoral education mirrors education more generally – importing scholars whose own research education was often in other fields (Mills et al 2006), and theoretical ideas from disciplines and fields whose primary focus is not learning. Figure 1.1 represents these in other collage groups, including one titled 'social' theories: theories of society, social interaction, identity, structure and agency. These have enriched doctoral education work in at least two key ways. First, they offer explanatory tools that researchers have connected directly with learning. The work of McAlpine and colleagues (for example, Turner & McAlpine 2011) on identity-trajectory (drawing on Tonso 2006) and agency exemplifies this, using these concepts to inform data collection that documents everyday practices and experiences, and then to infer findings about learning. Second, these 'social' theories prompt us to explore how doctoral education is a microcosm of society, a site at which broader social forces are in play. Concepts from Goffman's symbolic interactionism and Hochschild's emotional labour (Strandler et al 2014), and Bourdieu (Gopaul 2016) resource our understanding of the social dynamics of doctoral education and its relations to the societies and inequities in which it unfolds.

Power features strongly as a theoretical focus, often drawing on Foucault (e.g. Kendall 2002) but also Rose's technologies of the self (see contributions to Lupton et al 2018). Other work informed by theories of power and positionality (e.g. Acker & Haque 2015) has revealed tensions between everyday experiences of diverse student bodies and the academic labour market.

'Social' theories also lead us to issues of human being-ness. This has prompted researchers to investigate doctoral education in terms of affect (e.g. Burford 2014), gender (e.g. Johnson et al 2000; Sallee 2014), desire (Grant 2003) and sexuality (e.g. Lee 1998). Bendix Peterson's (2007) work exemplifies how theories of subjectification, category boundary work and performativity (with roots in feminism and other traditions) can be applied to reconceptualise doctoral education in general, and supervision in particular. Barnacle and Dall'Alba (2014) used a phenomenological perspective to tie together bodies, writing and lived experience. In such cases, theories offer necessary, sophisticated tools to dive deeply into subjective experience while maintaining a firm analytical grip on broader patterns and the conditions that shape those experiences.

The third group shown in Figure 1.1 comprises theories relating to language, systemic functional linguistics, writing, genre, discourse, narrative, and drama. The work represented here has drawn on theorists including Bakhtin and Halliday (Lamberti & Wentzel 2014), and Zimmerman (Stracke & Kumar 2010). Bendix Petersen (2012) worked with narrative through post-structural theorising of subject and subjectivity, linking selfhood, supervision and global forces influencing doctoral education, while Coperman (2015) explored principles for emotionally connected storytelling through concepts of drama. Within this theoretical group are approaches that bring doctoral writing into clear view. Paré (2014) uses genre theory as a basis for a pedagogy of academic writing, and his work with Aitchison (Aitchison & Paré 2012) conceptualises texts alongside the practices producing them through a notion of craft. These theories thus allow us to explore how the final and interim artefacts of doctoral education are produced, how they shape learning, and how we might develop curricula and pedagogical arrangements to assist students who struggle.

The fourth collage group in Figure 1.1 refers to theories focusing on knowledge, its organisation and higher education policy. Through these we have documented and called into question logics of disciplinarity and organisation of academic work. This work has drawn on Becher and Trowler's disciplinary cultures (Parry 2007), Kuhnian notions of paradigm (Evans 2014), and Boyer's domains of scholarship (Austin & McDaniels 2006). The effects of globalisation on doctoral education have been explored through Marginson's glonacal approach and Beck's ideas of the cosmopolitan turn (Pearson *et al* 2016), the knowledge economy (Simmonds & Du Preez 2014), and how the rise of neoliberal policy regimes has made us risk-averse (McWilliam 2009). Theories from the sociology of knowledge, particularly Bernstein, informed Walford's (1981) work on how doctoral projects are formulated in physics, and Clegg's (2014) more recent work, which connects with feminist theory in order to push boundaries in doctoral education. These theories connect the core of doctoral education – knowledge work – with the systems and frameworks we use to organise, regulate and produce this work, and generate questions and insights that are crucial in imagining alternative horizons.

The collages I constructed left a residue comprising theories that might well have been central or aggregated differently had alternative collages been put together. This 'cabinet of curiosities' (MacLure 2013) is useful because it reveals something important about the practices of theorising in our field. Here, we find familiar doctoral education scholars dabbling with unfamiliar ideas and theories. For example, Lee and Williams's (1999) 'Forged in fire' draws on psychoanalytic theory to reveal the traumatic nature of doctoral education. The theories in this group appear less widely taken up than those in the other groups. Frequency of use is doubtful as a proxy for quality of insight, raising questions about how and with what effects intellectual traditions and the communities and projects that build up around them cast shadows on our horizons just as they illuminate features of them, and what as a scholarly community we should do in response to this.

The remaining collage group in Figure 1.1 is labelled 'non-dominant' – this points to theories that explicitly adopt a disruptive standpoint, seeking to undermine hegemonic framings. They often address widely discussed issues through distinctive angles that problematise the framing of the issue. For example, Margolis and Romero's (1998) work revealed startling racial features of doctoral education, but did so through an educational theory (Jackson's school-based notion of hidden curriculum). The non-dominant approach drew on critical race theory, explicitly adopting a troubling and troublesome agenda (for example, Daniel 2007).

Exemplary of work in this group is Manathunga's (2012) research drawing on post-colonial or Southern theory, especially Bhabha, to imagine intercultural supervision as a contact zone. Grant (2010a, 2010b) drew on McClintock and Bell to offer de-colonising visions of doctoral education in terms of Māori-Pākehā relationships. Such work uses theory to sensitise the scholar/practitioner to contemporary manifestations of historical forces and the inequities and silences that result from them. Theory is also used to provide an analytical framework through which to connect detailed analyses of interactions with global geopolitical histories. Hopwood and Paulson's (2012) work on bodies brought broader arguments about the body as an absent presence in social research more generally into the specific domain of doctoral education, using theory to 'see' the body in narratives where it might otherwise have been overlooked. Bodies were also foregrounded in Burford's (2015a, 2015b) work, employing affective politics and queer theory. Manathunga (2014, 2015) imports concepts from geography (not a frequent source of theory in the past), and works with those concepts – space and time – in a way at odds with conventional understandings (referencing Massey and Adam). A multiplicity of perspectives is also reflected in Middleton and McKinley's (2010) work, which draws on Bernstein (sociology of the academy), Lefebvre (critical spatial theory) and Maori educational theory. These are excellent examples of the way emerging approaches often address problems by bringing plural theoretical horizons into view, rather than remaining within the intellectual landscapes on one perspective alone.

These non-dominant theories have enabled researchers to provoke and productively disrupt. They reveal horizons that are present but overlooked, or features of them that we may prefer not to see. They do so by adopting uncomfortable premises, embracing troublesome possibilities, and defamiliarising familiar ideas in a way that is often confronting and unsettling. It is precisely these destabilising aspects that give these approaches their distinctive value. My point is not to elevate this group as somehow 'above' the others – Figure 1.1 is deliberately non-hierarchical. However, I am arguing that the rips, intrusions and fault lines that these approaches offer are vital features of our theoretical repertoire if we are to realise a vision of doctoral education practice and research that is equitable and restorative, not just effective and efficient.

THE POTENTIAL OF PRACTICE THEORIES

Having drawn a rough map of theory use in the field, I now address some of the white spaces on Figure 1.1 In doing so, my own theoretical affinities (Clegg 2012) come to the fore. Much of the work mentioned above has address the practices of doctoral education – what students, supervisors, administrators and others do and say, and how they relate to one another. However, there remains untapped potential in researching and enacting doctoral education in ways informed by a theorisation of these doings, sayings and relatings as practices (Kemmis 2009).

Practice theories are themselves a collage. Nonetheless there is something distinctive about the 'practice turn' (see Schatzki et al 2001) that offers useful premises, lines of questioning and analytical tools for doctoral education. Practice theoretical work takes practices not just as a unit of analysis (an epistemological framework), but as a unit of social life (an ontological one). Troubling dichotomies between structure and agency are dislodged in a view that sees individuals enacting and upholding practices that at the same time prefigure and shape what they do. Contemporary practice theories explicitly emphasise the importance of materiality, the embodied performance of any particular practice, and the metaphor of emergence (as a counter to acquisition or participation, previously dominant metaphors of learning; see Hager 2011). A focus on practices is not new in doctoral education research (see prior mentions of Bourdieu, for example). However, recent developments open up productive new horizons. In what follows, I draw on my own work in other fields of inquiry to create a silhouette of these horizons and make a case for taking up practice theories more substantially in our field.

In relation to work on practices of supporting families with young children, I have argued that the learning of those involved has four essential dimensions: times, spaces, bodies, and things (Hopwood 2014, 2016). By essential I mean that they cannot be taken out (ontologically or epistemologically), and that they are the essence of learning: what it is made of, not just what it happens in or through. Each of these four dimensions is explicitly theorised as:

- enacted – they emerge through the performance of practices rather than being pre-existing; their bearing on human life only arises through practices;
- plural – unresolvable to a singular entity, but co-existing as a multiplicity;
- interconnected – mutually entangled and co-implicated such that changes in one have implications for the others – they produce the texture of practices (connectedness in action; see Gherardi 2006).

I now consider what might be offered by putting these ideas to use in relation to doctoral education research and pedagogic practices.

Time is conventionally understood as objective, something that gets used up. Pressures of time to completion are experienced in this way. Practice theories remind us that this time, the form that runs out, is an effect of particular practices and material conditions. They also remind us that the pace and nature of this unfolding is up for grabs – we can enact times as fast and slow, iterative and linear. A practical theoretical approach grounds an understanding of times in relevant histories. The pace of work, for example, reflects a moment in disciplinary and institutional histories in which technologies may accelerate work, while other conventions may act as potentially helpful brakes – the rules shaping doctoral practices mean the drive-through PhD completed in a week seems unlikely at present.

Practice theory might also be used to interpret what we know about students' everyday practices differently. Doing so could lead us to recognise, at least in some parts of the world, for some students, a PhD 3.0, where 1.0 is paper-based and slow, 2.0 is digitised and faster, and 3.0 places intense expectations on students to produce and not just consume throughout the journey (reciprocating peer support through social media, for example). Framed in terms of practice theory, these modes could co-exist, shaping and being produced by what students do. When thinking about times, we also think about doctorates in the time of life – enacted by bodies that age, carry different degrees and forms of embodied wisdom (what Schatzki 2002 calls "practical understandings"). This may be helpful in disrupting approaches that conceptualise doctoral trajectories as resolving a deficit that the doctoral newcomer inevitably embodies.

Spaces are not just physical containers or contexts in which doctoral education unfolds. The aforementioned work of Manathunga (2014, 2015) and Middleton and McKinley (2010) has taken up theories of space as a coming together of trajectories (Massey 2005) and as perceived, conceived and lived (Lefebvre 1991) respectively. A practice theoretical approach to investigating the Global South and North would compel us to address the material practices within and between these regions, to acknowledge different possible embodied understandings, rules, affective attachments, and shared understandings of doctoralness. Practice theories are well positioned to help us confront the reality of the de-centred university (see Francis 2011) by asking, What are the practices through which students cultivate, nurture and learn from 'globally distributed funds of living knowledge'? What pedagogic practices would support students in this respect, acknowledging their embodied location in particular spaces? Thinking about spaces in terms of practices also provides new angles on features of contemporary doctoral education such as distance study, offshore campuses, dual/joint degrees, and how institutions and students compete in international markets for places and scholarships.

INTRODUCTORY CHAPTER

Bodies have been acknowledged in the literature (see Burford 2015a; Hopwood & Paulson 2012), but bodies remain difficult to talk about, but an inevitable dimension of doctoral work. Regardless of physical co-presence or asynchronous digitally mediated interaction, there are always bodies doing the work. These bodies are gendered, raced, aged, differently able, positioned in social frames of judgements around preferred form, subject to physical and mental illness. Grosz's (1994) view of volatile bodies seems helpful: What if we embraced bodies as fleshy and fragile? What if we took forward Mol's (2002) idea of the body multiple, prompting us to explore how practices of doctoral education enact students' (and supervisors') bodies in different ways? Our field would be enriched by understandings that are grounded in experience and performance in ways that do not relegate the body as an absent presence. Such relegation problematically erases gender but assumes masculinity, erases race but assumes whiteness, erases age but assumes youth, erases difference but assumes healthy, able bodies. Practice theories help undo these erasures.

Things are another absent presence in many accounts of doctoral education. Unless we theorise them head-on, we risk taking the materialities of doctoral work and pedagogy for granted. To do so is to overlook a whole realm that shapes our practices, and which is produced by them. While prior research has addressed drafts and theses, these are approached in terms of words, writing, and communication. What about objects *as objects*? A practice theoretical approach would enable us to examine how objects 'act back' on us – think of the student who develops pain from extensive mouse work, or prolonged poor posture cultivated by relations between chairs, desks and screens. Knorr Cetina's (2001) notion of the *epistemic object* seems relevant. The epistemic object is something that pulls actors into complex knowledge work, provokes questions rather than provides answers, destabilises our understanding, leads us to consider what we know and the status of that knowledge, and forces us to be humble in relation to knowledge. Taking up Knorr Cetina's ideas might help us consider the thesis differently – not as a troublesome, often-delayed account of the past, but as a productively disruptive object/force connected with constellations of embodied practices.

Gherardi (2006) uses the term 'texture' to refer to connectedness in action. Most basically, this would prompt us to examine doctoral education in terms of how the actions of students are connected to those of other students, supervisors, disciplinary colleagues, and so on. We could trace those connections in embodied, materially and digitally mediated forms. Understanding texture in terms of four dimensions infuses this with a nuance that helps to specify demands and forms of learning.

Whichever dimension we take as a starting point, we inevitably end up confronting the other three dimensions, confirming their mutual connectivity, and essential status. The dimensions are thus not ontologically separable, but analytical points of departure, visibilising features of doctoral education that might not otherwise be noticed. Through these dimensions, our gaze refuses to sit still on one particular horizon, but is forced to shift, refocus, and super-impose.

The theoretical question of the relationship between practices and learning is complex and unresolved. I looked for moments in practices (reminder: these were not doctoral education practices) where the need to learn arose and required a response from those involved. Learning imperatives emerged when new textures were needed (that is, new connections in action were required), when existing textures had to be modified, adapted or repaired, when lost textures warranted restoration, or when other changes meant work had to be done to maintain textures and keep connectedness in action in place (see Hopwood 2016). Always, the connections in focus could be understood in terms of times, spaces, bodies, and things. These ideas might be useful as ways to develop novel conceptualisations of supervision, trace the impacts of policy, chart changing relationships between students and disciplines or fields, map the effects of dispersed networks of living knowledge, and the emergence of epistemic objects in students' study.

This case for practice theories does not reflect any inherently superior status or logic. It emerges from empirical work in which I have been engaging. Without displacing alternative horizons, I hope there is something enticing in the silhouettes I have cast here. I conclude by pointing to different horizons whose emergence into view reflects different forces, priorities and agendas.

CONCLUSION

New formations of the relationship between practice, theory and doctoral education may be initiated in many ways. Above, I outlined how developments in what are largely academic traditions from the Global North might open up new lines of inquiry and possibilities for practice. It thus seems fitting, in conclusion, to consider other sources of change.

There remain many countries in the world where doctoral education is not yet formalised. Rather than catching up with the rest of the world, these might be embraced as sites where new ideas and ideals might emerge, ahead of rather than behind the practices of others. This is precisely what is being attempted in Bhutan, where I have had a position of intimate outsider in relation to developing the country's first doctoral programme. Bhutanese doctoral education will be shaped by the notion of Gross National Happiness (GNH) (see Gross National Happiness Commission 2013; Phuntsho 2000). As far as I am aware this will be unprecedented as an approach to doctoral education that is based explicitly on four pillars of good governance, sustainable socio-economic development, preservation and promotion of culture, and environmental conservation. GNH might be regarded as a unique Southern theory, and these developments as an instance where theory is not just being used to research and understand doctoral education, but to shape it – from its core foundations to its institutional arrangements to the practices of admissions, supervision and assessment.

The assertion of spatially, historically and culturally specific values and priorities in reshaping doctoral education is happening elsewhere too. Auerbach (2017) describes how the African Leadership University has adopted seven commitments that constitute a radical, progressive basis for delivering higher education: use of open source material; languages other than English; balanced student exchange ratios; working beyond texts with music, food and other sources; collaboration with students in development of curricula and legal frameworks among other things; producing and shaping alternative discourses throughout candidature; and commitment to the highest possible ethical standards. These are a means to decolonise the social sciences, and speak to an assertion of African scholarship's historical place in the world and a vision of what this place might become.

These examples challenge the rough and partial map I have drawn, revealing its vagaries, inaccuracies and omissions. Nonetheless, the map is illuminative of a rich diversity of theoretical stances which may be collaged in particular ways to help us reflect on what theories have enabled us to do, what horizons they bring into view. My case for further work based on practice theories is sincere but shaped by my position as white, male, Anglo, privileged and so on. The horizons appearing in Bhutan and the African Leadership University are thrilling in their promise to unleash new ways of arranging doctoral education, support students, and formulate empirical inquiry. Theory and practice need not be separated by a chasm. In productive entanglement with research and practice, theories can inspire us, engage us affectively and bodily, expand what is possible, and hold us to the highest possible account.

ACKNOWLEDGEMENTS

I wish to thank Liezel Frick and Eli Bitzer for inviting me to contribute this chapter. I am grateful to the many IDERN-ers who responded to my request for details about theories in use in doctoral education. Without their contributions this chapter would have been a much more impoverished account.

REFERENCES

Acker S & Haque E. 2015. The struggle to make sense of doctoral study. *Higher Education Research & Development*, 34(2):229-241. https://doi.org/10.1080/07294360.2014.956699

Aitchison C & Paré A. 2012. Writing as craft and practice in the doctoral curriculum. In: A Lee & S Danby (eds). *Reshaping doctoral education: Changing programs and pedagogies.* London: Routledge. 12-25.

Auerbach J. 2017. What a new university in Africa is doing to decolonise social sciences. https://theconversation.com/what-a-new-university-in-africa-is-doing-to-decolonise-social-sciences-77181 [Retrieved 13 May 2017].

Austin AE. 2002. Preparing the next generation of faculty: Graduate school as socialisation to the academic career. *The Journal of Higher Education*, 73(1):94-122. https://doi.org/10.1353/jhe.2002.0001

Austin AE & McDaniels M. 2006. Using a doctoral education to prepare faculty to work within Boyers' for domains or scholarship. *New Directions for Institutional Research*, 129(51-65). https://doi.org/10.1002/ir.171

Barnacle R & Dall'Alba G. 2014. Beyond skills: Embodying writerly practices through the doctorate. *Studies in Higher Education*, 39(7):1139-1149. https://doi.org/10.1080/03075079.2013.777405

Bendix Petersen E. 2007. Negotiating academicity: Postgraduate research supervision as category boundary work. *Studies in Higher Education*, 32(4):475-487. https://doi.org/10.1080/03075070701476167

Bendix Peterson E. 2012. Re-signifying subjectivity? A narrative exploration of 'non-traditional' doctoral students' lived experience of subject formation through two Australian cases. *Studies in Higher Education*, 39(5):823-834. https://doi.org/10.1080/03075079.2012.745337

Botha N. 2014. The cohort supervision model: To what extent does it facilitate doctoral success? In: E Bitzer, R Albertyn, L Frick, B Grant & F Kelly (eds). *Pushing boundaries in postgraduate supervision*. Stellenbosch: AFRICAN SUN MeDIA. 133-152.

Burford J. 2014. Doctoral writing as an affective practice: Keep calm and carry on? In: E Bitzer, R Albertyn, L Frick, B Grant & F Kelly (eds). *Pushing boundaries in postgraduate supervision*. Stellenbosch: AFRICAN SUN MeDIA. 69-84. https://doi.org/10.18820/9781920689162/06

Burford J. 2015. Dear obese PhD applicants: Twitter, tumblr and the contested affective politics of fat doctoral embodiment. *M/C Journal*, 18(3).

Burford J. 2015. Queering the affective politics of doctoral education: Toward complex visions of agency and affect. *Higher Education Research & Development*, 34(4):776-787. https://doi.org/10.1080/07294360.2015.1051005

Clegg S. 2012. On the problem of theorising: An insider account of research practice. *Higher Education Research & Development*, 31(3):407-418. https://doi.org/10.1080/07294360.2011.634379

Clegg S. 2014. Knowledge questions and doctoral education. In: E Bitzer, R Albertyn, L Frick, B Grant & F Kelly (eds). *Pushing boundaries in postgraduate supervision*. Stellenbosch: AFRICAN SUN MeDIA. 11-24. https://doi.org/10.18820/9781920689162/02

Copeman P. 2015. Three Minute Theatre: Principles and practice for scripting and performing Three Minute Thesis presentations. *International Journal for Researcher Development*, 6(1):77-92. https://doi.org/10.1108/IJRD-09-2014-0028

Daniel C. 2007. Outsiders-within: Critical race theory, graduate education and barriers to professionalization. *The Journal of Sociology & Social Welfare*, 34(1):25-42.

Evans L. 2011. The scholarship of researcher development: Mapping the terrain and pushing back boundaries. *International Journal for Researcher Development*, 2(2):75-98. https://doi.org/10.1108/17597511111212691

Evans T. 2014. Doctoral work as boundary-riding and boundary-breaking. In: E Bitzer, R Albertyn, L Frick, B Grant & F Kelly (eds). *Pushing boundaries in postgraduate supervision*. Stellenbosch: AFRICAN SUN MeDIA. 25-37. https://doi.org/10.18820/9781920689162/03

Francis RJ. 2011. *The decentring of the traditional university: The future of (self) education in virtually figured worlds*. London: Routledge.

Gherardi S. 2006. *Organizational knowledge: The texture of workplace learning*. Oxford: Blackwell.

Gopaul B. 2016. Applying cultural capital and field to doctoral student socialization. *International Journal for Researcher Development*, 7(1):46-62. https://doi.org/10.1108/IJRD-03-2015-0009

Grant B. 2003. Mapping the pleasures and risks of supervision. *Discourse: Studies in the Cultural Politics of Education*, 24(2):175-190. https://doi.org/10.1080/01596300303042

Grant B. 2010. Challenging matters: Doctoral supervision in post-colonial sites. *Acta Academica Supplementum*, 2010(1):103-129.

Grant B. 2010. The limits of 'teaching and learning': Indigenous students and doctoral supervision. *Teaching in Higher Education*, 15(5):505-517. https://doi.org/ 10.1080/13562517.2010.491903

Gross National Happiness Commission. 2013. *Eleventh five year plan: 2013-2018*. Thimphu: Royal Government of Bhutan.

Grosz E. 1994. *Volatile bodies: toward a corporeal feminism*. Bloomington: Indiana University Press.

Hager P. 2011. Theories of workplace learning. In: M Malloch, L Cairns, K Evans & BN O'Connor (eds). *The SAGE handbook of workplace learning*. London: SAGE. 17-31. https://doi.org/10.4135/9781446200940.n2

Hopwood N. 2010. Doctoral students as journal editors: Non-formal learning through academic work. *Higher Education Research & Development*, 29(3):319-331. https://doi.org/10.1080/07294360903532032

Hopwood N. 2014. Four essential dimensions of workplace learning. *Journal of Workplace Learning*, 26(6/7):349-363. https://doi.org/10.1108/JWL-09-2013-0069

Hopwood N. 2016. *Professional practice and learning: Times, spaces, bodies, things*. Dordrecht: Springer. https://doi.org/10.1007/978-3-319-26164-5

Hopwood N & Paulson J. 2012. Bodies in narratives of doctoral students' learning and experience. *Studies in Higher Education*, 37(6):667-681. https://doi.org/10.1080/03075079.2010.537320

Hopwood N & Stocks C. 2008. Teaching development for doctoral students: What can we learn from activity theory? *International Journal for Academic Development*, 13(3):175-186. https://doi.org/10.1080/13601440802242358

Johnson L, Lee A & Green B. 2000. The PhD and the autonomous self: Gender, rationality and postgraduate pedagogy. *Studies in Higher Education*, 25(2):135-147. https://doi.org/10.1080/13601440802242358

Kemmis S. 2009. Understanding professional practice: A synoptic framework. In: B Green (ed). *Understanding and researching professional practice*. Rotterdam: Sense Publishers. 19-39.

Kendall G. 2002. The crisis in doctoral education: A sociological diagnosis. *Higher Education Research & Development*, 21(2):131-141. https://doi.org/10.1080/07294360220144051

Knorr Cetina K. 2001. Objectual practice. In: TR Schatzki, K Knorr Cetina & E von Savigny (eds). *The practice turn in contemporary theory*. London: Routledge. 175-188.

Lamberti P & Wentzel A. 2014. Integrating authoritative disciplinary voices in postgraduate writing. In: E Bitzer, R Albertyn, L Frick, B Grant & F Kelly (eds). *Pushing boundaries in postgraduate supervision*. Stellenbosch: AFRICAN SUN MeDIA. 85-107. https://doi.org/10.18820/9781920689162/07

Lee D. 1998. Sexual harassment in PhD Supervision. *Gender and Education*, 10(3):299-312. https://doi.org/10.1080/09540259820916

Lee A & Williams C. 1999. "Forged in fire": Narratives of trauma in PhD supervision pedagogy. *Southern Review*, 32(1):6-26.

Lefebvre H. 1991. *The production of space*. Oxford: Blackwell.

MacLure M. 2013. The wonder of data. *Cultural Studies – Critical Methodologies*, 13(4):228-232. https://doi.org/ 10.1177/1532708613487863

Manathunga C. 2012. Supervision and culture: Post-colonial explorations. *Nagoya Journal of Higher Education*, 12:175-190.

Manathunga C. 2014. *Intercultural postgraduate supervision: Reimagining time, place and knowledge*. London: Routledge.

Manathunga C. 2015. Transcultural and postcolonial explorations: Unsettling education. *International Education Journal: Comparative Perspectives*, 14(2).

INTRODUCTORY CHAPTER

Margolis E & Romero M. 1998. 'The department is very male, very white, very old, and very conservative': The functioning of the hidden curriculum in graduate sociology departments. *Harvard Educational Review*, 68(1):1-32. https://doi.org/10.17763/ haer.68.1.1q3828348783j851

Massey D. 2005. *For space*. London: SAGE.

McWilliam E. 2009. Doctoral education in risky times. In: D Boud & A Lee (eds). *Changing practices of doctoral education*. London: Routledge. 189-199.

Middleton S & McKinley E. 2010. The gown and the korowai: Maori doctoral students and the spatial organisation of academic knowledge. *Higher Education Research & Development*, 29(3):229-243. https://doi.org/10.1080/07294360903510590

Mills D, Jepson A, Coxon T, Easterbury-Smith M, Hawkins P & Spencer J. 2006. *Demographic review of the UK social sciences*. Swindon: Economic and Social Research Council.

Mol A. 2002. *The body multiple: Ontology in medical practice*. London: Duke University Press. https://doi.org/10.1215/9780822384151

Paré A. 2014. Rhetorical genre theory and academic writing. *Journal of Academic Language and Learning*, 8(1):83-94.

Parry S. 2007. *Disciplines and doctorates*. Dordrecht: Springer.

Pearson M, Evans T & Macauley P. 2016. The diversity and complexity of settings and arrangements forming the 'experienced environments' for doctoral candidates: Some implications for doctoral education. *Studies in Higher Education*, 41(12):2110-2124. https://doi.org/10.1080/03075079.2015.1019449

Phuntsho K. 2000. On the two ways of learning in Bhutan. *Journal of Bhutan Studies*, 2(2):96-126.

Sallee M. 2014. Performing masculinity: Considering gender in doctoral student socialization. *International Journal for Researcher Development*, 5(2):99-122. https://doi.org/10.1108/IJRD-10-2014-0034

Schatzki TR. 2002. *The site of the social: A philosophical account of the constitution of social life and change*. University Park PA: Pennsylvania State University Press.

Simmonds S & Du Preez P. 2014. The centrality of the research question for locating PhD studies in the global knowledge society. *South African Journal of Higher Education*, 28(5):1607-1624.

Stracke E & Kumar V. 2010. Feedback and self-regulated learning: Insights from supervisors' and PhD examiners' reports. *Reflective Practice*, 11(1):19-32. https://doi.org/10.1080/14623940903525140

Strandler O, Johansson T, Wisker G & Claesson S. 2014. Supervisor or counsellor? – Emotional boundary work in supervision. *International Journal for Researcher Development*, 5(2):70-82. https://doi.org/10.1108/IJRD-03-2014-0002

Tonso KL. 2006. Student engineers and engineer identity: Campus engineer identities as figured world. *Cultural Studies of Science Education*, 1(2):273-307. https://doi.org/10.1007/s11422-005-9009-2

Turner G & McAlpine L. 2011. Doctoral experience as researcher preparation: Activities, passion, status. *International Journal for Researcher Development*, 2(1):46-60. https://doi.org/10.1108/17597511111178014

Van Schalkwyk S. 2012. Graduate attributes for the public good: A case of a research-led university. In: B Leibowitz (ed). *Higher education for the public good: Views from the South*. London: Trentham Books. 87-99. https://doi.org/10.18820/9781928357056/07

Walford G. 1981. Classification and framing in postgraduate education. *Studies in Higher Education*, 6(2):147-158. https://doi.org/10.1080/03075078112331379402

Zuber-Skerritt O & Cendon E. 2014. Critical reflection on professional development in the social sciences: Interview results. *International Journal for Researcher Development*, 5(1):16-32. https://doi.org/ 10.1108/IJRD-11-2013-0018

SECTION A
SUPERVISORY SPACES

'SUCCESS' AND 'FAILURE' IN TWO POSTGRADUATE RESEARCH LEARNING SPACES

AN ACTIVITY THEORY ANALYSIS

Carolyn (Callie) Grant

BACKGROUND AND CONTEXT

The last few decades have seen a dramatic shift in the face of higher education across the world (Guerin, Picard & Green 2014) as the sector has had to respond to the massive global expansion of postgraduate education (Herman 2014). The internationally accepted approach to postgraduate supervision with the 'apprentice scholar' working with the 'master' has begun to be troubled (Clegg 2014) and, as Lee and Boud (2009:22) explain, "the iconic student-supervisor relationship" has become "subsumed into a diverse matrix of opportunities, resources, monitoring processes and expectations". In South Africa, as elsewhere, there is a groundswell towards alternatives to the traditional (dyadic) approach, referred to variously in the literature as group and team approaches (Bitzer & Albertyn 2011), communities of practice (Lotz-Sisitka, Ellery, Olvitt, Schudel & O'Donoghue 2010), cohort supervision (Botha 2014) and learning through community (Grant 2013). Against this backdrop, I have argued that while individual supervisor–student interaction still plays an important role in research learning and development, a communal approach to postgraduate research learning and supervision is a viable alternative (Grant 2013) as it opens up the supervisory space to a variety of different viewpoints or 'voices' (Ranson 2000) and creates the opportunity for an expansive and enriched teaching and learning process.

However, a closer look at the literature, globally and locally, reveals a preference for case studies of postgraduate supervision alternatives at the level of the doctoral degree. In direct contrast, research learning in community at the level of the master's degree is relatively unexplored. This chapter, emerging out of my experience of teaching and supervising several cohorts of master's students in Educational Leadership and Management (ELM) over a number of years (Grant 2014b), aims to contribute to this body of literature. The specific focus of this chapter is thus 'community research learning' in the Master of Education (M Ed) degree in ELM, offered through coursework and half thesis. The postgraduate students who register for this degree are non-traditional in the sense that they are mature-aged, experienced professionals, studying on a part-time basis, while teaching and, in some instances, leading schools (Grant 2014a). In particular, the chapter draws on two cohorts of this M Ed ELM degree, the first from University A, and the second from University B. Both are South African universities, currently classified as traditional universities.

At University A, the cohort consisted of 11 part-time students (practising educational professionals) registered for the M Ed degree in ELM in 2008–2009. I was the sole academic in the programme, responsible for coordination, teaching and supervision. In line with the recommendation of the National Research Foundation audit review calling for more large-scale research (Deacon, Osman & Buchler 2009), the research component of the degree was designed as a multi-case study of 'Teacher leadership in (in)action'. For the half-thesis component of the degree, each student was responsible for one of the 11 case studies.

At University B, the cohort again consisted of 11 part-time students (also practising educational professionals) registered for an M Ed degree in ELM in 2012-2013. By this time, I had relocated from University A to University B where I was similarly involved in the coordination, teaching and supervision of the M Ed ELM programme, together with a senior colleague. The philosophy, structure and model of delivery of this M Ed coursework/half-thesis programme at the two universities were comparable, although aspects of the coursework content and assessment differed slightly. Heeding the National Research Foundation audit review call, it was decided to invite students at University B to participate in a replicated study of the one successfully completed at University A. Thus, the half-thesis component of the degree at University B was also designed as a multi-case study of 'Teacher leadership in (in)action' with students responsible for their own case studies.

Using student results and throughput rates as a measure of success, the first of the community research learning cases was deemed successful with all 11 students at University A completing the degree with quality passes (65% and above) within the minimum two-year period. However, the second of the two cases was far less successful with no student at University B completing the degree within the minimum period. Moreover, only five of the original 11 students completed the degree at all, three within a three-year period and two within a four-year period. The remaining six students either withdrew from the programme or were excluded due to poor progress.

Given that the philosophy, structure and model of delivery of the two programmes was so similar, the question I grappled with was why 'community research learning' was successful at University A, but less so at University B. Using cultural historical activity theory (Engeström 2015) and relational models theory (Fiske 1991, 1992) as theoretical lenses, this chapter seeks plausible explanations for the relative 'success' of the community research learning at University A and the 'failure' of community research learning at University B.

THEORETICAL FRAMEWORKS AND METHODOLOGY

In my initial theorising of community research learning (Grant 2014a, 2014b), I drew on relational models theory (Fiske 1991, 1992) which argues that people across cultures are fundamentally sociable and commonly organise their social life in terms of their relations with other people. Social life, according to Fiske, is a process of "seeking, making, sustaining, repairing, adjusting, judging, construing and sanctioning relationships" (1992:689). Four basic types of elementary social relationships have been identified in this theory and these have been applied to the postgraduate supervision process (Hugo 2012; Grant 2014a). In 'communal sharing' relationships, the focus is on the similarities of the people in a group; they are viewed as equivalent and undifferentiated (Fiske 1992). For Fiske (1992), 'authority ranking' acknowledges the asymmetrical and linear positioning of people in a hierarchical social structure. 'Equality matching' relationships ensure fairness and balance in the group while 'market pricing' is based on socially meaningful values attributed to individuals "in proportion to the amount of effort they put into their work and the quality thereof" (Grant 2014a:117).

Relational models theory was particularly helpful to me in theorising the relational practices as they occurred in the first community research learning supervisory space; the success story at University A (Grant 2014a, 2014b). However, the subsequent 'failure' of the second community research learning space prompted a number of further questions that necessitated the adoption of an additional theoretical lens. I turned to cultural historical activity theory (Engeström 2015) which afforded me the necessary language and tools to describe and explain the different outcomes across the two research learning spaces at University A and University B.

Cultural historical activity theory seeks to analyse development in practical social activities (Engeström 2015; also see Chapter 6 and 20 in this volume for more information about Activity Theory methodology). The unit of analysis in activity theory is the concept of object-oriented, collective and culturally mediated human activity, or activity system (Blackler 2009). This activity system involves subjects working collectively towards the object (or objective) of the activity as its true motive, mediated by a range of artefacts, such as signs and tools (Roth & Lee 2007). The activity is carried out within a specific social context or community, informed by rules (explicit and implicit), and organised according to a division of labour (roles and responsibilities). These elements add the socio-historical aspects of mediated action and influence the outcome of the activity.

A fundamental principle in activity theory is the notion of contradiction as a source of change and development possibilities of the activity (Engeström 2015). Contradictions are historically accumulating structural tensions or forces within and between activity systems, which become the actual driving forces of expansive learning (Engeström & Sannino 2010). Each element of the activity system (e.g. a rule or a subject) can be regarded as a site of clash between forces, a primary contradiction. Secondary contradictions take place between two elements of the central activity system (e.g. between the rule and the community). Tertiary contradictions occur between an activity and a culturally more advanced form of the central activity while quaternary contradictions occur between the central activity and other neighbouring activities (Engeström 2015). By surfacing the contradictions, the dynamics and inefficiencies of the system are exposed, revealing opportunities for innovative ways of structuring and enacting the activity (Foot 2014).

Subjects, in activity theory, through their collective agency, are endowed with the power to act, communicate, solve contradictions and produce artefacts (Sannino, Daniels & Gutierrez 2009) and the ultimate goal is to transform social conditions in order to generate something new (Roth & Lee 2007). Thus, cultural historical activity theory is both practice-based and future-oriented, concerned to describe but also to intervene in social practice (Engeström 2015).

In the next section, cultural historical activity theory and relational models theory are used to analyse the two postgraduate research learning spaces at University A and University B in order to find plausible explanations for the 'success' of one and the 'failure' of the other. To do this, data were drawn from official university documentation such as pass rates, throughput rates and examiners' reports, as well as programme documentation, including course outlines, evaluations and student reflective journals. Data also included interviews with a sample of students from both universities. Two publications on the first case of community research learning at University A (Grant 2014a; Grant 2014b) were also used as sources of data.

AN ANALYSIS OF COMMUNITY RESEARCH LEARNING AT UNIVERSITY A: A STORY OF SUCCESS

In activity theoretical terms, the subjects at University A comprised the cohort of 11 M Ed ELM students and myself as academic. The object of our activity was community research learning within a supervisory space with the outcome evidenced in the successfully completed M Ed theses. The community included colleagues and other postgraduate students at the university as well as school colleagues in the different workplaces. The course outline, academic readings and a series of regular contact sessions constituted the mediating artefacts at the commencement of the activity.

From the outset of the programme, the existing division of labour of the group was given immediate attention. 'Authority ranking' by virtue of the hierarchical power relations of the schooling system was challenged and the voices of teachers and principals were equally valued in the academic space. Differences with respect to designation, gender and age were downplayed and the commonalities within the group brought to the fore. In common was that all were novice researchers with professional experience of school leadership and management, sourced from the mass media or from the workplace (Grant 2014a). Sharing of this tacit knowledge and opening it out to interrogation immediately drew these novice researchers into a relationship of 'communal sharing'. Communal sharing was further encouraged through the sharing of material artefacts such as academic articles, books, notes and meals (Grant 2014a).

However, communal sharing relationships were not conceived in insolation but were strengthened by virtue of the 'equality-matching' relationships embedded in the mediation process. Turn taking, a necessary principle of equality-matching relationships, was integral to the provision of shared lunches, the seminar presentations as well as talk-time during discussion and feedback sessions. One student wrote how "we used to debate the issues and everybody in the group had an opinion" (Student 5, journal entry). For another student, the discussions were invaluable and could only be so if every member read widely and critically" (Student 2, journal entry). Thus turn taking, or "the amount of 'air time' different members of the group may have in general discussions" (Guerin *et al* 2014) developed into a significant rule of the group. Other rules developed, including punctual attendance at, and active participation in, contact sessions as well as commitment to the submission deadlines negotiated for aspects of the research and writing processes (Student 5, journal entry). This unwritten contract was based on "the values of trust and respect, a healthy touch of competition, regular and open communication, the development of friendships and a strong work ethic" (Grant 2014b:93).

This safe collective supervisory space provided fertile ground for the emergence of distributed agency and leadership among students (a distributed division of labour). In terms of these 'market pricing' relationships, one student added value to the group when he introduced the idea of a group t-shirt, a mediating artefact, which helped with social cohesion. He was also instigator of a number of social activities, including a formal group photo-shoot and a celebratory post-graduation braai (Grant 2014b). Another two students added value to the learning process because "they shared a lively sense of humour and an infectious laugh, which contributed to a safe and relaxed pedagogical space" (Grant 2014b:95). Yet another student stood apart because of her courage to pose challenging intellectual questions; perceptively captured in an examiner's report:

> [This student] is neither intimidated nor constrained by the literature she has read and she shows remarkable insight into complex arguments, where she is able to extract the essence of validity for her study. She is not afraid of challenging what less competent students might feel they have no right to question. This is, in my opinion, a particular strength of this dissertation (M Ed Examiner's Report 4, 2010).

This case of community research learning was deemed successful, primarily because the subjects cohered socially in their achievement of the object, evidenced in the 11 completed M Ed theses in the minimum period. One examiner was impressed by "the level of critical scholarship" of the thesis (M Ed Examiner's Report 8, 2010) while another wrote of the "competent level of independent scholarship" of the work (M Ed Examiner's Report 8, 2010). Another examiner remarked, "This student's dissertation is an important contribution to the field" (M Ed Examiner's Report 4, 2010). Seven students were encouraged by examiners to publish their research while the student who attained the highest dissertation mark was encouraged to proceed immediately to doctoral studies. Subsequently, three students from this cohort have graduated with their doctoral degrees.

Student reflections on their community research learning experiences were also interesting: "Our group project only worked because each one of us as an individual was driven to succeed and finish and we were motivated by each other" (Student 1, journal entry). Another made the point that "as students we were encouraged to take charge of our own learning" (Student 5, journal entry) while another reflected on the tough work of the degree: "I toiled when I worked the dissertation! The many drafts were energy sapping but they were necessary to set a standard that we could be proud of" (Student 2, journal entry). The success of the activity was viewed by colleagues in the faculty as ground breaking in terms of cohort supervision within a collaborative research project (Peer-Review Report 1, 2010) and in terms of increased postgraduate throughput rates (Peer-Review Report 2, 2010). An outcome of this 'success' was the invitation to publish a chapter in the book *Pushing boundaries in postgraduate supervision*, edited by Bitzer, Albertyn, Frick, Grant and Kelly in 2014.

AN ANALYSIS OF COMMUNITY RESEARCH LEARNING AT UNIVERSITY B: A STORY OF DISAPPOINTMENT AND SUBSEQUENT DELIBERATION

In many ways, the case at University B was very similar to that at University A. The *subjects* at University B also comprised 11 M Ed students, similarly constituted in terms of designation, age, gender and experience. However, at University B, two academics, a senior colleague and I, constituted the staff component of the *'subjects'* element. Similar in terms of our race, level of privilege and commitment to ELM as a field of study, we differed in our gender, age and supervision practices. His 20-year postgraduate supervision experience revealed his preference for the traditional one-on-one approach to supervision, while I leaned more towards collaborative practices in my 10-year postgraduate experience. The *object* of the activity remained the same, community research learning within a supervisory space with the *outcome* the successfully completed M Ed theses. The *community* in both cases was also similar.

The course outline, academic readings and a series of regular contact sessions constituted the *mediating artefacts* at the commencement of the activity, and attempts to challenge the hierarchical power relations of the schooling system, inherent in the *division of labour* of the group, were also initiated. The structured face-to-face support offered to these part-time students during the coursework component of the degree was comparable across universities (Course outlines; University A, University B). The overview, purpose and format of the degree were specified in the course outline and, although content differed to some extent, the responsibilities of the students were made explicit with respect to participation and assessment (the *rules*). Assessment at both universities included written assignments and a self-reflective journaling process (Course outlines; University A, University B). However, a seminar presentation approach was not adopted at University B. The communal sharing of meals was also not introduced as a practice in this group and, as with many part-time postgraduate programmes, lunch breaks were considered a private responsibility. As a student explained: "… and during our lunch we used to go out and buy something for ourselves" (University B, Student 4, interview). Communal sharing relationships were only evident in the sharing of and engagement with scholarly texts, in preparation for the assignments, as noted by one student: "Most of the readings, if somebody is having the reading; he will give it to the other students, as well" (University B, Student 4, interview).

What this ultimately meant was that the principle of turn taking, integral to the provision of shared lunches, the seminar presentations as well as 'air time' during discussion and feedback sessions at University A, did not become a *rule* at University B. With so little opportunity for turn taking within the group, equality-matching relationships were not explicitly advanced. It was therefore left to University B students to be responsible for, and accountable to, the group of their own accord. This, unfortunately, did not happen and the group did not cohere. In the words of one student, "[W]e were apart. The problem is ... even though we were a group we didn't really work as a group" (University B, Student 1, interview). The unwritten *rules* of punctual attendance at, and active participation in, contact sessions as well as commitment to the submission deadlines negotiated for aspects of the research and writing processes were neither owned, upheld nor enforced (University B, Students 1 and 2, interviews). Furthermore, there was a general sense of anxiety among students; they often felt dejected and many grappled with their personal set of stresses (University B, Student 3, interview). The result was that only five of the original 11 students completed the degree, but none within the minimum period. A couple of students did not even manage to submit their proposals (University B, Student 2, interview).

WHY DID COMMUNITY RESEARCH LEARNING AT UNIVERSITY B FAIL?

By drawing on activity theory, three contradictions (one primary and two secondary) could be identified in the data, and this helped us explain why community research learning at University B 'failed'.

First, a primary contradiction within the *subject* element of the activity system was identified. Student investment in postgraduate studies (Van Schalkwyk 2014) and prioritisation of these studies differed amongst the students and influenced their level of contribution and commitment to the group. As one student explained: "... initially we used to come together in our first year and discuss things but later we sort of drifted apart" (University B, Student 1, interview). This same student acknowledged that she was not a team person but "more of a lone ranger" (University B, Student 1, interview). Another student explained how the group did not prioritise their M Ed studies, but instead favoured competing commitments such as SADTU[1] leadership or church leadership over their university commitments (University B, Student 4, interview). In

---

[1] South African Democratic Teachers' Union

her words, "… you can't be doing three or more things at the same time. So, if it's 'I am studying', it must be like that. You can't commit yourself to other things" (UB, Student 4, interview). Yet another student argued that "when you say you've come (to the university) to work, you must work. You must not get involved in moving right round this location[2] during the night … you see there are taverns there … there are ladies moving down there" (University B, Student 3, interview). These tensions within the 'subject' element resulted in a poor work ethic, exemplified by late coming, absenteeism, non-participation in class as well as the ignoring of deadlines and submission dates.

Second, this poor work ethic was reinforced by a secondary contradiction, a tension between the *rule* and the *object* of the activity. While community research learning was espoused as the object of the activity, this was in tension with the unwritten rules embedded in the institutional culture of University B, which still privileged traditional supervision practices. This tension was exacerbated by the differing histories of the two academics. Consequently, turn taking (in the form of meal sharing and rotational assessment practices) was not a prominent feature of the programme. Furthermore, in line with the liberal tradition, rules were underplayed and perceived more flexibly as guidelines, allowing for a fair amount of manipulation and misuse. As academics, we colluded in this process. One student bemoaned the fact that "we were not pressed by deadlines" (UB, Student 2, interview) while another was of the view that "the dates should be observed. I think so because, because if you keep on being lenient, obviously the people who you are working with will relax a bit" (University B, Student 3, interview). When reflecting on the shifting of the due date for proposal submission, Student 1's anger at our leniency around deadlines was palpable:

> Ja, and people got away with it and I felt terribly betrayed because here I was, I had stopped things (taking up her senior marking position during matriculation marking) that were important to me … only to realise in January that, no, some of us had gone for marking after all and weren't terribly worried. There were those who hadn't even started their proposal in the first place (University B, Student 1, interview).

Third, the tensions around *rules* had a direct impact on the *division of labour* in the activity system because, in the absence of turn taking, the hierarchical relations of the schooling system prevailed. This was particularly detrimental to equality-matching

---

[2] A South African term also known as 'township'. Locations or townships were built on the periphery of towns and cities and were often under-developed. Until the end of apartheid, they were reserved for race groups other than the 'white' population.

relationships as one member of the group, a senior official in the provincial department, wielded power over his colleagues, as suggested in the data. For example, this official referred to himself as "chief" in relation to his colleagues and claimed that many were "afraid of him". In an interview, one of the students quoted him as saying, "I used to joke with them (members of the group) that when you are here at University B, that is fine. But on Monday, I'll be in your school to check what it is that you are doing in terms of the policy." This student continued: "Some of them would just become angry, others would just laugh" (University B, Student 3, interview). A number of similar quotes from his interview speak to issues of power and hierarchical social relations prevalent in the schooling context, which played themselves out in the postgraduate space. As academics, we did not fully grasp these rather damaging undercurrents which, with hindsight, we now understand would have contributed to a loss of trust and the development of a supervisory space which was neither safe nor generative (Van Schalkwyk 2014). Indeed, intimidatory remarks such as these were at odds with the heterarchical relationships (Woods & Gronn 2009) we were trying to engender among our students in the pursuit of the goal of community researching learning.

HOW COMMUNITY RESEARCH LEARNING MIGHT BE EXPANDED: INSIGHTS FROM ACROSS THE CASES

A comparison of the two cases shows that there was more variation in the student group (*subjects*) in terms of race, language, ethnicity, religion and union representation at University A than at University B. Because the student group at University A was more diverse, individuals had to do the hard work of getting to know 'the other' and so group diversity became a catalyst for new learning, as well as new ways of "being and becoming" (Van Schalkwyk 2014:215). In contrast, the more homogenous student group at University B was able to take much more for granted in their interactions with others, resulting in fewer opportunities for new ways of being and becoming. Given that community research learning at University A was successful, one can argue that diversity (rather than homogeneity) within the subject element is more likely to contribute to its solidarity and ultimate success. Botha (2014:150) makes a similar claim when she argues that "accommodating diversity is at the centre of success" of the cohort supervision model.

Although all students across both cases held education honours degrees, the cases differed in terms of student preparedness for postgraduate study. A sobering observation was that not one of the five students who graduated with their honours degrees at University B was successful at master's level. We had to critically interrogate our own honours degree at University B and ask questions about its content and purpose: was it preparing our students sufficiently for postgraduate study? It was not, if we compared it to the honours programme at University A, which included a module introducing students to research and another requiring them to do a small independent research project.

In order to achieve the objective of community research learning, conscious investment in the process is required. This necessitates knowing in new ways (McKenna 2012) and implies identity work. As McKenna (2012:57) argues, "[T]aking on new ways of thinking, reading and writing entails taking on new ways of being." This, however, does not happen by chance, and concerted teaching is essential, teaching that pays attention to the different elements of the activity system; the scheduling of sessions and careful design and delivery of the programme (Botha 2014), the development of artefacts (signs and tools), the interrogation of the culture and division of labour and making explicit the rules of the activity. By so doing, the "shroud that obscures the inner workings of the supervisory relationship" (Van Schalkwyk 2014:225) will be disturbed. If successfully effected, the postgraduate students will be more able to critique the current situation, the taken-for-granted, and expand their learning. Though often marked by moments of dissonance, uncertainty and crisis, this process will ultimately lead to supervisory spaces of changes and growth.

In this reconceptualisation of the postgraduate research learning space, consideration of the *output*, the completed M Ed thesis, is also required. Students held contrasting perceptions of the M Ed half thesis in the two cases. At University B, the analogy of 'the quick and easy fast-food purchase' can be used to describe how some students viewed the thesis. These students were not sincere in their commitment to learning but instead wanted a 'quick fix' with the least amount of engagement possible. Their individual and collective motivation levels, so crucial to engaged research learning (Frick, Albertyn & Bitzer 2014), were largely inadequate. In contrast, students at University A were fully committed to the metaphor of the "gestation of the thesis" (Hounsell 2007), a two-year period during which the coursework component with its structured assessment fed forward into the research process of the second year of study (Grant 2013). The demanding work of this gestation process was aptly captured in an excerpt quoted earlier and which I repeat here: "I toiled when I worked the dissertation! The many drafts were energy sapping but they were necessary to set a standard that we could be proud of" (Student 2, journal entry).

GOING FORWARD: HOW CAN WE BETTER PREPARE FOR COMMUNITY RESEARCH LEARNING?

Social cohesion is at the heart of community research learning. Social cohesion can be defined as a cohesive group which "works towards the wellbeing of all its members, fights exclusion and marginalisaton, creates a sense of belonging, promotes trust and offers its members the opportunity of upward mobility" (Australian Human Rights Commission 2015). Within the postgraduate research learning space, social cohesion can be developed through a structured programme of regular, focused contact sessions, clarity and purpose of assessment tasks which demand of each individual some embodied contribution, as well as firm commitment to dates and deadlines. Furthermore, the purpose of the research learning community with its goal, rules, artifacts and division of labour must be made more explicit and negotiated with all subjects at the outset of the teaching process. Thus, in the postgraduate research learning space, social cohesion needs to be made explicit – it needs to be taught – just as disciplinary specific knowledge and research processes and practices also need to be taught (Figure 2.1). Additionally, as Frick, Albertyn and Bitzer (2014) remind us, momentum during this teaching process is essential.

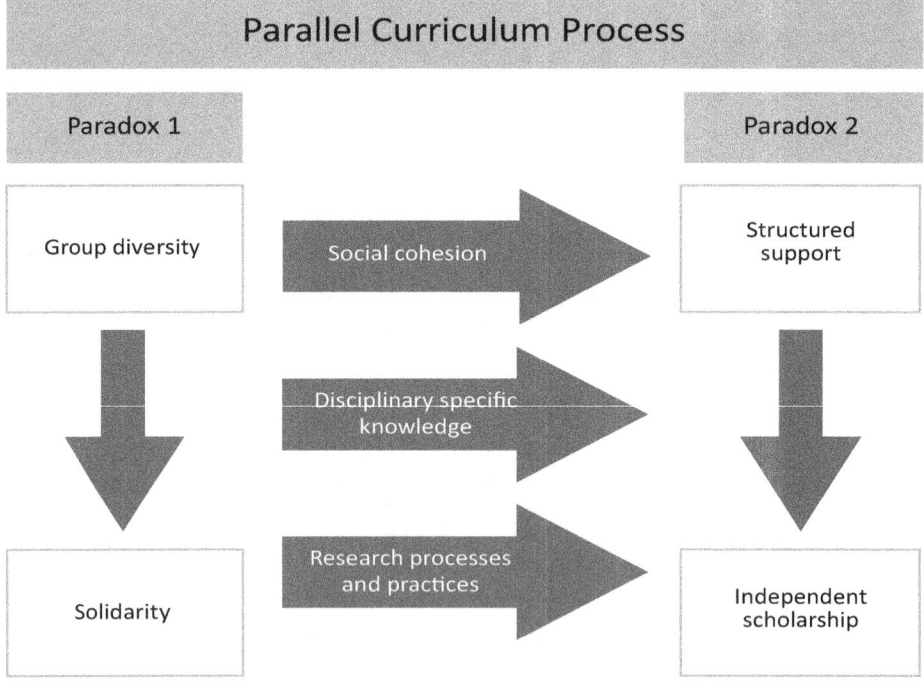

FIGURE 2.1 Parallel curriculum processes necessary in the accomplishment of the objective of community research learning

In summing up, the analysis of 'success' and 'failure' in the two post-graduate research learning spaces, discussed in this chapter, leaves us with two paradoxes (Figure 2.1). The first paradox is that group diversity ultimately leads to solidarity. Diversity within a social group opens up other ways of being and becoming, it challenges its members to question the taken-for-granted, and it offers opportunities for authentic 'collaborative critique' (Guerin et al 2014) and expansive learning. As an outcome of this engaged process, a (new) group identity is likely to emerge. The second paradox is that the more structured the support at the beginning of the postgraduate programme (the more 'glue' there is), the more likely students will learn the new ways of being and becoming. This structured support will provide a solid platform from which to learn to stand on one's own, develop the ability to critique and ultimately emerge as an independent scholar.

I have learnt much about community research learning from our 'success' and 'failure' at Universities A and B respectively, and this learning continues to inform subsequent iterations of the M Ed degree. Additionally, as a consequence of this research, the Honours ELM elective at University B has undergone a rigorous process of re-curriculation. In closing, I argue that while the two cases I have presented are locally inflected and understood, a picture of community research learning emerges that transcends the local and contributes to the international debates on postgraduate supervision.

ACKNOWLEDGEMENTS

I thank the M Ed students for their contributions to this chapter and my colleague and friend, Professor Hennie van der Mescht, for his enduring support of my work.

REFERENCES

Australian Human Rights Commission. 2015. *Building social cohesion in our communities*. www.acelg.org.au/socialcohesion [Retrieved 1 January 2017].

Bitzer EM & Albertyn RM. 2011. Alternative approaches to postgraduate supervision: A planning tool to facilitate supervisory processes. *South African Journal of Higher Education,* 25(5):874-888.

Blackler F. 2009. Cultural-historical activity theory and organisational studies. In: A Sannino, H Daniels & KD Gutierrez (eds). *Learning and expanding with activity theory*. Cambridge: Cambridge University Press. 19-39. https://doi.org/10.1017/CBO9780511809989.003

Botha N. 2014. The cohort supervision model: To what extent does it facilitate doctoral success? In: E Bitzer, R Albertyn, L Frick, B Grant & F Kelly (eds). *Pushing boundaries in postgraduate supervision*. Stellenbosch: AFRICAN SUN MeDIA. 133-152.

Clegg S. 2014. Knowledge questions and doctoral education. In: E Bitzer, R Albertyn, L Frick, B Grant & F Kelly (eds). *Pushing boundaries in postgraduate supervision*. Stellenbosch: AFRICAN SUN MeDIA. 11-24. https://doi.org/10.18820/9781920689162/02

Deacon R, Osman R & Buchler M. 2009. *Audit and interpretative analysis of educational research in South Africa: What have we learnt?* A research report submitted to the National Research Foundation, March 2009.

Engeström Y. 2015. *Learning by expanding: An activity theoretical approach to development research*. 2nd Edition. Cambridge: Cambridge University Press.

Engeström Y & Sannino A. 2010. Studies of expansive learning: Foundations, findings and future challenges. *Educational Research Review*, 5:1-24. https://doi.org/10.1016/j.edurev.2009.12.002

Fiske AP. 1991. *Structures of social life: The four elementary forms of human relations*. New York: The Free Press.

Fiske AP. 1992. The four elementary forms of sociality: Framework for a unified theory of social relations. *Psychological Review*, 99(4):689-723. https://doi.org/ 10.1037/0033-295X.99.4.689

Foot KA. 2014. Cultural historical activity theory: Exploring a theory to inform practice and research. *Journal of Human Behavior in Social Environments*, 24(3):329-347. https://doi.org/10.1080/10911359.2013.831011

Frick L, Albertyn R & Bitzer E. 2014. Conceptualising risk in doctoral education: Navigating boundary tensions. In: E Bitzer, R Albertyn, L Frick, B Grant & F Kelly (eds). *Pushing boundaries in postgraduate supervision*. Stellenbosch:AFRICAN SUN MeDIA. 53-66. https://doi.org/10.18820/9781920689162/05

Grant C. 2013. Using assessment strategically to gestate a student thesis: Learning through community. *South African Journal of Higher Education*, 27(5):1250-1263.

Grant C. 2014a. Pushing the boundaries of postgraduate supervision: Theorising research learning in community. In: E Bitzer, R Albertyn, L Frick, B Grant & F Kelly (eds). *Pushing boundaries in postgraduate supervision*. Stellenbosch: AFRICAN SUN MeDIA. 109-122. https://doi.org/10.18820/9781920689162/08

Grant C. 2014b. Postgraduate research learning communities and their contribution to the field of educational leadership and management. *International Studies in Educational Administration*, 41(1):89-100.

Guerin C, Picard M & Green I. 2014. A coordinated framework for developing researchers' intercultural competency. In: E Bitzer, R Albertyn, L Frick, B Grant & F Kelly (eds). *Pushing boundaries in postgraduate supervision*. Stellenbosch: AFRICAN SUN MeDIA. 169-183. https://doi.org/10.18820/9781920689162/12

Herman C. 2014. The South African doctorate: Where to now? In: E Bitzer, R Albertyn, L Frick, B Grant & F Kelly (eds). *Pushing boundaries in postgraduate supervision*. Stellenbosch: AFRICAN SUN MeDIA. 39-52. https://doi.org/10.18820/9781920689162/04

Hounsell D. 2007. Towards more sustainable feedback to students. In: D Boud & N Falchikov (eds). *Rethinking assessment in higher education: Learning for the longer term*. Oxon: Routledge. 101-113.

Hugo W. 2012. Supervision response. In: A Fataar (ed). *Debating thesis supervision*. Stellenbosch: AFRICAN SUN MeDIA. 107-113.

Lee A & Boud D. 2009. Framing doctoral education as practice. In: D Boud & A Lee (eds). *Changing practices of doctoral education*. Oxon: Routledge. 10-25.

Lotz-Sisitka H, Ellery K, Olvitt L, Schudel I & O'Donoghue R. 2010. Cultivating a scholarly community of practice. *Acta Academica Supplementum*, 1:130-150.

McKenna S. 2012. The context of access and foundation provisioning in South Africa. In: R Dhunpath & R Vithal (eds). *Alternative access to higher education*. Cape Town: Pearsons. 50-60.

Ranson S. 2000. Recognising the pedagogy of voice in a learning community. *Education Management and Administration*, 28(3):263-279. https://doi.org/10.1177/0263211X000283003

Roth W-M & Lee Y-J. 2007. Vygotsky's neglected legacy: Cultural-historical activity theory. *Review of Educational Research*, 77(2):186-232. https://doi.org/ 10.3102/0034654306298273

Sannino A, Daniels H & Gutierrez KD. 2009. Editors' introduction. In: A Sannino, H Daniels & KD Gutierrez (eds). *Learning and expanding with activity theory*. Cambridge: Cambridge University Press. xi-xxi.

Van Schalkwyk S. 2014. Evolving doctoral identities: Understanding 'complex investments'. In: E Bitzer, R Albertyn, L Frick, B Grant & F Kelly (eds). *Pushing boundaries in postgraduate supervision*. Stellenbosch: AFRICAN SUN MeDIA. 215-227. https://doi.org/10.18820/9781920689162/15

Woods PA & Gronn P. 2009. Nurturing democracy: The contribution of distributed leadership to a democratic organisational landscape. *Educational Management, Administration and Leadership*, 37(4):430-451. https://doi.org/ 10.1177/1741143209334597

SUPERVISING UP – A (FICTIONALISED) REPORT FROM THE RESEARCH TRAINING TRENCHES

Nick Mansfield & Sally Purcell

INTRODUCTION

This is less an academic essay than an attempt to exhibit the tangle that some candidates can get into during the course of their research. Although it is possible to put in place specific remedies for specific issues, candidature is always experienced as a uniquely complex whole where multiple issues intersect and cross-multiply to place the candidate in an always unprecedented situation. How do candidates navigate their way in such a unique space, and how possible is it to give them skills that will make them masters of their own academic destiny? Candidates' connection with the university has multiple facets. The university provides resources and funding and awards qualifications. But the most important thing it provides is the human connection to a research community. What graduate surveys indicate is that candidates who are happy with supervision are almost always happy with their whole research training experience. The quality of supervision, however, is highly variable, and often resistant to improvement. Supervisors also face new challenges. Because of the increasing specialisation of research, the projects candidates undertake are increasingly beyond the scope of their supervisors' knowledge and oversight. More research is being undertaken off-site, in industry, for example. Candidates end up with a number of people in a supervisory role, with different skills and different responsibilities. Yet these responsibilities are often fluid and unclear, and need to be managed carefully.

Using a number of case studies, in this chapter we first show some of the tangled problems that might be encountered with supervision, and the unique form in which they compound with one another in each individual case. We then look at different ways in which Macquarie University is responding to the complexity of these issues, to indicate how some of these challenges are being dealt with in one institution at least. We look at a way of helping candidates learn how to build greater self-agency so that they can have greater input and better manage their complex supervision teams. PhD candidates are the ones who will ultimately bear the consequences of the management of their higher degree by research (HDR) programmes and, as a result, they need to know how to take charge of their project and communicate assertively with their support teams. Learning how to manage projects assertively will also help PhD graduates to transition to post-PhD employment.

There is widespread acknowledgement in the literature of the complex web of relationships in which candidates are immersed while undertaking higher research degrees. Mantai and Dowling (2015), for example, reveal the networks on which successful candidates rely in order to make it through to completion with both academic quality and personal wellbeing intact, as exhibited in thesis acknowledgement pages. Some of the literature reports on and theorises these complex networks in relation to the agency candidates adopt in order to cope (see, for example, Deuchar 2008; Hopwood 2010). The focus, however, has been largely on the important work of how agency currently emerges when candidates are under pressure and need practical solutions on the spur of the moment or on how we can think about agency in research training. Other contributions see the development of agency as a way of cultivating transferable skills that will be useful in employment or are important in the development of the candidate's academic identity (see McAlpine & Asghar 2010; Baker & Pifer 2011).

In this chapter we adopt an unapologetically practical and programmatic approach in that we see the structured and positive cultivation of strong candidate agency and assertiveness as indispensable to successful candidature. This is especially important given that candidates are no longer looking only at academic careers or undertaking conventionally academic projects, and are building their candidature in multiple and complex environments, in which they must increasingly take charge of their own situations. It is widely recognised that the PhD candidate can no longer be seen as a junior player in a known academic environment of which their supervisor is a practised and confident citizen. Instead, candidates are shifting between different environments, many of which are well beyond their supervisors' knowledge and expertise, and in which they need to become the controlling party. In line with this practical approach, we approach this issue by way of a small set of hypothetical case studies.

CASE STUDIES

The cases described below are all fictional, although they have their origins and counterparts in our HDR management experience.

Mara

Mara has come to Australia to do her PhD on indigenous scientific knowledge, specifically the use of resin from native plants for medicinal purposes. Her research requires fieldwork because she needs to travel to remote locations on Aboriginal lands to interview practitioners and gather samples. Her university requires her to conform to strict protocols, and her supervisor must appear in all ethics documentation as the chief investigator on her project. Her supervisor isn't much help, however, and sees ethics applications as form-filling, and he tells her to "just get on with it". Mara recognises that she does need her supervisor's assistance yet she feels daunted by the thought of approaching him. Her associate supervisor was unaware he was on her project, and says he can't do anything as he is currently overseas. So she consults a junior staff member, an HDR academic writing advisor, who is really helpful, but keeps reminding Mara that helping candidates with ethics applications is not her responsibility.

Mara chooses to avoid having a difficult conversation with her supervisor, so, in order to get through the process she reduces her fieldwork to the bare minimum. After some feedback and re-drafting, she gets ethics clearance and heads into the field. In order to research on Aboriginal lands in western New South Wales, she needs clearance from the local Aboriginal authorities, which is given. While she is in the field, Mara is advised to talk to some practitioners across the border in South Australia, where she is likely to get the best data. She asks her supervisor what to do. He's keen to get data from this region for his own research, so he encourages her to go ahead. Her research goes well. She returns to campus and starts working on her draft. Later, during examination, one of Mara's examiners questions whether Mara had permission to research on Aboriginal Lands in South Australia, either in her ethics clearance or from the relevant authorities. The preliminary review by the ethics office looks likely to conclude that this fieldwork was not approved, and therefore cannot be included in her thesis. If she has to remove this data from her thesis, she won't have much left and might have to walk away without a degree …

George

George is lucky to secure an industry-based PhD scholarship. The stipend is higher than regular scholarships and he will be working in the R&D unit of an exciting electronics firm. His project focuses on a security algorithm that will increase the accuracy of facial recognition software. The university is very interested in his project as it may lead to a highly lucrative commercialisation opportunity. His supervisor at the university has his own start-up and is very keen to monitor George's research, as are both the innovation and corporate engagement offices of the university. In the lab at the electronics firm, where he's based, George has an official supervisor who's the corporate outreach manager (friendly and supportive but busy and ignorant of the science) and a lab supervisor (very good on the engineering, but impatient and snappy). Neither of them has a PhD, and the outreach manager does not even seem to be clear as to what a PhD involves. Everyone is interested in George's project but no one is giving him much help with the science. At a conference, George befriends an academic from another university in the same city where he is based who is very interested in what he's doing and understands the scientific issues. They begin to meet regularly. It turns out there is bad blood between this new mentor and George's supervisor, so he has to keep the relationship secret.

Although he'd like to, he can't change universities as the scholarship he's on is locked in between his current university and the firm he's working for. With this new support, the project progresses well. However, George's supervisor runs into him and his rival mentor in a coffee shop one day and starts to get suspicious and unhelpful. George feels that he would like to talk to his supervisor and explain what led him to seek additional assistance and guidance. However, he doesn't know how to go about having that conversation so he avoids it. The firm suddenly revises its R&D strategy, and is less invested in the area of George's research. His overseeing supervisor in the firm leaves and the lab supervisor starts to become disengaged. He can't get resources and he really needs a new industry support team, but he doesn't know how to go about asking for this. He is concerned that he may not be able to submit his thesis for examination, and lies awake at night fearing he may never get a PhD.

Jessa

Jessa is a successful documentary film maker. Her first feature on a sexual abuse case in the military won a set of national awards, and got honourable mention at one of the world's biggest documentary film festivals. Her partner is an academic and recommends to her that she enrol in a doctorate while making her next film. "You're going to make the film anyway," she says. "Why not get a PhD, as well, while you're doing it?" Jessa enrols in the department where her partner works, and is appointed a supervisor she doesn't really know, and about whom her partner is a bit dubious. Jessa is very experienced and capable, however, and feels she doesn't need much supervision. She attends the meetings her supervisor calls irregularly, but feels she is just going through the motions. Her thesis is a combination of creative output and academic exegesis. She intends to complete the film first and write the exegesis later. Her supervisor is a bit nervous about this plan, but is timid so lets her go ahead. She sets up a production company for her film, and appoints someone she has worked with in the past as her producer. The funding the university provides does not cover the production costs for her new film, which involves significant travel to remote locations, so she has to apply to a government funding body. Because of her reputation and the significance of the new project, she gets funding, even though the budget will be tight.

However, after she receives the first tranche of funding, the government announces a freeze on all support for the arts. The project stalls. Jessa and the producer she is working with head off overseas, without leave from candidature, in order to try and raise production money. The producer tells her the film is a higher priority than her degree, and the quest for funding has to come first. Meanwhile, back at the university, a factional dispute has bubbled to the surface in the department. Jessa's partner and her supervisor are on different sides. She's not unduly worried as she is relying on her partner for academic advice more than her formal supervisor. She knows she needs to sort out her own position in relation to her supervision, but it seems too tangled and she keeps putting it off. About half-way through her candidature, however, she is put under review by her supervisor, whose report says her plan for completion was never approved and no progress is being made on the academic side of her project.

PROBLEM: WEAK OR DISTRACTED SUPERVISION

These cases show a set of issues that can arise in the course of candidature and potentially threaten completion. The issue we want to focus on is supervision. In each of these cases, the candidate draws on advice from a variety of formal and informal mentors. They are working in a variety of contexts – industry, the field, the arts – each requiring types of expertise and access to different kinds of resources that are outside of the control and even the understanding of the university and its staff. In Mara's case, formal supervision is indifferent or absent, and she doesn't know how to confront her supervisor so she relies on staff who are helpful but neither qualified nor assigned to supervise. Her fieldwork is undertaken without awareness of the sensitivities of working in a specific cultural/political environment, and she neither seeks advice nor has a really qualified person appointed to advise her. In George's case, there are a series of interested parties with more of a stake in the product of

George's research than in his getting a PhD and George feels helpless and doesn't know how to negotiate a better supervision experience. The one academic who does help him has no formal appointment, and, in the end, his project is not sufficiently protected from developments in industry. In Jessa's case, her level of professional expertise is significantly higher than that of her appointed supervisor, who also has different ideas about how to proceed. Jessa would benefit from guidance on how to take advantage of the supervisor's expertise in negotiating the academic requirements of her candidature. She is relying on input and advice from a number of other parties in industry and on the technical side, but also on the personal side. In the end, because of a funding crisis, the advice from these different sources starts to conflict. What's worse, this is happening in an environment where relationships are already failing.

All of these projects are threatened with disaster, and each of the candidates may have to walk away without getting their degree. Part of the problem may be attributed to conflict of interest. In each case, some of the advice each candidate receives is influenced by the interests of other parties. Mara's supervisor wants to piggy-back on her fieldwork in order to progress his own research. George is working at the intersection of various parties who all want to benefit from what he comes up with. He's also trapped between two rival academics. Jessa's situation is complicated by the fact her partner is in the same department, and then ends up on the other side of a bitter factional dispute to her supervisor. It's arguable that these conflicts of interest could be mitigated by some reflection on the part of the parties involved, but each is also under significant pressure: from the need to produce their own research, generate research-related income, advance the university's relations with industry, or secure doctoral completions.

There are also serious issues of a lazy or casual approach to supervision. In Mara's case, the supervisor fails to support her properly through the ethics application, forcing her to rely on a junior staff member who provides help but outside of their proper role, and without the necessary expertise. This is an example of supervision without appointment or authority, something widespread in practice. In George's case, the actual science behind his research is a low priority for those who have been formally appointed as his supervision team. He finds expert supervision, which allows him to progress, but it is unofficial, and for reasons of academic politics, he has to pursue it on the sly. Finally, in Jessa's case, supervision is fraught by a lack of competence in her exact research area, another complicated institutional relationship and eventually ill-feeling between groups in the department where she is studying. She is also more committed to the project than the degree, so when a funding crisis develops, she lets her commitments to the university slide.

SOLUTION: POLICING SUPERVISION?

These are all potential instances of unprofessional or even unethical behaviour on the part of supervisors. Supervision quality and the professionalism of supervision have lagged behind analogous developments in learning and teaching, where teaching qualifications, certification and fellowship schemes, as well as a renewed emphasis on teaching in university promotions criteria, have all signalled especially to incoming academics, what the expectations are for quality in the classroom. Universities have tried to respond to the question of supervisor quality by mandatory supervisor training, but there are increasing calls for hard data on supervisor performance, including consequences for under-performing supervisors. The recent Review of the Australian research training system by the Australian Council of Learned Academies (ACOLA) stated: "Universities have a responsibility to monitor supervisor performance and drive excellence in HDR supervision through recognition mechanisms and performance management" (ACOLA 91). It went on: "Monitoring supervisor performance will require institutions to improve their performance data and to develop performance measures. Performance data should be collected at not only the individual level, but also at the level of supervisory committees. Performance measures could include candidate evaluations, completion times and rates and career outcomes of HDR graduates… allowing for legitimate breaks for the candidate; and recognising additional benefits gained, such as candidate publications" (ACOLA 91).

There is a risk here of drawing on metrics that are an unsubtle representation of what is happening during candidature. Good completion times may be the product of highly motivated candidates attracted to a strong research team, or an overly narrowly designed project, in which only output and not the broader development of the candidate is the focus. Many departments also have a supervisor of last resort, who may take on candidates who have struggled or are overtime, and succeed in getting them through. If judged purely on completion times, such supervisors would look like under-performers. Metrics too easily provoke judgements and judgements trigger consequences, often of a potentially draconian form. A culture of performance may emerge, but one still lacking a fully professional educational ethos, or indeed a coherent pedagogy.

There is also the problem of the over-individualisation of the problem of supervision quality. Supervisors are themselves under significant pressure to perform and be accountable in a range of areas, and on a day-to-day basis, something often has to give. Supervision, with its vague deadlines and flexible programme of work is always going to be at risk here. It's famously vulnerable to procrastination. Pretending supervisors are solely responsible for ideal outcomes simply adds to their burden while doing nothing to control their workloads or make them feel encouraged and supported, let alone providing them with practical strategies that will show them the way forward in tricky situations.

SOLUTION: MORE TRAINING?

There are also problems with supervision training. Universities have had problems in the past when they set mandatory requirements for workshop attendance that fail to acknowledge the different levels of experience of supervisors, and are also seen by staff as a compliance requirement rather than a contribution to their skills and professional development. At Macquarie University, we have tried in recent years to negotiate the shift from a compliance approach (where academics need to attend a minimum number of workshops per year) to cultivating a shared culture of supervision, in which not only supervision outcomes, but engagement with the research on supervision, mentoring and sharing experiences are valued. The promotions criteria at Macquarie have been re-written to include these expectations of supervision, not just in terms of outcomes but contribution to the university's research training life more generally. For example, those seeking promotion to professor are expected to have shown "leadership of a supportive research-training environment that enables learning and discovery and facilitates on-time completion" (see https://staff.mq.edu.au/work/strategy-planning-and-governance/university-policies-and-procedures/policies/academic-promotion/media1111118/documents11111/Criteria-Schedule_Academic-Promotion.pdf). Senior staff become responsible for developing a strong supervision culture within their departments.

THE PROBLEM OF DISPERSED SUPERVISION

The drama in each of the cases mentioned above, however, arises from another issue that reflects the transformation of supervision currently underway in many countries: dispersed supervision, where oversight of the research trainee needs to be undertaken in a number of different environments with people of different expertise and responsibilities. Of course, most prominent amongst these responsibilities are the academic ones: how is the research best undertaken in order to produce the academic outcomes required to pass examination? Some of these responsibilities are legal and ethical: what are the protocols for researching on Aboriginal lands, given the complexity of indigenous knowledges and the ugly ways in which they have been appropriated and exploited in the past? When does a casual approach to ethics clearance shade into legal liability? Others are industry-based, reflecting a corporation's reliance on university-quality research and a university's need to demonstrate its real-world impact. On top, around and beside all this is a kind of casual and *ad hoc* supervision: the staff that provide supervision without appointment or often any expertise, as well as the candidate's peers in their research training cohort, to whom they go for advice and support.

Part of the problem can be solved by expanding the number of categories of supervisor. At Macquarie University, we are redesigning our supervision policy to include several new categories, such as Higher Degree Research Cultural Advisor and Higher Degree Research Advisor. The HDR Cultural Advisor must be an Aboriginal or Torres Strait Islander person, and is appointed in order to show respect for the longstanding knowledge economies of indigenous culture, and especially to assist candidates in negotiating their way through their complex protocols without transgressing boundaries or causing offence. Candidates need to be aware not only of sensitive political boundaries but also of the complex ways in which knowledge is disseminated in indigenous cultures. This is how Mara got into trouble, in two ways: her ethics clearance did not allow her the flexibility of crossing into another jurisdiction, and the relevant authorities were not consulted, and therefore she lacked approval for the work she'd done. Her supervisor was casual about the ethics clearance process and because she was daunted by the prospect of confronting him, she went ahead unaware of the risk she was taking. The protocols around the ownership of knowledge and the right to teach in indigenous culture need to be negotiated carefully. An indigenous advisor appointed in Sydney will not necessarily have the deep knowledge of practices in other parts of the country, but will help in identifying risks and managing negotiations.

The problem for the other candidates is that they are in situations with multiple supervisors, both formal and casual, with a complex and fluid distribution of roles and responsibilities. George looks for supervision guidance to people on site whose background and skills equip them to deal with specific technical issues, but not candidature management, or really, academic science. George also appears to lack the communication skills to assertively address the issues with his supervisor. The HDR Advisor role aims to enlist specialists onto the project, acknowledging and specifying their capabilities, without requiring them to become substitute supervisors.

A major part of the problem is that it is unclear who has overall responsibility for managing or adjudicating the different supervisory roles in the project. It might be possible to set up a committee with a chair, who is able to direct staff on how to behave, let them know when they are failing their responsibilities and what the limits of their roles are. However, many of the people involved are not employees of the university and not answerable to it, even though they are significantly engaged with the project. Some are working beyond their responsibilities and mightn't want their involvement known. In two of the cases, the candidate gets caught up in complex institutional issues which are obscure to them, totally beyond their control and which involve significant risk to their work and their reputations.

In the cases above, each of the dimensions of the situation can be thought through and dealt with. How should the ethics process be run? What are the limits of an on-site industry-based supervisor without a PhD? How can candidates be protected when departmental relationships splinter? Universities can put in place all kinds of measures to deal with these different situations: recalcitrant supervisors can undergo more training about their responsibilities during the ethics application process, for example. Contracts between the university and industry can be used to clarify different roles, and finally, senior faculty staff can be more sensitive to HDR candidates caught in the crossfire of departmental disputes.

THE CANDIDATE'S AGENCY

Yet something risks being lost in such a piecemeal approach, and that is how it all looks from the point where all these dimensions of candidature intersect: the candidates themselves. Each solution is institution-led. This is appropriate in that the university is fulfilling its duty of care to candidates. However, it leaves the candidate passive. This encourages a sense of vulnerability even hopelessness, and provides them with no preparation for a career where they will have to negotiate their way through complex institutional arrangements. The important thing about the case studies above is not the individual dimensions of the candidates' situations, but how these compound one another. They all happen to the same person at the same time. What we would like to look at is a way of helping candidates learn how to manage their complex supervision situations, not relying solely on formal university procedures but helping them to take responsibility for their project.

SUPERVISING UP

There has been a shift toward building professional skills development into PhD programmes. During PhD candidature, there are opportunities to develop a range of professional and employability skills including communication, negotiation, teamwork, leadership, critical thinking, project management, problem identification, problem solving, adaptability and creativity. 'Managing Up' is a commonly used term in management circles. This concept can be effectively adapted to the PhD candidate experience. Managing Up, or in this case Supervising Up, is, at its most basic, about teaching PhD candidates to understand the communication and management styles of their supervisors and then to adjust their own communication styles to ensure that the best outcomes are achieved. The objective is to equip HDR candidates with the communication and negotiation skills to help them to effectively address issues as they arise so that they can avoid situations where small issues grow out of all proportion, potentially derailing their candidature or impacting negatively on their wellbeing.

With the impact of casualisation, the gig economy, automation, demographic shifts, geopolitical situations and the growth in artificial intelligence, there is an increasing need for individuals to take responsibility for managing the development of their own career as the old paradigm of 'a job for life' disappears (Savickas 2011). To enable the PhD candidates to gain more control and get the most out of their programme, the HDR Professional Skills Program in the Dean's Office at Macquarie University runs workshops on Managing Up. These workshops aim to equip PhD candidates with skills and tools to manage supervisory relationships more effectively, to understand how to develop a strong support network and to explore ways in which they can build their agency during their candidature (Goode 2010).

The participants explore strategies that can positively influence the supervision relationship. Using case studies, they work together in small groups to identify issues and brainstorm potential solutions and different approaches to solving problems. As the workshop progresses and greater trust is built within the group, participants begin to talk about their actual experiences and to raise the issues that concern them about supervision. Some of the issues include regularly cancelled appointments, irregular meetings, uncertainty about expectations, and unclear feedback.

Knowing the preferred methods of communication of the supervisor can help the candidate to achieve clearer and more regular feedback and, as a result feel more supported. A supervisor may prefer only occasional face-to-face meetings with more regular contact via email or they might prefer regular informal meetings over coffee (Hemer 2012). During the workshop, the participants are encouraged to identify their supervisor's communication styles and to consider how they might be able to adjust their own communication to get the best results. They break into pairs and role-play either the supervisor or the candidate. The participants start to appreciate the different styles of communication appropriate to, or enforced upon, different academic players. They thus begin to examine the effectiveness of their interactions with their supervisor and start to recognise what can result from poor communication. The group learns to judge when a more assertive or a more passive style may be warranted. Candidates can be resistant to the suggestion that, to achieve the best results, they may need to make the most compromises – at least in the early stages of their candidature – and yet, if they can shift their thinking and adjust their approach and communication style then their interactions with their supervisor may be much more productive. By making concessions early, and in the right way, the candidate may find that the supervisor will be more willing to make compromises and adjust their own style to better suit the candidate's needs.

During the workshop, there is discussion on managing difficult supervision relationships. The group explore the difficult types of supervisor – *hostile, manipulative, self-centred complainer, nice but no follow-through, pessimistic, indecisive, absent* – and the group are invited to add to the list. The participants work through scenarios where they might be working with a supervisor who fits one or more of the descriptors listed and they are also asked to consider when they have been the 'difficult' person in a specific situation. Breaking into pairs, the participants role-play a negotiation with someone playing the 'difficult' person. Prior to the role play the 'non-difficult' person is asked to write down their goal, and to then focus upon achieving the desired outcome.

The Communications and Managing Up workshops are part of the strategy to build a higher level of self-agency within the HDR cohort. Another initiative that supports Macquarie University HDR candidates is the HDR Mentors programme – a peer-to-peer mentoring programme supported financially and administratively by the HDR Support and Development Program within the Office of the Dean. The HDR mentors undergo training that includes cross-cultural communication, boundary setting and referral methods and resources. The HDR mentors are given clear guidelines on their role and understand the need for confidentiality and to gauge when other university services are needed to provide formal or informal support. The PhD candidate needs to be proactive in confronting issues at an early stage and to achieve good outcomes. They need to have a good understanding of university structures and processes and to have a clear knowledge of the formal requirements of the PhD programme. Universities need to commit to providing challenging experiences that assist HDR candidates in developing a range of skills that enhance HDR graduate employability and that deliver a high standard of research education. The aim of the Mentors programme is not only to provide support for candidates but to give the mentors themselves practice in taking the lead in negotiating the complex and obscure ways of big institutions, thus strengthening their own sense of agency.

The most conventional way in which to imagine the space of HDR candidature is to see candidates as occupying a fragment of a larger and uniform departmental academic environment. In such a model of space, the candidate's place would be enclosed by, consistent with and transparent to the larger departmental space. However, such a model can no longer be seen to apply. The candidate occupies a set of overlapping and interpenetrating spaces that are not only not part of the university environment, but not always visible to it or easily understood by it. These spaces have multiple occupants with different skills and qualifications, as well as different inhibitions and limitations, who move in and out of the space according to their own timelines and agendas. Only the candidate moves regularly between all these spaces, and their experience of these spaces may vary hugely from excitement and wonder to confusion and anxiety. At times, they share theses spaces with supervisors and mentors who can be their greatest inspiration and most frustrating impediment, with administrators and support staff who routinely save them but also add to their burden, and with peers who provide them with necessary encouragement and relief, but also comparison and competition. Given the increased complexity of the multiple spaces in which candidates move and that can never be simply homogenised or made orthodox in any consistent way, the strong agency of the candidates themselves is increasingly necessary, so the candidate can negotiate, mediate and succeed.

CONCLUSION

Each of the case studies we outlined at the start of this paper proposes a set of issues confronting the candidate all at once. In these situations, candidates often freeze or panic, because they are unused to taking the initiative in complex institutional situations. There are a range of things universities can put in place to make sure everyone on the supervision team is equipped for their roles, and aware of what is at stake. But a key circuit-breaker in each case could have been provided if the candidates had been able to assert themselves with their supervisors and others, in order to manage complex cultural and industrial protocols, get the support they need and modify the impact of hostility and relationship breakdown. Because of the increasingly complex situations candidates find themselves in, they will need sophisticated professional skills to help them protect themselves and advance their research. As work changes around us, this sense of agency will not only be necessary for them to gain their degrees, but also for managing their whole future careers.

REFERENCES

ACOLA (Australian Council of Learned Academies). 2016. *Review of Australia's research training system*. Melbourne: ACOLA.

Baker VL & MJ Pifer. 2011. The role of relationships in the transition from doctoral student to independent scholar. *Studies in Continuing Education*, 33(1):5-17. https://doi.org/10.1080/0158 037X.2010.515569

Deuchar R. 2008. Facilitator, director or critical friend?: Contradiction and congruence in doctoral supervision styles. *Teaching in Higher Education*, 13(4):489-500. https://doi.org/10.1080/13562510802193905

Goode J. 2010. 'Perhaps I should be more proactive in changing my own supervisions'? Student agency in 'doing supervision.' In: M Walker & P Thomson (eds). *The Routledge doctoral supervisor's companion supporting effective research in education and the social sciences*. New York and London: Routledge.

Hemer SR. 2012. Informality, power and relationships in postgraduate supervision: Supervising PhD candidates over coffee. *Higher Education Research & Development*, 31(6):827-839. https://doi.org/10.1080/07294360.2012.674011

Hopwood N. 2010. A sociocultural view of doctoral students' relationships and agency. *Studies in Continuing Education*, 32(2):103-117. https://doi.org/10.1080/015803 7X.2010.487482

Mantai L & R Dowling. 2015. Supporting the PhD journey: Insights from acknowledgements. *International Journal for Researcher Development*, 6(2):106-121. https://doi.org/10.1108/IJRD-03-2015-0007

McAlpine L & Asghar A. 2010. Enhancing academic climate: Doctoral students as their own developers. *International Journal for Academic Development*, 15(2):167-178. https://doi.org/10.1080/13601441003738392

Savickas ML. 2011. Constructing careers: Actor, agent, and author. *Journal of Employment Counselling*, 48:179-181. https://doi.org/10.1002/j.2161-1920.2011.tb01109.x

I AM A POSTGRADUATE RESEARCH SUPERVISOR: WHO AM I?

Nonnie Botha

INTRODUCTION

Supervising master's and doctoral research studies is internationally accepted as one of the tasks of academics at universities and would therefore constitute a space of academic identity. Some academics find research supervision to be challenging (Wadee, Keane, Diets & Hay 2010) and they might be hesitant to embark on it. These individuals need support to take the first step and also throughout the supervision journey until they have developed sufficient confidence and capacity to become independent supervisors.

De Lange, Pillay and Chikoko (2011:19) believe that supervision "requires the supervisor to reflect on his or her role" towards improving the supervision and co-developing "knowledge and identity production". Madileng (2014:2030) confirms this notion by indicating that reflective practice is "an important tool for understanding self-identity and professional identity". One of the conclusions drawn from research conducted by Halse (2011:568) is that the supervision of doctoral students is a continuous process of identity development.

In this chapter I explain how a framework for postgraduate research supervisor identity was developed by considering data that emanated from empirical research and applying a theoretical model for identity development to the data. The significance of this research lies in its potential to cultivate new insights into the supervisory space of identity development, capacity building and quality in postgraduate supervision.

The study set out to find an answer to the question: *In which way could an academic develop a personal postgraduate research supervisor identity?* Possible answers to several sub-questions, as articulated below, would incrementally lead to an answer to the main question:

- What is a postgraduate research supervisor?
- What is an identity?
- What is a postgraduate research supervisor identity?
- How is a research supervisor identity developed?

POSTGRADUATE RESEARCH SUPERVISOR AND SUPERVISION

For the purpose of this chapter I define a postgraduate research supervisor as a person – usually an academic – who supervises the research (and other work associated with it) of a master's student or a doctoral candidate at a higher education institution.

The supervision of the supervisor in such contexts is viewed as a journey of learning, growth and development for both supervisor and postgraduate student. In the course of this journey the novice supervisor gains experience, developing an identity as a research supervisor with increased confidence (Spooner-Lane, Henderson, Price & Hill 2007; Lee 2012) towards becoming a supervisor (Leshem 2013).

Good postgraduate research supervision is reported differently in various sources of literature. However, some consensus features could be identified, for instance as demonstrating

- strong relationships (Brew & Peseta 2004; Green 2005; Vilkinas & Cartan 2006; Manathunga 2007);
- relevant pedagogy (teaching) (Pearson & Brew 2002; Brew & Peseta 2004; Green 2005; Manathunga 2005; Hill 2010; Zeegers & Barron 2012; Fataar 2012);
- effective administration (Vilkinas 2002; Brew & Peseta 2004; Manathunga 2005); and
- original contribution to knowledge (Brew & Peseta 2004; Miller 2007; Hill 2012).

In the next section I briefly discuss the concept of identity and a theory of identity that was deemed appropriate for this study.

IDENTITY: CONCEPT AND THEORY

Erikson's work on identity (1950, 1968) contributed to a sound foundation for further scholarly work on this concept and the way in which it is acquired. His definitions focus on the elements of self-knowledge, consistency, synthesis and confusion as these appear across contexts and time.

Since then, there has been some agreement that the identity concept is difficult and almost impossible to define properly (Beijaard, Meijer & Verloop 2004; Lichtwarck-Aschoff, Van Geert, Bosma & Kunnen 2008; Beauchamp & Thomas 2009). Several authors have taken up this challenge by identifying characteristics of identity that resonate with a range of definitions in the literature. Akkerman and Meijer (2011:308) indicate that such common features found in definitions and perceptions of teacher identity are that it is multi-faceted, discontinuous and social in nature. They further advocate that these features need to be understood more deeply through their opposites, namely unity, continuity and individuality (Akkerman & Meijer 2011:309).

In order to arrive at a working definition of identity for their own work, Lichtwarck-Aschoff et al (2008:372) considered how others perceive identity and thereby identified common characteristics, concluding that identity "refers to a maintaining 'self-sameness' and continuity through changes and movements across time and space. Self-sameness is for one part determined by the person himself. For the other part it is largely defined and affected by others and the relationship with them."

The above-mentioned elements of identity, which crystallised from a selection of definitions, are also evident in theories on identity formation. One such theory is used in this chapter as a lens through which to analyse and interpret the work reported on, namely Marcia's (1980) paradigm of identity status, which was developed from Erikson's insights on identity.

Marcia initially defined the processes or dimensions of identity as exploration and commitment (1966). Exploration is characterised by the active questioning of different identity alternatives, while commitment is understood as adherence to a set of convictions, goals and values.

Subsequently, Marcia refined these two dimensions (1980) by defining four statuses that reflect individual differences in how identity-related issues are approached and handled. Two of these statuses clearly display commitment, while the other two statuses display relatively little commitment.

When a period of exploration is followed by commitment, Marcia calls this status 'achievement' and perceives it as the most optimal status. When little exploration takes place before the status of commitment is reached, the author labels the status 'foreclosure'.

If exploration is currently happening and commitment is relatively absent, the status is known as 'moratorium'. When a person does little to explore life choices and also does not really commit to any choice, the status is called 'diffusion', the least optimal status.

POSTGRADUATE RESEARCH SUPERVISOR IDENTITY: SOME LITERATURE PERSPECTIVES

Although not much work has been published on the identity of research supervisors, supervision as part of academic and professional identities is acknowledged in the literature. Dahan (2007) views supervision as a vehicle through which students are professionalised, while Wisker and Robinson (2016) explored the professional identity of supervisors. Moynihan (2013) conducted research that shed light on academic identities and Murphy states that supervision "made me focus on my identity", influencing his understanding of his academic identity (Murphy & Wibberley 2017:63).

Halse (2011:568) refers specifically to the supervisor's identity when she states that "doctoral supervision can be theorised as a perpetual process of subjective and identity formation – of 'becoming a supervisor'". Maritz and Prinsloo (2015) refer to the 'nomadic' identity of the supervisor because changes in the playing field (regular and unexpected) continually shape the identities of supervisors.

The empirical work described in the following section is an effort to add some insights to the seemingly limited body of knowledge on research supervisor identity.

POSTGRADUATE RESEARCH SUPERVISOR IDENTITY: EMPIRICAL STUDY

The empirical part of the study was embedded in an interpretive paradigm as it acknowledges the existence of multiple realities and varying interpretations of the same occurrence; it also supports the idea that participants in research co-construct knowledge that emerges from such research (Creswell & Plano Clark 2011; Merriam 2009). A qualitative approach to data was chosen for this research as it is appropriate when studying human experiences and situations (Ary, Jacobs & Sorensen 2010). The study focused on supervisors' reflections on their own supervisor identities, thus rendering rich qualitative data.

DESIGN AND METHODOLOGY

A case study design was employed as it allowed me to explore a real-life, contemporary bounded system over a period of time (Yin 2009), namely the development of a postgraduate research supervisor identity. Ary *et al* (2010) identify three types of case studies: intrinsic case study (to better understand a particular case), instrumental case study (when a particular case represents the issue of interest) and collective case study (investigating multiple units to better understand a phenomenon). My research could be understood as both intrinsic and collective, as I studied personal reflections on supervision practices and supervisor identity of a number of supervisors. However, the supervisors all belonged to one particular bounded system and they wrote their reflections after exposure to the same intervention. This study only generated, analysed and interpreted qualitative data.

Ary *et al* (2010) define a population as all members of any well-defined class of people, events, or objects used in a study. The population for this study was all the portfolios submitted for assessment by a cohort of participants at the end of a one-year capacity-building programme for postgraduate research supervisors. The cohort comprised a total of 29 research supervisors and the level of their supervision experience varied significantly as academic staff of four African universities – one each in Kenya, South Africa, Tanzania and Uganda.

In qualitative research a sample is selected with the purpose of "obtaining rich descriptions of people's beliefs, behaviours and experiences" (Springer 2010:109). The sample for this study consisted of portfolios of those supervisors in the population who voluntarily agreed to allow me to analyse their written reflections on their own postgraduate research supervisor identities and supervision practices; these reflections formed part of their portfolios. Of the original 29 participants in the cohort, only 24 submitted portfolios for assessment. I requested written permission from these 24 participants to analyse their portfolios and 11 granted me permission for the analysis. To ensure that permission would be granted voluntarily, I did not send a follow-up request, as it could be construed as coercion.

When I started analysing the documents, it became clear that one of the documents could not be analysed for this purpose as the particular participant had no research supervision experience.

The distribution of participants among the four universities is set out in Table 4.1 below.

TABLE 4.1   Target population and sample

	Kenyan University	SA University	Tanzanian University	Ugandan University	Total
Original number of participants in capacity-building programme	8	11	4	6	29
Number of portfolios submitted for assessment	6	11	3	4	24
Number of non-responses to permission request	3	4	2	4	13
Number of positive responses to permission request	3	7	1	0	11
Number of reflections analysed	3	6	1	0	10

The written reflections were anonymised by allocating a code to each reflection in the sample. The data were handled and stored confidentially and safely.

The required ethical clearance for the empirical study was obtained from the university that hosted the research. The ethical principles of respect of persons, beneficence and justice, expressed as requirements for informed consent, communication of potential risks and benefits of the research and fair selection of participants (Springer 2010) were adhered to throughout the study, in line with the Belmont Report (The National Commission for the Protection of Human Subjects of Biomedical and Behavioral Research 1979).

Data analysis

The reflections written by the participants were analysed twice:

- In line with Marcia's theory of identity status, the purpose of the first analysis was to identify statements that would indicate the extent of exploration and commitment of each participant, typical of one of four possible identity statuses, namely achievement, foreclosure, moratorium or diffusion. For this first analysis I used inductive coding (Maree 2012:107) to identify relevant statements.
- Supervision practices could be perceived as manifestations of supervisor identity, therefore the purpose of the second analysis was to identify themes that emerged spontaneously from the individual writings about supervision practices

and identity. I again used inductive coding, this time to identify significant statements and axial coding to group these statements into themes or units of meaning (Creswell 2013).

The quotes presented for both analyses below each have a code that refers to the number allocated to the participating supervisor and the page number of the portfolio where the quote appears.

First data analysis and interpretation: Applying Marcia's theory

Marcia's theory of the four statuses that reflect differences in how individuals tackle identity-related issues (1980) was superimposed on the reflective writings, thus using it as a lens through which to analyse and interpret the writings.

Participant 1

There is evidence of exploration in this writing, as the participant is "always interrogating my identity in relation to my practice" (1:5), also acknowledging the importance of communities of practice and research excellence (1:5). This exploration has happened only for about two years, with limited supervision opportunities for exploration. In spite of this, commitment has come about as the supervision challenges described have all been reflected on and where solutions have not been found yet, they are continuously being considered and re-considered (1:5, 6). This supervisor is committed to be the kind of supervisor she never had (1:9). This case of relatively brief exploration and high commitment displays the status of foreclosure.

Participant 2

This participant has explored the supervisory activity over an extended period of time (2:4) and "strived to become a better supervisor" (2:4) by pushing herself "to enhance my theoretical and creative levels" (2:5). She committed herself to being a better researcher (2:4) to help others, and "facilitate their development on their own terms" (2:6). The extended exploration and resulting commitment are typical of an identity status of achievement.

Participant 3

Before working as an academic and a supervisor, this participant made a conscious decision to develop her area of expertise which she links to the development of her academic identity (3:4). Once she started supervising postgraduate students, she invested much effort into this through playing a supportive role (3:7), setting out clear expectations for both parties (3:8), developing her scholarship and other such activities. These are some examples of her commitment to the task of supervision. The extended and deliberate exploration which was followed by commitment displays an identity status of achievement.

Participant 4

This participant has explored and "actively interrogated ways in which my practice" might not be humanising (4:4). She worked "to integrate the scholarship of research" (4:4), engaged in critical self-evaluation (4:4), accepted responsibility for the guidance of her students (4:7) and, facing her fears, worked on finding ways to counteract them (4:10). Although her exploration seems limited, she demonstrated commitment to the work, which reflects an identity status of foreclosure.

Participant 5

This participant believes that constant "thinking and re-thinking and unlearning" are necessary when reflecting on the way in which he deals with his students (5:2). He seeks advice from more experienced colleagues (5:2) and explores various other ways through "constant iterative reflection" and "re-thinking my epistemological position" (5:6). As he has not yet supervised many students, the opportunities for exploring have been limited. Additionally, this participant states that he is "extremely committed" (5:2), which is confirmed by his accepting "responsibility to guide my students" (5:3), being a "careful listener" (5:8), providing prompt and meticulous feedback to students (5:9) and discussing mutual expectations with students (5:10). The relatively brief period of exploration, coupled with commitment to the work, is typical of an identity status of foreclosure.

Participant 6

The data in this case was not suitable for analysis as explained above

Participant 7

During many years of supervising postgraduate students, this participant has worked with students from different countries and has migrated from one set of specialisations to another based on scholarly developments in his life (7:2). His exploration therefore comprised a diversity of contexts. He perceives himself as "able to learn and grow", and his role as "multi-faceted" and enhancing transformation (7:3). His extended and deep exploration of postgraduate supervision culminated in a deep commitment by, for example, providing prompt feedback to students (7:5), including much discussion, deliberation, interrogation and negotiation in the supervisory process (7:7), providing a space for sharing (7:8) and by making an effort to "use supervision practices that enhance student development" (7:10). The extensive exploration and resulting commitment displayed by this participant reflects an identity status of achievement.

Participant 8

Much exploring has taken place over an extended period of time by participating in communities of practice (8:6), having "learnt time management" (8:6), and having to "change my views" once the workload increased (8:8). Commitment is demonstrated through providing "constructive feedback" (8:5), "organizing and managing the research process and in providing support for the candidate" (8:5), working on student documents when travelling (8:6), having an effective submission and feedback cycle in place (8:7) and thinking through supervisory challenges to the point where workable solutions are found (8:12). All of these provide evidence of an identity status of achievement.

Participant 9

The written reflection of this participant included only one example of exploring the supervisory activity. Due to very large student numbers this participant coped by being "rigid, strict and less attached" (9:4). However, reflection resulted in changed supervision strategies that provide focused support to students through dedicating a "whole day to supervision", doing rotational consultation and group discussions (9:4). Many manifestations of commitment were mentioned, such as negotiating availability, developing student expertise, planning ahead, enhancing student emancipation and negotiating responsibilities (9:6). These are typical of an identity status of foreclosure.

Participant 10

Some students expect this supervisor to identify a topic, set objectives and find suitable literature, but after reflection the supervisor decided that "students should be independent and proactive to design their own study" (10:3), thus displaying an attitude of exploring supervisory practice. Another example of exploration is the realisation that procrastination is detrimental to both parties and it is better to attend to things immediately (10:5). No further examples of exploration were offered, and this fact, coupled with the relative inexperience of the supervisor, implies limited exploration. Commitment is displayed in that the supervisor gives "every student room to make decisions" (10:3), planning meetings ahead of time (10:4), "assisting students to transform their weaknesses into competencies" (10:4), meticulous record-keeping (10:4), working with students in small groups to promote peer consultation (10:6), and numerous other examples. The relatively brief exploration, together with commitment, indicates an identity status of foreclosure.

Participant 11

Although this participant has many years of supervision experience, limited evidence of exploration is provided in his writing. I could find only one example of exploration, namely that he uses both face-to-face and group supervision, depending on the context (11:6). In contrast to this, the supervisor's commitment is evident from his meticulous application of the institutional policies (11:6), student involvement in the choice of methodologies (11:7), his personal approach to providing feedback (11:7), encouraging failing students (11:8) and many more. The limited exploration, paired with commitment, is matched with an identity status of foreclosure.

The analysis and interpretation provided above show that six of the ten participants displayed an identity status of foreclosure (limited exploration coupled with commitment) and the remaining four participants provided evidence of an identity status of achievement (extensive exploration paired with deep commitment) – the latter being the most optimal status in Marcia's theory. None of the participants were found to have a status of moratorium (exploration currently happening, little commitment) or of diffusion (little exploration, not really committed). This is hardly surprising, as the sample was drawn from a population who voluntarily participated and submitted portfolios for assessment in a supervision capacity-building programme, and it is unlikely that people who are not committed to supervision would be part of this population.

Second data analysis and interpretation: Themes that emerged spontaneously from the data

Below I present the evidence of the six themes and their concomitant sub-themes that emerged spontaneously from the analysis of the assessment portfolios.

Theme 1: What I bring to the table

Some of the participants reported on how their experiences as a student shaped their own supervision practice, for example: I supervise "how I was supervised" (10:3), and I "try to be the kind of supervisor I never had" (1:9). Several other participants indicated how life experiences other than being supervised (positive and negative) shaped their own supervision, namely that a background in project management helps in meeting deadlines in supervision (9:7), and being a broken person promotes supervision that ensures that students appreciate themselves with all their flaws (1:8).

Evidence that participants' attitude to research influenced the way in which they fulfilled their supervision role is provided in statements such as "I believe in research that makes a difference in people's lives" (1:11), and "I had to reconstruct and renegotiate my academic identity to integrate the scholarship of research" (4:4). Participating supervisors perceived their area of specialisation as integral to their supervision role, for example: "… before an academic can become a successful supervisor he or she must be a scholar in his/her field of specialisation" (3:8), and "I cannot always supervise in my area of expertise … have to supervise students across disciplines" (2:7).

This theme thus unfolded into three sub-themes, namely own life experiences, attitude to research and area of specialisation.

Theme 2: What is supervision?

Participants described supervision as creating "a space for learning in a certain context" (2:6); a "pedagogical space" (2:8), or a "safe learning space" (3:9). They also indicated that supervision is a "mutually symbiotic relationship" (7:7), or a "partnership" (4:9). Moreover, they described supervision as being "like a roller-coaster" (8:15), a "wonderful journey" (8:15), and they commented that there is "not one perfect way to supervise" (5:6).

Words used to describe supervision ranged from positive to neutral to negative: "enjoy" (11:3), "keen" (3:8), rewarding" (8:9), "exciting" (11:4), "supportive" (4:5), "respect" (5:8), "commitment" (8:6), "professional" (11:4), "multi-faceted" (7:3), "sacrifice" (10:6), "rigid" (9:4).

Sub-themes that emerged related to a space and a relationship, with both positive and negative emotions being associated with supervision.

Theme 3: Attitude to students

In this theme ownership came out strongly as a sub-theme, as participants made statements such as "sense of ownership of the research project" (7:8), "students are empowered to take ownership of the academic practices" (2:7), "the research project is his/her responsibility" (4:11), and students must "own their progress" (1:13).

Fostering growth, development and transformation was regarded as important, constituting a second sub-theme. This emerged when participating supervisors stressed that postgraduate students "need to grow" (8:7), that supervisors must "facilitate their development on their own terms" (2:6) (referring to students), and that the supervisory relationship must "stimulate and enhance their personal and professional development" (2:7).

A third sub-theme is the humanising dimension of supervision, which was expressed in many ways: "I strive to establish a humanising learning environment" (2:7), "I have embraced a humanising approach" (5:3), "I regularly ask students what their needs are" (5:9), and "I use coffee conversations with great effect" (5:9).

The final sub-theme in this theme involved the conflict between control and independence. This emerged from statements such as "If students are allowed too much freedom … it may lead to laxity" (10:3), "I give every student room to make decisions" (10:3) and "They need frequent checks" (10:3).

Theme 4: Supervisory challenges

In some cases participants merely mentioned or described the challenge without offering a solution or sharing how they deal with the challenge. Examples of these were:

- Power issues: "I struggle to relinquish power … I need to figure out what my actions should be" (2:8).
- Stressing about progress: "I still find myself getting more stressed than the students in terms of the progress … I am not sure how I will unlearn this habit" (1:13).

Supervisors also indicated how they handled a challenge:

- Power issues: "The first challenge I faced was the power dynamics involved … This encounter forced me to keep my emotions in check … I decided to stay calm and vowed to myself that they will learn from my actions and guidance … that I have the expertise to supervise them" (1:5, 6).
- Students would make inappropriate choices: "sometimes … a supervisor has to … allow the student to do what they are doing" (8:13).
- Supervising outside area of expertise: "I have to read and study just as much" as the student (2:7).
- Over-supervising: "I steer solutions that were appropriate to the limitations and capabilities of my students" (4:10).
- Large numbers of students: "I dedicate the whole day to supervision, I group the students according to cohorts and within specific stages … I do rotational consultation in groups and thereafter subject them to discussion within their groups based on the raised comments in their individual work … peer consultation" (9:4).

Theme 5: Awareness of self

Three sub-themes could be distinguished in this theme, namely a sense of vulnerability, reflection on practice and an openness to change.

Supervisors expressed their vulnerabilities in various ways: "not to be afraid to admit to my students that I don't have all the knowledge" (5:8), "I have to believe more in my capabilities without overestimating it" (5:3), feedback "is the area that makes me feel most vulnerable … because I am so conscious that this is the area where the most 'power discourses' are situated" (4:14).

Reflective practice was regarded as important by several supervisors: "to engage with critical self-evaluation" (4:4), "I reflect for days … in collaboration with my students … this is cognitively and emotionally exhausting" (5:2). When supervisors reflect on their own practice they sometimes find ways to improve their supervision: "I have actively interrogated ways in which my practice may be reproducing exploitive, or oppressive patterns or relationships" (4:4), "constant iterative reflection is key to grow my academic supervision" (5:6). One supervisor indicated that identity development benefits from reflection (1:5).

Many supervisors wrote on their openness to change: "I am always prepared to learn from others" (7:4), "not afraid to ask for assistance from my main mentors" (5:2), "some students can challenge your emotions and so I found out that I need to be more understanding and patient" (10:4). Some supervisors indicated the kind of measures they have taken to promote this change. Communities of practice came to the fore: "I learnt the importance of communities of practice" (1:5), "build an academic network with other supervisors" (3:9), "importance of critical academic debate" (5:5). Improving supervision was an important outcome of change measures: "I changed my supervision working style to become more of a listener" (8:8), "avoid focussing on emotions and blaming people" (10:5), "I pushed myself to cross conceptual thresholds to enhance my theoretical and creative levels" (2:5).

Theme 6: Awareness of work

The final theme has to do with how supervisors go about their supervision work relating to six matters that are intricate parts of supervision, namely planning and record-keeping, time management, feedback, dialogue, roles of students and supervisors, and co-supervision.

On planning and record-keeping supervisors indicated "I develop a research plan" (2:10), trying to find a balance between the different roles an academic has to play "has taught me the value of planning and keeping track of all activities" (1:4),

"I keep records of meetings, but I leave the bulk of this work with the students to write out what was achieved in the previous meeting" (1:12).

Some comments regarding time management were: "struggling with maintaining deadlines ... I need to find new ways of ensuring that we stick to the timelines that we agree on from the beginning" (1:12), "I sit with my students and we negotiate and renegotiate realistic timeframes" (5:9).

Of interest in all of the above is the oscillation of the focus being on either the student or the supervisor.

Speedy feedback was regarded as important: "small chunks ... of work ... allows me to provide feedback immediately" (8:9). Good feedback was characterised as "supportive" (3:7), "prompt, meticulous and explicit" (5:9).

Dialogue opportunities included face-to-face meetings and online discussions (4:8), with an "open style of supervision ... rather than a paternalistic style" (7:3) being advocated.

Supervisors supported a "working agreement" that would outline the different expectations of students and supervisors and they acknowledged that each student and supervisor "has different roles to play" (3:8). They identified the following as being part of their supervisory role: "to create participatory learning environments" (1:6), "to introduce the student to the 'rules of the game'" (2:10), "building their confidence" (7:3), "provide a space for the student to share his/her concerns" (7:8), "agent of change" (2:6). Although supervisors stated that the "student has also various responsibilities" (9:6), they did not clearly indicate what exactly these are. Similarly, supervisors referred to "co-responsibility and shared roles" (5:10) between students and supervisors, but these were not identified.

Although co-supervision was supported, "universities assume that everyone can supervise with anyone" (1:8); however, the parties need to be "carefully matched" (7:4). Other challenges associated with co-supervision included power issues (1:7); students following the advice of only one of the supervisors, ignoring the inputs from the other one (1:7); conflicting guidance from the co-supervisors to the student, and different approaches to supervision, e.g. it is "difficult to work with a co-supervisor who does not share my compassion with the students" (7:4).

The twofold data analysis presented above provides insights that are integrated with each other in the next section, culminating in a framework for a postgraduate research supervisor identity.

A framework for a postgraduate research supervisor identity

The first data analysis in the previous section illustrated how Marcia's identity theory could be applied to supervisor writings on their own supervision. As a result of the application, an identity status could then be associated with each supervisor. By combining this application of Marcia's theory with the themes and sub-themes from the second data analysis in the previous section, a framework for postgraduate research supervisor identity emerges. The framework is presented in Table 4.2.

The themes from the second analysis are re-perceived to become dimensions of the framework, while the sub-themes are re-perceived as elements of the dimensions. The framework can be used to determine an individual's supervisor identity by answering the questions in the third column, either by him-/herself or by somebody else through analysis of supervisor writings on each of the elements of the different dimensions. The framework therefore customises Marcia's general identity theory to become more relevant for research supervisors.

TABLE 4.2 A framework for postgraduate supervision identity

Identity dimensions of the framework	Identity elements of each identity dimension	Exploration and commitment
Dimension 1: What I bring to the table	Element 1.1: Own life experiences Element 1.2: Attitude to research Element 1.3: Area of specialisation	To what extent have I explored each element? To what extent have I committed to a choice?
Dimension 2: What is supervision?	Element 2.1: As a space Element 2.2: As a relationship Element 2.3: Positive/negative emotions	To what extent have I explored each element? To what extent have I committed to a choice?
Dimension 3: Attitude to students	Element 3.1: Ownership Element 3.2: Grow/Develop/Transform Element 3.3: Humanising Element 3.4: Control vs Independence	To what extent have I explored each element? To what extent have I committed to a choice?
Dimension 4: Supervisory challenges	Element 4.1: Power issues Element 4.2: Stress regarding progress Element 4.3: Inappropriate student choices Element 4.4: Supervising outside area of expertise Element 4.5: Over-supervision Element 4.6: Large numbers of students	To what extent have I explored each element? To what extent have I committed to a choice?

TABLE 4.2 A framework for postgraduate supervision identity (continued)

Identity dimensions of the framework	Identity elements of each identity dimension	Exploration and commitment
Dimension 5: Awareness of self	Element 5.1: Vulnerability Element 5.2: Reflection on practice Element 5.3: Openness to change	To what extent have I explored each element? To what extent have I committed to a choice?
Dimension 6: Awareness of work	Element 6.1: Planning and record-keeping Element 6.2: Time management Element 6.3: Feedback Element 6.4: Dialogue Element 6.5: Roles Element 6.6: Co-supervision	To what extent have I explored each element? To what extent have I committed to a choice?

Notes on the framework in practice:

- The answers to the exploration/commitment questions for each element in the framework will provide detail about the supervisor's identity regarding each of the elements. This detail could assist with identifying areas for further exploration and capacity building.
- The nature of the dimensions seems to be chronological; however, at closer inspection this does not necessarily hold true.
- The way in which supervisor behaviour manifests in the different identity dimensions through the various elements is cyclical rather than linear in nature.

CONCLUSION

This chapter illustrates how an identity framework for postgraduate research supervisors was developed from two pieces of empirical work: first, the application of Marcia's identity theory to supervisor reflections on their own supervision, and second, the thematic analysis of the same reflections. A framework such as this might shed considerable light on the supervisory space of identity development, for example by identifying personal supervision identities, determining areas for supervision capacity building, and facilitating appropriate matches of co-supervisors with each other and supervisors with students. In applying the framework one might expect that more ways would be identified whereby the notion of supervisor identity can be of use.

REFERENCES

Akkerman SF & Meijer PC. 2011. A dialogical approach to conceptualizing teacher identity. *Teaching and Teacher Education,* 27:308-319. https://doi.org/10.1016/j.tate.2010.08.013

Ary D, Jacobs LC & Sorensen C. 2010. *Introduction to research in education.* 8th Edition. Wadsworth: Belmont.

Beauchamp C & Thomas L. 2009. Understanding teacher identity: An overview of issues in the literature and implications for teacher education. *Cambridge Journal of Education,* 39(2):175-189. https://doi.org/10.1080/03057640902902252

Beijaard D, Meijer PC & Verloop N. 2004. Reconsidering research on teachers' professional identity. *Teacher and Teacher Education,* 20 (2004):107-128. https://doi.org/10.1016/jtate.2003.07.001

Brew, A & Peseta, T. 2004. Changing postgraduate supervision practice: A programme to encourage learning through reflection and feedback. *Innovations in Education and Teaching International,* 41(1):5-22. https://doi.org/10.1080/1470329032000172685

Creswell JW. 2008. *Research design: Qualitative, quantitative, and mixed method approaches.* 3rd Edition. Thousand Oaks: SAGE.

Creswell JW. 2012. *Educational research: Planning, conducting and evaluating quantitative and qualitative research*. 4th Edition. Pearson: Lincoln.

Creswell JW. 2013. *Qualitative inquiry and research design: Choosing among five approaches.* 3rd Edition. Thousand Oaks: SAGE.

Creswell JW & Plano Clark VL. 2011. *Designing and conducting mixed methods research.* Thousand Oaks: SAGE.

Dahan A. 2007. Supervision and schizophrenia: The professional identity of PhD supervisors and the mission of students' professionalization. *European Journal of Education,* 42(3):335-349. https://doi.org/ 10.1111/j.1465-3435.2007.00310.x

De Lange N, Pillay G & Chikoko V. 2011. Doctoral learning: A case for a cohort model of supervision and support. *South African Journal of Education*, 31:15-30. https://doi.org/10.15700/saje.v31n1a413

Erikson EH. 1950. *Childhood and society.* New York: Norton.

Erikson EH. 1968. *Identity: Youth and crisis.* New York: Norton.

Fataar A (ed). 2012. *Debating thesis supervision: Perspectives from a university education department.* Stellenbosch: AFRICAN SUN MeDIA.

Green B. 2005. Unfinished business: Subjectivity and supervision. *Higher Education and Development,* 24(2):151-163. https://doi.org/10.1080/07294360500062953

Halse C. 2011. 'Becoming a supervisor': The impact of doctoral supervision on supervisors' learning. *Studies in Higher Education,* 36(5):557-570. https://doi.org/10.1080/03075079.2011.594593

Hill GW. 2010. *Making use of pedagogic models as reflective catalysts for investigating pedagogic practice.* In: The 5th International Inquiring Pedagogies Conference (iPED), 15 September, Coventry, United Kingdom.

Hill G. 2012. *What happens when a student wants to do something different in their dissertation: Cabaret as academic* writing. Inaugural Global Storytelling Conference. Prague, Czech Republic.

Lee A. 2012. *Successful research supervision: Advising students doing research*. London: Routledge.

Leshem S. 2013. The self-made supervisor: Learning experiences of MEd supervisors in teacher education college. *Journal of Teacher Education and Educators*, 2(1):7-30.

Lichtwarck-Aschoff A, Van Geert P, Bosma H & Kunnen S. 2008. Time and identity: A framework for research and theory formation. *Developmental Review*, 28 (2008):370-400. https://doi.org/ 10.1016/j.dr.2008.04.001

Madileng MM. 2014. Critical reflections: Experiencing discrimination, disrespect and disregard; forming a professional identity. *South African Journal of Higher Education*, 28(6):2027-2040.

Manathunga C. 2005. The development of research supervision: "Turning the light on a private space". *International Journal for Academic Development*, 10(1):17-30. https://doi.org/10.1080/13601440500099977

Manathunga C. 2007. Supervision as mentoring: The role of power and boundary crossing. *Studies in Continuing Education*, 29(2):207-221. https://doi.org/10.1080/01580370701424650

Marcia JE. 1966. Development and validation of ego-identity status. *Journal of Personality and Social Psychology*, 3(5):551-558. https://doi.org/10.1037/h0023281

Marcia JE. 1980. Identity in adolescence. In: J Adelson (ed). *Handbook of adolescent psychology*. New York: Wiley. 159-186.

Maree K (ed). 2012. *First steps in research*. Pretoria: Van Schaik.

Maritz J & Prinsloo P. 2015. *The new normal: Nomadic identities and the future of doctoral supervision*. Slide show. www.slideshare.net/Gremlins1/the-new-normal-nomadic-identities-and-the-future-of-doctoral-supervision [Retrieved 27 September 2017].

Merriam SB. 2009. *Qualitative research: A guide to design and implementation*. San Francisco: John Wiley.

Miller P. 2007. Problematising 'good' HDR supervision: A case study of an international pilot of an on-line HDR supervisor professional development program. *The International Journal of Research Supervision*, 1(1):29-38.

Moynihan TJ. 2013. Covert Conversations: Disciplined Improvisation and Meaning-making in the Masters (MA) Supervisory Relationship. PhD thesis. Ireland: University College Cork.

Murphy N & Wibberley C. 2017. Development of an academic identity through PhD supervision – An issue for debate. *Nursing Education in Practice*, 22:63-65. https://doi.org/10.1016/j.nepr.2016.12.002

Pearson M & Brew A. 2002. Research training and supervision development. *Studies in Higher Education*, 27(2):135-150. https://doi.org/1080/03075070220119986c

Spooner-Lane RS, Henderson DJ, Price RA & Hill GW. 2007. Practice to theory: Co-supervision stories. *The International Journal of Research Supervision*, 1(1):39-51.

Springer K. 2010. *Educational research*. New Jersey: John Wiley & Sons, Inc.

The National Commission for the Protection of Human Subjects of Biomedical and Behavioral Research. 1979. The Belmont Report: Ethical Principles and Guidelines for the protection of Human Subjects of Research. DHEW Publication No (OS) 78-0012. Washington DC: The US Government Printing Office.

Vilkinas T. 2002. The PhD process: The supervisor as manager. *Education and Training*, 44(2):129-137. https://doi.org/10.1108/00400910210424337

Vilkinas T & Cartan G. 2006. The integrated competing values framework: Its spatial configuration. *Journal of Management Development*, 25(6):505-521. https://doi.org/10.1108/02621710610670092

Wadee A, Keane M, Diets T & Hay D. 2010. *Effective PhD supervision: Learning, meaning and identity*. Cambridge: Cambridge University Press.

Wisker G & Robinson G. 2016. Supervisor wellbeing and identity: Challenges and strategies. *International Journal for Research Development*, 7(2):123-140. https://doi.org/10.1108/IJRD-03-2016-0006

Yin R. 2009. *Case study research*. Thousand Oaks, California: SAGE.

Zeegers M & Barron D. 2012. Pedagogical concerns in doctoral supervision: A challenge for pedagogy. *Quality Assurance in Education*, 20(1):20-30. https://doi.org/10.1108/09684881211198211

FIBONACCI POWER IN A DESCRIPTIVE EQUATION FOR POSTGRADUATE THROUGHPUT

Sanchen Henning

INTRODUCTION

Roald Dahl's eccentric character, the Big Friendly Giant (BFG) is famous for saying, "I is fluckedgungled" when he is caught in a hopeless situation (Dahl 2016) – so hopeless that he cannot speak or write correctly. His words mirror the feelings of hopelessness, disempowerment and isolation that master's degree research students often express regarding their research dissertation (Cilliers & Harry 2012): "I just want to give it up and get my life back" and "I realise how little I know, it is intimidating." The construction of a quality dissertation within a restricted period, often with additional challenges such as limited research methodology experience and knowledge; insufficient academic literacy and language proficiencies, seems to contribute to low completion rates of postgraduate qualifications in South Africa (Cilliers & Harry 2012:2). An expected outcome of the research module in the master's degree at the business school where the current study was conducted is formulated as "the learner must be able to do *independent* research". Some students interpret this outcome as *doing research in solitary confinement,* thereby contributing to their agony and isolation during their research journey. Descriptions such as "it is daunting", "out of control" and "I am out of my comfort zone" reveal postgraduate students' anxieties about failure. I argue that a compelling reason to conduct research may create a sense of meaning and inspire students to complete a quality dissertation.

Context and meaning

In an attempt to explain the concepts 'context' and 'meaning' to my adult and working research students, I ask them the following question (which seems quite appropriate within wine-drinking cultures, but might be less so or even offensive in cultures where alcohol is a taboo): A certain postgraduate supervisor habitually rewards his doctoral student with a bottle of wine after the completion of each chapter. What additional information would you need to be able to predict whether the student will:

a. come to love or hate wine,
b. love or hate working on a chapter, or
c. love or hate the supervisor?

The many ramifications of the question confirmed my argument: that all the needed additional information concerned the *context* and *meaning* of the interaction between the supervisor and the student. Without the contextual information, that is, the conditions or dynamics that surround the interaction or behavioural exchange, any interpretation, explanation or prediction may be inaccurate (Bateson 2000). If we know that the student *really* dislikes wine because he suffers severe allergic reactions from it and, as a self-sponsored student, *really* wants to complete his doctoral studies, then we can predict with reasonable certainty that the supervisor's 'reward' will be meaningless to the student. If we know that the supervisor rewards his student, who is a serious wine connoisseur, with a limited edition of a unique cultivar and vintage, then we can predict that the student will love his supervisor for it. Additional information regarding context and meaning could make accurate predictions possible through deeper insight and understanding of the situation. Similarly, if students understand the context and meaning of their research projects they seem to be less anxious and more engaged, which may contribute to higher levels of postgraduate throughput.

Learning occurs in a specific context and supervisors of postgraduate students should ask themselves, What should be learnt? and How can context and meaning be created to enhance learning? Bartlett and Mercer (2002:2) state that none of the manuals on postgraduate supervision "include or even imagine the variety of possible situations that may arise between a supervisor and a candidate". Despite attention to research methods; limited academic engagement with pedagogic knowledge for research capacity building exists (Nind, Kilburn & Luff 2017). Academics who teach research methods rely mostly on a network of peers, scattered research literature and much trial and error. Furthermore, current research is mostly reflective case studies of pedagogical practice development including themes such as 'varied backgrounds', 'the teacher as a learner', 'the role of methods software', 'the lack of a pedagogical culture' (Nind, Kilburn & Luff 2017).

In an effort to improve master's student completion rates, I established a collaborative and continuous learning space for business research students to encourage the development of critical thinking skills and scholarly voices.

Collaborative research culture

Education in Africa currently takes place in both a globalising and a post-colonial context (Msila & Gumba 2016). African philosophies traditionally value concepts such as *context* and *meaning* as expressed in the principle of Ubuntu which describes the significance of human interdependence and group solidarity as vital to the survival of a community. Malungu (2006) states that the sharing and collective ownership of opportunities, responsibilities and challenges as well as the importance of people and relationships over things are two of the interrelated principles of Ubuntu. I will argue that there is a pattern that connects human interconnectedness and interdependence to meaning and context, to South Africa's philosophical heritage of Ubuntu and to social learning.

In this spirit a series of seminars as a community of practice (Lave & Wenger 1991) was arranged by the author as the supervisor of a group of postgraduate research students. Learning as a social and not an individual practice, based in a specific situation or *context,* is congruent with the values of Ubuntu and the seminars were designed to create a meaningful learning space for students. The supervisor as a facilitator organises a sequential series of seminars where eight to ten students are invited to present their research as they progress from the proposal phase to the final chapter. Supervision becomes a conversational process where constructive feedback is encouraged and insights are discovered or invented, often in an unpredictable manner as students present their research. As in jazz music, so in collaborative learning seminars we all become improvisers in real time, co-constructing new possibilities and scholarly connected.

The purpose of this chapter is to present a descriptive equation for postgraduate research throughput. The equation, as opposed to a quantitative formula, is a collation of themes based on the qualitative analysis of the experiences of postgraduate research students who took part in the research seminars. My aim is to address the perceived gap in pedagogical knowledge and discourse regarding research and dissertation writing skills.

A SYSTEM PSYCHODYNAMIC FRAMEWORK

The theoretical paradigm in which the study was embedded is the System psychodynamic framework of psychological wellness (Henning 2009). This framework is a fusion of system psychodynamic theory and positive psychology theory and provides a lens for deep insights into individual, team or organisational behaviour. For this study, the framework was applied to analyse a research support programme for postgraduate students.

System psychodynamic theory and methodology

System psychodynamic theory integrates concepts from both system theory and psychodynamic theory. The paradigm evolved at the Tavistock Institute in the UK in the 1950s and 1960s to gain a better understanding of the conscious and unconscious dynamic behaviours in teams and organisations (Henning 2009). It can be understood as a combination of a 'working outside in' (systems) perspective as well as a 'working inside out' (psychodynamic) perspective (Czander 1996). The theory offers a depth psychology perspective while also acknowledging unpredictable emerging patterns of relationships within all living systems. Concepts such as 'identity', 'power', 'containment' and 'boundary management' and how they influence or are expressed in various systems such as an individual, group or an organisation are central themes. When it is said that a person, or in this context the lecturer, acts as a 'container' for the group's emotions it is meant that he or she is holding, bounding, confining and fencing in the effect of that system (Henning 2009:116). System psychodynamic theory also accepts anxiety as the basis for and driving force of relationship and relatedness behaviour (Armstrong 2005) and behaviour manifestations are interpreted as defences against anxiety. The series of seminars provides containment for the emotional states of the students to enable more task-oriented behaviour within the time boundaries of the module.

As a central characteristic of system theory, the whole is described as more than the sum of its parts (Gharajedaghi 2011) or in 'lay' terms, two turkeys will not make an eagle. This implies that the synergy between the different parts of a system may co-create an unexpected emerging whole and that uncertainty and ambiguity are valued where a network of relationships, connectedness and context is important (Henning 2009). This is true during the seminars where a student often experiences a collective 'Aha!' moment that is valuable and exciting to all other students:

> I'm just amazed that we come up with these ideas. I mean, I'm just like sitting here and listening and thinking wow, you know, I never in a million years would have thought of half of this stuff.

Emerging properties of an interacting system – in this case the seminar – cannot be measured directly or predicted with certainty; only their manifestations can be measured. A quality research dissertation delivered on time is the manifestation of success, and instead of trying to describe a student or group of students in terms of *being*, we can also try to understand them as part of a process of *becoming*. The interactive discourse generates spontaneous new insights, cumulatively contributing to the complex process of each student becoming a master in research. This process of becoming or developing is descriptive of what is known as the Fibonacci sequence.

The Fibonacci sequence

From a system theory paradigm, the Fibonacci sequence is introduced as a metaphor of growth as it describes the emerging scholarly development of students during the sequence of seminars. Leonardo Pisano, best known as Fibonacci, first described the sequence and ratio that constitute the ideal properties of beauty and growth patterns in all living organisms (Lehman & Posamentier 2007). It is a series of numbers where a number is found by adding up the two numbers before it: 1 1 2 3 5 8 13 and so forth (Campbell 2010). That is: $1 + 1 = 2, 2 + 3 = 5, 5 + 3 = 8, 8 + 5 = 13$ and so on and on, *ad infinitum*.

The Fibonacci sequence as a growth factor in all living systems is referred to as *Phi* [pronounced *fi*] and should not be confused with Pi, the sixteenth letter of the Greek alphabet which represents the ratio of a circle's circumference to its diameter. *Phi* is the twenty-first letter of the Greek alphabet and also represents the Golden Ratio of 1.618. As the perfect measure for beauty and perfection it has unique properties in architecture, music, theology, physiology and anatomy and even in financial markets. It explains the 'pattern that connects' and interdependency in the bigger web of life (Bateson 1979). Figure 5.1 depicts how the Fibonacci numbering is hidden behind the spiral pattern in the growth of living things from DNA structures on microscopic level to the pattern formation of other non-living phenomena on macroscopic level such as in weather patterns and galaxies.

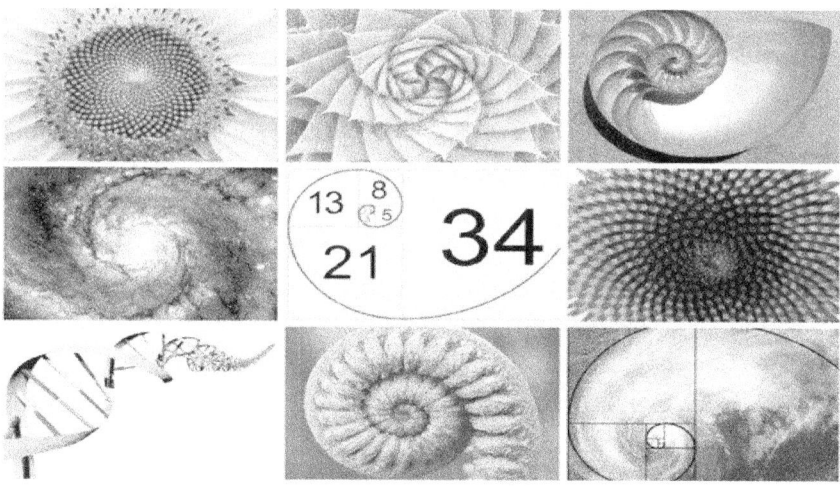

"Where there is matter, there is geometry."
~ Johannes Kepler

FIGURE 5.1 Fibonacci patterns in nature

The sequence of five seminars follows the logical steps of writing a dissertation; each progressively building on the previous event. Scholarly development may be illustrated in a spiral shape, ever-expanding as the year progresses and students master the skills of research from one unit to the next. The scholarly growth of the research students, meaning the insights of students presented from one seminar to the next, seems to be the sum of the new information learned from the previous seminars. The interaction between the students and the supervisor has the potential to contribute collectively and cumulatively to unexpected outcomes and a synergy of social and academic capital, that is, the positive development of students and their final research reports. Over a period of 11 months, the students progressed from making indiscriminate generalisations of personal experiences during the first seminars to articulating well-reasoned and complex academic discourse during the last sessions. This pattern of growth or blueprint plan for development is also acknowledged by the psychologist Erikson (1968:91) who referred to the development of the self as the 'epigenetic principle':

> Whenever we try to understand growth, it is well to remember the epigenetic principle which is derived from the growth of organisms in utero … this principle states that anything that grows has a ground plan and that out of this ground plan the parts arise each having its time of special ascendancy, until all parts have arisen to form a functioning whole.

The researcher is recursively part of the observed and in a sense one can speak of an 'observing system' which is created by the observer and that which is observed. Such an observing system is self-referential as the observer, in this case the author, and the observed (postgraduate students) interact and influence one another. That implies the supervisor as part of the system recursively develops and grows with the students as they progress together through the year and co-create research outcomes. The emphasis on the expansion of theoretical knowledge is also reflected in practice, where the sequence of the seminars – the emphasis on progress from a literature review to a problem statement to a research question – creates a space where there are various conversations about possibilities. The students accept that the seminar conversations are everyone's responsibility and the opportunity to present research is not just about a turn to talk, but it is about being authorised with the power to initiate a topic that others join in reviewing.

Positive psychology

Positive psychology focuses on the study of humans' positive subjective experiences and the study of individual traits, character strengths and virtues (Peterson & Seligman 2006).

It has its roots in humanistic psychology where concepts such as 'self-actualisation' and 'self-efficacy' are relevant and psychodynamic thinking, where the concepts 'hope' and 'wisdom' exist. It can be defined as the study of optimal human functioning with the aim of changing the focus of theories and practices from a preoccupation with disease and healing to wellbeing and the enhancement or fostering of strengths and virtues (Peterson & Seligman 2006). Diverging from the old disease paradigm of human functioning that asks, 'What went wrong?' a positive psychology approach asks, 'What went right?' Some of the concepts in positive psychology theories are 'gratitude', 'forgiveness', 'compassion', 'courage', 'purpose in life', 'humour', 'spirituality', 'humility' and 'appreciation'. Selected concepts such as 'hope' (Snyder & Lopez 2005), 'meaning' and 'mastery' (Joseph 2015) were included in the study as they related to the research question and objectives and were expressed in the students' evaluations of the programme. The subdomains of the concept 'mastery' include 'autonomy', 'independence', 'problem solving' and 'adaptation' (Joseph 2015) and these behaviours are all expected outcomes of the research dissertation module at the learning institute. Hope, mastery and meaning as positive psychology concepts were confirmed in this study as they contributed to student completion rates.

SCAFFOLDING THE STEPS TO AN ECOLOGY OF MIND

Structure and regularity are important elements in human existence and a lack of structure may have negative effects such as depression and a lack of motivation. The sequential support programme consists of five stepwise seminar style events arranged throughout the year at the business school. Each seminar is at the same time a stepping stone towards the next seminar and a building block from the previous seminar. The seminars aim to keep students' motivation levels high with challenges and variety in the five events, following a logical flow in writing a dissertation. These five seminars are structured and named as follows:

a. Seminar 1: Proposal Chat
b. Seminar 2: Literature review – Reading to Write
c. Seminar 3: Research methodology – Tools of Trade
d. Seminar 4: Data analysis – Keeping the Golden thread
e. Seminar 5: Research results – Telling the Story

Each seminar consists of two or three parts, based on the identified needs of the students. During the first seminar, Proposal Chat, the students reflect and motivate the purpose or meaning of their research projects:

Why do I? – A reflexive exercise: Think-pair-share (20 minutes)

During this activity the facilitator poses the question to all students: 'Why did you decide on your research topic?' to consider briefly. Next each person turns to the student next to them for discussion, where after a few students self-select to report their thoughts to the group.

All seminars include a lecture and student presentations:

What do I? – A lecture on the relevant topic of the seminar (45 minutes)

This activity is a formal short lecture presented by the faculty member in line with the milestone phase of the research programme.

How do I? – Student presentations (2-3 hours)

Students self-select to present their research to the rest of the group for peer review and constructive feedback.

Contributions are voluntary and the seminars, as an additional support strategy, do not replace the traditional one-to-one relationship between the supervisor and the student.

A DESCRIPTIVE EQUATION FOR THROUGHPUT: NOT JUST A PHI IN THE SKY

The primary themes that emerged from the qualitative responses of the student's programme evaluation were combined to construct a 'formula' or 'descriptive equation' for postgraduate student throughput:

T = PHI + (Me + Ma) CpaC, where T = Throughput, P = Power, I = Identity, Me = Meaning, Ma = Mastery and CpaC = Continuous proactive communication

Phi (pronounced *fi*), apart from being the name of the Fibonacci sequence or Golden ratio, is an acronym for the themes 'power', 'hope' and 'identity' as they emerged from the students' qualitative responses. These three concepts seem to be intertwined as part of the dynamics between the students themselves and the supervisor as they all share power, authorise each other and create hope that transcends their initial anxiety and fears at the start of the research module.

P = Power

Power is closely related to authority and the context of the study implies the authority of the supervisor over students, how the supervisor authorises students and how students authorise one another in their conversations during the seminars. Power or authority is progressively de-centralised throughout the year away from the supervisor to the students. Robertson (2016) refers to three power 'states', namely 'power to', 'power with' and 'power over' regarding postgraduate supervision. The three power states are described below as they pertained to this study:

Power to: The main purpose of the supervisor as facilitator is to empower students to enter the conversation and to acquire an own voice in the scholarly dialogue. Comments reflecting students' experiences of being authorised were categorised under this theme:

> It fast-tracked my growth and was an extreme confidence booster.
>
> Through the workshops I am now equipped to interrogate and critically evaluate research results at work which is usually done by research specialists.

Being authorised from the top (the supervisor) as well as from the sides (peers), students often position themselves as a being an authority to speak about a particular topic. For example, when introducing an idea in conversation a student might say, "As an engineering consultant …" or "As a brand manager …" I often give power to a student by positioning them through giving them a particular status. For example: "Megan, you can probably speak to this since you have been in the same industry."

Power with: Responses that express how students experience being authorised specifically by their peers are categorised under this theme. The formation of a group identity is closely related to this theme. It happens in the moment-to-moment negotiations that are always present in seminars where it is clear how authority as power intertwines with identity:

> I was exposed to a great team from different spheres with different backgrounds. Team members were able to assist one another and learn from others. We were allowed to present our work to team members and the supervisor who gave value inputs.
>
> The interaction with others students provided an exceptional experience.

Strong group cohesion was evident at the end of the year and students were reluctant to leave the last seminar and go their separate ways.

Power over: Perceptions of the increase of cognitive distance and the decrease of an over-dependency that progressively develops between the supervisor and the student are categorised under this theme. As the year progresses, the power relationship between the students and the supervisor changes from an asymmetrical power relationship where the supervisor has more authority and power 'over' students to a more symmetrical power relationship where students become empowered in a more vertical structure of shared power.

H = Hope

Hope through a systems thinking lens offers a theory that is 'hopeful' because of concepts such as 'self-organisation' and 'complex adaptation' as opposed to the traditional deterministic psychological approaches (Henning 2009). The ever-changing state of a system – be it a despondent supervisor, a rebellious student, a team or organisation with low morale, any system in flux – has the potential to adapt to a changing environment. The seminars offer opportunities to students to set goals, find pathways to reach their desired goals and become motivated to reach those goals. In short, students can adapt and 'self-organise' to rise to the challenges of writing a dissertation. Snyder and Lopez (2005) state that hope flourishes under probabilities of intermediate goal attainment, pathways thinking in order to reach the goals, and agency thinking, which is the motivational component in hope theory. It reflects the self-referential thoughts about starting to move along a pathway and continuing to progress along that pathway (Henning 2009). From their conversations, students seem to be very effective at suggesting alternative routes when their peers encounter obstacles in planning and executing their research activities. The supervisor as facilitator took up the role of a "merchant in hope", making sure the end remains in sight and within reach of all students: "The dissertation is not an unsurpassable hurdle and not so daunting if you work diligently and follow the process" (Kets de Vries 2007:211).

Human relationships, the ability to generate new life opportunities and actively seeking an open mind to absorb new knowledge and experiences may create hope (Cameron & Spreitzer 2012) as some students reflected:

> I experienced many life perspective altering learnings.
>
> There are many students who suffer in silence. I always looked forward to the next session.

Students' initial anxiety and feelings of loneliness seem to have reduced over time. They experienced a growing sense of personal agency that creates hope that the desired outcome will realise.

I = Identity

Responses regarding engagement with scholarly dialogue as a new voice or new 'kid on the block' were categorised under this theme. Our identities come from our personal experiences and social interactions over time. Fiksdal (2014) contends that we are always negotiating multiple social identities as we talk, and although we actively construct our identities in our interactions with others, negotiation remains part of this process as our listeners validate or reject that identity.

The task of the supervisor is to be sensitive to 'below-the-surface' dynamics to determine whether the group as whole is productive or if anti-task behaviour hinders the growth of the group. Behaviour such as pairing, me-ness as withdrawal, dependency and fight-or flight conduct (Bion 1961) is often counter-productive to the growth of individual members towards a scholarly identity. The development of a scholarly identity was evident in all the students as they engaged in the dialogues:

> The last two workshops made me feel like I really owned the dissertation and I felt proud of my work.
>
> My interactions with other fellow students added value to me and that cemented relationships with fellow students that I am still in contact with.

Me = Meaning

Responses that describe how the seminars supported students to find purpose and meaning in their research projects are categorised under this theme. The existentialist Victor Frankl (1959) coined the term 'logotherapy' which means 'therapy through meaning', implicating there is a healing force in meaning. He remarked that ever more people have the means to live but no meaning to live for. Once the students become aware of the purpose and meaning of their research projects and what their specific roles and tasks relating to that purpose are, enthusiasm and progress are activated. The knowledge that they will be able to make a difference at work by applying their research recommendations in business seems to be a powerful source of inspiration to students to complete their dissertations.

Ma = Mastery

Mastery refers to the strength of managing oneself as well as one's environment (Henning 2009). It refers to the acquisition of new skills and knowledge through experiential learning as students present their work and discuss it with each other and the supervisor. In this regard, one student responded:

> I didn't know I had a paradigm!

The sequential structure of the seminars builds the skills and knowledge of the research process and methodologies in a stepwise manner to enable the mastering of difficult concepts. The cognitive and emotional trajectories of the students are evident as they do peer reviews of the research presentations. The supervisor increasingly authorises students to take the lead in feedback, guide less as the students master the basic research skills, and advise one another towards the end of the module:

> I read a lot of academic journals and can proudly say that my life will never be the same.

CpaC = Continuous proactive communication

Reflective diary notes throughout the year and students' comments regarding communication with the supervisor between the events are categorised under this theme. A proactive approach in contemplating the needs and questions of students and the provision of a continuous virtual presence is necessary to complement the time between the series of seminars.

Implications

The seminars as a learning space for supervisors and master's degree students have numerous positive implications. A supervisor may gain more control and experience and less pressure regarding the complete supervisory process when power is decentralised and assigned to students during the seminars. The collective value of the sessions is more effective than individual supervisory sessions. The need for lengthy individual sessions is moderated through mutually shared understandings. The students share a common goal and find a sense of purpose and fulfilment in their research projects. They become more task-oriented, read in a more focused manner and manage their time more efficiently. They share information and provide social media support and, in greater solidarity, also learn how to agree to disagree. To some extent aspirations towards a doctoral degree become part of the dialogue as students progressively master each phase of the research process, gain confidence, expand their understanding of business research and identify gaps in the body of knowledge.

In sum, the academic workloads of supervisors and students may be relieved as is evident in the timeous production of quality dissertations and the establishment of a virtuous cycle of knowledge production between academia and industry leaders.

CONCLUSION

A 'one-size-fits-all' magic formula for an effective supervisor–student space does not exist. However, there seems to be value in the seminar as a collaborative learning space combined with the concepts proposed in the descriptive equation for throughput. Living systems are integrated wholes whose properties cannot be reduced to those of smaller parts. There are things that emerge only together or in interaction with other things at a certain time and place and the seminar as a supervisor–student space is one of many different options where learning may take place.

Fibonacci (Phi) power in postgraduate supervision offers a blueprint development plan, sequentially arranged and cumulatively contributing to an ecology of mind to the benefit of all the stakeholders involved. In conclusion, teaching and learning within the African context should adopt learning practices that do not view a challenging situation as a closed world from which there is no exit, but rather as a collaborative process of constructing possibilities of *Phi*, that is, empowerment, *hope* and scholarly *identities*.

REFERENCES

Armstrong D. 2005. *Organisation in the mind. Psychoanalysis, group relations and organisational consultancy.* London: Karnac Books.

Bateson G. 1979. *Mind and nature.* New York: Dutton.

Bion WR. 1961. *Experiences in groups.* London: Tavistock. https://doi.org/ 10.4324/9780203359075

Bitzer E, Albertyn R, Frick L, Grant B, & Kelly F (eds). 2014. *Pushing boundaries in postgraduate supervision.* Stellenbosch: AFRICAN SUN MeDIA. https://doi.org/10.18820/9781920689162

Cameron SK & Spreitzer GM. 2012. *The Oxford handbook of positive organisational scholarship.* New York: Oxford Press.

Campbell SC. 2010. *Growing patterns: Fibonacci numbers in nature.* Pennsylvania: Boyds Mills Press.

Cilliers F & Harry N. 2012. The systems psychodynamic experiences of first-year master's students in industrial and organisational psychology. *SA Journal of Industrial Psychology/SA Tydskrif vir Bedryfsielkunde,* 38(2), Art. #992, pp. 1-9.

Czander WM. 1997. *The psychodynamics of work and organisations: Theory and application.* New York: Guilford Press.

Dahl R. 2016. *The BFG.* Penguin Random House: South Africa.

Erikson EH. 1968. *The life cycle: Epigenesis of identity. Identity, youth and crisis.* New York: Norton & Company.

Fiksdal S. 2014. *A guide to teaching effective seminars.* New York: Routledge.

Frankl V. 1959. *Man's search for meaning.* New York: Beacon Press.

Frost N. 2011. *Qualitative research methods in psychology: Combining core approaches.* New York: McGraw Hill.

Gaskell A & Mills R. 2014. The quality and reputation of open, distance and e-learning: What are the challenges? *Open Learning: The Journal of Open, Distance and e-Learning*, 29(3):190-205.

Gharajedaghi J. 2011. *Systems thinking: Managing chaos and complexity*. London: Elsevier.

Henning S. 2009. Towards a System Psychodynamic Model of Psychological Wellness. DPhil thesis. Pretoria: UNISA.

Joseph S. 2015. *Positive psychology in practice: Promoting human flourishing in work, health, education and everyday life*. New Jersey: John Wiley & Sons, Inc. https://doi.org/10.1002/9781118996874

Kets de Vries MFR. 2007. *The happiness equation: Meditations on happiness and success*. Lincoln: iUniverse Press.

Nind M, Kilburn D & Luff R. 2017. *The teaching and learning of social research methods*. London: Routledge.

Peterson C & Seligman MEP. 2004. *Character strengths and virtues: A handbook and classification*. New York: Oxford Press.

Posamentier AS & Lehmann I. 2007. *The (fabulous) Fibonacci numbers*. New York: Prometheus Books.

Robertson MJ. 2016. Team modes and power: Supervision of doctoral students. *Higher Education Research & Development*. https://doi.org/10.1080/07294360.2016.1208157

Snyder CR & Lopez SJ. 2005. *Handbook of positive psychology*. New York: Oxford University Press.

Wissing M, Potgieter J, Guse T, Khumalo T & Nel L. 2014. *Towards flourishing: Contextualising positive psychology*. Pretoria: Van Schaik Publishers.

6 'MORE THAN WRITING A THESIS'
REFLECTIONS ON COHORT RESEARCH SUPERVISION

Christine Winberg & Simon Winberg

INTRODUCTION: EXPANDING THE SUPERVISION SPACE

An important shift has occurred in the purpose of doctoral education: from preparation for a life in academia towards more interdisciplinary programmes that prepare students for different kinds of work both in and out of universities. A key factor driving this change is greater participation, which has resulted in doctoral programmes becoming increasingly diverse with regard to student demographics and pedagogies, as well as in terms of programme and degree types (Åkerlind & McAlpine 2017). Enlarging the field of postgraduate supervision in these multiple ways creates opportunities for "expansive learning" (Engeström 1999). This chapter reports on a study of how the supervision space at two research sites expanded to include project-based cohort supervision, a practice that involved more supervisors, more peer learning, and a larger research community. Project-based cohort supervision is a model that is more common in engineering and the applied sciences than in the social sciences. It is usually organised in terms of projects that have been funded or commissioned, with the purpose of building and applying knowledge in a specialised field, as illustrated in Figure 6.1:

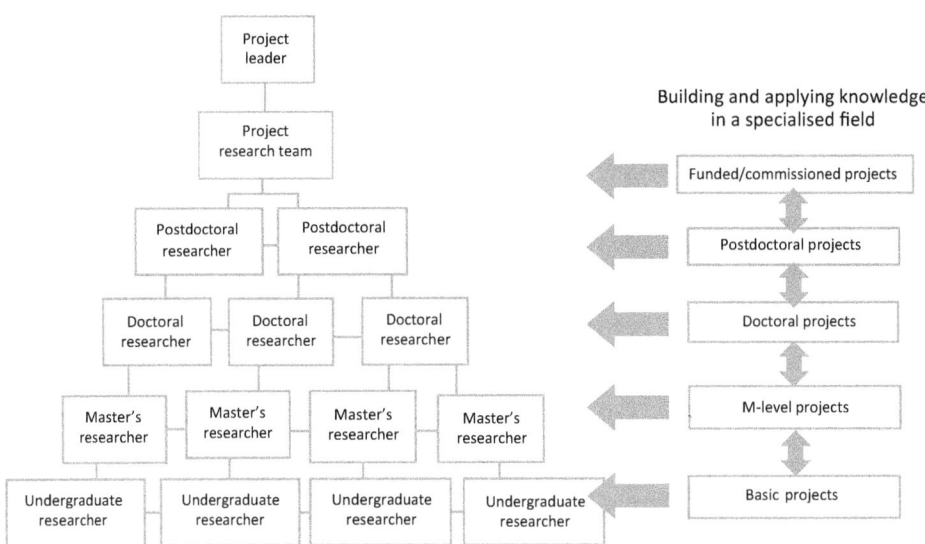

FIGURE 6.1 Cohort supervision showing the scaffolding of projects and researcher roles at different research levels

Figure 6.1 simplifies the knowledge-building process in cohort groups to a hierarchy, but in practice it is more of a network of multiple projects that is fluid and dynamic as different researchers move in and out of the project team, and more and less researchers work together on different projects, with the common cause of growing a specialised field.

BRIEF OVERVIEW OF THE LITERATURE ON FORMS OF GROUP-BASED SUPERVISION

Much of the literature assumes that research supervision is dyadic, comprising interactions between supervisor and student (Bastalich 2017). Thus the literature on doctoral supervision has tended to focus on supervisor–candidate relationships (McCallin & Nayar 2012), the process of supervising research (Manathunga & Goozée 2007) and the postgraduate experience (Åkerlind & McAlpine 2017). A number of studies suggest that postgraduate pedagogies should be re-evaluated. There is, for example, evidence that student isolation and marginalisation are linked to attrition and low completion rates (Janta, Lugosi & Brown 2014) and that successful doctoral students often find support in a wider learning community and interaction with peers (McCulloch et al 2016). Group supervision processes rarely feature in institutional quality assurance policies or guidelines for doctoral supervision (Fenge 2012); it was this that inspired Boud and Lee's (2005) critique of the apprentice model and call for a new emphasis on postgraduate pedagogy, with a focus on peer learning and the wider research environment.

There is an emerging interest in alternative models of research supervision that have the potential to enhance effectiveness by promoting scholarly cohort interaction in a context of social and academic support (McCulloch et al 2016; Choy, Delahaye & Saggers 2015). Doctoral writing groups, for example, have been shown to improve candidates' writing outputs (Lee & Kamler 2008). The literature also suggests that many candidates are under-prepared for doctoral studies and need support in the development of research skills, such as information finding (McCallin & Nayar 2012), working with texts (Kamler & Thomson 2007) and research methodology (Hutchings 2017). In group-based supervision, supervisors and collaborators offer workshops that cover topics such as reviewing the literature, referencing, research design and methods, and research problem-solving – all of which support learning (McCallin & Nayar 2012). Some studies suggest that group supervision models are more suited to 21st century doctoral attributes, such as high level teamwork (Manathunga et al 2012). Interdisciplinary research studies are increasingly common and are better facilitated by an interdisciplinary supervision team (Winberg et al 2011). Some studies suggest that candidates' satisfaction is more likely when there are two (or more) active supervisors (Watson 2012). There is thus emerging evidence that the supportive scholarship of group supervision can improve the postgraduate experience.

In practice, research supervision is often 'blended' (De Beer & Mason 2009), comprising infrastructural resources and academic communities that are intellectually, socially and geographically dispersed. A blended supervision approach combines supervisor and candidate meetings with a virtual classroom that offers teleconferences, online exemplars, discussion groups and self-paced online courses. Blended models of supervision are particularly effective for strengthening relationships between supervisors and candidates (Watson 2012) and in creating communities of practice (McCulloch et al 2016). Blended research supervision reflects recent changes in higher education and the move towards combining face-to-face contact with online learning (McCallin & Nayar 2012).

Theoretical framework

In order to explore more fully the process and outcomes of cohort postgraduate supervision, we drew on the resources of Activity Theory (Engeström 1999). Activity Theory understands that human activity is always undertaken by subjects, mediated by cultural tools and embedded within a social context. These interactions are known as the activity system. Activity Theory is useful in educational research for developing a deep understanding of how individuals produce and reproduce themselves as members of an academic community through the social interactions of production, exchange, consumption and distribution (Roth 2004).

The activity system has zones of production, exchange, consumption and distribution. The zone of production comprises subjects, their tools, and the object of the activity. In this study of cohort supervision, the postgraduate students, supervisors and collaborators are multiple subjects involved in the achievement of the object. The tools can be physical, cultural or conceptual; in this case they are the technical, textual, virtual and symbolic research tools needed to undertake research work. The first principle of activity is that the object drives the activity (Engeström 1999). Activity Theory distinguishes between the object and the outcome. The object of an educational activity system is always the transformation of the subject (Edwards & Daniels 2004). Identity formation could thus be understood as both the object and the process of the postgraduate supervision activity system. A focus on the object (building researchers) enables outcomes, such as the production of a thesis, a research report, or published article, to flow out of the system.

There are three additional zones in the activity system: exchange, consumption and distribution. The exchange zone is governed by tacit and explicit rules that determine how the subjects (the postgraduate researchers, their supervisors and collaborators) may act, and are a result of socio-historical processes. Conventions and guidelines in postgraduate study have their roots in academic traditions, and are slow to change to accommodate new objects. The zone of consumption is determined by the community, that is, the broader social context in which the postgraduate study occurs. Members of the community will, for example, examine the thesis, accept a report or review an article. The community is part of the activity system, and can advance or block the achievement of the object. The zone of distribution is the arrangements made for the division of labour, that is, the hierarchical structures and task distributions within the research supervision activity system.

The four zones anchor the subjects, tools, objects, rules and communities, and controls how work is done. In order to understand postgraduate research supervision and its outcomes, the whole activity system, both process and outcome, has to be studied (Granata & Dochy 2016). By studying the whole system, researchers can identify the interactions that postgraduate researchers have to negotiate, as well as the tensions and contradictions. Finding these 'sticking points' indicates ways of improving practices within doctoral programmes (Beauchamp, Jazvac-Martek & McAlpine 2009).

A RESEARCH DESIGN FOR STUDYING COHORT SUPERVISION

The broad research question guiding the study was: How do postgraduate researchers, their supervisors and collaborators understand the benefits and challenges of cohort supervision? As activity system is inherently dynamic, continuously undergoing change and bringing about change, the research design needed to capture changes in the system over time.

Research sites

The first site is an interdisciplinary research centre that studies professional, vocational and technical education. Almost all of the postgraduates are part-time students in full-time employment as lecturers or managers at universities, technical and vocational education colleges, government departments, non-governmental organisations, or other workplaces. Collaborative forms of supervision have evolved over the centre's 15-year history; currently each postgraduate researcher has a main supervisor and additional co-supervisors linked to a project that has both local and international collaborators. The postgraduate researchers are thus introduced to a wider community of researchers from the outset. The centre has a website, where readings, videos, podcasts, and presentation slides are available. The research centre conducts quarterly workshops and breakaways that bring the project teams, postgraduate researchers, supervisors and external collaborators together to focus on the theoretical and practical aspects of building knowledge in the field of professional, vocational and technical education.

The second site is an interdisciplinary research group that develops specialised software applications. Each student (whether doctoral or master's) has two or three supervisors. The main supervisor is usually a software engineer and the co-supervisor is a specialist in the application domain. About half the students in the group are industry-based and have an additional workplace supervisor. Additional local and international academic and industry-based collaborators provide training workshops and supervision. The group activities include structured lectures and workshops, referred to as 'research training sessions'. Writing workshops are also offered; these are based on campus and facilitated by an experienced technical editor and members of the supervisor team. The supervision strategy is a blended approach that includes group and individual training, both in-person and via Skype, online tools and email correspondence.

Research participants

Each cohort has different kinds of members, broadly divided into internal team members, who are more closely associated to the groups concerned, and external team members, who are less frequent collaborators from other institutions. The different participant categories and their roles are listed in Table 6.1.

TABLE 6.1   Participants and their roles

Role	Internal team member	External team member
Master's researcher	Master's researchers	N/A (all are internal team members)
Doctoral researcher	Doctoral researchers	N/A (all are internal team members)
Supervising team	Academic supervisors and co-supervisors, postdoctoral researchers, research officers	Co-supervisors (unofficial or official) from industry or other university affiliated to the team
Collaborators	Research assistants, internal academic staff members (not supervising students)	Research collaborators from other organisation or university, visiting researcher/scholar, invited trainers

Data sources and data collection

There were three sources of data available for the study: 1) data from formative feedback (usually elicited at the end of a group training session or breakaway), 2) survey data, and 3) the project email archive. Most of the data were collected in the form of group reflections following cohort supervision activities. These reflections were elicited over a two-year period (2016-2017) at different stages across the doctoral journeys. Open questions were asked about how the group had experienced cohort supervision, in particular what they had found useful in their research work. Feedback and suggestions were used to plan subsequent cohort supervision activities. During 2016/2017 an external evaluator was appointed to facilitate the group reflections and record the feedback data. These data were professionally transcribed and then sent to participants for verification. An online survey was distributed at the end of 2016 to 26 participants at Site 1 and 22 participants at Site 2. The survey asked questions about the benefits and difficulties experienced, preferred supervision strategies, preferred ways of giving or receiving feedback, types of supervision or support that may have occurred outside of group meetings, as well as suggestions going forward. The third data source was the projects' email archive. The email archive is an important document in project work: it contains what Engeström (2009) calls the "germ cell" – the ideas, insights and concepts that could potentially develop

CHAPTER 6 • 'MORE THAN WRITING A THESIS': REFLECTIONS ON COHORT RESEARCH SUPERVISION

TABLE 6.2   Coding the data

Data source	Attribution	Data	In vivo codes	Coder 1	Coder 2	RESEARCHERS' COMMENTS
Survey	Master's	I thought that the session on the literature review and the guest presentation on Mendeley was really useful. The three-day writing retreat at [place] was of huge benefit – it was an opportunity to kick start the thesis.	Literature review, Mendeley, Writing retreat	TOOLS & COMMUNITY	TOOLS & COMMUNITY	Cohort supervision seems to link TOOLS to COMMUNITY – in fact because everything is group-based it could be that everything has this community slant.
Survey	Doctoral	I think there should be some more input on methodology, and also some input on the writing process – such as how to write up findings. I think the [training] weeks should continue 1 x term – but maybe only individual meetings in the last term.	(more) Methodology, writing process, [training] Weeks Individual	TOOLS & COMMUNITY	TOOLS & COMMUNITY	Different kinds TOOLS imply different kinds of learning and different COMMUNITIES for group meetings and individual meetings and online meetings ... not one COMMUNITY but many ...

into research proposals, published articles, conference presentations, or arguments in a thesis.

Data analysis

We drew on the categories of activity both to develop the data collection tools and to frame the data analysis and interpretation. A database was created for the feedback transcriptions, survey responses, and the project email archive. These data were coded, firstly with *in vivo* codes, and subsequently with the categories of activity, as shown in Table 6.2.

Each researcher coded the data separately, and then consolidated the codes and comments. Patterns began to emerge from the analysis about what constituted depth and growth in collaborative learning, as well as the more everyday needs and challenges of cohort supervision.

Ethical issues

This study was part of a larger research project involving six universities, funded by the South African National Research Foundation and the Swedish Foundation for International Cooperation in Research and Higher Education. The project obtained ethical clearance from the lead institution, and permission to conduct research activities from each participating institution. Participants provided informed consent for the use of feedback and survey data and the project email archives.

FINDINGS: A COHORT ACTIVITY SYSTEM

The data obtained from the research participants enabled us to model cohort supervision practices as an activity system, and to see where tensions and contradictions arose.

Outcome: Building knowledge in new fields

The expected outcome of the cohort research supervision activity system was building knowledge in new fields and making a knowledge contribution to these fields. The proxy for this outcome was the production of research proposals, theses-in-progress or completed, research articles, conference presentations, and project reports.

Expanding the object: More than the thesis

The primary object that drove cohort-based supervision was the transformation of candidates into independent researchers, which entailed building their expertise in specialised fields of study. As one supervisor put it, "[A] central component of …

postgraduate studies is … development as a researcher …" (Supervisor 1). For both the supervisors and the candidates there was more at stake than writing a thesis; they were becoming researchers and contributing to new and specialised fields. A focus on the developing researchers meant that that there were many activities beyond thesis-writing, such as attending project meetings, co-authoring research articles, co-presenting at conferences, seminars and workshops, and co-authoring of funding proposals.

The email archive gives evidence of the kinds of activities that drove the project cohort. The email archive for both groups contains ideas for new projects and research proposals, funding opportunities, and ways to disseminate research findings. In the email extract below a supervisor responds to a suggestion from a co-supervisor to contribute to a call for a special edition:

> This is a great find … It is just what [we] should be writing about. [Doctoral 1], if you are up for a first draft of a paper on [topic] I am definitely willing to do some reading … and contribute (Supervisor 2).

The following email correspondence, between two supervisors in different departments, proposes interdepartmental collaboration to build knowledge in the new field:

> Dear [Supervisor 3], Please find attached descriptions of the two projects … I would be very keen to know if the students are interested in this … we can co-supervise as we did with [Doctoral 2]. We can meet with [Supervisor 4] and the students to explain [the application] further (Supervisor 1).

The above emails show how the object driving the system expanded to take on "a great find" or a new "project", which created opportunities for new research work. As Engeström (1999) explains, object-oriented actions are, explicitly or implicitly, characterised by "ambiguity, surprise, interpretation, sense making, and potential for change".

Subjects: The research team

The postgraduate researchers in both groups were not traditional students; many were employed, had professional experience, and several held important positions in their industries or universities. The supervisors and collaborators were busy people who had to manage their time carefully. Thus all were well aware that when several days were allocated to group supervision meetings, the expectation was that the meetings would be useful and advance the research studies. Many letters were written to employers, explaining that the group meetings would "benefit their progress and allow them to engage more effectively with their research projects" (Supervisor 1). For many of the postgraduate researchers there was a gap between their previous academic studies and their current studies, and they required support to get back into academic ways of thinking and writing. For example, there were requests for "workshops on research methodologies and theories" (Master's 1). As one postgraduate researcher put it: "[T]here is a lot about the [discipline] … I guess I'm expected to know but don't" (Doctoral 3). The collective subjects of the activity system enabled the postgraduates to develop their identity as researching professionals and motivated them on their "doctoral journey" (Doctoral 4).

Tools for collaborative knowledge building

Busy research team members and postgraduate candidates used a variety of individual and collaborative tools to support their work. An important tool was the cohort supervision meetings, which typically involved presentations (often by external experts on aspects of thesis writing or topics in the field), training on specialised tools (for example Mendeley, concept mapping, statistical packages) and seminars or round table discussions led by the postgraduate researchers. The postgraduate researchers found the topics "relevant" (Masters 2), whether for "rethinking" the study (Doctoral 5) or for focusing on a particular aspect, such as "methodologies" (Doctoral 3). While it might be thought that attending group meetings might slow down progress, the postgraduates found these meetings to be opportunities to "kick-start" (Doctoral 2) or "jumpstart" (Doctoral 6) their thesis work. For supervisors, the week-long group sessions provided "dedicated time to meet with postgraduate students" (Supervisor 5).

Outside of the group sessions, there was time for the postgraduate researchers to have "one-on-one interaction" (Doctoral 1) with supervisors, peers and visiting scholars. Face-to-face group and individual meetings were supplemented by online collaborative using Google Docs, Dropbox (for written feedback) and Skype meetings; in the case of the engineering group, additional specialised on-line collaborative tools to support software development were made available online. In both case studies, the project website was an important resource where relevant readings and resources for thesis writing could be uploaded (by team members and postgraduate researchers), and where researchers could 'catch up' if a meeting had been missed:

> Thank you so much! I watched [video recording of external expert] last night, and really enjoyed his talk. The paper that I presented at [conference name] … resonated with this approach (Doctoral 7).

Mastering the tools was sometimes difficult for the supervisors who had to become familiar with multiple online project management tools and version control systems. Postgraduate researchers also found new tools challenging; one researcher explained the difficulty of "doing research to understand the application and Hardware/Software development for a computer platform I haven't used before all at the same time" (Doctoral 8). Some participants tried some of the tools, and decided not to continue using them, but almost all participants found some of the tools useful for some functions:

> Definitely [the online collaboration tool] was very useful! Especially for the last progress report – I admit I used some of the logs and code traces to remind me what I actually did :-) (Doctoral 9).

The division of labour: Flattening the hierarchy

Cohort-based supervision is highly collaborative; task distribution is fluid as supervisory team members and postgraduate researchers take on different roles. For example, a postgraduate researcher might be the first author on a particular article, and the first to call for additional meetings, and set up a collaborative writing platform to which supervisors and collaborators could contribute; or a postgraduate researcher might be a presenter at a cohort supervision meeting. The postgraduate researchers appreciated receiving "feedback from more people than [the] main supervisor" (Master's 3); while supervisors found value in the "balance between experts presenting and … students present[ing] and run[ning] discussions to build them as academics and keep the focus on their research" (Supervisor 2). Postgraduate researchers, supervisors and collaborators thus changed roles as they worked together on academic papers, presentations, and on research proposals to secure funding for their work. The postgraduate researchers in both case studies did not feel isolated or alienated; they were part of a research community that exchanged ideas and that offered many varieties of supervisory input. Such flexibility in the division of labour was not without its challenges, for example:

> Cooperating with many other teammates, it's sometimes hard to follow who has done what, ordering components/materials/parts … (Master's 4).

When asked what was particularly challenging, one of the supervisors responded:

> Coordinating the efforts of multiple contributors to a larger project. High productivity in an academic environment for a large project is a challenge because goals are not always clearly defined, not enough planning done, stakeholders pulling in different directions ... (Supervisor 3).

Achieving flexibility to maintain high participation and avoiding over-burdening busy team members needed an effective strategy:

> There should be a 'critical mass' of postgraduates at the [training] weeks – when there are few there isn't a good group dynamic – although there is the benefit that the facilitators can give individual feedback or support. Also I think that as some people power ahead and others lag behind, the group will not be as coherent going forward – for example, everyone starting out benefited from the focus on proposal writing as they were at an early stage, but as the postgrads get into their studies group supervision might not be as relevant – so we'll need to shrink the circle for the newcomers, but also widen it so everyone gets the benefit of the ideas and the work (Supervisor 5).

The cohort supervision strategy created opportunities for postgraduate researches to receive guidance and support from a variety of team members, besides their supervisors. Flattening the hierarchy was of particular importance when supervising colleagues. In some cases, postgraduate researchers were reluctant to request assistance from their main supervisors and preferred to meet with peers. In other cases supervisors needed to call on the assistance of particular experts. What emerged from the data is the importance of being able to both "shrink the circle ... and widen it" (Supervisor 5) to meet different needs.

A community of scholars

In Activity Theory, the community comprises individuals or groups, other than the subjects, who have the same general object, and with whom subjects can interact (Engeström 1999). Postgraduate researchers interacted with these wider communities when they wrote to an editor, interacted with reviewers' feedback, or presented papers at conferences. As the quote below shows, obtaining advice from an expert in the wider community of scholarship can significantly benefit research progress:

> With kind assistance from [names expert], we have cracked the synchronisation problem between the carrier detector and the digitiser. It seems the occasional missing samples glitch is fixed ... Thanks again for getting us in touch (Doctoral 9).

Supervisors brought postgraduates to the expert community through their own networks. In the email below a postgraduate writes to a scholar in the field, following an email introduction by a supervisor:

> Please find attached a very rough layout of my thinking. I would value your input on whether I am on the right track, please (Doctoral 1).

Rules: Contradictions in the system

A concern raised by many of the research participants was that institutional policies and guidelines were not particularly supportive of cohort-based research supervision. This included petty annoyances (such as forms that only have place for a main supervisor and co-supervisor), or more serious difficulties such as locating the study in an appropriate department; in fact finding departmental homes for interdisciplinary work is, as many will attest, a considerable difficulty and a major cause of delay and demotivation (see, for example, Winberg et al 2010). While some departments work around these difficulties and make their own arrangements for sharing FTEs and publication subsidies, this study identified 'rules' as the main source of contradiction in the activity system of cohort supervision – and thus a place where change is needed if cohort supervision is to be successful.

CONCLUSION

This chapter highlights the distinctiveness of cohort supervision, and argues its potential to address some of the difficulties associated with more traditional forms of supervision. It also raises further questions, particularly with regard to changing deeply ingrained supervision practices. When supervisors, in their roles as researchers, work collaboratively, it is usual to bring postgraduate students into such a research community. But for supervisors who have a more traditional approach, such expansion of the supervisory space may prove challenging.

The study offers four key research findings that contribute to the expansion of the supervisory space. The first is the expansion of the object in cohort supervision activity systems, which arises as the subjects develop researcher identities and begin to pursue additional research goals. Engeström (1999:65) explains: "[The object] is truly a horizon: as soon as an intermediate goal is reached, the object escapes and must be reconstructed by means of new intermediate goals and actions."

Project-based cohort research teams are laboratories of expansive learning. Large teams require coordination to ensure that needs at different levels of progress are met and that the postgraduate researchers are included as participants in the activities of the cohort

The second key finding relates to supervisory practice; postgraduate researchers generally had positive experiences as a result of mentoring and their inclusion into a research team. The cohort system builds a community of researchers through the giving and receiving of support, feedback and guidance from a wide variety of sources: peers, postdoctoral scholars, non-supervising collaborators and external experts, as well as supervisors and co-supervisors. The contribution that this study makes with regard to supervisor–candidate relationships is the potential of project-based cohort supervision to address the often "uneasy association between supervisory engagement and student 'dependence'" (Bastalich 2017).

A third finding is that, among the several benefits and opportunities offered by cohort supervision, postgraduate researchers also have a productive experience in the form of co-publication of research articles and co-presentation of conference papers, seminars and workshops. Most doctoral researchers would have published on aspects of their study prior to the examination of the thesis and received peer review from international experts. They therefore tend to produce good theses because they have had input and feedback from experts before submission for external examination. Cohort-based supervision enables an enriched learning environment through peer support and supervision teams.

Expansion has its difficulties, and over-expansion could result in a "runaway object" (Engeström 2009) – such as responding to external pressure around increasing the numbers of PhD graduates, without reducing academic integrity and quality. A final finding is that while an experienced team of experts and postdoctoral scholars can supervise a relatively large number of postgraduate researchers and produce high quality research outputs, they require institutional support. Suggested recommendations for the support of cohort supervision include clear institutional guidelines for cohort supervision, including arrangements for interdisciplinary and inter-institutional cooperation. There should be adequate resources to support students and the additional costs involved for team meetings, off-campus breakaways and external experts or visiting scholars.

An activity system is inherently dynamic; the elements of the activity system interact with one another and may conflict. Such contradictions are necessary for "expansive learning" (Engeström, 1999) and can result in the generation and integration of new practices into the activity system. Cohort supervision embodies a form of collaboration consistent with the view that research supervision is an inherently social practice extending beyond the relationship between candidate and supervisor, and having implications for individual and group transformation. Postgraduate researchers produce outcomes that are distributed, exchanged, and consumed, but also, in the same process, produce and reproduce themselves as members of a research community.

ACKNOWLEDGEMENT

This research was funded by the South African National Research Foundation and the Swedish Foundation for International Cooperation in Research and Higher Education under grant No. STINT160829186851

REFERENCES

Åkerlind G & McAlpine L. 2017. Supervising doctoral students: Variation in purpose and pedagogy. *Studies in Higher Education*, 42(9):1686-1698. https://doi.org/10.1080/03075079. 2015.1118031

Bastalich W. 2017. Content and context in knowledge production: A critical review of doctoral supervision literature. *Studies in Higher Education,* 42(7):1145-1157. https://doi.org/10.1080/03075079.2015.1079702

Beauchamp C, Jazvac-Martek M & McAlpine L. 2009. Studying doctoral education: Using activity theory to shape methodological tools. *Innovations in Education and Teaching International*, 46(3): 265-277. https://doi.org/10.1080/14703290903068839

De Beer M & Mason RB. 2009. Using a blended approach to facilitate postgraduate supervision. *Innovations in Education and Teaching International*, 46(2):213-226. https://doi.org/10.1080/14703290902843984

Boud D & Lee A. 2005. "Peer learning" as pedagogic discourse for research education. *Studies in Higher Education*, 30(5):501-516. https://doi.org/ 10.1080/03075070500249138

Choy S, Delahaye BL & Saggers B. 2015. Developing learning cohorts for postgraduate research degrees. *Australian Educational Researcher*, 42(1):19-34. https://doi.org/10.1007/s13384-014-0147-y

Edwards A & Daniels H. 2004. Using sociocultural and activity theory in educational research. *Educational Review*, 56(2):107-111. https://doi.org/10.1080/0031910410001693191

Engeström Y. 1999. Activity theory and individual and social transformation. In: Y Engeström, R Miettinen & RL Punamäki (eds). *Perspectives on activity theory*. New York: Cambridge University Press. https://doi.org/10.1017/CBO9780511812774

Engeström Y. 2009. The future of activity theory: A rough draft. In: A Sannino, H Daniels & KD Guitiérrez (eds). *Learning and expanding with activity theory*. New York: Cambridge University Press. https://doi.org/10.1017/CBO9780511809989.020

Fenge LA. 2012. Enhancing the doctoral journey: The role of group supervision in supporting collaborative learning and creativity. *Studies in Higher Education*, 37(4):401-414. https://doi.org/10.1080/03075079.2010.520697

Granata SN & Dochy F. 2016. Applied PhD research in a work-based environment: An activity theory-based analysis. *Studies in Higher Education*, 41(6):990-1007. https://doi.org/10.1080/03075079.2014.966666

Hutchings M. 2017. Improving doctoral support through group supervision: Analysing face-to-face and technology-mediated strategies for nurturing and sustaining scholarship. *Studies in Higher Education*, 42(3):533-550. https://doi.org/10.1080/03075079.2015.1058352

Janta H, Lugosi P & Brown L. 2014. Coping with loneliness: An ethnographic study of doctoral students. *Journal of Further and Higher Education*, 38(4):553-571. https://doi.org/ 10.1080/0309877X.2012.726972

Kamler B & Thomson P. 2007. Rethinking doctoral work as text work and identity work. In: B Somekh & TA Schwandt (eds). *Knowledge production: Research in interesting times*. New York: Routledge. 166-179.

Lee A & Kamler B. 2008. Bringing pedagogy to doctoral publishing. *Teaching in Higher Education*, 13(5):511-523. https://doi.org/10.1080/13562510802334723

Manathunga C & Goozée J. 2007. Challenging the dual assumption of the "always/already" autonomous student and effective supervisor. *Teaching in Higher Education*, 12(3):309-322. https://doi.org/10.1080/13562510701278658

Manathunga C, Pitt R, Cox L, Boreham P, Mellick G & Lant, P. 2012. Evaluating industry-based doctoral research programs: Perspectives and outcomes of Australian Cooperative Research Centre graduates. *Studies in Higher Education*, 37(7):43-858. https://doi.org/10.1080/03075079.2011.554607

McCallin A & Nayar S. 2012. Postgraduate research supervision: A critical review of current practice. *Teaching in Higher Education*, 17(1):63-74. https://doi.org/10.1080/13562517.2011.590979

McCulloch A, Kumar V, Van Schalkwyk S & Wisker G. 2016. Excellence in doctoral supervision: An examination of authoritative sources across four countries in search of performance higher than competence. *Quality in Higher Education*, 22(1):64-77. https://doi.org/10.1080/13538322.2016.1144904

Roth W. 2004. Activity theory and education: An introduction. *Mind, Culture & Activity*, 11(1):1-8. https://doi.org/10.1207/s15327884mca1101_1

Watson T. 2012. Colleague supervision – "ignored and undervalued"? The views of students and supervisors in a new university. *Journal of Further and Higher Education*, 36(4):567-581. https://doi.org/10.1080/0309877X.2011.644774

Winberg C, Barnes V, Ncube K & Tshinu S. 2011. Postgraduate students' experiences in interdisciplinary research studies. *South African Journal of Higher Education*, 25(5):1003-1019.

RECONCEPTUALISING THE SUPERVISORY ROLE

BORDER CROSSINGS AND BOUNDED SPACES

Rebekah Smith McGloin

INTRODUCTION

Research is increasingly inter-connected, crossing discipline, sector, institutional and national boundaries. Doctoral education is an integral part of this wider trend. As the landscape of the doctorate has evolved and developed — crossing boundaries and inhabiting new spaces — policy makers, funders, university senior managers and academics have set out to codify the doctorate and to articulate competency frameworks for the role of the supervisor.

The spaces that supervisors inhabit are increasingly prescribed and circumscribed by frameworks and regulations. Yet the borders, boundaries and hierarchies that frame the 'traditional' supervisory domain are ever more tested and made more permeable and contingent by the complexities, challenges and opportunities of negotiating collaborative, cross-cultural and cross-sectoral working.

In this chapter I consider a range of external forces — from the macro to the individual — that are reshaping supervisory spaces and re-examines the changing role and development needs of the supervisor set against the skills, competencies and training that currently predominates. The focus of many of the examples given is the UK, where applicable common trends in policy and practice are highlighted from other countries and regions.

I explore in turn growing trends towards research consortia and researcher mobility, the evolution of the doctorate and growth areas such as collaborative programmes and professional doctorates, the expansion of overall numbers of doctoral candidates and the drive to increase participation at doctoral level of a diverse group of people. I also discuss the impact of these key trends on the role of the supervisor and contrast the ideas of connectedness, community, collaboration and complexity that underpin them with the development of national codes, competency frameworks and a dominant role set for doctoral supervisors.

I then specifically consider recent examples of codification of the supervisory role from the UK: the UK Professional Standards Framework – Dimensions of the Framework for Doctoral Supervisors (Taylor 2016) and the criteria for two national awards for doctoral supervision (one from the UK and one from Australia). I conclude the chapter by comparing and contrasting the activities, values, knowledge and attributes set out in the framework and the award criteria with the contemporary demands on the supervisor and the spaces they inhabit within the changing doctoral landscape.

COLLABORATION AS THE NEW COMPETITION

Excellent research is collaborative, often necessarily international, preferably cross/inter-disciplinary and with guaranteed high impact on business, industry and society. At an organisational and an individual level, research and researchers are responding to the policy imperative to broaden access to research findings, the high costs of conducting research, and the philosophical questioning of knowledge production – where and how new knowledge can be generated and by whom. In a 'post-industrial society',[1] where factory workers have been replaced by knowledge workers as the most significant producers of wealth, access to knowledge is posed (Merle & Meek 2013) as central to the ability to generate wealth. Amplifying the reach and impact of new knowledge and widening the circle of actors involved in creating it is therefore framed as central to economic growth. At the same time, the escalating cost of research infrastructure in the sciences and engineering restricts investment into a smaller number of centres of excellence. There is increasing diversity in what counts as knowledge-producing institutions as universities, industry and government seek to work together in a triple helix to drive the knowledge economy (Etzkowitz & Leydesdorff 1997; Halse & Malfroy 2011; Gemme & Gringas 2004; Enders 2005).

Access to research funding is increasingly predicated in many fields on extensive networks at an organisational level – between higher education institutions and between universities and business, industry and third sector where networks act as "knowledge bridges" (Welch & Zhen 2008:519) – and at an individual level, where researchers can function as "knowledge conduits" (Turpin, Woolley, Marceau & Hill 2008:263). Just at the point that competition for research investment

---

[1] This term was first-coined by the American Sociologist, Daniel Bell in 1962. Cited in Merle and Meek (2013:332).

has arguably become most fierce, collaboration is being put forward as the key to success.

Two key trends in research organisation, policy and practice emerge from this: the increase in size, scale and number of formal research consortia and a proliferation in schemes and initiatives to support researcher mobility.

In the UK, there have been trends towards multi-institutional consortia of research-intensive universities in the form of transregional university alliances. Harrison, Smith and Kinton (2016) identified over 50 transregional alliances between UK universities which were either research consortia or what they term 'doctoral training centres'; that is, cohort-based PhD programmes that operate across a number of institutions.

The development of these consortia was supported by the UK government's undertaking to provide extra funding for research in larger, better-managed research units (Department for Education and Skills 2003), and to recognise the value of collaborations between organisations (Department for Business, Innovation and Skills 2011). Allowing for some lag between policy and practice, the six major para-regional research consortia identified by Harrison et al were established within a six-year period (2007-2013) following the publication of the policy papers.

As well as securing access to funding, there is also some evidence (Smith McGloin & Wynne 2015:50-51) in case-study data that these kinds of consortia support capacity building and people development through a variety of means including increased opportunities for co-supervision, access to training, resources and research networks for doctoral students. Working together in this way also facilitates best practice sharing and co-delivery of skills training.

Alongside these multi-institutional, semi-fixed groupings, individual universities around the world are seeking multiple bilateral strategic partnerships with other universities, both nationally and internationally, either institution-wide or at a faculty level. Mission groups in the UK, Europe and Australia, formed as alliances of universities with similar aims and aspirations to lobby and shape higher education policy, have also begun to drive research collaborations between members and with major multinational partners in business. For example, the Australian Technology Network (ATN) of five business-facing universities in Australia leads several consortia-based initiatives including online research skills training and a jointly delivered industry doctoral training centre. The group were also able to collaborate on a Science and Research Priorities Seed Funding scheme which was designed to connect leading ATN researchers with industry and international collaborators to address global research challenges.

Gunn and Mintrom (2013) point to a number of multilateral global university alliances such as the Association of Pacific Rim Universities (APRU), Universitas 21 (U21), and the Worldwide Universities Network (WUN), established between 1997 and 2000. The WUN was set up to create opportunities for multilateral research collaborations. Key programmes of activity include promoting research networks and encouraging researchers to collaborate with peers in other high-performing and aspiring universities around the world. Gunn and Mintrom's analysis of the efficacy of these alliances points to the need for substantial individual commitment in order for the consortium to achieve these aims. It also highlights other work showing that close proximity is most helpful for creativity and discovery in research (Travaille & Hendriks 2010) and is a strong predictor of the likelihood of the co-authored research publications that are most sought after in institutional research strategies (Lee, Brownstein, Mills & Kohane 2010).

Personal investment as a knowledge conduit in the collaboration game – for doctoral researchers and supervisors alike – is facilitated and encouraged by a proliferation of mobility schemes.

RESEARCHERS ON THE MOVE

Researcher mobility is promoted by Organisation for Economic Co-operation and Development (OECD 2000, 2008) as fundamental to the advancement of knowledge and society, and this imperative can be traced through to national and transnational policies in all income brackets.

Within the European Research Area (ERA), mobility is considered a so-called 'fifth freedom' (EC 2007) and is one of ERA's five priorities (Borell-Damian 2009). It is described as movement between universities (national and international), between sectors (to business and industry) and virtual mobility – collaboration using the internet. European Union (EU) policy makers are seeking to develop mobility further and couple international movement to knowledge exchange activity; creating mobility between universities and business, industry and the third sector as well as between universities and countries, at all career stages. This approach has produced a series of initiatives designed to facilitate researcher mobility both within and from outside ERA. These initiatives have included removing obstacles to cross-border mobility of researchers and movement between public and private research centres. There

CHAPTER 7 • RECONCEPTUALISING THE SUPERVISORY ROLE: BORDER CROSSINGS AND BOUNDED SPACES

has also been a programme of joint funding calls (see, for example, Horizon 2020) and specific schemes to support transnational, inter-sectoral and interdisciplinary mobility (Marie Skłodowska-Curie actions). In addition, the European Commission has invested in joint infrastructure such as EURAXESS, which is a network of over 500 service centres in 40 European countries that offer advice and information to researchers on employment rights and responsibilities across Europe.

Outside of the EU, the USA has the prestigious Fulbright Exchange programme that operates in more than 160 countries to support academic mobility. China, South Africa, Brazil and Chile are among the developing countries that have specific international mobility programmes to support the development of their research funding portfolios and internationally co-authored papers. These programmes include both inward and outward mobility. China and India have also used mobility policies to enhance their local research capacity as well as to benefit from distributed or diaspora knowledge networks (Meyer & Wattiaux 2006; OECD 2010) that have been established.

Positive outcomes predominate in review and analysis of empirical data on researcher mobility for the individual and include the development of transnational networks that sustain productive international collaborations (Woolley, Cañibano & Tesch 2016), enhanced productivity (De Filippo, Casado & Gomez 2009), access to equipment and technology (Guth 2008), production of new knowledge, international transfer of existing knowledge, and establishment of research collaborations (Ackers 2005; Van de Sande, Ackers & Gill 2005; Jöns 2011; O'Hara 2009). However, loss of networks and esteem in the home institution (Gaughan & Robin 2004; Cruz-Castro & Sanz-Menendez 2010; Pezzoni, Sterzi & Lissoni 2012), decrease in productivity (Van Heeringen & Dijkwel 1986) and inequality of engagement with mobility (Hansen, Avveduto & Inzelt 2004; Leemann 2010; Weert 2013) are highlighted as negative consequences for the individual researcher in some analyses. At the level of national research or global research systems there is also some anxiety regarding the impact of researcher mobility; particularly in terms of the movement of researchers from countries with less well established research infrastructures towards the traditional scientific hubs in the north – the USA and Europe. The prevailing counter-discourse to the negative conceptualisation of the south–north brain drain is the positive impact of collaboration and mobility in leveraging 'metropolitan science' to address local development issues (Merle & Meek 2013).

Trends in policy and practice are also manifest in career theory related to researcher progression. In the literature review of theories by Woolley *et al* (2016) which set out to describe researchers' careers, two principal theories place mobility and collaboration as central to career progression for all researchers – including PhD students. Laudel and Gläser (2008) characterise three parallel strands of development that are necessary to progress as a researcher: cognitive development (technical, analytical skills); standing in the institution; and esteem in the peer community (of academics in the discipline or cognate areas). Mobility is put forward as a key factor in developing all three strands. Bozeman, Dietz and Gaughan (2001) describe a similar three-dimensional approach that shapes and frames researchers' career. According to Bozeman et al (2001:718), to be an effective researcher one needs scientific (or academic), technical and human capital, where human capital is expanded to include a "productive social capital network". These three dimensions are directly affected by participation in research collaboration, networking and inter-sectoral mobility.[2]

There is an underpinning principle of connectedness which is manifest in patterns of collaboration and mobility, and driven by policy imperatives that are premised upon wealth-equalling access to knowledge. As we have seen, the benefits are evidenced in the literature both at an individual and a national level. This affects supervisors directly. Researchers seeking success, development and career progression in their own right are increasingly encouraged and expected to navigate, broker and negotiate multiple networks and partners. Supervisors are also affected by trends and changes in doctoral education at a policy, structural and practice level which have mirrored to some extent those I have just outlined in the wider research community.

EVOLUTION IN DOCTORAL EDUCATION

At a doctoral level, one might relate connectedness to recent key trends in doctoral education. Such trends include the move away from the Humboldtian master-apprentice model of the doctorate (Kehm 2007; Jackson 2009; Lee & Kamler 2008) towards a more team-based approach to supervision; the importance of process (doctoral training) as well as product (thesis) (Park 2005); the growth in popularity of cohort-based delivery at a doctoral level; the development of a range of collaborative programmes, including professional doctorates; the massification of the research degree and the related changing profile of the doctoral population.

---

[2] Bozeman et al (2001) also highlight the role of institutional changes, such as oversupply of researchers, funding issues and discrimination, in researcher career trajectories.

CHAPTER 7 • **RECONCEPTUALISING THE SUPERVISORY ROLE: BORDER CROSSINGS AND BOUNDED SPACES**

Teams and training

Doctoral candidates are increasingly being supported and guided by supervisory teams that are drawn from across a number of disciplines, institutions and/or countries. The more complex arrangements include dual or joint doctoral degrees from more than one university. Although no comprehensive data have been published to date, there have been a number of national publications in recent years pointing to an increase in the number of these collaborative programmes (Obst, Kuner & Banks 2011; Hall 2012).

In addition, there are, increasingly, a significant number of other actors involved in supporting the doctoral candidate, outside of the formal supervisory team. These range from pastoral tutors and mentors, to subject-specialist librarians, to researcher development managers. Many of these roles are incorporated into 'doctoral colleges' or equivalent, which are strategic units that offer professional support, training and development. Their growth in recent years has been evident in many countries and has been a Europe-wide phenomenon.[3] It has been concurrent with the rise of the training agenda more generally within doctoral education. In the UK, this was in response to the Roberts report (2002) on the supply of people with science, technology, engineering and mathematics skills. In the EU there were major policy initiatives such as the Bologna communiqués, the Salzburg Principles (EC 2005; 2010b), the Innovation Union (EC 2010c), and the Principles for Innovative Doctoral Training (EC 2011) to support generic skills development among the postgraduate researcher population.

For the supervisor, this can mean an increase in time spent navigating institutional regulations and negotiating co-supervisory working arrangements across disciplines, institutions and international borders. At the same time supervisors play less of a role in recruitment, induction, and development of needs analysis and training (at the level of the individual doctoral researcher), as these functions are taken up by academic-allied staff.

Cohorts and communities

Alongside connections out to a wider variety of supervisors and other adjunct academic and professional service staff, we have also seen growth in a cohort-based delivery model at a doctoral level which has built from educational

---

[3] In 2007, 30% of European universities had doctoral schools (Crosier, Purser & Smidt 2007) whereas in the latest European Commission Research Area Survey (EC 2013) they were almost ubiquitous.

theories around peer-learning and it is designed to develop communities of practice and learning communities among doctoral students (Nerad 2012; Smith McGloin & Wynn, 2015). Peer-learning (specifically in North America, the UK, Europe and Australia) is becoming a sought-after mode of development and knowledge acquisition at a doctoral level (Boud & Lee 2005; Sweitzer 2009; Flores & Nerad 2012). Cohort-based doctoral training programmes are now almost the only mechanism through which research councils in the UK fund doctoral candidates and there is evidence of more widespread adoption of the cohort-based method, through national mission-group-led consortia such as the Doctoral Training Alliance. Cohort-based doctoral training is also central to some European initiatives designed to strengthen the quality of doctoral training and enhance industry engagement. In Spain, Estrategia Universidad 2015 (Ministro de Educación 2010) was a university modernisation strategy that included the establishment of International Campuses of Excellence Initiative (CEI) where cohort-based doctoral programmes of excellence were incentivised. In Germany, one of the three key foci of the 'Excellence Initiative' was the creation of thematically-organised graduate schools to provide an enhanced research environment for the training of groups of highly qualified doctoral researchers and scholars.

In addition to the trend towards communities of collocated doctoral researchers there is also an increase in the use of online training and remote supervision (Clarke & Lunt 2014; Smith McGloin & Wynn 2015) across a growing number of non-laboratory-based doctoral programmes that are delivered at distance. These programmes are almost exclusively part-time and target mid-career candidates who wish to undertake a doctorate alongside their job. Doctoral researchers on these programmes communicate with their supervisors and other students via e-mail, electronic forums, videoconferencing, chat rooms, bulletin boards, instant messaging and other forms of computer-based interaction. The programmes often include online training and the use of virtual classrooms.

For the supervisor, this can require negotiating the complex social dynamics of cohort programmes, where the supervisor is one voice among many (peers, other supervisors, other academic colleagues and allied professionals). It can also require participation in the many-to-many model of research supervision where a group of doctoral candidates is supervised by a team of supervisors, and supervisions become more akin to small-group teaching. In the case of at-distance programmes, supervisors will need to adapt and develop their skills to manage supervisions via electronic means, using synchronous and asynchronous modes. They will need to ensure that doctoral candidates have the same quality of experience and have the same access to a quality research environment as their campus-based peers in a context.

Cohort-based delivery – whether real or virtual – is also a key feature in a growing number of collaborative doctoral programmes; that is, those developed and sometimes delivered in partnership with business and industry.

Business and industry

Collaborative programmes are a relatively new type of doctorate where candidates are supervised by a team which includes academics and business, industry or third-sector specialists. The research question has relevance to the collaborative partner and candidates may spend at least some time carrying out their research in the business, industry or third-sector organisation. These programmes have developed in response to government policy that focuses on a more collaborative stance between higher education and the wider community.[4] This desire to facilitate knowledge transfer and knowledge exchange through doctoral researchers is incentivised in the UK through research councils funding schemes such as Collaborative Doctoral Partnerships, Collaborative Awards in Science and Engineering, and Cooperative Awards in Science and Technology, and in Europe through Horizon 2020. Alongside these schemes there is also an increased level of activity in industry placements for 'standard' PhDs. An example from Australia is the finding of the Australian Council of Learned Academies (ACOLA) 2015 review of the Australian research training system which recommended Australian Government funding of $12.5 million per annum be provided to support universities to increase numbers of industry placements for PhD students.

In addition, the sector has also seen a rise in the number of professional doctorates. A professional doctorate can be broadly defined as a programme of advanced study and research which meets both the specific needs of a professional group (such as engineers or business leaders) and university criteria for the award of a doctorate. This type of doctorate tends to offer candidates the opportunity to develop research skills that are then applied to project(s) within business, industry or the third sector. Many professional doctorates have a taught element with a transition into a research stage.

These professional doctorates emerged in the UK in the late 1980s (Donn Routh & Lunt 2000); around the same time as in Australia and significantly later than in

---

[4] In the UK and European context, see Wilson (2012) Borrell-Damian (2015), Witty (2013), Group of Eight (2013), Dowling (2015).

the USA, where the educational doctorate emerged in the first half of the twentieth century (Kot & Hendel 2012). The professional doctorate has seen a rapid increase in programmes between 1990 and 2010 in the UK and in Australia. Mellors-Bourne (2016) infers that this pattern of growth has continued at a steady rate from 2010 to 2015 (although the data are not directly comparable). Professional doctorates are not widespread in Europe. With the exception of a small number of publications (2006-07) that call for further exploration of the professional doctorate in the European context (Huisman & Naidoo 2006; Kehm 2006; EC 2007) little has been published (in research or policy) that specifically addresses professional doctorates. In practice, variations on industrial PhDs are in evidence across Europe. The Marie Curie European Industrial Doctorate Programme offers pan-European funding for collaborative doctorates between industry and universities.

For the supervisor, this can mean moving outside of their area of direct expertise to support a doctoral candidate in a more applied research project. Supervisors may also find themselves in a supervisory team with an external supervisor from business, industry or the third sector who is more 'expert' in the research project. In addition, the supervisor may also be required to supervise mid-career doctoral researchers who are significantly more experienced and more senior than the supervisor, though new to research. Other challenges that the supervisor may need to overcome in collaborations with business and industry are managing competing expectations between the university and the external partner in terms of, for example, frequency and style of output (the thesis after three to five years versus regular report-style updates) and the research question (where partner organisations might seek validation rather than novelty).

Massification and diversification

> What can governments do to unleash innovation?
> Build the stock of researchers.
> (OECD 2010:82)

There has been a major trend towards growth in the population of doctoral researchers over recent decades. Arguably this is driven by the neo-liberal interpretation of education as a driver for wealth through economic growth.[5] Data show significant average annual growth in doctoral degree completions (termed

---

[5] This is not an uncontested assertion: Rizvi and Lingard (2006) relate this policy theme to functionalist assumptions made at OECD level which then flows through to the educational policies of OECD member; and Servage (2009) questions the validity of this approach, particularly in relation to doctoral education.

'PhD outputs') from the end of the twentieth century onwards (Cyranoski Gilbert, Ledford, Nayar & Yahia 2011); particularly (although not exclusively) in countries with developing research infrastructures. Between 1998 and 2006, China, Mexico and India saw an average annual growth of doctoral degrees across disciplines of 40%, 17.1% and 8.5% respectively. India, according to figures compiled by the University Grants Commission, has subsequently seen an uplift of over 50% of the number of research degrees awarded, from 10 781 in 2008-09 to 16 093 in 2011-12. In South Africa, the Department of Higher Education and Training has projected targets of an eight-fold increase over 15 years (from 2014) in doctoral scholars.

Inevitably, alongside up-lift of in-country output of doctorates there is also significant in-flow of international students to countries with the most developed research infrastructure. The British Council (2014)[6] for example, predicts annual average growth in outbound postgraduate mobility to Australia, Canada Germany, Japan, the UK and the USA from Nigeria (+8.3%), India (+7.5%), Indonesia (+7.2%), Pakistan (+6.4%) and Saudi Arabia (+5.2%). China is expected to account for 338 000 outbound international postgraduate students (to the destination countries listed above) in 2024. India will account for 209 000.

As much as connectedness characterises bridge-building in doctoral education – as outlined previously, between doctoral researchers, across and between institutions and with business and industry – it is also associated with boundary-breaking in terms of engagement with new types of doctoral researchers. This includes internationalisation of the doctoral population but also equality and diversity in recruitment and retention among home populations.

Policy drivers for equality and diversity have included in the UK the Vitae "Every Researcher Counts" initiative which aimed to change recruitment practices and spotlight issues of equality and diversity in working practices within research, from doctoral level to principal investigator. New doctoral loans in the UK (from 2018) are designed to open up access to doctoral education to a greater number of potential candidates. In South Africa, the Department of Higher Education and Training funds a New Generation of Academics Programme (nGAP) which provides targeted investment to support under-represented communities to complete a doctorate and transition into an academic career. In New Zealand, the Māori and Indigenous (MAI) programme is a national network and capability building programme that supports Māori and indigenous students to undertake doctoral research.

---

[6] Note, this report does not disaggregate numbers of taught postgraduate students from research postgraduates.

For the supervisor, this poses a need to develop not only intercultural competencies but also new ways of working with doctoral candidates from a variety of backgrounds in terms of gender, ethnicity, sexuality and socio-economy.

COMPLEX, CONNECTED, CONTINGENT VERSUS CODES AND COMPETENCIES

As the landscape of research and doctoral education evolves and develops it has become more connected, more complex and more contingent. Arguably, supervisors – as researchers and as directors and guides of doctoral candidates (the next generation of researchers) – are central (or peripheral?) to these moving boundaries. Yet, within broadly the same period, a parallel trend can be seen in doctoral education which has sought to define and codify the doctorate and doctoral supervision. National codes such as the UK Quality Code, the Australian Qualifications Framework, the National Research Council's Assessment of Research Doctorate Programs (2010), pan-continental agreements (the Bologna Framework) and other more specific initiatives (the Carnegie Project on the Education Doctorate Framework for the EdD (2013), and the League of European Research Universities (2016) have begun to set out what the doctorate is. At the same time a dominant role set (Laudel & Glaser 2008) has begun to emerge through competency frameworks for the role of the supervisor, most notably in the UK Professional Standards Framework (UKPSF) Dimensions of the Framework for Doctoral Supervision (HEA 2016).[7] Recently, criteria have also been developed for national awards for supervision which were introduced in the UK in 2016 and in Australia in 2017. Excellence awards are also being developed in Austria, China, Germany, and the Netherlands.[8]

Although it is early days in the formulation and articulation of the supervisory role, perhaps the obvious question in a changing environment is to what extent the emerging supervisor role sets capture the evolving nature of supervision.

It is interesting to note that in the most comprehensive framework published to date – the UKPSF Dimensions – a significant proportion of the activities, values and knowledge descriptors are in areas affected by the trends in research and doctoral education that I have set out in this chapter. That is, areas in which supervisors'

---

[7] A comprehensive framework of list of competencies that supervisors can gain, strengthen, and be measured by was also by Hyatt and Williams based on their empirical research into the issue (Hyatt & Williams, 2011:58-60).

[8] This comes from the preliminary findings of a research project currently being undertaken by Dr Stan Taylor (Honorary Fellow of the School of Education, Durham University) and Prof. Alistair McCulloch (University of South Australia).

CHAPTER 7 • RECONCEPTUALISING THE SUPERVISORY ROLE: BORDER CROSSINGS AND BOUNDED SPACES

control, responsibility and influence have been or are beginning to diminish due to new practices and ways of working that have been directed by policy or funding.

These areas can be summarised as follows:

- recruitment (often centrally-managed on cohort-based programmes or with significant input from business, industry or the third sector in the case of collaborative programmes);
- research design (projects can be restricted to particular areas or may be impacted by the constraints of access of equipment in at-distance programmes, collaborative partners may take responsibility for setting out the research question according to business need);
- direction (more commonly decision-making is undertaken across supervisory teams which may include external supervisors);
- progression and completion (increasingly doctoral colleges or equivalent institutional structures have some level of responsibility for monitoring progression and delivering relevant training and development to ensure timely completion);
- face-to-face interaction (limited in cotutelle arrangements when the doctoral candidate is located at the partner institution and in collaborative programmes when the candidate is at the partner organisation, and non-existent in at distance programmes);
- pedagogical leadership (possible, but more commonly a model of negotiated expertise in a group supervision); and
- pastoral care (increasingly support is offered either by the Doctoral College or equivalent or a specific postgraduate tutor role).

Figure 7.1 below maps these changes to a summary of the UKPSF Dimensions document.

Activities	Values	Knowledge
Support student learning to help understand research*	Every PGR is different	Match doctoral research project with expertise*
Help student to find a suitable topic *	Diversity in recruitment*	Support student in research design*
Work as part of a supervisory team	Strategies to support all students	Awareness of disciplinary frameworks
Give feedback/act as examiner	Familiarity with PedR on doctoral supervision	Awareness of how students become independent researchers
Inform student about research integrity*	Awareness if PGR career development needs and employability agenda*	Use of technology to maintain contact
Ensure access to resources*		Support students to build research networks*
Reflect on practice		Support students to develop technical skills*
		Engage with evaluation of supervision
		Awareness of regs, monitoring, exam policies, mentoring and monitoring (at a higher level)*

*Examples where the activity, value or knowledge can be considered as currently under erosion as a result of changes in policy and practices

FIGURE 7.1 UK professional standards dimensions of the Framework for Doctoral Supervisors (2016): Summary elements

At the same time, the framework does not capture areas in which the supervisor role is expanding, such as co-supervising with non-academic colleagues, negotiating across institutions, increased administration to demonstrate compliance, supervising at a distance (new ways of working, use of technology, adapted pedagogy), supporting research students with a wider range of academic backgrounds, and supervising in emerging areas and areas outside of their main expertise.

More work is required to understand the impact of codes such as the UKPSF Dimensions document and the extent to which it may (or may not) shape institutional supervisor training and academic reward and progression. Little research has been completed to date on the form and content of supervisor development. However, it is clear that comparable competency frameworks such as the UK Researcher Development Framework (focused on supporting doctoral candidates) and the UK Professional Standards Framework (focused on higher education teaching and learning support) have had a significant impact on shaping training and development content for its target groups.

At a national level, supervisor awards criteria do give some small insight into sector engagement with the changing supervisory role. In the UK, the criteria include evidence of support for students from a range of backgrounds, help(ing) students navigate through difficulties, and providing additional support and facilities to give greater scope to their (the doctoral candidates') research. In Australia, the criteria incorporate promotion of industry engagement.

Neither the framework nor the national awards criteria seem wholly to capture the contemporary demands placed on supervisors. This raises important questions that institutions, funders and governments need to consider if the value of doctoral research (and researchers) to universities, the economy and society is to be realised through high-quality support for doctoral candidates.

CHANGING SPACES/CHANGING PLACES

The supervisory space is shifting because research is evolving and doctoral education is responding to this changing context. Policy imperatives and funding incentives are driving a connectedness which is demanding that supervisors play a different role. Territories (only recently codified) that were once familiar have become eroded by new structures, programmes and types of doctorate. Supervisors, like researchers in general, are navigating these new, connected spaces and developing the skill sets required to support doctoral candidates in a variety of situations that are off the map. More work is needed to understand the impact of the changing doctoral landscape on supervisory spaces and to examine how best we understand this new space and support supervisors who have to locate themselves within it.

REFERENCES

Ackers L. 2005. Moving people and knowledge: Scientific mobility in the European Union. *International Migration*, 43:99-131. https://doi.org/10.1111/j.1468-2435.2005.00343.x

Aksnes DW, Rørstad K, Piro FN & Sivertsen G. 2013. Are mobile researchers more productive and cited than non-mobile researchers? A large-scale study of Norwegian scientists. *Research Evaluation*, 22(4):215-223. https://doi.org/10.1093/reseval/rvt012

(AQF) Australian Qualifications Framework. 2013. *Australian qualifications framework*. 2nd Edition. http://www.qaa.ac.uk/publications/information-andguidance/publication?PubID=2674#.U8T35XJwbIU [Retrieved 18 September 2017].

Borrell-Damian L. 2009. *Collaborative doctoral education: University-industry partnerships for enhancing knowledge exchange*. http://www.eua.be/eua-work-and-policy-area/research-and-innovation/doctoral-education/doc-careers.aspx [Retrieved 18 September 2017].

Borrell-Damian L, Morais R & Smith J. *Collaborative doctoral education in Europe: Research partnerships and employability for researchers report on doc-careers II project*. Brussels: European Universities Association. http://eua.be/Libraries/publications-homepage-list/EUA_Doc_Careers_II_web.pdf?sfvrsn=6 [Retrieved 18 September 2017].

Boud D & Lee A. 2005. Peer learning as pedagogic discourse for research education. *Studies in Higher Education*, 30(5):501-516. https://doi.org/10.1080/03075070500249138

Bozeman B, Dietz J & Gaughan M. 2001. Scientific and technical human capital: An alternative model for research evaluation. *International Journal of Technology Management*, 22(7/8):636-655. https://doi.org/10.1504/IJTM.2001.002988

Clarke G & Lunt I. 2014. *International comparisons in postgraduate education. HEFCE.* http://www.hefce.ac.uk/pubs/rereports/Year/2014/pginternational/Title,92156,en.html_ [Retrieved 18 September 2017].

Crosier D, Purser L & Scmidt H. 2007. *Trends V: Universities shaping the European higher education area report. EUA.* http://www.eua.be/eua-work-and-policy-area/building-the-european-higher-education-area/trends-ineuropean-higher-education/trends-v.aspx [Retrieved 18 September 2017].

Cruz-Castro L & Sanz-Menéndez L. 2010. Mobility versus job stability: Assessing tenure and productivity outcomes. *Research Policy*, 39(1):27-38. https://doi.org/10.1016/j.respol.2009.11.008

Cyranoski D, Gilbert N, Ledford H, Nayar A & Yahia M. 2011. Education: The PhD factory. *Nature News*, 472(7343):276-279. https://doi.org/10.1038/472276a

De Filippo D, Casado ES & Gómez I. 2009. Quantitative and qualitative approaches to the study of mobility and scientific performance: A case study of a Spanish university. *Research Evaluation*, 18(3):191-200. https://doi.org/10.3152/095820209X451032

Department for Education and Skills. 2003. *The future of higher education White Paper.* London: Government Publishers. http://webarchive.nationalarchives.gov.uk/20040117000548/http://www.dfes.gov.uk/highereducation/hestrategy/ [Retrieved 24 September 2017]

BIS (Department for Business, Innovation and Skills). 2011. *Innovation and research strategy for growth.* London: Government Publishers. https://www.gov.uk/government/publications/innovation-and-research-strategy-for-growth--2 Last [Retrieved 24 September 2017].

BIS. 2013. *Exploring student demand for postgraduate study.* London: Government Publishers. https://www.gov.uk/government/uploads/system/uploads/attachment_data/file/264115/bis-13-1319-exploring-student-demand-for-postgraduate-study.pdf [Retrieved 18 September 2017].

BIS. 2015. *The Dowling review of business-university research collaborations.* London: Government Publishers. https://www.gov.uk/government/uploads/system/uploads/attachment_data/file/440927/bis_15_352_The_dowling_review_of_business-university_rearch_collaborations_2.pdf [Retrieved 18 September 2017].

Donn JE, Routh DK & Lunt I. 2000. From Leipzig to Luxembourg (via Boulder and Vail): A history of clinical psychology training in Europe and the United States. *Professional Psychology: Research and Practice*, 31(4): 423-428. https://doi.org/10.1037/0735-7028.31.4.423

EC (European Commission). 2005. Paper presented at Bologna seminar. 3-5 February, Salzburg. Bologna seminar doctoral programmes for the European Knowledge Society., Conclusions and Recommendations. *Salzburg, 3-5 February 2005.* Brussels: European Commission.http://www.eua.be/eua/jsp/en/upload/Salzburg_Conclusions.1108990538850.pdf [Retrieved: 15 September 2017].

EC. 2007. Strategic Report on the Renewed Lisbon Strategy for Growth and Jobs: Launching the New Cycle (2008-2010) – Keeping up the Pace of Change. Brussels: European Commission.

EC. 2010a. Salzburg II recommendations: European universities' achievements since 2005 in implementing the Salzburg principles. Brussels: European Commission. http://www.eua.be/Libraries/Publications_homepage_list/Salzburg_II_Recommendations.sflb.ashx [Retrieved 18 September 2017].

EC. 2010b. *Developing the European research area: Improving knowledge flows via researcher mobility.* Brussels: European Commission. https://ec.europa.eu/jrc/en/publication/eur-scientific-and-technical-research-reports/developing-european-research-area-improving-knowledge-flows-researcher-mobility [Retrieved 18 September 2017].

EC. 2010c. *Communication from the commission to the European parliament, the council, the European economic and social committee and the committee of the regions: Europe 2020 Flagship Initiative Innovation Union.* Brussels: European Commission. http://ec.europa.eu/research/innovation-union/pdf/innovation-union-communication_en.pdf#view=fitandpagemode=none [Retrieved 18 September 2017].

EC. 2011. *Principles for innovative doctoral training.* Brussels: European Commission. http://ec.europa.eu/euraxess/pdf/research_policies/Principles_for_Innovative_Doctoral_Training.pdf [Retrieved 18 September 2017].

EC. 2013. *European research area progress report.* Brussels: European Commission. http://ec.europa.eu/research/era/pdf/era_progress_report2013/era_progress_report2013.pdf [Retrieved 18 September 2017].

Enders J. 2005. Border crossings: Research training, knowledge dissemination and the transformation of academic work. *Higher Education*, 49(1-2):119-133. https://doi.org/10.1007/s10734-004-2917-3

Etzkowitz H & Leydesdorff L. 1997. Introduction to special issue on science policy dimensions of the Triple Helix of university-industry-government relations. *Science and Public Policy*, 24(1):2-5.

Flores E & Nerad M. 2012. Peers in doctoral education: Unrecognized partners. *New Directions for Higher Education*, 157:73-83. https://doi.org/10.1002/he.20007

Gaughan M & Robin S. 2004. National science training policy and early scientific careers in France and the United States. *Research Policy*, 33(4):569-581. https://doi.org/10.1016/j.respol.2004.01.005

Gemme B & Gringas Y. 2004. *Training a new breed of researchers, inside and outside universities.* Working paper presented on colloquium on research and higher education policy, December 2004. Paris: UNESCO.

Grant BM & McKinley E. 2012. Expanding pedagogical boundaries: Indigenous students undertaking doctoral education. In: A Lee & S Danby (eds). *Reshaping doctoral education: Changing programs and pedagogies.* London and New York: Routledge. 204-17.

Group of Eight. 2013. *The changing PhD: A discussion paper.* https://go8.edu.au/sites/default/files/docs/the-changing-phd_final.pdf [Retrieved 18 September 2017].

Gunn A & Mintrom M. 2013. Global university alliances and the creation of collaborative advantage. *Journal of Higher Education Policy and Management*, 35:179-192. https://doi.org/10.1080/1360080X.2013.775926

Guth J. 2008. The opening of borders and scientific mobility: The impact of EU enlargement on the movement of early career scientists. *Higher Education in Europe*, 33(4):395-410. https://doi.org/10.1080/03797720802522601

Guthrie S, Lichten C, Harte E, Parks S & Wooding S. 2016. *International mobility of researchers: A survey of researchers in the UK.* https://royalsociety.org/~/media/policy/projects/international-mobility/researcher-mobility-report-survey-academics-uk.pdf [Retrieved 18 September 2017].

Hall F. 2012. *Best practices regarding international dual/double and joint degrees: A paper prepared for the Canadian Association for Graduate Studies.* http://www.cags.ca/documents/publications/best_practices/Best_Practices_Dual_Joint_Degrees.pdf [Retrieved 18 September 2017].

Halse C & Malfroy J. 2010. Retheorizing doctoral supervision as professional work. *Studies in Higher Education*, 35(1):79-92. https://doi.org/10.1080/03075070902906798

Hansen W, Avveduto S & Inzelt A. 2004. *The brain-drain-emigration flows for qualified scientists.* http://www.rcuk.ac.uk/documents/publications/hocdexeucommittee-negotiatingobjectives-rcukresponse-pdf/ [Retrieved: 11 September 2017]

Harrison J, Smith DP & Kinton C. 2016. New institutional geographies of higher education: The rise of transregional university alliances. *Environment and Planning A*, 48(5):910-936. https://doi.org/10.1177/0308518X15619175

Higher Education Academy. 2016. *UK professional standards framework for doctoral supervisors.* https://www.heacademy.ac.uk/system/files/ukpsf_dof_ss_final_270716.pdf [Retrieved 24 September 2017].

Huisman J & Naidoo R. 2006. The professional doctorate. *Higher Education Management and Policy*, 18(2):1-13. https://doi.org/10.1787/hemp-v18-art11-en

Hyatt L & Williams PE. 2011. 21st Century competencies for doctoral leadership faculty. *Innovative Higher Education*, 36(1):53-66. https://doi.org/10.1007/s10755-010-9157-5

Jackson C. 2009. Changing practices of doctoral education. *British Journal of Educational Studies*, 57:339-341. https://doi.org/10.1111/j.1467-8527.2009.437_7.x

Jacob M & Meek VL. 2013. Scientific mobility and international research networks: Trends and policy tools for promoting research excellence and capacity building. *Studies in Higher Education*, 38(3):331-344. https://doi.org/10.1080/03075079.2013.773789

Jessop B. 2007. *State power.* Cambridge: Polity.

Jöns H. 2011. Transnational academic mobility and gender. *Globalisation, Societies and Education*, 9(2): 183-209. https://doi.org/10.1080/14767724.2011.577199

Kehm BM. 2006. *Doctoral education in Europe and North America: A comparative analysis.* London: Portland Press. https://doi.org/10.1111/j.1465-3435.2007.00308.x

Kehm BM. 2007. Quo vadis doctoral education? New European approaches in the context of global changes. *European Journal of Education*, 42(3):307-319.

Kot FC & Hendel DD. 2012. Emergence and growth of professional doctorates in the United States, United Kingdom, Canada and Australia: A comparative analysis. *Studies in Higher Education*, 37(3):345-364. https://doi.org/10.1080/03075079.2010.516356

Lambert R. 2003. Lambert review of business-university collaboration: Final report. University of Illinois at Urbana-Champaign's Academy for Entrepreneurial Leadership Historical Research Reference in Entrepreneurship.

Laudel G & Gläser J. 2008. From apprentice to colleague: The metamorphosis of early career researchers. *Higher Education*, 55(3):387- 406. https://doi.org/10.1007/s10734-007-9063-7

Lawson C & Shibayama S. 2015. International research visits and careers: An analysis of bioscience academics in Japan. *Science and Public Policy*, 42(5):690-710. https://doi.org/10.1093/scipol/scu084

League of European Research Universities. 2016. *Maintaining a quality culture in doctoral education at research-intensive universities.* http://www.leru.org/files/publications/LERU_AP19_maintaining_a_quality_culture_in_doctoral_education.pdf [Retrieved 24 September 2017].

Lee K, Brownstein JS, Mills RG & Kohane IS. 2010. Does collocation inform the impact of collaboration? *PloS One*, 5(12):1-6. https://doi.org/10.1371/journal.pone.0014279

Lee A & Kamler B. 2008. Bringing pedagogy to doctoral publishing. *Teaching in Higher Education,* 13(5):511-523. https://doi.org/10.1080/13562510802334723

Leemann RJ. 2010. Gender inequalities in transnational academic mobility and the ideal type of academic entrepreneur. *Discourse: Studies in the Cultural Politics of Education*, 31(5):605-625. https://doi.org/10.1080/01596306.2010.516942

Leitch S. 2006. *Leitch review of skills: Prosperity for all in the global economy – World class skills.* London: HM Treasury.

Melin G. 2005. The dark side of mobility: Negative experiences of doing a postdoc period abroad. *Research Evaluation*, 14:229-37. https://doi.org/10.3152/147154405781776102

Mellors-Bourne R, Robinson C & Metcalfe J. 2016. *Provision of professional doctorates in English HE institutions: Report for HEFCE by the Careers Research and Advisory Centre (CRAC), supported by the University of Brighton: January 2016.* http://dera.ioe.ac.uk/25165/1/Professional_doctorates_CRAC.pdf [Retrieved 18 September 2017].

Meyer JB & Wattiaux JP. 2006. Diaspora knowledge networks: Vanishing doubts and increasing evidence. *International Journal on Multicultural Societies*, 8(1):4-24.

Ministro de Educación. 2010. *Estrategia Universidad 2015. Madrid: Ministro de Educación.* http://www.mecd.gob.es/docroot/universidad2015/flash/eu2015-flash/document.pdf [Retrieved 18 September 2017]

National Research Council of the National Academies. 2010. *A data-based assessment of research-doctorate programs in the United States.* http://www.virginia.edu/vpr/docs/nrc_report.pdf [Retrieved 24 September 2017].

Nerad M. 2012. Conceptual approaches to doctoral education: A community of practice. *Alternation*, 19(2):57-72.

Obst D, Kuder M & Banks C. 2011. *Joint and double degree programs in the global context: Report on an international survey. Institute of International Education.* http://ecahe.eu/w/index.php/Joint_and_Double_Degree_Programs_In_The_Global_Context# [Retrieved 18 September 2017].

OECD (Organisation for Economic Co-operation and Development). 2000. *Science, technology and innovation in the New Economy, OECD policy brief.* Paris: OECD.

OECD. 2008a. *Open innovation in global networks.* Paris: OECD.

OECD. 2008b. *Data collection on careers of doctorate holders: State of the art and prospects.* Paris: OECD.

OECD. 2010. *Measuring innovation: A new perspective.* Paris: OECD.

OECD. 2012. *Transferable skills training for researchers: Supporting career development and research.* Paris: OECD.

O'Hara S. 2009. Internationalizing the academy: The impact of scholar mobility. Second in a series of global education research reports. *Higher Education on the Move: New Developments in Global Mobility,* 3:29-47.

Park C. 2005. New variant PhD: The changing nature of the doctorate in the UK. *Journal of Higher Education Policy and Management,* 27(2):189-207. https://doi.org/10.1080/13600800500120068

Pezzoni M, Sterzi V & Lissoni F. 2012. Career progress in centralized academic systems: An analysis of French and Italian physicists. *Research Policy,* 41:704-19. https://doi.org/10.1016/j.respol.2011.12.009

(QAA) Quality Assessment Agency. 2004. *Code of practice for the assurance of academic quality and standards in higher education, Section 1: Postgraduate research programmes.* Bristol: QAA. http://www.qaa.ac.uk/publications [Retrieved 12 September 2017].

QAA. 2015. *Doctoral degree characteristics.* Bristol: QAA. http://www.qaa.ac.uk/en/Publications/Documents/Doctoral-Degree-Characteristics-15.pdf [Retrieved 12 September 2017].

Rizvi F & Lingard B. 2006. Edward Said and the cultural politics of education. *Discourse: Studies in the Cultural Politics of Education,* 27(3):293-308. https://doi.org/10.1080/01596300600838744

Roberts G. 2002. *Set for success: The supply of people with science, technology, engineering and mathematical skills.* London: HM Treasury. http://webarchive.nationalarchives.gov.uk/+/http://www.hm-treasury.gov.uk/d/robertsreview_introch1.pdf [Retrieved 12 September 2017].

Sainsbury (Lord). 2007. *The race to the top: A review of government's science and innovation policies.* London: HM Treasury. http://www.rsc.org/images/sainsbury_review051007_tcm18-103118.pdf [Retrieved 12 September 2017].

Servage L. 2009. Alternative and professional doctoral programs: What is driving the demand? *Studies in Higher Education,* 34(7):765-779. https://doi.org/10.1080/03075070902818761

Smith A, Bradshaw T, Burnett K, Docherty D, Purcell W & Worthington S. 2010. *One step beyond: Making the most of postgraduate education.* Report for UK Department for Business, Innovation and Skills. London: HM Treasury.

Smith McGloin R & Wynne C. 2015. *Structural changes in doctoral education in the UK – A review of graduate schools.* Lichfield: UKCGE.

Sweitzer V. 2009. Towards a theory of doctoral student professional identity development: A developmental networks approach. *The Journal of Higher Education,* 80(1):1-33. https://doi.org/10.1080/00221546.2009.11772128

Taylor S. 2016. *UK professional standards framework (UKPSF) dimensions of the framework for doctoral supervisors.* York: Higher Education Academy.

Travaille AM & Hendrik PH. 2010. What keeps science spiralling? Unravelling the critical success factors of knowledge creation in university research. *Higher Education,* 59(4):423-439. https://doi.org/10.1007/s10734-009-9257-2

Turpin T, Woolley R, Marceau J & Hill S. 2008. Conduits of knowledge in the Asia Pacific: Research training, networks and country of work. *Asian Population Studies,* 4(3):247-265. https://doi.org/10.1007/BF01599727

University Alliance, National Council for Universities and Business and Innovation UK. 2014. *The contribution of university research to economic growth.* London: University Alliance. http://www.ncub.co.uk/index.php?option=com_docmanandview=downloadandcategory_slug=reportsandalias=139-contribution-to-growthandItemid=2728 [Retrieved 12 December 2016].

Van de Sande D, Ackers HL & Gill B. 2005. *Impact assessment of the Marie Curie fellowships under the 4th and 5th framework programmes of Research and Technological Development of the EU (1994-2002).* Brussels: European Commission.

Van Heeringen A & Dijkwel PA. 1986. Mobility and productivity of academic research scientists. *Czechoslovak Journal of Physics,* 36(1):58-61.

Warry P. 2006. *Increasing the economic impact of research councils: Advice to the Director General of Science and Innovation DTI, from the Research Council Economic Impact Group.* London: HM Treasury. http://webarchive.nationalarchives.gov.uk/20070603164510/http://www.dti.gov.uk/files/file32802.pdf [Retrieved 12 September 2017].

Weert E. 2013. *Support for continued data collection and analysis concerning mobility patterns and career paths of researchers. Final report of the MORE 2 project.* Brussels: European Commission.

Wilson T. 2012. A review of business-university collaboration. London: HM Treasury.

Witty A. 2013. *Final report and recommendations: Encouraging a British invention revolution: Sir Andrew Witty's review of universities and growth.* London: HM Treasury.

Woolley R, Cañibano C & Tesch J. 2016. *A functional review of literature on research careers.* INGENIO (CSIC-UPV). Brussels: European Commission.

SECTION B
SUPERVISORY JOURNEYS

PHD EMPLOYABILITY IN CORPORATE SOUTH AFRICA[1]

Amaleya Goneos-Malka

INTRODUCTION

Modern economies are increasingly based on knowledge and information production. The Organisation for Economic Co-operation and Development (OECD) stresses the importance of a highly-skilled competent labour force to generate economic growth: "In the new economy where knowledge is the source of wealth creation, human capital becomes as important as financial capital" (OECD 2010:78).

Blankley and Booyens (2010) concur that a highly skilled workforce is crucial to developing a country's capacity to become a knowledge-based economy, and argue that the total number of full-time equivalent (FTE) researchers per thousand of the overall employed population is a reliable indicator of the penetration of high-level skills across a country's labour pool. The relative state of a country's knowledge economy may be gauged by indexes such as the World Bank's Knowledge Economy Index (KEI). The KEI is calculated as an average of four sub-indexes that underpin knowledge economies, namely education, innovation and technology adoption, economic incentive and institutional regime, and information communication technology infrastructure (World Bank 2007). The correlation between select countries' highly skilled workforce and knowledge economy ranking have been paired in Table 8.1: the lower the index value the higher the country's knowledge economy capacity. For example, South Africa's ratio of FTE researchers is considerably lower than that of the UK, Japan and Denmark; correspondingly South Africa's KEI measure is significantly higher, which implies it has a lower capability to utilise knowledge for economic development. In comparison to other developing BRICS countries, South Africa is ahead of China and India but lags behind Russia and Brazil.

TABLE 8.1 Relationship between select countries' full-time researchers and knowledge economy readiness

	COUNTRY							
	Russia	Brazil	China	India	South Africa	United Kingdom	Japan	Denmark
Full-time equivalent researchers per 1 000 total employment (Blankley & Booyens 2010)	(Data not provided from source)				1.4	8.2	> 10	> 10
Knowledge Economy Ranking (World Bank 2012)	54	59	83	109	67	14	22	3
Knowledge Economy Index (World Bank 2012)	5.78	5.58	4.37	3.06	5.21	8.76	8.28	9.16

Source: Blankley and Booyens (2010); World Bank (2012)

In 2007, South Africa was ranked 50th on the KEI (World Bank 2007) out of a total of 144 countries, but by 2012 the country had slipped 17 places to 67th position (World Bank 2012). This decline in rankings should be a point of concern for a nation that has publically articulated its intent to transform into a knowledge-based economy (Department of Science & Technology 2008; National Planning Commission 2011). If highly skilled human capital is vital to drive the economy forward, one question that comes to mind is how South Africa's limited number of highly skilled individuals are distributed in the labour force.

PhD holders are the most educated cohort in societies and arguably contribute to knowledge creation for economic growth (Auriol, Schaaper & Felix 2012; Bogle 2010). In this chapter I unpack details of an independent study that I ran in 2014, which addressed PhD employability in corporate South Africa. It consisted of a nationwide cross-industry study on the distribution of South Africa's highly skilled talent, its PhDs, in leading companies that drive the South African economy. This survey encompassed the top 350 companies (top 200 Johannesburg Stock Exchange listed businesses and 150 other leading corporations, both international and local, operating in South Africa, such as Samsung, Microsoft, Procter & Gamble, BP, Coca-Cola and Toyota), and covered more than 1 500 000 permanently employed employees.

PHD EMPLOYMENT IN INDUSTRY: THE PROBLEM STATEMENT

For some PhD graduates, finding suitable employment after graduation is a challenge. Although the level varies from discipline to discipline, it seems to be compounded for those seeking positions in industry. There is a tendency for some organisations to label doctoral graduates as overqualified, too academic, too technical and too expensive, thus penalising these candidates in the hiring process. This discriminatory point of view has arisen because corporate South Africa does not necessarily recognise or understand the potential value contribution of PhDs to their business, their industry and ultimately the country's economy. The extent of this situation will be compounded as the supply of PhDs increases, which is an expectation of the National Development Plan (National Planning Commission 2011:319).

> Produce more than 100 doctoral graduates per million per year by 2030. South Africa currently produces 28 doctoral graduates per million per year ... If South Africa is to be a leading innovator; most of these doctorates should be in science, engineering, technology and mathematics. Double the number of graduate and postgraduate scientists and increase the number of African and women postgraduates, especially PhDs...

Despite the positive merits of this plan, one cannot ignore the contradictory scenario of increasing the number of PhD graduates if market demand for these individuals does not match the supply of PhDs.

UNDERSTANDING PHD EMPLOYMENT CHALLENGES AND PLACEMENT

The purpose of this research was to improve the understanding of PhD employability in corporate South Africa through the following objectives:

- Firstly, to identify some of the barriers experienced by recent PhD graduates when seeking suitable employment
- Secondly, to assess the distribution of PhD graduates permanently employed by the top companies that drive the South African economy

A two-phased approach was used for the study. The initial phase was designed to address the first objective. This exploratory descriptive investigation targeted PhD holders who had graduated in the past two years from 14 universities in South Africa (Cape Peninsula University of Technology, Durban University of Technology, North-West University, Rhodes University, University of Cape Town, University of Free State, University of Johannesburg, University of KwaZulu-Natal, University of Pretoria, University of South Africa, Stellenbosch University, University of Western Cape, University of Witwatersrand, and University of Zululand). Respondents were invited to complete a self-administered questionnaire, which was issued electronically and accessible on the Internet.

The second phase of the study sought to determine the number of PhD graduates that were permanently employed across different economic sectors in South Africa. This exploratory quantitative study followed non-probability purposive sampling, and targeted the Top 200 Johannesburg Stock Exchange listed companies, as well as an additional 150 other leading companies (international and local) operating in South Africa, as mentioned above.

PHASE I: RESULTS AND DISCUSSION

Understanding PhD employment challenges: The graduate perspective

For Phase I, a total of 359 usable responses were received. The demographic profile of respondents was deemed representative of PhD graduates from South African universities, due to consistencies with data reported by the Council for Higher Education for PhD graduates in 2012. In terms of gender, 56% were male and 44% were female. The largest age category was 31-40 year olds representing 34% of respondents, and the second largest age group, accounting for 28%, was the 41-50 year old segment. In terms of nationality, two-thirds were South African; 18% were comprised of other African nationalities and the rest were from Europe, the Americas, Asia and Australia. Respondents earned doctoral qualifications from over 200 different subject areas (including economics, management, education, engineering, built environment, health sciences, humanities, law, natural sciences, and theology). The most dominant fields of study were engineering, management sciences, psychology, and education.

The majority of respondents were employed while completing their PhD qualifications; just under 30% studied full-time. Most of the respondents who were employed while undertaking their PhD remained with their incumbent employer after completing their doctorate. Almost one third of respondents pursued further academic studies after earning a PhD, in the main taking up postdoctoral research positions. The latter finding is not surprising when considering the respondents' sectors of employment, as two thirds worked in the education sector, with 62% in higher education and 4% in other education sectors. Only 17% worked in business enterprise, 11% were employed by government and 6% worked for private non-profit organisations. Notably, 21% of PhD graduates were not employed in their field of specialisation.

Half of the respondents had either directly experienced difficulties finding appropriate employment, or knew of other PhD graduates that had encountered the same challenges. Additionally, 25% of PhD graduates took up to one year to find employment, 3% took up to two years, and 11% stated that they were still unemployed.

Specific barriers to employment for PhDs appeared to rest with prevailing employer assumptions, as indicated by the fact that 68% of PhD graduates stated that when applying for jobs employers considered them to be overqualified for positions; 58% stated that employers thought that appointing them would be too costly from a remuneration perspective; and 40% indicated that employers thought that they would not remain with the organisation for long. A doctoral tracer study undertaken in 2009 (Cloete, Mouton & Sheppard 2015) concurs with the finding that the majority of people undertaking their doctoral studies in South Africa were employed, and more than half worked in higher education. However, Cloete et al (2015) did not elaborate on whether PhD graduates were employed in their sector of choice, as opposed to working in a position to generate an income rather than be unemployed, or if these individuals sought non-academic roles what types of challenges they encountered, if any.

Following the closed-question portion of the survey, respondents were invited to offer suggestions to improve the employment prospects of PhD graduates. Key themes emerging from these inputs are educating industry about PhD graduates, greater collaboration with companies in industry, and marketing PhDs more effectively. Several statements from respondents are provided below to highlight potential options.

The most pertinent theme emerging from the qualitative data was the need for educating industry on the value of PhDs:

> Industries need to be made aware of the value that a PhD graduate brings. PhD graduates are dedicated and passionate; this needs to be highlighted. Since the Master's degree is now commonplace, the PhD really does give the candidate an edge over the general population. This really needs to be realised and appreciated.

> Better understanding regarding the abilities of PhD graduates. These professionals are mostly under-utilised due to a lack of understanding from the employer or by the graduate being forced to accept employment below their training level.

> Companies can/should be more aware of the value of PhD candidates and it might help to have training programmes aimed at giving candidates with strong academic backgrounds good industry experience without sacrificing their level of education.

> In South Africa industry should realise the potential and skills of people with a PhD and not be threatened by it. In Europe it is normal for people with a PhD to work in industry and it is also encouraged.

> Most developing countries, including South Africa, still think in very narrow terms as far as PhD skills are concerned. There is too much focus on the discipline as opposed to transferable skills.
>
> Perhaps trying to get the message out to HR and recruitment consultants that a PhD teaches you more than just the topic you are researching. It gives you tools that make you adaptable to change, able to learn fast, time management etc.
>
> Since so few people know what studying a PhD involves, they don't appreciate the skills acquired in the process and therefore, organisations don't offer these candidates the opportunity for a position they deserve.
>
> Promote the fact that the process of obtaining a PhD can be usefully employed to solve business problems.
>
> The misconception that PhDs are over-qualified for many positions needs to be addressed. These graduates can make significant contributions given the opportunity.
>
> The perception that we are too specialised should be challenged. People don't realise the skills are transferable.
>
> We need to increase the level of innovation across corporations operating in South Africa. Innovation brings change and encourages competitiveness. PhDs can be the differentiator in the world of work and industry.

Respondents furthermore saw the value in conducting applied research and collaborating with industry as ways in which to enhance their employability beyond academe, as the following quotations suggest:

> Companies need to view PhD graduates as more than super-specialised Honours/Master's graduates. This should be done by (i) offering PhD students career guidance/mentoring from when they start their graduate studies – maybe by getting former PhD students who are working in industry to act as 'Big Doctor' mentors and (ii) as a university/faculties/departments finding ways to interact with potential employees in a way that adds value to the companies without looking for some kind of sponsorship/funding. In this way companies start to see what benefits there are to having this higher level of expertise in-house.
>
> A lot of collaboration with the industry instead of mere conference presentations and journal article writing.
>
> Both the private sector and government departments need to forge closer links with universities to monitor PhD studies in the various faculties/schools. This would facilitate needs analysis exercises on a continuous basis and, ultimately, benefit all the stakeholders.

One way in which a closer alignment to industry could be forged was through fostering industry internships, as suggested below:

> Linking prospective PhD candidates to employers who have certain needs and are willing to fund graduates in finding innovative solutions to their needs; matching the commercial needs for innovation, R and D with the pool of prospective students.

> Involve industry in research topics.

Respondents also suggested leveraging PhD intellectual property as a way in which to contribute to commercial developments:

> The developed world (US, Europe …) hires PhDs to solve problems and maybe providing these stats to local business could help.

> With respect to PhD graduates, many overseas PhDs start businesses after completing their studies and I think we need a local fund/venture capitalists which could help graduates pursue commercialising their research. How much IP is sitting at universities not being exploited?

Respondents additionally saw a need for matching study outputs with skills demand:

> Aligning skills needs

> Do not embark on studies before you investigate the possibility of employment once you qualify.

Finally, respondents indicated a need to market the potential value PhDs could add to industry more explicitly:

> Place more emphasis on marketing PhD graduates as people who add extra value, and have exceptional growth potential within organisations.

> PhDs have to market themselves and build a profile as a spokesperson in their specific field.

> Better understanding of what a PhD can offer to employers. I found that if your boss has a PhD then they have a better understanding of what you can offer. It is when your boss does not have a PhD that they get threatened by your presence.

Both the quantitative and the qualitative findings from Phase I provided an understanding about recent PhD graduates' experiences when seeking employment, as well as potential interventions to improve industry perceptions of PhDs to make these individuals more appealing as prospective hires. It is important to acknowledge the limitations of the study, primarily due to its exploratory nature. In this phase, a non-probability sampling strategy was applied to access recent PhD graduates, whereby participating universities distributed the survey to PhD alumni listed on their email databases. The limitation of this method is that particular groups in the sample may either be under- or over-represented, which prevents one from making population generalisations. Nonetheless, the insights from Phase I were useful in developing the second phase of the study.

Before delving into Phase II, it would be pertinent to reflect on some of the implications of the above findings. The results highlight that for economies to be globally competitive, universities, industries and governments can no longer operate in silos, and universities should evolve their practices to compete in a changing world. ASSAf (2010) uses the analogy of a triple helix to denote the complexity and interdependence of the relationships between these entities. The reciprocity between some research universities and industries has led to successful innovative commercial developments and the establishment of entrepreneurial hubs in places such as Silicon Valley in the USA and Bangalore in India (UNESCO 2015). Bogle (2010) contends that the modern doctorate should produce highly skilled individuals who are equipped with transferrable skills that are applicable to academic and non-academic roles. Given the present findings, the idea of promoting professional/industrial PhDs (ACOLA 2016; Danish Agency for Science, Technology & Innovation 2012) might seem a reasonable alternative to the traditional PhD, however this is considered a moot point as currently industry appears unaware of the distinctions among doctorate qualifications.

PHASE II: RESULTS AND DISCUSSION

PhD distribution in corporate South Africa: The view of industry

The purpose of Phase II was to determine a) the number of people holding PhD qualifications that are permanently employed in the top 200 companies listed on the Johannesburg Stock Exchange as well as 150 other leading companies (international and local) operating in South Africa, and b) the proportion of PhDs permanently employed by these companies as a percentage of their permanently employed workforce.

The results from participating companies showed that only 0.07% of the 1 408 173 permanent employees working in these corporations held a PhD, which equated to 955 PhDs. For example, Shoprite had 104 000 employees, but only three held PhD qualifications; Anglo Gold Ashanti had 31 499 employees, with three PhDs; Harmony had 30 000 employees, with two PhDs; Lonmin had 28 485 employees, but only one PhD; Woolworths had 25 752 employees, but no PhDs; Massmart had 21 549 employees, with two PhDs; Netcare had 21 149 employees, with two PhDs; Pick n Pay had 17 668 employees, but no PhDs; MMI Holdings Limited had

15 336 employees, but only one PhD; Mr Price had 13 583 employees, but no PhDs; Group Five Limited had 13 022 employees, with two PhDs; McDonald's had 10 000 employees, but no PhDs.

Low levels of PhD hires were reported across all sectors of industry. However, two companies, ABSA and Sasol, countered the private sector trend of low PhD employment within the workforce. ABSA had 31 000 employees of whom 120 held a PhD, and Sasol had 30 500 employees of which 283 held a PhD. These two companies accounted for 43% of all permanently employed PhDs observed in the study. Due to the stark differences in the numbers of PhDs employed by ABSA and Sasol compared to other companies in the report, these outliers warranted further investigation. ABSA, unlike other banking counterparts, has a strong self-development philosophy and has positioned itself as a learning organisation; the majority of employees with PhDs acquired their doctorates while working for the organisation. Sasol is a petrochemical entity that is active in research and development and consciously pursues candidates with scientific expertise – particularly chemists. However, Sasol does not limit its PhD hires to chemistry; for example, at the point of data collection 18 PhDs worked in the human resource division.

BARRIERS TO HIRING PHDS IN CORPORATE SOUTH AFRICA

From the findings in Phase I, three specific barriers to employing PhDs were noted: respondents indicated that prospective employers perceived PhDs would be overqualified for the position on offer, too expensive to employ, and would move if a better opportunity arose. One should consider that the most common point of access to organisations sits with the human resource or human capital function. Human resource departments are gatekeepers that tend to control the hiring processes in companies. This begs the question, with the exception of ABSA and Sasol, how plausible is it that human resource personnel in other leading companies in South Africa have not come across nor hired PhDs? The following statements from human resource personnel illustrate the negative sentiment towards PhDs during the hiring process:

> We consciously screen PhDs out of the selection process. [Fast-Moving Consumer Goods. Multinational firm]

> I've worked in executive human resources for the past 25 years, across FMCG, packaging, engineering and construction, a PhD has never been part of any job spec. [Construction firm]

> We don't look at PhDs; there has never been a requirement to appoint a PhD. [Multinational – Fast-Moving Consumer Goods Electronic firm]

Discriminatory remarks such as these point to a lack of understanding about the potential value of PhDs to corporate South Africa. In contrast, in Germany the perception of PhDs by businesses is markedly different: in this country PhDs' skills are marketed for industry (Cyranoski, Gilbert, Ledford, Nayar & Yahia 2011). According to the Consortium for the National Report on Junior Scholars (2013), Germany produces 25 000 PhDs per year; 95% are employed, almost half work in the private sector and approximately 20% are self-employed. Similarly, in Denmark almost 80% of industrial PhDs and 50% of conventional PhDs work in the private sector (Danish Agency for Science, Technology & Innovation 2012). Additional evidence of PhDs working in industry is documented by the Royal Society (2010), which reported that 53% of UK science PhDs pursue careers outside academia as soon as they earn their doctorate. For the remainder that choose an academic path, 17% switch to industry following a period of early career work, thereafter another 26% leave academia for industry. This raises the question as to where South African PhDs find employment.

WHERE ARE SOUTH AFRICA'S PHDS?

According to the South African Qualifications Authority and the Council for Higher Education, in the 20-year period from 1992 to 2012, South African higher education institutions produced 21 399 PhDs. The Council for Higher Education reported that in 2012 South African universities permanently employed 6 957 PhDs. Research entities such as the Council for Scientific and Industrial Research employed 284 PhDs, the *Human Sciences Research Council* employed 23 PhDs and the National Research Foundation employed 141 PhDs. With regard to government employment of PhDs, records from the Department of Public Service and Administration, as of 31 July 2014, which were re-extracted for this period in October 2017 by Bandt (2017), showed that provincial and national government departments (excluding the Defence Department) permanently employed 1 708 PhDs. The results from this current study reported 955 PhDs across the country's top 350 companies. Based on the above information, Figure 8.1 illustrates an estimate for the distribution of 21 399 PhDs by sector. According to this study, PhDs employed in the top 350 companies in South Africa represented just 4% of South Africa's PhD population. The proportion of PhDs employed by industry in South Africa falls far below that of developed nations such as Germany and Denmark.

The data used to estimate the number and proportion of permanently employed PhDs in South Africa by sector were gathered from several sources which provided qualification information on their employees. These sources included the companies that participated in the study, research entities, and records from government as well as education bodies. This census-like approach differs from the destination study used by Mouton in ASSAf (2010), which used a sample of 1 076 doctoral graduate respondents to map out their sectors of employment. Similar proportions of PhDs employed in education and government sectors were reported at just over 50% and 9.4% respectively (ASSAf 2010). However, variances have been noted between the ASSAf (2010) study and this report in terms of PhD employment patterns observed in industry and research institutions; with ASSAf (2010) recording 18.8% in industry, 8% self-employed and 10% working for science councils or the not-for-profit sector. The discrepancies in findings arose in part from different methodological approaches; my study focused on permanently employed PhDs in corporate South Africa rather than general industry employment and self-employment; and as per the distribution pyramid constructed in Figure 8.1 the study recognised that it was not able to account for the full-time employment of 35% or 7 483 of an assumed population of 21 399 PhDs.

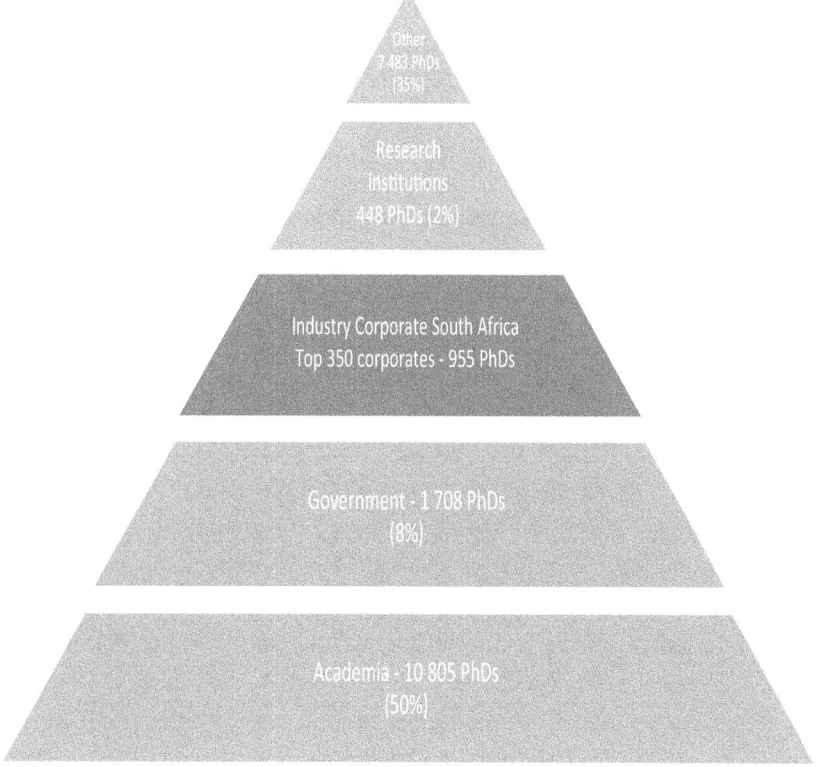

FIGURE 8.1 Distribution of 21 399 PhDs in South Africa by sector of employment (**Source:** Author's conceptualisation)

IS SOUTH AFRICA REAPING RETURN ON INVESTMENT FROM ITS PHDS?

One has to consider the tremendous resource invested in producing PhD graduates (in terms of time, money and future economic outputs) and the loss of this investment if doctoral graduates are not working in their area of specialisation, or worse if South Africa's intellectual talent is emigrating as a result of not finding suitable employment. According to the Department of Higher Education and Training (R. Cilliers, personal communication, 30 July 2014), during the period of inquiry universities received subsidies in the region of R345 000 for each PhD they produce; that is, three times the value of a publication output unit (DHET 2016). Therefore, the South African government invests approximately R645 million each year to produce ± 1 800 PhDs, or in other words, about R5 billion in the last 10 years. Has this investment proven to be a good return for taxpayer's money? Are PhDs benefiting the economy in their current positions? Van Heerden, Giesecke, Makochekanwa and Roos (2007) simulated a model to demonstrate the impact of higher education on the economy in South Africa. Their model proposed that through a combination of increasing government spending on higher education, producing more higher education graduates and generating more professionals to work in the economy, for every Rand invested into higher education, the economy would grow by R11, on the assumption that training 1% more professionals raises productivity by 0.1%.

The contribution of an academic education to wealth generation was illustrated at the beginning of the chapter in the discussion on knowledge-based economies. It is further emphasised by the Wealth-X and UBS Billionaire Census (2014), which indicated that of the world's 2 325 billionaires (who have a collective net worth US$7.3 trillion) 65% had a university degree and 11% possessed a PhD. This segment of the population is responsible for generating scalable economic wealth, through job creation, infrastructure development and service provision. Their wealth is a measure of their achievement, and this measure of success is increasingly being adopted by universities who pride themselves on the number of billionaires they produce. For example, Harvard University had 52 billionaire alumni with a net worth of $205bn, the University of Pennsylvania had 28 billionaire alumni with a net worth of $76bn, Stanford University had 27 billionaire alumni with a net worth of $68bn, New York University had 17 billionaire alumni with a net worth of $96bn, and Columbia University had 15 billionaire alumni with a net worth of $114bn. These universities are producing graduates that contribute to the global economy. Imagine what this type of talent could do for South Africa's economy.

CONCLUSION

The research findings confirm the problem statement of low PhD employability across all sectors of industry in South Africa. It was found that only 0.07% of the 1 408 173 permanent employees working in the top 200 companies listed on the Johannesburg Stock Exchange as well as 150 other leading companies (international and local) operating in South Africa held a PhD.

The resulting low penetration of PhDs across the private sector in South Africa is detrimental to the country's economy. Industries are responsible for generating financial wealth and one of the contributing elements to sustain a competitive outlook is appointing the country's top talent to drive innovation and productivity. There are many questions to ask; one that is difficult to contemplate is whether the low representation of South Africa's top talent, its PhDs, across industries, is due to deliberate discrimination, as a result of inadequate understanding about the value contributing potential of PhDs, or a failure to market them effectively.

Today's global economy is a knowledge-based one. The primary objective of a doctoral education is to create new knowledge to drive progress and development in all spheres of life, and in the new economy this is a source of wealth creation. If developed countries, such as the USA, Denmark, the UK, Germany, among others, have succeeded in cultivating and utilising their collective academic knowledge to drive their countries' economies further, so can South Africa. As a developing country, South Africa cannot move forward and become globally competitive in the knowledge-based economy without deploying the valuable talent that it has cultivated but underutilises.

I believe that it is possible to create alternatives to the current situation and offer more options to PhDs and other postgraduates in pursuing their careers – options that combine academic institutions, private and public sectors, and different industries and in so doing increase South Africa's competiveness on a global level and boost the economy by leveraging the assets of its knowledge generators.

In 2017, I commenced with a second study on PhD employability. The intention is to attain new information on PhD graduates employed in corporate South Africa and to start trending the data points to assess whether any changes have occurred regarding PhD employability. Comparisons between periods will provide important information on the extent of the absorption of new PhD graduates into the economy.

In relation to the title of the book, studies into the employment of doctoral graduates suggest challenges to postgraduate supervision on the one hand. On the other hand, it urges candidates to assume certain responsibilities to collectively strive for optimal career outcomes where the value of a PhD qualification becomes universally recognised, both by academe and non-academe sectors, to break new knowledge frontiers and advance developments, whether theoretical or commercial.

REFERENCES

ACOLA (Australian Council of Learned Academies). 2016. *Review of Australia's research training system*. Melbourne: ACOLA.

ASSAf (Academy of Science for South Africa). 2010. *The PhD study: An evidence-based study on how to meet the demands for high-level skills in an emerging economy*. Pretoria: ASSAf.

Auriol L, Schaaper M & Felix B. 2012. *Mapping careers and mobility of doctorate holders: Draft guidelines, model questionnaire and indicators*. 3rd Edition. Paris: OECD Publishing. https://doi.org/10.1787/5k4dnq2h4n5c-en

Blankley WO & Booyens I. 2010. Building a knowledge economy in South Africa. *South African Journal of Science*, 106:15-20. https://doi.org/10.4102/sajs.v106i11/12.373

Bogle D. 2010. *Doctoral degrees beyond 2010. Training talented researchers for society*. Leuven: League of European Research Universities.

Brandt R. 2017. PhD employees: National development plan 2030, e-mail to AC Goneos-Malka [Online], 4 October 2017.

Cloete N, Mouton J & Sheppard C. 2015. *Doctoral education in South Africa: Policy, discourse and data*. Cape Town: African Minds.

Consortium for the National Report on Junior Scholars. 2013. *National report on junior scholars*. Bielefeld KG: Bertelsmann VerlagGmbH & Co.

Cyranoski D, Gilbert N, Ledford H, Nayar A & Yahia M. 2011. Education: The PhD factory. The world is producing more PhDs that ever before. Is it time to stop? *Nature* 472:276-279. https://doi.org/10.1038/472276a

Danish Agency for Science Technology and Innovation. 2012. *The effect of the industrial PhD programme on employment and income*. https://ufm.dk/en/publications/2013/files-2013/the_effect_of_the_industrial_phd_programme_on_employment_and_income_v4.pdf [Retrieved 12 July 2015].

Department of Science and Technology. 2008. *Innovation towards a knowledge-based economy: Ten-year plan for South Africa (2008-2018)*. http://www.esastap.org.za/download/sa_ten_year_innovation_plan.pdf [Retrieved 5 October 2017].

DHET (Department of Higher Education). 2016. *Ministerial statement on university funding: 2017/18 and 2018/2019*. http://www.dhet.gov.za/Financial%20and%20Physical%20Planning/161214-MinisterialStatement.pdf [Retrieved 5 October 2017].

National Planning Commission. 2011. *National development plan 2030: Our future make it work*. http://www.dac.gov.za/sites/default/files/NDP%202030%20-%20Our%20future%20-%20make%20it%20work_0.pdf [Retrieved 12 January 2015].

Organisation for Economic and Cultural Development. 2010. *Higher education in regional and city development: State of Victoria, Australia*. www.oecd.org/edu/imhe/46643288.pdf [Retrieved 12 July 2015].

The Royal Society. 2010. *The scientific century: Securing our future prosperity*. London: The Royal Society.

UNESCO. 2015. *UNESCO science report: Towards 2030*. http://unesdoc.unesco.org/images/0023/002354/235406e.pdf#page=6&zoom=90,-2,282 [Retrieved 5 December 2017].

Van Heerden J, Giesecke HJ, Makochekanwa A & Roos L. 2007. *Higher education impact: Universities in the South African economy*. Report for Higher Education South Africa.

Wealth-X. 2014. *Wealth-X and UBS billionaire census*. http://inequalities.ch/wp-content/uploads/2014/10/BCensus-2014_latest.pdf [Retrieved 12 July 2015].

World Bank. 2007. *Knowledge economy index (KEI) 2007 rankings*. http://siteresources.worldbank.org/KFDLP/Resources/461197-1170257103854/KEI.pdf [Retrieved 1 October 2017].

World Bank. 2012. *Knowledge economy index*. https://knoema.com/WBKEI2013/knowledge-economy-index-world-bank-2012 [Retrieved 1 October 2017].

'CROSSING OVER' INTO RESEARCH ON TEACHING AND LEARNING

Brenda Leibowitz, Gina Wisker & Pia Lamberti

INTRODUCTION

This chapter focuses on academics teaching in higher education institutions who choose interdisciplinary projects for their postgraduate studies that link their own discipline with that of education or with teaching and learning. They face opportunities and challenges that are similar to other part-time postgraduate students as well as issues that are specific to them as a group. They encounter the usual challenges, such as of time management, but they experience specific opportunities and achievements related to academic identity and the research process. The focus for this volume, 'spaces, journeys and new horizons' aptly conveys the experiences of 'crossing over', as these academics travel between their own disciplines and the field of education, journeying inwards to focus on their own practice and teaching and learning contexts in order to move ultimately, towards 'new horizons'.

Our understanding about the issues faced by academics moving from their own discipline base to engage with research and innovation in education or learning and teaching areas can be theorised using the literature on the scholarship of teaching and learning (SoTL). A major element of the work of SoTL focuses on valuing teaching and learning, researching, innovating and evaluating our practice in teaching, learning and assessment. The literature on SoTL signposts the topics to investigate, the methods to use, as well as the potential and challenges faced by academics in the disciplines who pursue postgraduate studies in teaching and learning. Expert researchers can feel at sea in this new field, its literature, its discourses and practices. Thus expert teachers can find theorising and researching their effective practice and innovations challenging.

Each needs to learn social science based (education) research processes to carry out the research effectively and in a way that can be shared with others who are also concerned with learning, teaching, assessment, curriculum development, the student experience and the various related areas on which this field and its research processes focuses.

LITERATURE REVIEW

While there is ample literature on research into innovative learning and teaching practice in general and in specific disciplines, such as Mick Flanagan's website focusing on using threshold concepts in the disciplines as a basis for understanding and innovating in teaching and learning,[1] there is little exploration of the challenges to academics' established capabilities and theorising, as they engage with a new field of knowledge to theorise practice in their own disciplines.

Engaging in research in areas of one's professional practice as a teacher in higher education can be intellectually invigorating (Leibowitz & Holgate 2012) and can enhance professional practice (Brew 2002; Hutchings, Huber & Ciccone 2011), perhaps because of the approach of questioning, problematising, theorising and then systematically and rigorously exploring, and identifying what problems there are, their causes, and how innovations and interventions might address these. Similar use of theory and a systematic, rigorous research approach helps identify which developments work so one can learn to transfer one's insights to other contexts.

The insights offered by research approaches can enhance understanding about the breadth and depth of learning, teaching, assessment and curriculum development processes and practices. For those involved in the research there are issues which emerge concerning academic identity development and the research–teaching nexus (Leibowitz, Wisker & Lamberti 2016; Fanghanel, Pritchard, Potts, Wisker 2015; Fung & Gordon 2015). Much of this can be theorised within the bounds of SoTL. SoTL traces some of its history back to the work of Boyer (1990) and the Boyer Commission on Educating Undergraduates in the Research University (1998). Boyer argued that the "tired old teaching versus research debate" (1990:xii) needed challenging so that higher education functions and the focus and talent of academic colleagues could be seen as moving beyond this historical divide. Boyer defined four forms of scholarship: the scholarship of discovery, the scholarship of integration, the scholarship of application and the scholarship of teaching, the latter which he saw as involving pedagogical learning and research. The interdisciplinary

---

[1] Available at: https://www.ee.ucl.ac.uk/~mflanaga/

research orientation that he called for, especially with regard to the scholarship of integration, maps well onto the work of those undertaking research into their own disciplinary practice as well as onto learning and teaching more broadly. His call for the scholarship of teaching and learning has led to a range of work, notably, for example, that by Caroline Huber (Huber 2010) based in and funded by the Carnegie Academy for the Scholarship of Teaching and Learning.

Recent work on SoTL includes contributions by Hutchings, Hubert and Ciccone (2011), Kreber (2001, 2013), McKinney (2013), and Murray (2008). In the UK, Fanghanel *et al* (2015) explored issues to do with positioning, support, student engagement with SoTL, and rewards and recognition within institutional contexts, thus the conditions of the researchers, rather than the focus on the learning and teaching itself. The latter is the kind of research in which colleagues involved in EdDs and PhDs, the subject of this chapter, are engaged. However, the contextual theoretical and methodological issues are the same.

Undertaking inquiry into one's teaching can enhance an academic's sense of autonomy and purpose, as it often requires a reflection on the values that inform one's practice (Kreber 2013; Rowland 2000). Higher education is an interdisciplinary research field (Tight 2012; Brennan & Teichler 2008) in which, apart from notable university research groupings (such as at Lancaster University in the UK, or the Centre for Higher Education Studies at the University of London) and internationally the IDERN (International Doctoral Education Research Network) for example, there are few full-time, long-established higher education researchers. In terms of the focus of this chapter, those researching on higher education practice, as against policy, are a sub-set of that group. Many of those researchers in the field of higher education practice remain in their disciplines. Many, particularly the group on whom we focus, that is, insider researcher practitioners in higher education undertaking higher degrees within their own institution, return to their discipline base with an enhanced sense of what works (in terms of teaching, learning, assessment, student engagement, curriculum and so on) and how it might be researched rigorously in that practice. They are not necessarily undertaking this form of research in order to join, for example, educational or academic development teams or the higher education section of a school or department of education (although they might).

One of the positives of this temporary focus is that these postgraduate students bring with them to their postgraduate study methodologies and methods from their own disciplines, their discourses and worldviews, research designs and processes, and a variety of literature and philosophy of learning theoretical frameworks that enhance both their studies and the field of SoTL. Interdisciplinary research processes most often focused on interpreting practice can follow, which enriches both fields. For some, however, the transitioning between and splicing of fields can be challenging.

There can be challenges in relation to conducting research in the unfamiliar knowledge domain of education (Adendorff 2011; Leibowitz & Bozalek 2016) and using social science and educational research processes and practices that are unfamiliar, that is, that are not from the candidate's 'home' discipline base (Fanghanel, Pritchard, Potts & Wisker, 2015). Some have had prior engagement with teaching and learning theories and methods, but others are essentially autodidacts in important dimensions of their study.

Being, for example, a scientist or an artist brings with it its own disciplinary language and research approaches. In exploring their own learning practice or context, such academics are required to become social science researchers. This presents challenges as they engage with unfamiliar research processes, including problems of identification of a methodology and methods, and the discourse of the education field. Some dangers of working with new disciplinary approaches could be to oversimplify or overcomplicate, seeing the area as straightforward and descriptive, secondary to the discipline in which one teaches, or as a wall of excessively complex impenetrable discourse.

There could also be managerial and administrative challenges, such as having to secure line manager approval or support (Leibowitz, Wisker & Lamberti 2016; Wisker 2012), or having to register in a faculty that is not the academic's home faculty.

Academic identity issues also present a potential challenge. Candidates engaged in education research studying within their own institution, and perhaps researching within their own institution, are also transitioning between being an academic, or administrator or other staff member with one version of status within a university to the identity of a researcher, with a different status, and then back again. The different roles and the different kinds of status, access, and identity that accompany them can be troubling, not least when a supervisor is a colleague. Some aspects of this complex set of transitions resemble those experienced by educational or academic developers who also move from being researchers, administrators, teachers with a discipline base and a university position, to being expert advisors on the development of mostly discipline-based teaching and learning (on the latter group, see Handal 2008). This is not unlike the researcher exploring teaching and learning from their own discipline base as a practitioner. Each is engaged in identity work, "exploring all facets of their practice in order to better understand and define their role, position and influence within their institution" (Hanson 2013:388). However, the researcher is not necessarily focusing on their own role transition, but rather the learning and teaching, development of their students, and their position within that. Little and Green (2012) look at the identity struggle of academic developers as resembling that of migrant workers moving between homes and safe familiar and unfamiliar locations, and so it is for these EdD and PhD researchers. Adendorff (2011) reports on the isolation associated with a focus on one's teaching, when there is not a critical mass of researchers in a department or faculty who are interested in this field.

Another of the issues of undertaking such professional practice based research into one's own learning and teaching or student learning, or that of one's colleagues, is the issue of 'insider research' (Hanson 2013). One can have privileged access to information and experience but one is also quite often in an ethical bind since that insider knowledge and access makes one privy to some information, attitudes and behaviours that might make one vulnerable to the ethical constraints that are so plentiful in this work, as Hansen (2013) and Trowler (2012) explore. For some, the move to research their own practice in a course of study can offer a challenge to their established status as an academic. For some the insider research to which this often leads enables them to gain access to their subjects of study but presents ethical issues that need to be dealt with (Hanson 2013), including those of trust and confidentiality. Researching one's own practice can be untidy and too close to home, and specific cautionary practices are necessary to make it manageable and to minimise risk to the participants, the candidate and the context.

There are also potential problems more common to any postgraduate student or busy career professional. Many of those undertaking research into their own teaching and learning practice tend to be mid- or later career academics. Therefore there is the challenge of time management (Leibowitz, Wisker & Lamberti 2016; Motshoane & McKenna 2014; Bitzer 2011): working and studying, and having a large work burden and caring responsibilities are significant features for this group as well.

METHODOLOGY AND METHODS

We three authors work with colleagues at our universities as academic developers, leaders of postgraduate study, and active researchers. In these roles we regularly work with other researchers who are academic staff researching their own professional practice in higher education. This shared experience initiated our interest, enabled understanding of the context and helped us in gaining the trust of participants, ensuring that we mutually understood and adhered to the ethical regulations and expectations concerning confidentiality, data protection, no harm, and duty of care. We conducted our study in two universities, each with a history of a focus on teaching as well as research. The University of Johannesburg is a merged university comprising a university and a former 'technikon' (or polytechnic), in South Africa. The University of Brighton is a merged university which was once a polytechnic, college of education and college of art in the UK. Both universities are actively seeking to raise the number of their staff qualified to PhD or EdD.

The interview method with semi-structured open-ended interview questions was decided on as it would allow in-depth discussions with the research participants and so that the specific experiences of the participants could be recognised and valued. In all there were thirteen interviews, with nine lecturers at the University of Johannesburg, and four lecturers at the University of Brighton. We read and re-read through the transcripts, then analysed the data in relation to our research questions and the literature, to identify themes. We identified the following themes from the data:

- Pressure
- Identity crisis
- Credibility
- Confidence
- University politics
- Insider research
- Time
- Threat to career enhancement
- Leaving the research and rebalancing
- Discovering and using different approaches to research
- Theorising practice
- Improvement in teaching practices

Further, the research topics pursued by participants were the following: students' learning including student engagement and inequality; teaching methods including assessment; curriculum development; the use of technology in teaching; and evaluating effectiveness.

Instead of merely representing the results of the data analysis in terms of these themes, we chose specific cases whose experiences seemed to represent recurrent and familiar issues and stories arising from both our research and our experiences in role.

The project will continue as we intend to consider the strategic decision making of executive management colleagues. This should provide rich information about the strategies in practice of the universities and their support for such insider learning and teaching research for doctoral qualifications. Ultimately, interviews will be at three levels:

a. Lecturers undertaking Masters EdDs or PhDs who 'cross over'
b. Their heads of department or heads of school
c. Executive management

Thus far we focus only on section a.

Having analysed the data for themes, we have chosen five emblematic cases to share.

The case studies

Case 1: Understanding student learning (Mark, University of Johannesburg)

Mark is a radiography lecturer who is investigating computer-aided tool design. He always wanted to understand learning from the point of view of learners and how he can enhance his delivery. His sense of needing to understand why he teaches the way he does echoes the words of Savory *et al* (2007) that benefits of undertaking SoTL research are taking more informed actions and developing rationales for practices:

> I joined Education as a radiographer, as a professional, so I have always been aware that there is so much to learn in terms of the educational approaches. The other thing that I noted is that generally when people join higher education as professionals not as previous educators they tend to do things the way that their educators did them without fully understanding the pedagogical aspects behind why they do what they are doing, etc. So, I have always had this desire that I want to broaden my understanding of the educational concepts, improve my teaching, improve the understanding by the learners.

As with several other interviewees in the study, such as Lindi, this was not Mark's only foray into the educational paradigm. Alongside his PhD study, he was nominated to join a prestigious programme encouraging good teachers to engage with SoTL and change strategies:

> When I started looking at the issues of student engagement I had limited knowledge, so being involved in TAU[2] you know, there were issues around student engagement. And I also looked at projects that other people are doing using different approaches. … so I think it has opened my mind to see different approaches, to see things I can incorporate in terms of my writing as such which before I got involved with TAU I honestly will say I wouldn't have thought of them. But being involved with TAU I sort of now know wider and it forced me to even read wider because it was a new environment for me.

These engagements with SoTL, the PhD study and TAU complemented each other and suggest that 'crossing' over in research on teaching and learning is facilitated by multiple engagements with educational paradigms.

Case 2: The benefit of prior engagement with educational theory (Lindi, University of Johannesburg)

Lindi completed a Post-Graduate Certificate in Education (PGCE) and learned research practices through that and subsequent research projects. His research centred on working-class learners' experience of the visual arts curriculum in high schools:

> The PGCE course, I was very lucky to be actually involved in a very good PGCE course that went way beyond the remit; we did field research as part of that. We also had to do some research into the visual arts curriculum, how it was constructed, who constructed it, and so on, but we did do field research as part of that, ja. And then my master's had a kind of educational component because I was looking at education in community centres, and then as a result of my PGCE I was actually commissioned to do quite a big study in artists in schools, projects, in Johannesburg and internationally.

This complementarity of SoTL engagements raises the question of whether it is feasible or suitable to embark on a postgraduate study in this domain without prior or concomitant engagement with the educational paradigm.

---

[2] This was the Teaching Advancement at University (TAU) programme.

There was much competing pressure on Lindi's time with domestic pressures, teaching, and faculty expectations of his publishing within his disciplinary field and not in learning and teaching:

> Well, teaching is a full-time job and doing a PhD is extremely difficult, with a family, but I think probably the biggest difficulty is, you know, the university expects you to publish, and in its own cycles, and kind of has a disregard for your own trajectory, and your own kind of development as researchers, so and that kind of stalls you and so instead of being able to devote yourself to a PhD, there are other pressures to publish, to teach, there are too many things that are required of us.

He comments on having an identity crisis through moving between disciplines and researching learning and teaching:

> That decision, not to do the Visual Arts PhD, was like, I have always found that it's a kind of crisis, making one decision or the other, it's a full on identity crisis. You know, What am I? What am I going to be? Where am I going to invest all my energy? At one point I just realised it is kind of a cathartic moment where I said, 'Actually I don't want to be a professional visual artist and I don't want to be part of this world, anymore, I want to be part of a different world'", you know. And it was a big decision, you know, like ethically and the whole, politically, there is a lot of thinking that goes into making that choice.

However he is able to see improvement in his teaching, and at the same time, to engage with bigger, systemic issues and purpose and value of teaching:

> My teaching has improved, I think quite dramatically. I also understand the bigger issues in education … I understand kind of institutionally how things work … I think, if I get kind of caught up in the discipline I forget about the teaching. And the teaching is a really really important aspect of what I do and I have found that, you know, just having a supervisor who is in education I have got a much more bigger picture of what is happening and I can locate my teaching in the discipline within a bigger kind of context which I wasn't able to do before.

Case 3: SoTL research is risky and potentially isolating
(Clare, University of Johannesburg)

Clare registered for a PhD in her own field in the faculty of science, but changed to a PhD in Education and graduated in 2016. Her research focused on an intervention to support students in a first-year 'risk' module with a high failure rate.

Echoing the challenges reported by Adendorff (2011), she experienced identity challenges to her sense of professional competence and to credibility in her home department disciplinary community on entering a new field of scholarship:

> It was a very very lonely hard road … It was extremely overwhelming … I didn't realise the extent and the depth of the discourse and the discipline. … when I went across I didn't even know who Vygotsky was, to give you an idea. I knew absolutely nothing. … It was quite tricky in the beginning, because I couldn't just write, I didn't have extensive background, so it was quite limiting, or limited, and I think even today it's limited … I will always be a bit on the back foot, I think, because I don't have that, you know, 20 years of experience … there is just something that comes from having 20 years of education behind you.

Credibility and appreciation of what she was doing – or lack thereof – was an issue:

> … the University somehow sees Education as … not a university discipline … They just seem to see it as some sort of soft skill. I know people look at me and think, 'Oh, she did an easy PhD' … in a meeting someone said, 'You can publish so much in a year because your discipline is far easier than the hard sciences.'

Again echoing Adendorff's findings (2011), this was also perceived as a threat to career advancement:

> When we had a change of HoD … any of us coming from education, he says we are not allowed to supervise PhD students because we don't have the qualifications and I was told in the department that I was committing career suicide.

However, Clare is also aware of broad benefits of her studies, which encouraged insight and her sense of vocation (cf Rowland 2000):

> I must admit it has given me a lot of insight, which I never had before … because I was passionate about what I was doing, things just started happening. I got NRF[3] funding, I started publishing, I just really did well.

Case 4: Challenges of confidence, politics and time (Anita, University of Brighton)

Anita is undertaking an EdD alongside a full-time job and the duties of looking after two small children (she took one year off to have a second child). She is exploring elements of her own practice in her own university. She is confident in own professional practice which is the basis of the research, but this is undermined by supervisory conversations concerning theoretical perspectives, language, and

---

[3] The South African National Research Foundation.

the sense of starting and continuing with something insecure and new. Theorising practice was another issue:

> I feel like because I'm so busy with the practice that I don't get a lot of time to read and theorise as much as I would like and I feel that really exposes me when I'm in a meeting or supervision or something like that because I feel that I don't have a proper handle on the theory and just recently its really made me feel like I've gone back to being a first year undergrad.

She felt she lacked confidence in the discourse, theorising, and research in practice, and this undermined her confidence in her writing:

> That's been a wake-up call because now I feel like … I don't know how to write, how do I not know how to write this thing and it's because the compounding issue is not having a good handle on the theory and so I can't just read a chapter on identity and then translate it into my research plan because I'm not getting enough depth or time to think about the application of the theory or even having that thread, the single thread that a lot of books talk about when you're writing proposals or a theorise plan that you need so I'm coming a bit unstuck really.

The need for sufficient time is critical, especially when one is crossing over into such new intellectual territory. University politics and insider research also became pressing. Anita does not want to get the insider research caught up with university politics:

> I think it comes with its challenges because as soon as you're allocated a supervisor it's usually someone that you know.

Case 5: Leaving a doctorate (Jane, University of Brighton)

Time, identity and priority conflicts meant doing the doctorate was one conflicted task too many in this time of performativity and instrumental approaches to delivery. Jane terminated her doctorate and later cut her working week from five to three days.

Talking of her own leaving she said:

> [The] emphasis is all on retention and actually in some cases the student leaving the university is a perfectly positive outcome and actually the best thing for them but in the sort of discourse that we have there's no allowance for that it's just seen as a negative thing, it's like we didn't manage to keep hold of them or they weren't up to it, but whichever one of those things it is, it's like someone's being blamed for something not happening.

Jane felt at odds with the priorities and values of the university and is much happier now that she is working three days at the university and two days elsewhere (in therapeutic practice).

> If you focus entirely on numbers and if your achievement markers are about 'finish and come with the so-and-sos', then that's what you're stuck with, aren't you, since numbers relate to money.

DISCUSSION AND QUESTIONS FOR CONSIDERATION

The professional colleagues undertaking research journeys into the fields of learning, teaching, student engagement, curriculum and their own practice experienced a range of hurdles in their work. Time and pressure were familiar ones, but university politics, insider research and the undermining of the worth of researching one's teaching and learning practice were perhaps specific to them as individuals pursuing SoTL research. They faced identity crises and learned to conduct research in ways that differed from their previous practice, including tackling issues about discourse, theorising and methodology. There were clear needs expressed about more support, and recognition. Several did mention the enhancement of their own practice resulting from this research and clearly benefited, as did their students, from conducting it. What we have found corroborates our own hunches, previous research, the literature about SoTL and postgraduate study in the field of teaching and learning. The group of individuals who cross over into education to pursue PhDs are working in a nontraditional area that is somewhat hidden from view. In order to support them we need to better understand this complex and murky research path. Our aim is not to gate-keep, but to raise awareness and consider implications. Some of the difficult questions that remain for us are:

Are we doing our colleagues who come from fields other than education a disservice by uncritically promoting higher degree study in teaching and learning?

What works or would work for this group of academics to support and recognise their work in researching teaching and learning?

We hope some of the pertinent questions will be further addressed when focusing on the senior management responses.

REFERENCES

Adendorff H. 2011. Strangers in a strange land – On becoming scholars of teaching. *London Review of Education*, 9(3):305-315. https://doi.org/10.1080/14748460.2011.616323

Bitzer E. 2011. Doctoral success as ongoing quality business: A possible conceptual framework. *South African Journal of Higher Education*, 25(3):425-443.

Boyer E. 1990. *Scholarship reconsidered: Priorities of the professoriate*. The Carnegie Foundation. San Francisco: Jossey Bass.

Boyer Commission. 1998. *Reinventing undergraduate education: A blueprint for America's undergraduate research universities*. New York: Carnegie Foundation.

Brennan J & Teichler U. 2008. The future of higher education and of higher education research. Higher education looking forward: An introduction. *Higher Education*, 56:259-264. https://doi.org/10.1007/s10734-008-9124-6

Brew A. 2002. Research and the academic developer: A new agenda. *International Journal of Academic Development*, 2:112-122. https://doi.org/10.1080/1360144032000071332

Fanghanel J, Pritchard J, Potts J & Wisker G. 2015. Defining and supporting the scholarship of teaching and learning (SoTL): A sector wide study. https://www.heacademy.ac.uk/resource/sotl-sector-wide-study. [Retrieved on 12 June 2017].

Fung D & Gordon C. 2015. Rewarding educators and education leaders. Higher Education Academy. https://www.heacademy.ac.uk/resource/rewarding-educators-and-education-leaders [Retrieved 13 March 2017].

Handal G. 2008. Identities of academic developers: Critical friends in the academy? In: R Barnett R & R Di Napoli (eds). *Changing identities in higher education: Voicing perspectives*. Abingdon: Routledge. 55-68.

Hanson J. 2013 Educational developers as researchers: The contribution of insider research to enhancing understanding of role, identity and practice. *Innovations in Education and Teaching International*, 50(4): 54-71. https://doi.org/10.1080/14703297.2013.806220

Huber M. 2010. Editorial: CASTL has concluded. Long live the scholarship of teaching and learning! *Arts and Humanities in Higher Education*, 9(1): 5-8. https://doi.org/10.1177/1474022209357660

Hutchings P, Huber M & Ciccone T. 2011. *Scholarship of teaching and learning reconsidered: Institutional interaction and impact*. San Francisco: Carnegie Foundation for the Advancement of Teaching. Jossey Bass.

Kreber C (ed). 2001. *Scholarship revisited: Perspectives on the scholarship of teaching. New directions for teaching and learning*, No 86. San Francisco, CA: Jossey-Bass.

Kreber C. 2013. *Authenticity in and through teaching in higher education: The transformative potential of the scholarship of teaching and learning*. London: Routledge.

Leibowitz B & Bozalek V. 2016. The scholarship of teaching and learning from a social justice perspective. *Teaching in Higher Education*, 21(2):109-122. https://doi.org/10.1080/13562517.2015.1115971

Leibowitz B & Holgate D. 2012. Critical professionalism: A lecturer attribute for troubled times. In: B Leibowitz (ed). *Higher education for the public good: Views from the South*. Stoke on Trent: Trentham Books/SunMedia. 165-178. https://doi.org/10.18820/9781928357056/13

Leibowitz B, Wisker J & Lamberti P. 2016. Postgraduate study in uncharted territory: A comparative study. In: M Fourie-Malherbe, R Albertyn, C Aitchison & E Bitzer (eds). *Postgraduate supervision: Future foci for the knowledge society*. Stellenbosch: AFRICAN SUN MeDIA. 189-202. https://doi.org/10.18820/9781928357223/11

Little D & Green D. 2012. Betwixt and between: Academic developers in the margins. *International Journal for Academic Development*, 17(3): 134-147. https://doi.org/10.1080/1360144X.2012.700895

McKinney K (ed). 2013. *The scholarship of teaching and learning in and across the disciplines*. Bloomington IN: Indiana University Press.

Motshoane P & McKenna S. 2014. More than agency: The multiple mechanisms affecting postgraduate education. In: E Bitzer, R Albertyn, L Frick, B Grant & F Kelly (eds). *Pushing boundaries in postgraduate supervision*. Stellenbosch: AFRICAN SUN MeDIA. 185-202.

Murray R (ed). 2008. *The scholarship of teaching and learning in higher education*. Maidenhead: Open University Press.

Rowland S. 2000. *The enquiring university teacher*. Buckingham: SRHE and Open University Press.

Savory P, Burnett A & Goodburn A. 2007. *Inquiry into the college classroom; A journey toward scholarly teaching*. Bolton, Massachusetts: Anker Publishing.

Tight M. 2012. *Researching higher education*. 2nd Edition. Maidenhead: Open University Press.

Trowler P. 2012. *Doing insider research in universities*. Kindle version.

Wisker G. 2012. *The good supervisor*. Basingstoke: Palgrave Macmillan. https://doi.org/10.1007/978-1-137-02423-7

WRITING THE INTRODUCTION CHAPTER OF PHD THESES
COMPARATIVE INTERNATIONAL PERSPECTIVES

Shosh Leshem, Eli Bitzer & Vernon Trafford

INTRODUCTION

The issue of investigating the style of introductory chapters in doctoral theses emerged from our joint experience in conducting doctoral workshops and encountering doctoral candidates from different disciplines, universities and countries. Questions regarding the Introduction chapter to theses that always emerge include, 'What should the introduction section contain? How long should it be? Can we choose the structure or style of writing?'

Another issue that arises is the tension between conventional thesis presentation and the challenge of these conventions for candidates' research journeys. Most research candidates seek advice in relation to the structure of the thesis to ensure they meet the examination requirements (Fisher & Phelps, 2006). The traditional approaches to structuring theses are to adopt the 'five chapter model' comprising introduction, literature review, methodology, analysis and conclusions. Do students who challenge these conventions risk examiners' alienated judgement? We chose to collect evidence on this issue, hopefully to assist candidates and their supervisors on research journeys.

THEORETICAL PERSPECTIVES

The introductory chapter is often considered to be the most difficult part of a thesis for writers, since it forces them to grapple with decisions ranging from selecting an organisational framework to making adequate word choices (Swales 1990). Doctoral candidates are sometimes unclear on what is expected of them and what the 'entry' to their thesis should contain.

The difficulty may be due to the fact that authors know implicitly that beginnings are important in conditioning how readers view their work and influencing how their writing will progress once they are launched into text production (Dunleavy 2003:91). The point of the lead-in text is simply to frame, highlight and lead up to the core aspects of the thesis. In particular, such text should ensure that readers can appreciate the originality and the usefulness of what the particular student has done in his or her central research activities. Dunleavy (2003:51) further claims that "students spend so much time and effort on writing lead-in materials that they create a long, dull, low value sequence of chapters before readers come across anything original" (also see the chapter by Frick in this volume).

Likewise, Oliver (2004) maintains that the introductory chapter is a very significant chapter in the thesis as it is usually the first chapter that is read by the examiners and creates first impressions of style and the broad nature of the thesis. Studies of PhD theses have emphasised the crucial function of introductions to justify the study being reported (Swales 1990; Bunton 2002). It is a site where the interplay of the student's agency in the research being reported and the role of previous research are manifested. It sets up readers' expectations and orients the reader to what will follow (Bunton 2002). In the same vein, Hart (2009) suggests that the introductory chapter has a particular purpose; it provides the reason for the research and an overview of what the reader can expect to find in more detail in succeeding chapters. He therefore advises that the chapter includes answers to what the thesis is about, the reasons for the research, the kind of research, and how and where it was done.

Most literature on thesis writing consists of handbooks and guides but there is little literature on the analysis of texts (Mauch & Birch, 1998). Likewise, no studies have been done on faculty's expectations for the different components or tasks of a dissertation (for example introduction/problem statement, literature review, theory, methods, results/analysis, discussion/conclusion). However, a very small body of literature exists on the nature, but not quality, of research article introductions, as asserted by Lovitts (2007). For example, in her research on making explicit the performance expectations of faculty regarding different components of theses, Lovitts (2007:64) presents their views on the Introduction chapter in four levels of quality:

> **Outstanding introductions** have a hook, an element of surprise that draws people in and makes them want to read the dissertation. They provide a clear statement of the problem, identify the contribution up front, and address its importance and significance. They are written with authority, and show insight into and command over the argument/ material.

Very good introductions lack the "Wow!" factor. They pose a clear research question or problem, but are less interesting and less well motivated than outstanding ones.

Acceptable introductions do the things that an introduction needs to do. They state, 'This is a study of … " but do not convince the reader that the question/problem is interesting or important.

Unacceptable introductions are poorly written. The problem is not well stated or well motivated. They often contain a lot of extraneous material. After reading the unacceptable introduction, *the reader does not know what the dissertation is about and does not know (or care) where it is going.*

Yet, in recent years significant disciplinary-based analyses of thesis sections in particular disciplines have appeared (Swales, 2004; Bunton, 2005; Samraj, 2008; Carbonell-Olivares & Soler-Monreal, 2009; Choe & Hwang, 2014; Trafford, Leshem & Bitzer, 2014). One of the reasons for the lacuna in text analysis of theses might be the variation in expectations across disciplines, fields of study, supervision and controversies on what a thesis should look like and also the size of theses as texts for analysis (Thompson, 1999; Swales, 2004). Paltridge's research reinforces this notion by highlighting that there is a wider range of thesis types than the guide books suggest and there is a gap between what the books offer and what actually happens in practice (Paltridge 2002). Similarly, Booth, Colomb and Williams (2008) claim that different research communities do things in different ways, but nowhere do those differences seem greater than in their introductions. This view is supported by Bui (2014) who claims that variations in structure of introductory chapters may occur, depending on the nature of the study and institutional or supervisor preferences.

It has become something of a truism that all genres are embedded in their sociohistorical contexts. There are several layers of shaping context that determine the construction and creation of theses: institutional regulations, expectations of graduate schools as a whole, disciplinary conventions, and situated localities of advisor–advisee relationships. These types of influences are highly variable in their impacts between particular cases (Swales 2004).

Theses have a common commitment to producing and distributing knowledge, yet the way knowledge is communicated is shaped by different determinants. Doctoral students are sometimes at a maze on what is expected of them and what the 'entry' to their thesis should look like. Thus the overall aim of the study was to identify how, if at all, introductions orient the reader to the thesis and the topic and, especially, *what the writer appeared to convey to the academic reader.*

THE RESEARCH

The study scrutinised a total of nine theses – three from each country: Israel, South Africa, and the UK. All nine theses were in education in order to avoid disciplinary variability. We assumed that theses within a single and common field of study would exhibit similar approaches to research, methodology and presentation. Since their respective examiners had judged each thesis to have met the criteria to pass, they were in the public domain and chosen from university library shelves; therefore, neither the consent of authors nor ethical approval was required in order to use the theses. Only PhD theses written in English were selected with certain types of thesis being excluded (professional doctorate theses and at the Israeli University where theses are mainly written in Hebrew). Thus the selection was not random (Bryman 2001:81).

The selected theses were in the year range of 2015-2016 and dealt with aspects of higher education, primary and secondary education, teacher education, learning disabilities, inclusive education, educational leadership and policy, adult education, and community learning. We have to acknowledge the small scale of the cases (3) representing each university. Also, factors such as the supervisor, the candidate and the topic can explain basic indications of variance. However, as our primary sources were only the theses and we did not include supervisors' or candidates' views, we cannot attest to the reasons for variability.

Collection of data took place in three phases. Firstly, the pagination shown in the contents pages was checked against the text to confirm the total pages of text (excluding Roman pages, reference list, appendices) and the number of pages in the introductory chapter. This provided the relative size of introductory chapters within each thesis. The second phase involved inductive documentary analysis identifying sections, headings, references, intertextual styles, rhetorical patterns. Each component was coloured differently and then compared to identify further differences and similarities. The third phase involved an in-depth scrutiny of the chapter. Each researcher articulated understandings of *how* and *if* the text of the three theses from his/her context had *'the readers in mind'* in conveying the assumed entry information to the thesis. Categories were compared within countries (between theses) and across countries (between theses of each country). Data were presented in tables to facilitate the comparison.

WHAT DID WE FIND?

The following section describes what we found in the introductory chapters of nine theses from three different national contexts, as described above. Our observations refer to page numbers, sections and titles, and a readers' impression of the chapter. Theses are referred to by letters according to the order which the theses introductions were scrutinised.

South Africa

The length of the introductory chapters in the South African theses ranged between 23 and 40 pages. Each introductory chapter has the same title: 'Orientation to the study', or 'Contextualisation and orientation to the study'. All chapters contain between 9 and 18 sections. The headings of sections are quite similar in all these theses. The theses differentiate between research problem and the research question, where the statement of the problem provides the theoretical gap as an underpinning of the specific research questions. The theoretical perspectives also appear in all three theses with a slight difference in structure. While thesis A contains a separate section of theoretical perspectives, which follows the problem statement and the research questions, thesis B discusses the theoretical background as part of the statement of the problem and contains a short subheading defining the key concepts, and thesis C provides a section on theories and models to illuminate the possible answers to the research questions.

The chapters all contain a section on research paradigm/design and methodology. In thesis A, this section contains two subheadings: 'Data collection process' and 'Data analysis process'. In thesis B, the subheading is divided into more sections: 'Paradigm, design and methodology', 'Population sample', 'Data collection', and 'Data analysis', while in thesis C they appear as separate subheadings. The first thesis (Thesis A) contains a subheading titled 'Role and limitations of the researcher' written in the first person, the second thesis has a subheading titled 'Scope and limitations of the study' and the third thesis contains a subheading titled 'Ethical considerations'; it appears at the end of the Introduction chapter.

Each thesis contains a description of textual structure or outline. In the first two (A and B) it appears at the end of the Introduction chapter, while in thesis C it appears before the limitations and ethical considerations, which are the last part of the chapter.

The first thesis is written mainly in the first person, but fluctuates between the personal and impersonal. Thesis B and C are written in the third person where the author refers to himself as 'the researcher'. Each chapter ends with a short conclusion indicating the role of the introduction.

Reader's impression of the introductory chapter in thesis A

The chapter is comprehensively written, but is probably too long with too much detail. It does more than orientating the reader. It is somewhat of 'overkill'. It contains too much theory, which could have easily been included in later chapters. The role and limitations of the researcher are over-emphasised and could have featured better in the methodology chapter. However, the presentation is very meticulous and my impression is that the student was probably required to do more than less.

Reader's impression of the introductory chapter in thesis B

This is an appropriate orientation chapter to a study that provides sufficient information without going into too much detail. The balance among sections is excellent, but the chapter could have been shorter without doing injustice to its purpose. It is clear that institutional guidelines were followed closely.

Reader's impression of the introductory chapter in thesis C

In the introduction the author contextualises the study well by describing the national and institutional contexts. A graphical representation of the outline of the complete study sets the tone for a more holistic understanding of the research project. The background and motivation for undertaking the study is clear and again highlighted by the educational requirements of the particular higher education system. The orientation chapter moves successfully to explaining the research issue and problem in terms of student pass rates and the deficiencies related to progressing in the particular higher education system. The research question is well formulated and supported by applicable subsidiary questions. A number of definitions of key terms assist in setting the tone for a better understanding of the importance and relevance of such terms within the study.

The IQA (Interactive Qualitative Analysis) research design is explained in brief terms and sufficient information is provided to basically understand how the researcher has empirically investigated the problem. Key terms related to the IQA methodology are also explained, which helps the reader early on to get to grips with the model. Data collection measures are explained, but in my view the quality criteria for data interpretation discussed here could have rather featured in the methodology chapter of the study. An outline of the rest of the study is provided (perhaps in too much detail), while the limitations and ethical considerations are briefly touched upon. Overall the orientation chapter serves its purpose well, but a few sections, especially those with methodological detail, could have been reserved for the applicable methodology chapter later. I also think to have included some stronger theoretical foundation for the study (theoretical context) could have been useful – this was not observed in the orientation to the research.

United Kingdom

The length range of the Introduction chapter in the UK theses is from 10-15 pages. The main titles of the introduction are: thesis A – Introduction (15 pages), thesis B – Introduction to homework and to the school (10 pages), thesis C – Introduction to this research project (12 pages). Thesis A and B have no sections, thus a short overview of each chapter will be provided and they will be presented separately.

Reader's impression of the introductory chapter in thesis A

The author uses first person for emphasis. The chapter states *the focus of the research*, supported by some sources. It also explains the *context of the topic*. It indicates *how the topic will be investigated* and presents the *research questions*. It briefly explains the *research methodology*, and offers claims that the findings will *contribute to knowledge*. It also introduces the writer to show her affinity to, and understanding of, the topic. It introduces the primary theoretical sources which guide the entire research approach, research design and analysis of findings. It offers a very brief comment on what the fieldwork generated and how the data was analysed. The structure of the thesis is explained through a brief outline of each chapter.

The chapter has no sections or headings to guide the reader and this detracts from the flow of the text. Using the first person through the chapter emphasises family links in the research. Reasons for choosing the topic are not stated clearly but the chapter displays understanding of the proposed research as an integrated process

Reader's impression of the introductory chapter in thesis B

This chapter contains four subheadings: 'Homework in national policy and practice', 'The school context/culture', 'The homework challenge', and 'An outline of the thesis'. The chapter establishes the need for the research. It introduces primary sources and explains the context of the school and its policy. It also provides the theoretical context and research questions. There is an account of each chapter's content and its function in relation to the whole thesis.

The writer shares a personal quest and purpose with his readers. The chapter presents the topic descriptively without using the lexicon of doctoral research. Gaps in knowledge and contributing to knowledge are not mentioned. However, such aspirations are just about implicit in the text. By the end of the chapter readers have been introduced to the topic and shown why it is important in its demographic context. Thus, moving onwards in the thesis readers should be equipped to appreciate and understand the issues that appear. The writer established his familiarity with appropriate literature to show that he understands the concepts that are associated with his topic. Readers could therefore expect that his handling of theoretical perspectives would be informed and positive.

Reader's impression of the introductory chapter in thesis C

This chapter has no sections but one box presenting chapter titles with their respective content and another box outlines the methodological approach. The introduction presents the primary intention of this research through its research questions. The writer's own definitions of terms are provided and the methodological approach is asserted. It also describes the context of the research, the contribution to both theoretical knowledge and pedagogical practices that are shared with local schools. The writer touches on an array of theories and research findings are explained. The chapter presents an extended table listing certain stages in the research process and their accompanying activities plus a diagram of the conceptual links. It also lists the chapter titles with one or three lines that describe their respective content. The author uses a first person writing style to describe these issues.

The interconnections between ideas are not sufficiently evident, as if the writer assumes that readers would be able to make their own connections between issues and other components of the thesis. The writer does not use the lexicon of research and the chapter does not explain the scope or the nature of the research. The orientation to the thesis is not sufficient.

Israel

The title of the Introduction chapter in all theses is 'Introduction/general introduction'. The length range of chapters is from 2-8 pages. They all contain sections within the chapter.

Reader's impression of the introductory chapter in thesis A

The introduction chapter is divided into two sections: 'Motivation for the research' and 'Development of ideas'. In 'Motivation for the research' the writer tells the reader *how the topic emerged*. He also explains the gap that the research 'unlocks'. In the second sub-title: 'Developing of ideas', the author provides a short account of the evolvement of his thinking through processes of collecting and analysing data, testing and discussing ideas with others, and reading the literature. However, there are no references to the literature. The author indicates the theories that influenced his thinking, but does not explain them. The author also explains the novelty in his research and how it adds to existing knowledge. The chapter ends with research questions.

The writer establishes a strong authorial presence by using the first person as if conversing with the reader. He shares with the reader the motives for choosing the research topic, the gap and how the ideas evolved until research questions were formed. The style of writing is personal and engaging so that it sets the scene, arousing interest and expectations. There are no references to the literature. The author indicates the theories that influenced his thinking, but does not explain them.

Reader's impression of the introductory chapter in thesis B

The chapter is divided into four sections: 'Reading and the brain', 'Reading training', 'Cognitive interventions and reading' and 'Cognitive warm-up'. The structure of the thesis does not follow the conventional pattern and the chapters of the thesis are devoted to experiments conducted within the research. The introduction provides the theoretical underpinning of the experiments and the hypotheses. The contribution of the research is also indicated.

The structure of the thesis is unconventional and the introduction lends itself to the structure. It explains each of the concepts very thoroughly and provides the theoretical basis to the study in order to understand the experiments which are described in the following chapters. It orients the reader to what will follow and also provides the hypotheses that emerge from each of the concepts and are the basis for the experiments.

Reader's impression of the introductory chapter in thesis C

The chapter contains five sections: 'Rationale', 'Research goal', 'Main goal', 'Specific goals', and 'Contribution of the research'. The first part of the introduction explains the concept of transnational negotiations and what the study probes within this phenomenon. The next part of the introduction is the rationale for investigating the topic. It indicates the gap by stating how this study is different from previous studies and its contribution to studies on transnational children. It indicates the study's goals and is divided into main goals and specific goals. Within the main goals the author provides the questions that will guide the investigation. Each of these questions comprises additional components leading to more specific goals which are indicated in the following subsection. The last part of the introduction is the contribution of the research. It indicates its global and also local (Israel) contribution. The introduction includes reference to the literature. Methods, tools and the research paradigm are mentioned in general terms.

The writer provides the sufficient orientation to the chapters that follow. It explains the concepts so that the reader understands who the research is about and what is special about the phenomena. The research goals are meticulously explained and so is the research approach.

INTERPRETING THE FINDINGS

The introductory chapters in the South African university seem to be very similar in structure, style and content. They are much longer than in the two other universities and the section headings within the chapter are almost identical and seem to follow a particular pattern. They provide detailed background information of all the critical components most guide books suggest that an introduction should include (Wisker 2008; Bui 2014).

The UK introductions do not seem to follow a particular structure. One introduction is divided by sections; one does not contain sections; one includes tables to display the conceptual links, research framework and process of research. As far as content is concerned, each thesis provides an overview of what the reader should expect to find in more detail in succeeding chapters (Hart 2009; Bunton 2013).

The Israeli introductions differ in style, content and structure. One thesis adopts a very personal style of addressing the reader. It is only two pages long and leaves the details that are often included in this opening chapter to be handled in succeeding chapters. Another introduction provides the reader with a theoretical background of three experiments that make up the thesis. It also provides the explanation of the hypotheses and how they emerged. The structure of the introduction lends itself to the entire design of the thesis.

Some introductory chapters fail to consider the readers, regardless of scope. Longer chapters do not necessarily meet the reader's expectations. In a 12-page UK introduction the reader felt that the chapter did not introduce the readers to the doctoral thesis, by not explaining the scope and the nature of the research. However, in a two-page introduction (Israel) the reader felt that the chapter set the scene and aroused interest in the reader. In a South African 40-page chapter, the reader felt that it was 'overkill'. Thus the notion of 'engagement with presumed expectations of readers' in introductory chapters is a critical component which is not always taken into consideration by authors. This aligns with Lovitts's research where the 'Wow' factor was quite prominent in all levels of quality as evidenced by faculty (Lovitts 2007). Theses which did not capture the reader's interest were not considered outstanding, even though they 'do things introductions need to do'.

SO, WHERE DO WE GO FROM HERE?

Our limited, but novel investigation shows that there is versatility of styles and scope of chapters among theses and nationalities. There could be respective implications of cultural differences, institutional regulations, disciplinary conventions, supervisor's style, supervisor–supervisee agreement(s), candidate's autonomous choice, or a gap between staff expectations and students' interpretation of what is expected and required of them. We could assume that in theses where the structure more or less followed a particular pattern (South Africa), the candidates and supervisors were following institutional regulations. Where introductions did not seem to follow a particular structure (Israel, the UK) we assume that it might have been the candidate's choice or based on supervisor–supervisee agreement. The question still remains: if introductions should meet the reader's expectations, how should we guide our candidates? Should there be a 'one-size-fits-all' approach, or should there be space for creativity? To what extent does an implied psychological contract exist between authors and their readers? (Schein 1956).

Studies on postgraduate writing from an ethnographic perspective conclude that writing in the academy is highly situated (Prior 1998; Gao 2012). Prior (1998), for example, claims that we need to develop students' communicative flexibility in order to be able to manoeuvre in the dynamic situations of rules and conventions in the arena of academic writing. It is sometimes not an easy task and entails tensions, conflicts and even struggles with issues of identity (Casanave 2002).

We propose that reading a thesis successfully will depend on how the writer introduces the readers to the thesis. The writer establishes a social contract with the readers in the introduction to think about what the readers *know*, what they *don't know*, and what they *should know* and *why they should know* something. In and during their research journeys, writers should be concerned about readers' interest, their expectations and their understanding of the work. Our study may thus draw PhD students' attention to the complexity and variation in writing introductory chapters. This view supports Paltridge's research about the gap between the theory in the guide books and the actual practice (Paltridge 2002). The rules and expectations for theses are not necessarily binding nor fixed in time, as instances of academic genres are never exactly the same. That which is seen as appropriate changes over time as views of research change, and that which is considered acceptable research changes (Paltridge, Starfield & Tardy 2016). This notion, we argue, could benefit supervisors and academic writing workshops by introducing candidates to different styles and values of diversity to appreciate the 'what', 'how' and 'why', when choosing a particular style of writing.

As a follow-up of this exploratory research, evidence from interviews with authors of theses and supervisors from different disciplines and genres of research could provide answers to some of the questions posed above. It could also shed light on the authors' perspectives, and their choice of words and structure to make their intentions visible in the writing.

REFERENCES

Booth WC, Colomb GG & Williams JM. 2008. *The craft of research*. Chicago and London: The University of Chicago Press.

Bryman A. 2001. *Social research methods*. Oxford: Oxford University Press.

Bui YN. 2014. *How to write a master's thesis*. Los Angeles: SAGE. 2nd Edition. 93-118.

Bunton D. 2002. Generic moves in PhD thesis introductions. In: J Flowerdew (ed). *Academic discourse*. London: Longman.

Bunton D. 2005. The structure of PhD conclusion chapters. *Journal of English for Academic Purposes,* 4:207-224. https://doi.org/10.1016/j.jeap.2005.03.004

Carbonell M, Olivares LG & Soler-Monreal C. 2009. The thematic structure of Spanish PhD thesis introductions. *Spanish in Context*, 6(2):151-175. https://doi.org/10.1075/sic.6.2.01car

Casanave CP. 2002. *Writing games: Multicultural case studies of academic literacy practices in higher education*. Mahwah, New Jersey: Lawrence Erlbaum Associates.

Choe H & Hwang BH. 2014. A genre analysis of introductions in theses, dissertations and research articles based on Swales' CARS model. *Korean Journal of Applied Linguistics* 30(1): 3-31. https://doi.org/10.17154/kjal.2014.03.30.1.3

Dunleavy P. 2003. *How to plan, draft, write and finish a doctoral thesis dissertation*. New York: Palgrave Macmillan.

Fisher K & Phelps R. 2006. Recipe or performing art? Challenging conventions for writing action research theses. *Action Research*, 4(2):143-164.

Gao L. 2012. Investigating ESL graduate students' intercultural experiences of academic English writing: A first person narration of a streamlined qualitative study process. *The Qualitative Report*, 17(12):1-25. http://nsuworks.nova.edu/tqr/vol17/iss12/2 [Retrieved on 12 November 2016].

Hart C. 2009. *Doing a literature review*. London: SAGE.

Lovitts BE. 2007. *Making the implicit explicit: Creating performance expectation for the dissertation*. Los Angeles: Stylus Publications, LLC.

Mauch JE & Birch JW. 1998. *Guide to successful theses and dissertations. Conception to publication. A handbook for students and faculty.* 4th Edition. New York: Marcel Dekker Inc.

Oliver P. 2004. *Writing your thesis.* London, Thousand Oaks: SAGE.

Paltridge B. 2002. Thesis and dissertation writing: An examination of published advice and actual practice. *Journal of English for Specific Purposes,* 21:125-143. https://doi.org/10.1016/S0889-4906(00)00025-9

Paltridge B, Starfield S & Tardy CM. 2016. *Ethnographic perspectives on academic writing.* Oxford: Oxford University Press.

Prior PA. 1998. *Writing disciplinarity: A sociohistoric account of literature activity in the academy.* Mahwah, NJ: Lawrence Erlbaum.

Samraj B. 2008. A discourse analysis of masters' theses with a focus on introductions. *Journal of English for Academic Purposes,* 7:55-67. https://doi.org/10.1016/j.jeap.2008.02.005

Schein EG. 1965. *Organizational psychology.* Englewood Cliffs, NJ: Prentice Hall.

Swales JM. 1990. *Genre analysis: English is academic and research setting.* Cambridge: Cambridge University Press.

Swales JM. 2004. *Research genres: Explorations and applications.* Cambridge: Cambridge University Press. https://doi.org/10.1017/CBO9781139524827

Thompson P. 1999. Exploring the contexts of writing: Interviews with PhD supervisors. In: P Thompson (ed). *Issues in EAP writing research and instruction.* Reading, UK: CALS. 37-54.

Trafford VN, Leshem S & Bitzer E. 2014. Conclusion chapters in doctoral theses: Some international findings. *Higher Education Review,* 46(3):52-81.

FACTORS AFFECTING TIME TO COMPLETION OF MASTER'S MINI-DISSERTATIONS

Sumari O'Neil & Carla dos Santos

INTRODUCTION

Postgraduate research inspires growth, innovation, competitive edge and sustainability in any economy. It is a key contributor in driving the generation of new knowledge and research output (Halse & Mowbray 2011), and is paramount for the growth and sustainability of especially developing countries, as it should "enhance the human capital of communities and nations, and thereby contribute to the creation of a more competitive economy" (Bolli, Agasisti & Johnes 2015:396). Unsuccessful or prolonged completion results in economic and intellectual drain. Expenses accumulate over the period of enrolment. Resources such as supervision time and effort are wasted. This is especially a concern given the shrinkage of resources at institutions worldwide (King & Williams 2014). Given the cost of postgraduate programmes, delayed completion and non-completion may lead to financial losses and growing debts for the student, not to speak of the psychological effect it may have on them both during and after their supervision journey (Lovitts 2001).

TIME TO COMPLETION FACTORS AS INDICATED BY THEORY

Given the importance of successful completion (implying not only completing but also within a given timeframe), it is important to understand the reasons behind failure or prolonged completion. Some theories have aspired to explain the complexities and intricacies related to the supervision journey that may lead to prolonged completion. For instance, McAlpine and Norton (2006) note that the research related to postgraduate student attrition and time to completion (TTC) is either not theory driven, or focuses on specific discrete aspects of the issue. These authors propose an integrated theoretical framework which puts the student's experience at the centre. In their framework, learning occurs within multiple nested contexts, each of which presents factors that influence attrition and retention (see Figure 11.1). The nested systems represent different contexts or stakeholders that may influence student success. At the centre is the student–supervisor relationship which resides in the departmental context and within a departmentally specified programme. The departmental context is nested in the institutional context, which is nested in the societal or supra-societal context. Because the contexts are nested they influence each other, with those closest to each other exerting the most influence.

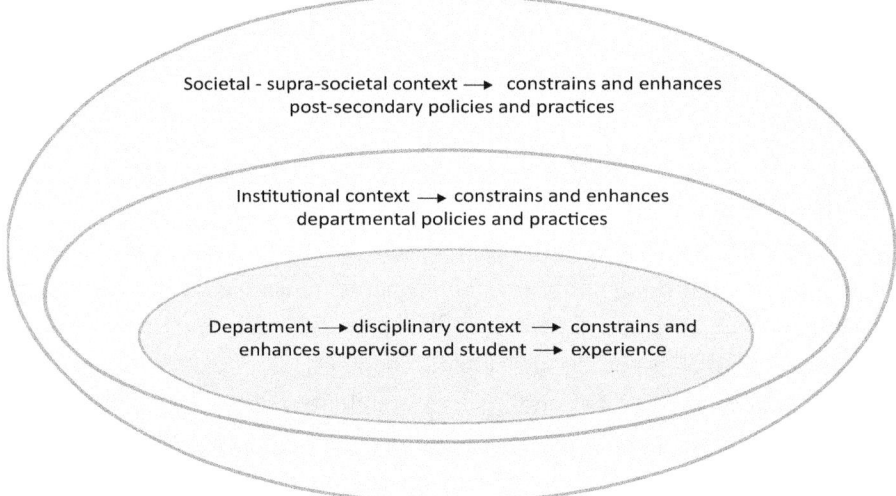

FIGURE 11.1 Nested contexts influencing retention and completion (McAlpine & Norton 2006:6)

The most well-known theoretical framework is the Social Integration Model (SIM) of Tinto (1975). According to the SIM, the successful completion of a degree is reliant on a student's academic and social integration and institutional commitment. Institutional commitment is the degree to which an individual is motivated to complete the degree. Integration can take place on both a social and an academic level, and occurs when the student shares information, perspectives and values with his or her academic community.

While the SIM was developed to understand undergraduate student attrition, Tinto (1993) later applied the theory to doctoral students (that is, the doctoral persistence theory). Accordingly, the difference between doctoral and other degree levels is the intensity of the social and academic integration needed to persist to completion. Doctoral students should also experience a sense of belonging, not only to the department or institution, but also to the field of study. Weidman, Twale and Stein (2001) noted in their 'graduate socialisation framework' that it is not only the relationship with faculty and advisors that is central to the successful completion of a degree, but also a student's personal communities (such as family, friends and employers) who stand outside the academic programmes.

Koen (2007) proposes a model to understand postgraduate student attrition by combining aspects of Tinto's work with a number of context-specific influences. Accordingly, Koen (2007) highlights seven factors that impact students' decisions to continue with the research, namely the institutional context (physical setting, social and academic spheres), household factors (socioeconomic group, educational background, domestic obligations, work responsibilities and financial situation), personal factors (ability, psychological motivation and commitment levels and student qualities), organisational factors (appointment policies, financial allocations, institutional resources, departmental structures, intellectual environment, supervision and academic progress), socio-political influences (allocation of state resources, scholarships and laws and regulations for higher education), academic performance factors (academic progress, mode of study and faculty affiliation), and research factors (teaching and supervision, research challenges and student qualities).

Lovitts (2005, 2008) notes the importance of creativity as inherent in and integral to successful graduate education. She highlights the difference between a successful undergraduate and a successful postgraduate student in the move towards independent research. This transition specifically refers to moving from a course-taker who receives specified tasks and reading lists to an independent researcher who has to function with no structure and much uncertainty. Accordingly, five individual resources are needed for creative work, namely intelligence, knowledge, thinking styles, personality and motivation. These resources can be inherent in the individual, but can also be developed through the educational programme, which constitutes the micro-environment within which the student is located and influenced, and may include the university and the department. The micro-environment in turn is embedded in, and influenced by, the macro-environment, which is the larger cultural context in which the student lives and works. Figure 11.2 shows the model developed by Lovitts (2005, 2008).

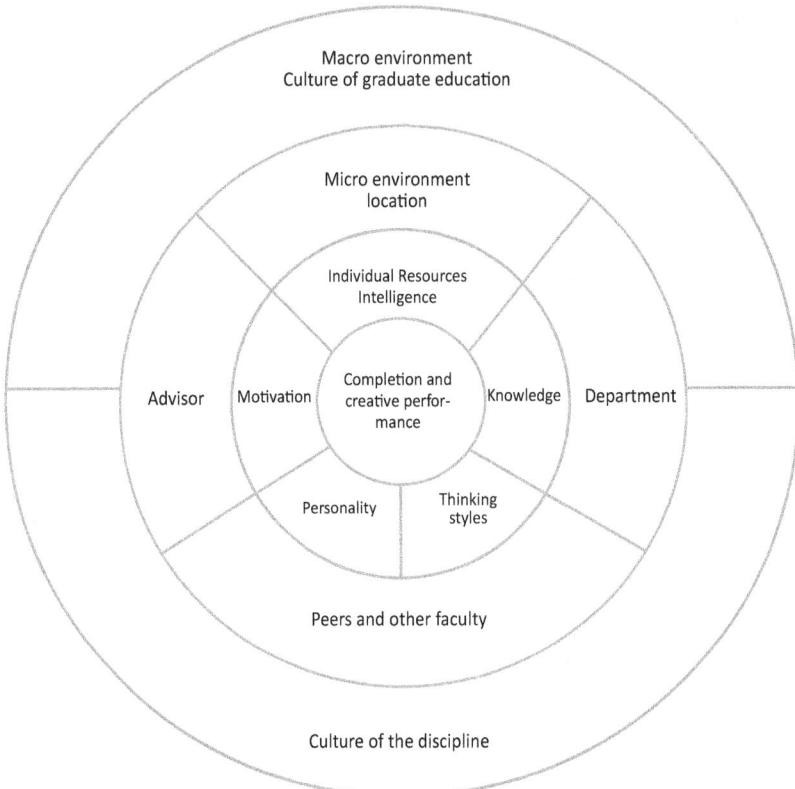

FIGURE 11.2 The model of factors influencing degree completion and creative performance (Lovitts, 2008:298)

Bitzer (2011) proposes a conceptual framework to investigate doctoral study success. He utilises the individual resources indicated by Lovitts (2008) but proposes a four-tiered framework (see Figure 11.3). The first tier of Bitzer's framework broadly highlights the student's personal environment, abilities and characteristics (that is, Lovitts's individual resources), and the second tier largely encompasses the immediate social and support context, which includes the student's location, the academic department, peer groups, and knowledgeable others such as supervisors or family members. In this latter tier there are four factors that may lead to potential success or failure: the potential for academic isolation, independence, student diversity and financial support and immediate resources. The third tier entails the programme context and includes the mode of study (that is, full-time or part-time registration), the nature of the degree structure (for example including coursework or not), the infrastructure provided to the students and the opportunities for academic socialisation. The last tier covers the institutional context which is mainly responsible for academic integration into the scholarly community.

CHAPTER 11 • FACTORS AFFECTING TIME TO COMPLETION OF MASTER'S MINI-DISSERTATIONS

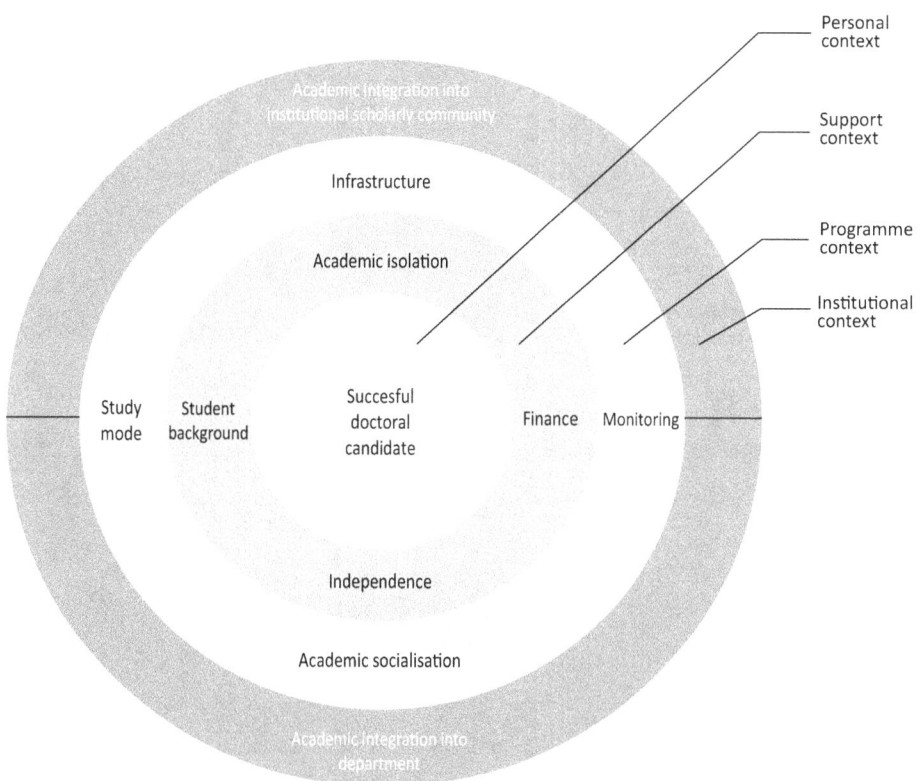

FIGURE 11.3 Bitzer's conceptual framework for exploring doctoral success (Bitzer 2011:438)

The chain of response model of Cross (1981) was developed to explore barriers to mature-aged students' participation in tertiary education. Although not specifically focused on postgraduate students, Carroll, Ng and Birch (2009) applied this model to postgraduate students' response to certain situational, institutional and dispositional (attitudinal) factors, by continuing, continuing with prolonged time, or discontinuing their studies. The barriers are crucial to students' decision to participate in an educational programme or not, and also to how students re-evaluate their ongoing participation throughout their studies. Although the original theory focused on barriers as such, Caroll et al also included enablers of student success. The adapted model is presented in Figure 11.4.

SECTION B • SUPERVISORY JOURNEYS

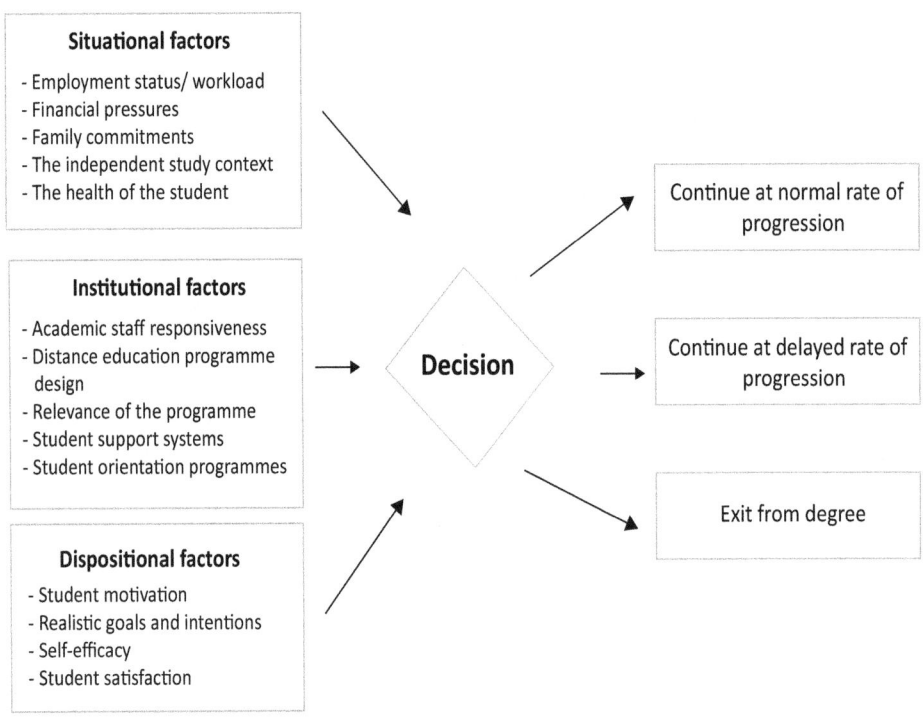

FIGURE 11.4 Carroll et al's (2009:200) framework for doctoral success

It is evident from the relevant theories that multiple factors on various levels are involved in understanding student TTC. As highlighted by Halse and Mowbray (2011), it is important to avoid adopting a narrow approach to interpreting the impact on postgraduate studies and instead to consider different stakeholder groups and identify different aspects of TTC.

Other theories that are used in explaining postgraduate student attrition or TTC are multidisciplinary and were not developed exclusively for understanding student attrition. Furthermore, all of the theories explained thus far focused on doctoral and master's by research students. In the next section the master's coursework is explained and contextualised, followed by a section explaining how the factors highlighted here are applicable to the master's mini-dissertation student.

THE MASTER'S BY COURSEWORK CONTEXTUALISED

The master's by coursework (also referred to as coursework master's or taught master's) has a coursework component that should constitute at least a half of the programme. Traditionally, the research component leads to a dissertation (referred to as a mini-dissertation or mini-thesis) as output, but it can also be an artefact such as a musical composition (Goodchild *et al* 2016).

The research component is of limited scope compared to the output expected from master's by research or doctoral level study. It is the student's first attempt to conduct independent research (Sayed *et al* 1998). Although it is described as research of limited scope, students invest so much time and resources in its completion that it is sometimes difficult to distinguish the mini-dissertation from a full dissertation (O'Neil 2016).

The coursework master's is a preferred programme for professions, especially those following a scientist-practitioner model (such as psychology) (Anderson *et al* 2008). Ward and Dixon (2014) note the popularity of the coursework master's degrees, leading to declining enrolment for research-orientated master's degrees.

Owing to issues of TTC, Pillay and Kritzinger (2007) argue that the inclusion and format of a dissertation should be reconsidered for some coursework programmes. Atkins and Redley (1998) argue that the dissertation should not be taken out of the coursework master's degree as it fosters the skills and abilities required of a master's student and also provides the means of displaying them. These skills include the ability to work autonomously, to be self-directed and self-reflective, to develop and present an argument, to put theory into practice, to work with uncertainty, to think critically, and to solve problems (Atkins & Redley 1998; Drennan & Clarke 2009). Since the research on master's coursework programmes should be aimed at "the application and utility of research in professional practice" it should also lead to "a deepening of understanding of a specific area of practice in the subject field" (Drennan & Clarke 2009:484), although the link between the mini-dissertation and practice on master's level is still being debated (Anderson *et al* 2006).

Governmental funding to higher education institutions for coursework master's may have an effect on the supervision journey depending on the funding model followed. For instance, in South Africa, funding from the Department of Higher Education Training to institutions is directly linked to teaching and research outputs (Mouton 2011). The funding system consists of two components, one of which provides funding for research publications. The subsidies provided by the state are based on the number of publications in accredited journals as well as the number of research master's and doctoral students (Mouton 2012). The second component is based on the teaching outputs. Subsidy is granted for completed non-research degrees, diplomas and teaching inputs for full-time student enrolment. Research done in partial fulfilment of a master's coursework degree falls into this category.

Since it is not funded as research output it tends to be discounted and is expected to be completed within the same time as the coursework (usually 1-2 years). The time available for it outside of the coursework may amount to 9-10 months at most, taking into account time for language editing and administration of evaluation. However, if the supervisor or student manages to publish from the work of a coursework master's study, there is a reward for the publication in addition to the allocated coursework funding.

Depending on the institutional reward system, funding for research has an added advantage for the supervisor in that the author can receive either cash or a credit in a university-based research fund. Supervisors will therefore often link coursework master's projects to their own. Although this is not the intention of a mini-dissertation, the pressure to publish, especially at research-intensive universities, along with the competing roles of academic staff and consequent lack of time to devote to research, leads academic staff to use any available opportunity to deliver a research output (O'Neil 2016). To be fit for publication, the work would exceed the requirements for a master's mini-dissertation in quality and breadth. Quality and TTC seem to be two conflicting pressures. On the one hand, one is pressured to produce high-quality research that can be published, while on the other the completion should be within a specific timeframe (Van Biljon & De Kock 2011).

TTC FACTORS UNIQUE TO MINI-DISSERTATIONS

Although the mini-dissertation is not on the level of a master's by research or a doctoral degree, the issue of TTC is still relevant. Many students who complete a coursework master's struggle to complete within the specified time, specifically because of the research component (Shaw & Le Roux 2016). Pillay and Kritzinger (2007) note that it took students in their study (N=137 of various institutions) between six months and 14 years to complete their mini-dissertations, while Sayed et al (1998) reported that only 10% of the master's by coursework students completed within the specified time. Recently, Dos Santos (2017) pointed out that although TTC may be decreasing for master's coursework students, many of them still complete very late, if at all. In the case of her research, a significant number of students at a particular department took more than three years between 2006 and 2014 to complete their research, despite many efforts to reduce time.

The delay in completion has serious repercussions for students if it is part of the requirements for professional registration. For instance, in the case of health professionals in South Africa, they are generally trained with a government subsidy and in accordance with the country's needs for them (Pillay & Kritzinger 2007). When fewer students than intended complete their degrees within a specified time, fewer practitioners than desired are in the field and this reflects a poor return on investment in terms of government funding. For instance, students specialising in psychology are unable to register and practise as psychologists if they did not complete all components of their degree, including the mini-dissertation. This implies fewer students practising their profession in the community. Where community service can be completed only after registration with a professional board (for example the Health Professions Council of South Africa), delayed completion leads to fewer practitioners than needed at community service institutions. Especially in developing counties, these institutions provide valuable services to disadvantaged and poor communities. As such the effect of extended periods for completion of their degrees (or no completion at all) affects the greater community as well.

Despite the growth in research related to postgraduate student attrition and time to completion in the past two decades, relatively few studies have focused on coursework master's students (Goodchild, Cadman & Hammond 2016). Table 11.1 summarises published studies focusing specifically on coursework master's.

TABLE 11.1 A summary of studies focusing on coursework master's students

Focus of the study	
Supervision practices	Anderson, Day & McLaughlin (2006, 2008); Chikte & Chabilall (2016); De Kleijn, Bronkhorst, Meijer, Pilot & Brekelmans (2016); Drennan & Clarke (2009); Ismail & Hussain (2010); Lessing & Schulze (2002); McFarlane (2010); Ngcongo (2000); O'Neil, Schurink & Stanz (2016)
Diversification of the research project	Goodchild, Cadman & Hammond (2016)
Quality assurance across programmes	Atkins & Redley (1998)
Research skills development	Schulze (2009); Shaw & Le Roux (2016)
Student support needs	Ward & Dixon (2014)
Constraining factors experienced by students	Morton & Worthley (1995); Sayed, Kruss & Badat (1998)

Anderson *et al* (2008:33) comment that "[w]hile there may be some similarities in students' experiences of undertaking a research project at whatever level (undergraduate, masters or doctoral), differences will also exist on account of contrasts in intellectual demands and time-frames". The factors discussed below emerged from studies of the TTC of coursework master's students. For the ease of discussion, factors are grouped according to their allocation on a macro-, meso-, or micro-level.

On a macro-level, financial support for research activities, especially in the current climate in higher education, seems to be a prominent factor (Drennan & Clarke 2009). There are fewer bursaries for students both directly and via supervisors, who potentially provide bursaries to students through their funding. The priority may also be to fund doctoral students and master's by research students rather than coursework master's students, especially at research-intensive universities.

On a meso-level, factors revolve around the institutional support, prior learning of especially research-related skills and the supervision. Students need access to resources such as library resources, writing centres and sometimes a place to work on their dissertation (Dos Santos 2017). Statistical support for mini-dissertation students is often lacking. O'Neil (2016) points out that when there is a lack of support resources, master's by research and doctoral level students are prioritised over coursework master's students, who do not always receive institutional support or the necessary resources to complete their dissertations. When support is needed, students may need to seek outside the boundaries of their institution or rely on the supervisor.

Despite sometimes extensive training during their coursework (Schulze 2009), students are inadequately aware of the research requirements for a mini-dissertation (Ngcongo 2000) or of research methods (Sayed et al 1998). Those who find the research modules difficult during their coursework year perform poorly in methodology, leading to anxiety when engaging in research. Negative experiences in previous years, if not reframed, lead to cemented attitudes towards research in future.

Admission and selection requirements for a master's by coursework student often do not include advanced academic reading and writing skills. These aspects of academic literacy are central to gaining and producing knowledge and to thinking (Shaw & Le Roux 2016). Students who do well in the tests and assignments of the coursework component, which do not rely heavily on these skills, may nevertheless struggle to complete the mini-dissertation (Dos Santos 2017).

Supervisors and examiners often expect more than they should of mini-dissertation students (Pillay & Kritzinger 2007). O'Neil (2016) attributes this tendency to a lack of interfaculty and interinstitutional standards for the mini-dissertation and the pressure on supervisors to publish.

Often insufficient supervision poses a further barrier to the quick completion of mini-dissertations (Pillay & Kritzinger 2007). Highly structured supervision may aid in quicker completion (McFarlane 2010), but may at the same time lead to less learning on the part of the student (O'Neil 2016). Dos Santos (2017) argues that it may not necessarily be bad supervision, but rather the lack of clear role clarification between supervisor and student that leads to delays in mini-dissertation completion.

Another factor, according to Chikoko (2010) and Drennan and Clarke (2009), is a lack of social and academic integration because the university does not provide opportunities for contact between students and between staff and students. During the preceding coursework year, students rely heavily on their peers and lecturers for guidance and support. This network provides an important resource to facilitate progress in the dissertation phase (Sayed et al 1998). However, when students start working or move away from campus they often lose contact with the networks established during their coursework year. This may be one of the core reasons why a group supervision approach is highly preferable for coursework master's students, as shown in the studies of Dysthe et al (2006), McFarlane (2010) and O'Neil et al (2016).

On a micro-level, students themselves may have a faulty perception of the requirements of the mini-dissertation, either in exaggerating what is expected (Pillay & Kritzinger 2007), or underestimating what is required (Sayed et al 1998). Students also find it difficult to adjust to the unstructured nature of the dissertation phase of their studies (Dos Santos 2017). Up to and including the coursework year, students have had structured training. The transition to independent study is difficult and leads to uncertainty or over-reliance on supervisor guidance (O'Neil 2016).

Master's students are more dependent on their supervisors for technical and structural guidance and require more guidance (Lessing & Schulze 2002). They begin their research "with the impression that throughout the research project the supervisor would 'hold their hand' and actively direct their work" (Sayed et al 1998:280). Some students expect functional and overly structured support (O'Neil 2016). Either owing to the lack of time, or skill, or owing to a supervisor's particular supervision style, students often do not receive this type of supervision, and then struggle to work with the supervisor. Students expecting this type of support view their supervisor as an authority figure for whom they are completing the dissertation. This also shows a lack of ownership of the dissertation from the student's side.

Mini-dissertation students are often fixated on completing their dissertation and are therefore overly concerned with its structural and technical requirements instead of focusing on the learning process. This often leads to their requiring structured and functional supervision (O'Neil 2016). When students receive contradictory feedback from different supervisors or in discussion with peers or mentors, they are unable to integrate the comments. Sayed et al (1998:280) ascribe this inability to the lack of developed intellectual skills to "shift focus to maintain logical coherence of their work".

The open-ended nature of research also presents a challenge, with multiple correct answers to a single problem, depending on methodology and reasoning. This epitomises the difficulty students have in adjusting to unstructured courses. Most coursework assignments have specific 'correct' answers, whereas research is experienced as a "journey to the unknown" (Sayed et al 1998:279). These authors hold that students enjoy the "security of the structured coursework component with pre-defined objects, aims and requirements for successful completion" (Sayed et al 1998:281). Students therefore often view the mini-dissertation as overwhelming and do not know where to start (Dos Santos 2017). The academic conventions and writing style required for writing a mini-dissertation pose an added challenge to student completion (Sayed et al 1998), while methodological problems, for example with gathering data or doing analysis, are also problems experienced by coursework master's students (Pillay & Kritzinger 2007).

When mini-dissertation students feel overwhelmed by the research, they usually also experience a sense of incompetence and a lack of self-esteem (Ngcongo 2000) as well as low research self-efficacy (Pillay & Kritzinger 2007). Although this may also be the case for students on other levels of study, it may be more so for the coursework master's students who encounter research for the first time in the form of their mini-dissertation. Most of them are unprepared for this task.

A major factor impeding TTC is that students in full-time employment have insufficient time to spend on the dissertation (Chikoko 2010). Some professional programmes (for example programmes in psychology) require students to complete an internship as a requirement for registering with a professional board. Frequently these internships are completed the year after the coursework, concurrently with the dissertation. Employers of interns are mostly not concerned with the student's dissertation completion (Dos Santos 2017).

Family obligations (Chikoko 2010; Sayed et al 1998) are another factor that may delay completion. Especially female students with children have conflicting role demands. O'Neil (2016) notes that the age of most students completing with a mini-dissertation coincides with the time students get married, start a family or start their first serious job – all different roles, each with a set of expectations for the student to fulfil. Dos Santos (2017) found, however, that if the family acted as a support structure and actively helped the student (through critical reading, for instance) it assisted students in completing their mini-dissertations.

A negative attitude towards research for the dissertation and a lack of motivation to work on it is especially prevalent on the master's coursework level (Pillay & Kritzinger 2007). O'Neil (2016) says that most students enrol for the coursework master's in order to qualify and register for professional practice. They are less motivated to conduct research than students enrolling for a master's by research or a doctoral degree. However, Anderson et al (2008) found that students had intrinsic motivation to complete their degrees outside of their professional practice. It is possible that the students included in the study by Anderson et al did not complete the degree for the sake of professional registration, as was the case in O'Neil's (2016) study.

Although the mini-dissertation is supposed to be an application of theory in practice, many students do not see the relevance of the research in their current or future practice (Dos Santos 2017; Pillay & Kritzinger 2007) and lose interest in the dissertation work, particularly if the workplace does not require the degree for registration (O'Neil 2016). As has been shown in the studies of Dos Santos (2017) and Anderson et al (2008), motivation and focusing on completing the task is vital for completion. This includes developing a strategy to work around challenges and set aside time to work on the dissertation.

As is visible from the theories presented earlier in this chapter, isolation is a major concern related to TTC. Regardless of the programme or supervision structure, completing a dissertation will always have some component of isolation, because it is an individual task. The study by Dos Santos (2017) demonstrates that some students have better tolerance for academic and social isolation than others. Therefore isolation may or may not be a barrier in the journey of mini-dissertation students.

CONCLUSION

Lengthy TTC has long troubled higher education and continues to do so. Although TTC issues affecting doctoral and master's by research students are also relevant for the coursework master's student, there are other contextual factors that plague their supervision journeys, such as the student's life stage, motivation to study, and research self-efficacy. In addition, students are under severe time limitations, they have greater research inexperience and they work full-time.

The fact that master's coursework students are mostly not interested in becoming researchers or in proceeding to doctoral study further distinguishes them from other levels of study in respect of student experiences and expectations and supervision experience. It is extremely important for the training of coursework master's students to include the requirements and expectations of the mini-dissertation, and that the roles of the supervisors and students be clarified before supervision commences. Standards of coursework master's research dissertations should be standardised to ensure that student, supervisor and examiner expectations are similar.

The professional field of study may also retard research progress, particularly where students have to be registered with a specific professional board or governing body in order to practise. Professional bodies have established criteria and training paths with which students are required to comply in order to be eligible for registration. Such requirements impact students' performance on their research either positively, by motivating them to complete more quickly, or negatively, by becoming a distraction during the research process.

REFERENCES

Anderson C, Day K & McLaughlin P. 2006. Mastering the dissertation: Lecturers' representations of the purposes and processes of master's level dissertation supervision. *Studies in Higher Education,* 31(2):149-168. https://doi.org/10.1080/03075070600572017

Anderson C, Day K & McLaughlin P. 2008. Student perspectives on the dissertation process in a master's degree concerned with professional practice. *Studies in Continuing Education,* 30(1):33-49. https://doi.org/10.1080/01580370701841531

Atkins MJ & Redley M. 1998. The assurance of standards at master's level: An empirical investigation. *Higher Education Quarterly,* 52(4):378-393. https://doi.org/10.1111/1468-2273.00106

Bitzer EM. 2011. Doctoral success as ongoing quality business: A possible conceptual framework. *South African Journal of Higher Education,* 25(3):425-443.

Bolli T, Agasisti T & Johnes G. 2015. The impact of institutional student support on graduation rates in US PhD programmes. *Education Economics,* 23(4):396-418. https://doi.org/10.1080/09645292.2013.842541

Carroll D, Ng E & Birch D. 2009. Retention and progression of postgraduate business students: An Australian perspective. *Open Learning,* 24(3):197-209. https://doi.org/10.1080/02680510903201599

Chikoko V. 2010. First year Master of Education (MEd) students' experiences of part-time study: A South African case study. *South African Journal of Higher Education,* 24(1):32-47.

Chikte UME & Chabilall JA. 2016. Exploration of supervisor and student experiences during master's studies in a health science faculty. *South African Journal of Higher Education,* 30(1):57-79. https://doi.org/10.20853/30-1-559

Cross KP. 1981. *Adults as learners. Increasing participation and facilitating learning.* San Francisco: Jossey-Bass.

De Kleijn RA, Bronkhorst LH, Meijer PC, Pilot A & Brekelmans M. 2016. Understanding the up, back, and forward-component in master's thesis supervision with adaptivity. *Studies in Higher Education*, 41(8):1463-1479. https://doi.org/10.1080/03075079.2014.980399

Dos Santos C. 2017. Towards a South African model of TTC of Postgraduate Industrial Psychology Research. Master's mini-dissertation. Pretoria: University of Pretoria.

Drennan J & Clarke M. 2009. Coursework masters programmes: The student's experience of research and research supervision. *Studies in Higher Education*, 34(5):483-500. https://doi.org/10.1080/03075070802597150

Dysthe O, Samara A & Westerheim K. 2006. Multivoiced supervision of master's students: A case of study of alternative supervision practices in higher education. *Studies in Higher Education*, 31(3):299-318. https://doi.org/10.1080/03075070600680562

Goodchild B, Cadman L & Hammond C. 2016. Diversifying the master's research project: Reflections on an initiative in architecture, planning and environmental management. *Student Engagement and Experience Journal*, 5(1):2074-9476. https://doi.org/10.7190/seej.v4e1l.108

Halse C & Mowbray S. 2011. The impact of the doctorate. *Studies in Higher Education*, 36(5):513-525. https://doi.org/10.1080/03075079.2011.594590

Ismail S & Hussain N. 2010. Learning, re-learning and un-learning: Our journey across the dissertation process – Reflection of two student teachers. *Reflective Practice*, 11(2):197-204. https://doi.org/10.1080/14623941003665869

King SB & Williams FK. 2014. Barriers to completing the dissertation as perceived by education leadership doctoral students. *Community College Journal of Research and Practice*, 1(38):275-279. https://doi.org/10.1080/10668926.2014.851992

Koen C. 2007. *Postgraduate student retention and success: A South African case study.* Cape Town: HSRC.

Lessing AC & Schulze S. 2002. Postgraduate supervision and academic support: Students' perceptions. *South African Journal of Higher Education*, 16(2):139-149. https://doi.org/10.4314/sajhe.v16i2.25253

Lovitts BE. 2005. Being a good course-taker is not enough: A theoretical perspective on the transition to independent research. *Studies in Higher Education*, 30(2):137-54. https://doi.org/10.1080/03075070500043093

Lovitts BE. 2008. The transition to independent research: Who makes it, who doesn't, and why. *The Journal of Higher Education*, 79(3):296-325. https://doi.org/10.1080/00221546.2008.11772100

McAlpine L & Norton J. 2006. Reframing our approach to doctoral programs: An integrated framework for action and research. *Higher Education Research and Development*, 25(1):3-17. https://doi.org/10.1080/07294360500453012

McFarlane J. 2010. Group supervision: An appropriate way to guide postgraduate students? *Acta Academica*, 42(4):148-170.

Morton KR & Worthley JS. 1995. Psychology graduate program retention, completion and employment outcomes. *Journal of Instructional Psychology,* 22(4):349-362.

Mouton J. 2011. Doctoral production in South Africa: Statistics, challenges and responses. *Perspectives in Education,* 29(3):13-29.

Mouton J. 2012. An analysis of the state of research at UP. Unpublished research report. Pretoria: University of Pretoria.

Ngcongo RP. 2000. Self-esteem enhancement and capacity building in the process of supervising master's students. *South African Journal of Higher Education,* 14(1):211-217.

O'Neil SM. 2016. Constructing a More Effective Postgraduate Supervision Practice: An Autoethnography. PhD Thesis. Pretoria: University of Pretoria.

O'Neil SM, Schurink W, Stanz K. 2016. The benefits of using small supervisor-initiated groups to supervise master's research. *South African Journal of Higher Education,* 30(4):210-30. https://doi.org/10.20853/30-4-613

Pillay AL & Kritzinger AM. 2007. The dissertation as a component in the training of clinical psychologists. *South African Journal of Psychology,* 37(3):638-55. https://doi.org/10.1177/008124630703700315

Sayed Y, Kruss G, & Badat S. 1998. Students' experience of postgraduate supervision at the University of Western Cape. *Journal of Further and Higher Education,* 22(3):275-285. https://doi.org/10.1080/0309877980220303

Schulze S. 2009. Mentoring in higher education to improve research output: An ethnographic case study. *Acta Academica,* 41(4):138-58.

Shaw C & Le Roux K. 2017. From practitioner to researcher: Designing the dissertation process for part time coursework masters students. *Systemic Practice and Action Research,* 30(4):433-46. https://doi.org/10.1007/s11213-016-9402-7

Tinto V. 1975. Dropout from higher education: A theoretical synthesis of recent research. *Review of Educational Research,* 45(1):89-125. https://doi.org/10.3102/00346543045001089

Tinto V. 1993. *Leaving college: Rethinking the causes and cures of student attrition*. 2nd Edition. Chicago IL: University of Chicago Press.

Van Biljon JA & De Kock E. 2011. Multiplicity in supervision relationships: A factor in improving throughput success? *South African Journal of Higher Education,* 25(5):987-1002.

Ward G & Dixon H. 2014. The research masters experience: The impact of efficacy and outcome expectations on enrolment and completion. *Journal of Further and Higher Education,* 38(2):163-81. https://doi.org/10.1080/0309877X.2012.706804

Weidman JC, Twale DJ & Stein EL. 2001. Socialization of graduate and professional students in higher education: A perilous passage? ASHE-ERIC Higher Education Report, Volume 28, Number 3. Jossey-Bass Higher and Adult Education Series. Jossey-Bass: San Francisco, CA.

MENTORING FOR STUDENT SUCCESS

THREE STAGES IN THE PHD JOURNEY

Suzanne T Ortega & Julia D Kent

INTRODUCTION

Transition points on the path to a PhD can be fraught with uncertainty: a prospective PhD student may not understand what makes a competitive application; a current student may struggle to navigate choices about research topics and professional development opportunities; and a recent PhD may not be aware of the range of careers and employers available to him or her. Good mentors provide critical support through these periods – not making decisions for students, but rather helping them to navigate their own studies and careers with success. To support this work, the Council of Graduate Schools (CGS), a membership organisation composed of approximately 500 US and Canadian universities and 25 international members, organises much of its best practice work around three critical phases of the graduate student experience: the point of entry into graduate school, the pathway through graduate school, and the transition to early career scholar or scientist. In this chapter we discuss three major CGS projects that represent these stages, addressing the implications of each for both mentors and mentees. We begin with a consideration of why we must change our current approach to one that better illuminates the journeys of current and prospective doctoral students.

WHY DOES GRADUATE MENTORING NEED TO CHANGE?

Mentoring models vary by country, but across most systems there are at least three reasons why the traditional apprenticeship and mentoring model of doctoral education is no longer sufficient. First, in an era of increasing calls for transparency and accountability, universities, doctoral programmes, and faculty must shift the focus from input factors on quality evaluations – such as performance on high-stakes tests – to evaluations that are good predictors of degree completion and career success. In the USA, and increasingly elsewhere in the world, prospective students want to know what the return on their investment in graduate education is likely to be. They are interested in the probability of completing the degree in a timely manner and of securing well-remunerated, rewarding careers. Likewise, governments and other funding agencies that invest in graduate education want to be assured that their investments lead to an advanced scientific and scholarly workforce that contributes both to the economy and the larger social good. Over time, this means that programme quality will be increasingly judged not only by the research productivity of the faculty and the promise of the students they admit but also by the faculty members' success in ensuring that students successfully navigate doctoral study and the transition to the first jobs and careers of the future.

The United States Bureau of Labor Statistics estimates that the average American entering the workforce today will hold 11 jobs and four careers over the course of his or her working life. Estimates indicate that future cohorts will experience even more job mobility. Tellingly, it is also estimated that nearly 40% of the jobs that students entering college today will secure upon graduation do not yet exist. Collectively these figures suggest that today's doctoral students will embark on careers so dynamic that we can only begin to approximate their contours. Thus, a second reason for rethinking the nature of mentoring (and perhaps the doctoral curriculum, itself) is the need to ensure that graduates are prepared to navigate career pathways that are less linear and less predictable than in years past.

Finally, there is compelling evidence that the quality of research depends on the diversity of the individual and the teams that produce it (Page 2007). Diverse cohorts of students help graduates develop the global competences, the multicultural and interdisciplinary perspectives, and the collaborative skills that make team-based, high-impact science and scholarship possible. We cannot achieve this diversity if mentors are not flexible in their approaches to providing support. This means that mentors must provide support and guidance appropriate to the different levels of preparation, interest, and lived experiences of their mentees.

In the USA, as in most countries, mentoring of PhD candidates has been limited in two major ways: supporting the success of well-represented or 'majority' students to the exclusion of students from more diverse backgrounds, and focusing too exclusively on academic career preparation. In the following sections we offer strategies for improving mentoring at three stages in the PhD journey – admissions, progress toward completion, and preparation for careers – each the focus of a CGS Best Practice initiative. We give particular attention to developing a more diverse group of doctoral degree holders prepared for the career pathways of the future.

PROMOTING DIVERSITY THROUGH HOLISTIC ADMISSIONS REVIEW

In the USA, considerable attention has been given to 'holistic' or 'whole-file' review in the context of university admissions. While multiple definitions exist, holistic review is generally understood to be a practice of considering a broad range of factors, including personal and non-cognitive attributes such as persistence and resilience, in the evaluation of candidates for admission (Kent & McCarthy 2016). A holistic admissions process does not necessarily exclude the consideration of student grades and standardised test scores; rather, it may consider those scores as valuable criteria among others in the assessment of a student's potential.

Holistic admissions processes have been tied to diversity initiatives for a number of reasons. First, students underrepresented in graduate education may under-perform on standardised tests. If tests and grades are used too exclusively, or if 'cut-off' scores are used to winnow down an applicant pool, then programmes may be deprived of the opportunity to recruit underrepresented students with the talent and motivation to succeed. Second, students from underrepresented backgrounds may possess characteristics such as resilience that help position them to succeed in graduate education. More research is needed to determine what traits are linked with successful outcomes in master's and doctoral education, and how best to measure them.

CGS conducted preliminary research on the practices associated with holistic review in a 2015 study supported by Hobsons. One of the main findings of this project was that graduate institutions need more data demonstrating the link between admissions criteria and student outcomes. A survey conducted as part of the project revealed that 81% of graduate deans and staff respondents believed that such data were needed at their own universities (Kent & McCarthy:iii).

How does holistic review relate to good mentoring? One of the main conclusions to emerge from this research is that we need to think beyond the admissions process when developing strategies for diversity and inclusion. We can recruit a diverse and talented cohort of students, but our work is not done unless our students successfully navigate their degree programmes and pathways to meaningful careers. We will now turn our attention to strategies for supporting these pathways.

CGS DOCTORAL DEGREE COMPLETION INITIATIVES

In 2004, in response to growing national concern about high doctoral attrition rates, CGS launched a major initiative to document degree completion rates by gender, race/ethnicity, and discipline. With the support of Pfizer Inc and the Ford

Foundation, 21 major US and Canadian research universities collected baseline attrition and completion data (representing academic years 1992-1993 through 2003-2004) and piloted interventions aimed at improving completion. This pool of universities was expanded in phase II (2007-2010) to include 22 research partners and 21 project affiliates. The wide range of participating universities produced robust completion and attrition data, ensuring that any promising practices emerging from the project would be relevant to the full range of doctoral-conferring universities in North America.

Results from this study indicated that only 57% of the doctoral candidates in the study completed their degrees within 10 years. However, this overall figure masks considerable variation by broad field of study, ranging from a high of 64% in engineering to a low of 49% in the humanities (Council of Graduate Schools 2008a). Furthermore, men, international students and white majority students had higher 10-year completion rates than women, US domestic students and those from non-majority races and ethnicities. While there was some field variation in the overall pattern, women and underrepresented minority students had higher late completion rates (from years 8-10) than men and white students, respectively (Council of Graduate Schools 2008b). Universities participating in the PhD Completion project were also asked to administer surveys to all students completing or otherwise leaving doctoral study. While the number of responses from those withdrawing from study was too few to analyse, 1 406 PhD completers provided useable responses.

With respect to mentoring and advising relationships, the key findings were as follows:
- While 90% of all students reported having access to an advisor during the dissertation writing and defence stages of doctoral study, only 82-83% reported having regular advising at early stages of study.
- Eighty-five per cent of respondents reported receiving regular feedback about their academic progress, but only about three-quarters of all students reported having access to a mentor, that is, someone who provided advice on academic and professional matters beyond the immediate research project.
- Among those with mentors, satisfaction was uniformly high, varying from 91% in social sciences to 94% in both the life sciences and the humanities.
- Respondents were also asked what they most valued about their mentors' guidance. Of those reporting having a mentor, 83% reported research guidance as highly valuable; 67% of respondents also mentioned career/professional advice. While only 15% indicated that mentoring was most valuable for 'other' reasons, those

who provided this response elaborated that personal and emotional support, advice on work-life balance and 'spiritual' support were highly valued.

- Although more than 90% of respondents indicated real satisfaction with their mentors, about two-thirds of respondents indicated ways in which mentoring could have been improved. Of these, 40% wanted more time with their mentors and a nearly identical number – 39% – indicated more career and professional advice would have been useful. Less than a third mentioned better quality of time and research advice (Council of Graduate Schools 2009a).

It is important to make a distinction here between 'mentors' and 'advisors'. An advisor may be formally assigned, but may not be perceived by the candidate to be a source of guidance or support on topics beyond the dissertation or thesis. Indeed, many of the doctoral candidates surveyed reported that they did not have access to someone who could provide advice and professional matters beyond the immediate research project.

Taken together, results from this exit survey suggest quite high levels of satisfaction with PhD advising and mentoring. Nevertheless, it is noteworthy that students reported less access to advising in the critical early stages of doctoral study, when they must become socialised to the norms and expectations of the university, the programme, and their research advisor. A second point worth noting is that while access to advisors was nearly universal, at least during the dissertation stage, access to mentors was far less ubiquitous; even for those with mentors, many new PhDs expressed interest in spending more time with, and receiving more career advice from, their mentors. In light of the rapidly changing labour market, such career advice is essential to helping new PhDs move smoothly into their roles as faculty members or scholars and scientists working in government, business, and non-profits.

How can graduate programmes and universities address these gaps? In the USA, many graduate programmes are now offering comprehensive orientation programmes to supplement advisor efforts during this formative period. In addition, many US graduate schools are providing handbooks and workshops to improve the capacity of mentors to make available good career and professional advice to their students (see for example, CGS 2009b; www.rackham.umich.edu/mentoring). One particularly promising practice is the use of individual development plans (IDPs) as a way of focusing mentoring conversations on students' career aspirations, what they must accomplish in order to reach them, and how mentors can help. Indeed, several major funding agencies, including the National Institutes of Health, are widely encouraging, and in some cases requiring, use of IDPs with trainees and postdoctoral students. However, many North American graduate schools are supplementing the work of individual mentors by offering career-focused programmes, seminars, and services for doctoral students (see for example, Denecke, Feaster & Stone 2017).

One final point is in order here. The exit survey results summarised above come from those who successfully completed their doctoral programmes. Many studies point to the absence of mentoring as a key reason for students leaving without the degree (Lovitts 2001; Nettles & Millett 2006). For many students, including those who are the first in their families to attend graduate school or who are from less affluent or racially and ethnically underrepresented groups, the absence of a mentor or conflict with a mentor or advisor may be the key factor that inhibits their ability to complete the degree.

In a 2015 study of doctoral attrition and completion among racially and ethnically underrepresented science, engineering, and mathematics students, Sowell, Allum, and Okahana found results that in many ways mirror those of the PhD Completion project described above. Overall, students reported real satisfaction with their advisors and mentors, highlighting their important role in supporting their ability to complete the PhD For these underrepresented STEM students, it is at the dissertation stage that a significant minority (30%) report that faculty do not seem to understand the unique challenges they face.

Survey results from these underrepresented students offered a number of recommendations for improving mentoring and advising. First, students felt strongly that programme expectations from initial enrolment through dissertation defence needed to be made clear. They suggested that these expectations could be communicated via online resources but also that student progress should be tracked and reviewed periodically with advisors so that students clearly understood how they were progressing. Second, students emphasised the importance of 'fit' with their advisors and the institution's role in helping them find the 'right match'. Students distinguished between advisors – those who were primarily responsible for directing research, finding funding, and advising on coursework – and mentors, or those who were more interested in the overall well-being of the student above and beyond their performance in courses, on exams, or in the research lab. Students noted that the advisor and mentor role were sometimes played by the same person but more frequently were played by different individuals. They noted that there was an added advantage when the mentor was someone not directly involved in the lab, programme, or department in which they were studying. Finally, students noted the key role that peer mentoring and peer networks played in doctoral success (Sowell *et al* 2015).

The overarching conclusion of both the earlier PhD completion work and the Sowell *et al* study is that doctoral student success depends on an environment that embraces diversity and inclusion. A critical part of creating such an environment is acknowledging that not all students come to PhD study with the same awareness of implicit norms. To create a more level playing field, we must make expectations clear and provide the peer, advising, and mentoring resources necessary to help all students complete degree requirements and launch successful careers.

PHD CAREER PATHWAYS

For at least two decades, the majority of new PhDs in the USA have entered first jobs in business, government, non-profit or other non-academic sectors. Nevertheless, relatively little is known about the career pathways of research doctorate holders. Why are these data important? First, the decision to pursue a graduate degree is often driven by career aspirations. For example, nearly 88% of students intending to pursue graduate study agreed that a post-baccalaureate degree would provide them with better career opportunities and over 84% agreed that it would enhance their earning potential (Wendler *et al* 2012). Enhanced job prospects may be particularly important for students from low-income or racially/ethnically underrepresented groups who appear to be particularly sensitive to incurring additional student-related debt and forgoing income to enter graduate study (Dowd & Malcom 2012).

However, knowledge about career pathways is not only important as students make the decision to enter doctoral study; it has implications for the way in which they progress through (or leave) the degree programme. Evidence suggests that available programme-led PhD career information may reduce attrition by clarifying the programme's alignment with the student's career goals (Council of Graduate Schools, 2009a; Kamas *et al* 1995); providing clearer pathways into a diversity of careers (MLA 2014; Rutledge *et al* 2011,) and decreasing the sense of isolation that PhD students sometimes report when considering a career beyond the academy (Golde & Dore 2001; Sauermann & Roach 2012). Additionally, information about prospective first, second, and third jobs may actually reduce time to degree by motivating students reluctant to leave graduate study for what may have seemed an uncertain job market (Woodrow Wilson Foundation 2005). In sum, data on the diversity of career pathways can help mentors and programmes prepare students for timely entry into the full range of rapidly changing, rewarding careers.

As noted above, advisors and mentors play a key role in giving students 'permission' to explore the full range of career options but they are also a key source of information about the nature and requirements for those same careers. Students desire more information and more and more graduate schools and mentors are attempting to provide it. Their efforts are hamstrung, however, by the paucity of information about the actual career outcomes of research doctorate recipients – what first jobs PhDs held, where they are now working, the career pathways that lead to current employment, the nature of the work they do and the academic and professional skills necessary to execute it. As Cassuto (2015) notes, availability of such data would allow faculty to provide better mentorship by giving them a clearer understanding of the real and potential impact of graduate training on their students' career trajectories.

In order to better understand how doctoral student career aspirations evolve over the course of study and to develop the programmes that can more effectively support 21st century career development, CGS has recently launched a major data collection effort. Beginning in Fall 2017, and made possible by the generous support of the Andrew W Mellon Foundation and National Science Foundation (#1661272) CGS, in collaboration with more than 60 major research universities, which began collecting career pathways data on doctoral students and doctoral alumni across all fields of science and the humanities. Over the course of the five-year project, data will be collected from second- and fifth-year doctoral students and from doctoral alumni three, eight, and fifteen years after graduation. Information about career aspirations and experiences will be used to inform career and professional development initiatives and doctoral programme improvement at participating universities.

Data will permit a deeper understanding of the efficacy of existing professional development efforts, and will also highlight those intellectual and transferrable professional skills not currently included in the graduate curriculum, via research mentoring, or through university-wide professional development efforts. By providing mentors and programmes with clear evidence of the range and quality of positions open to doctoral students, this study is designed to assist mentors and doctoral degree programmes in tailoring professional development efforts to each of the major stages of the doctoral student life cycle.

CONCLUSION

Studies conducted over the last 15 years or more routinely point to the critical role that mentors play in the success of students at each phase of their doctoral careers. Undergraduate mentors are extremely important in encouraging students, particularly students of colour, to pursue advanced study (DeAngelo 2009). At the doctoral level, a PhD candidate may receive relatively little to no formal coursework, with variations depending upon the country and university. Thus, supervision can 'make or break' a student's experience. Whether mentoring within or across gender and racial/ethnic difference, faculty mentors serve as both role models and the source of cultural and social capital, especially in fields where women and minorities are particularly underrepresented.

While it is quite possible that every faculty member will not or cannot be an extraordinary mentor, all faculty members and advisors can become better at fulfilling this role. Universities in all countries play an important role in the provision of the resources needed to support good mentoring, including workshops and publications and information that support constructive, support-seeking behaviour on the part of student mentees. As DeAngelo *et al* (2015) note in the context of undergraduate study, universities also must create the infrastructure that encourages and rewards good mentorship, including recognition of mentoring in tenure and promotion and compensation processes. This observation applies equally to an institutional recognition of innovative, high-quality doctoral mentorship. Of course, implementing such an infrastructure will depend on the local context and the behaviours that are valued and rewarded within it. For example, national and local systems seeking to diversify the knowledge workforce may provide incentives to graduate programmes and institutions that broaden the preparation of PhD candidates.

Most students understand that no single faculty member may be able to meet all of their academic, personal, and career development needs; they also recognise the critical role that peer mentoring and peer networks play in both academic and subsequent career success. For this reason, universities and programmes should consider supplementing the traditional one student-one advisor apprenticeship model with team mentoring approaches; on the latter model, the advisor becomes one mentor among several. In addition, providing a physical space for students to meet with one another and the programmatic space that allows them to meet across disciplinary boundaries are among the promising practices now being adopted by many North American universities. For example, Virginia Tech offers a Graduate Life Center, which houses graduate student residences, office space, study and meeting rooms, a computer lab, and a café. Having a larger network of colleagues and peers may be particularly important for underrepresented students who may feel greater isolation than their majority peers.

Graduate students need mentors, but they also need a community of fellow students and faculty who can provide different types of feedback and support. Giving our students the opportunity to build a network of colleagues not only supports healthy relationships; it is also excellent preparation for professional life. To be clear, such a network cannot replace great advisors and mentors. Rather, great mentors will help students create this network – and the future professional communities he or she will be a part of – with confidence and success.

REFERENCES

Cassuto L. 2015. *The graduate school mess: What caused it and how we can fix it.* Cambridge, MA: Harvard University Press. https://doi.org/10.4159/9780674495593

Council of Graduate Schools. 2008a. *PhD completion and attrition: Analysis of baseline program data from the PhD Completion Project.* Washington DC: Council of Graduate Schools.

Council of Graduate Schools. 2008b. *PhD completion and attrition: Analysis of baseline demographic data from the PhD Completion Project.* Washington DC: Council of Graduate Schools.

Council of Graduate Schools. 2009a. *PhD completion and attrition: Findings from exit surveys of PhD completers.* Washington DC: Council of Graduate Schools.

Council of Graduate Schools. 2009b. *Research student and supervisor.* Washington DC: Council of Graduate Schools.

DeAngelo L. 2009. Can I go? An exploration of attending a less selective institution on students' aspirations and preparation for the PhD. In: MF Howard-Hamilton, CL Morelon-Quinanoo, SD Johnson, R Winkle-Wagner, & L Sintiaque (eds). *Standing on the outside looking in: Multiple causes, implications, and potential remedies to address underrepresentation among minorities in graduate programs.* Sterling VA: Stylus Publishing, LLC. 25-44.

DeAngelo L, Mason J & Winters D. 2015. Faculty engagement in mentoring undergraduate students: How institutional environments regulate and promote extra-role behavior. *Innovative Higher Education*, 41(4):317-332. https://doi.org/10.1007/s10755-015-9350-7

Denecke D, Feaster K & Stone K. 2017. *Professional development: Shaping effective programs for STEM graduate students.* Washington DC: Council of Graduate Schools.

Dowd AC & Malcom LE. 2012. *Reducing undergraduate debt to increase Latina and Latino participation in STEM professions.* Los Angeles CA: University of Southern California.

Golde C & Dore T. 2001. *At cross purposes: What experiences of today's doctoral students reveal about doctoral education.* http://www.phd-survey.org/report%20final.pdf [Retrieved on 12 September 2017].

Kamas L, Paxson C, Wang A & Blau R. 1995. *PhD student attrition in the EECS department at the University of California, Berkeley.* http://www-inst.eecs.berkeley.edu/~wicse/index.php/papers/lindareport2.pdf [Retrieved on 12 September 2017].

Kent J & McCarthy M. 2016. *Holistic review of graduate admissions: A report from the Council of Graduate Schools.* Washington DC: Council of Graduate Schools.

Lovitts B. 2001. *Leaving the ivory tower.* Lanham, MD: Rowman & Littlefield.

MLA (Modern Language Association of America). 2014. *Report of the MLA task force on doctoral study in modern languages and literature.* http://www.mla.org/pdf/taskforcedocstudy2014.pdf [Retrieved on 14 June 2017].

Nettles MT & Millett CM. 2006. *Three magic letters: Getting to PhD.* Baltimore MD: Johns Hopkins Press.

Page SE. 2007. *The difference: How the power of diversity creates better groups, firms, schools, and societies.* Princeton NJ: Princeton University Press.

Rutledge J, Carter-Veale W & Tull R. 2011. Successful PhD pathways to advanced STEM careers for black women. In: H Frierson & W Tate (eds). *Beyond stock stories and folktales: African Americans' path to STEM fields.* Washington: Emerald Group Publishing Limited. 165-209. https://doi.org/10.1108/S1479-3644(2011)0000011013

Sauermann H & Roach M. 2012. Science PhD career preferences: Levels changes, and advisor encouragement. *PLOS ONE,* 7(5). https://doi.org/10.1371/journal.pone.0036307

Sowell R, Allum J & Okahana H. 2015. *Doctoral initiative on minority attrition and completion.* Washington DC: Council of Graduate Schools.

Wendler C, Bridgeman B, Markle R, Cline F, Bell N, McAllister P & Kent J. 2012. *Pathways through graduate school and into careers.* Princeton NJ: Educational Testing Service.

Woodrow Wilson National Fellowship Foundation. 2005. *The responsive PhD: Innovations in US doctoral education.* Princeton, NJ: Author. https://files.eric.ed.gov/fulltext/ED536859.pd [Retrieved on 12 September 2017].

FUNCTION OF SUPERVISORY AND RESEARCHER COMMUNITY SUPPORT IN PHD AND POST-PHD TRAJECTORIES

Kirsi Pyhältö

INTRODUCTION

A significant body of prior research on early career experience shows that both the quantity and the quality of social interactions with the academia play a central role in PhD and post-PhD trajectories. It has, for instance, been shown that good integration into the researcher community include frequent and positive interactions with supervisor(s), contributes to doctoral students' decision to launch their studies (see Brailsford 2010), timely progress (Ives & Rowley 2005), reduced risk for study abandonment, skills, knowledge and attitudes developed during the studies, and satisfaction with overall doctoral experience (Meyer, Shanahan & Laugksch 2005; Pyhältö, Vekkaila & Keskinen 2015). Similarly, although less studied, post-PhD researchers have also been shown to benefit from supervisory support and close connections and opportunities to engage in practices of researcher community. It is suggested that such benefits include more immediate employment after earning the degree, satisfaction with one's work and increased research productivity (Montserrat, McAlpine & Pyhältö 2016; Scaffidi & Bergnaman 2011).

Although the literature on supervisory and researcher community interaction is extensive, and hence evidence on its impact for PhD and post-PhD experience is convincing, the field of research is also quite fragmented. For example, different elements of supervision in a variety of combinations are explored separately, some studies focusing more on structure or organisation while others explore the quality of supervisory interaction. Naturally, different concepts and frameworks are applied, depending on the focus on the study. Though useful in understanding different aspects of researcher community and supervisory interactions, the diversity also provides a challenge in building a comprehensive picture of the interrelations between the different aspects of these interactions, both empirically and conceptually.

This chapter[1] aims to contribute to bridging the gap in the literature by proposing a model for analysing supervisory and researcher community support in PhD and post-PhD trajectories. The chapter proposes a conceptual tool for analysing different dimensions of supervisory journeys. First, a theoretical model for conceptualising supervisory and researcher community support is proposed. The model specifies forms, sources, support dynamics and fit as complementary components of supervisory and researcher community support. Next, empirical evidence for key components of this framework are discussed by summarising the results of a series of recent empirical studies that investigate the supervisory and researcher community support and the importance of social support for doctoral and postdoctoral researchers. Finally, possible future directions for this research in this area as well as implications for developing doctoral and postdoctoral trajectories are outlined.

RESEARCHER COMMUNITY AND SUPERVISORY SUPPORT MODEL

Drawing on a socio-constructivist view on learning (for example Sfard 1998), social support (Cobb 1976; House 1981) and working-environment fit theory (Holland 1985), as well as empirical evidence on doctoral and post-PhD experience, our presumption in building the model on researcher community and supervisory support was that social interaction is the primary determinant of early career researcher experience and researcher development. The *social support* itself refers to the resources both perceived to be available, and used by the doctoral students and post-PhD researchers in their social environment. These comprise both formal and informal relationships, including dyadic and group relationships within the researcher communities, with peers, that is, PhD students and post-PhD researchers, supervisor(s), other senior researchers and staff members (Vekkaila, Virtanen, Taina & Pyhältö 2016) as well as research groups, international researcher networks or special interest groups, and relationships with institutional representatives, for example funding agencies (Pyhältö, McAlpine, Peltonen & Castello 2017). They

---

[1] The chapter summarises previous work of the From PhD Student to Academic Expert research group on the different aspects of researcher community and supervisory support on early career researchers, that is, doctoral students and post-PhD researchers (referring to PhD degree holders less than 8 years from degree completion). The group is led by Prof. Kirsi Pyhältö. Read more about our research from https://researchondoctoraleducation.wordpress.com/

provide the primary sources of support for their work as researchers. At the same time, it is important to note that the potential sources of support are not limited to the researcher communities, but are often extended to close friends, family and other professional networks, specifically the support and co-investment of significant others, close family and friends that also serve as an asset in pursuing an academic career (Chen, McAlpine & Amundsen 2015). In fact, lack of such support is often perceived as problematic, and occasionally leads to career abandonment (McAlpine & Amundsen 2015; McAlpine & Amundsen 2016). Equally important for sufficient support utilisation is how well doctoral students and post-PhD researchers are able to identify the social resources available, how they perceive them, and their ability to utilise them.

Having several sources of support available is central, but not by itself a sufficient condition for functional support. In order to solve different kinds of problems, doctoral students and post-PhD researchers need different types of support. In extant literature, distinctions between three complementary *forms of support*, including *emotional*, *informational* and *instrumental* forms of support have been made (see Cobb 1976; Väisänen, Pietarinen, Pyhältö, Toom & Soini 2016). Emotional support entails empathy, trust, listening, caring, and belonging to a network of researcher communities with mutual obligation, whereas informational support is characterised by information, such as advice, feedback, affirmation, suggestions, and problem solving that enable an early career researcher to cope with problems. Instrumental support, referring to more concrete forms of help such as sufficient time allocation, writing recommendations or providing funding from different sources or research facilities, directly helps doctoral students and post-PhD researchers to manage their work. Since collective knowledge creation is typically at the core of scientific endeavour, we have proposed that emotional, informational and instrumental support should be complemented with a fourth form: *co-constructional* support, characterised by working on shared objects of activity resulting in new knowledge, that is, original scientific discovery (see Vekkaila *et al* 2016). Co-constructional support involves engaging in collaborative thinking and shared knowledge construction. Such activities are especially typical in the STEM (Math, Engineering, Technology, and Science) fields where solving complex research problems through laboratory or field research often requires intensive collaboration among researchers possessing different types of expertise (Cumming 2009; Delamont & Atkinson 2001). Yet, it can be argued that co-constructional support is essential for any research activities that strive to create new knowledge and innovations. Naturally, both the sources and needed forms of support can vary depending on individual competences, career phase and tasks at hand. Accordingly, a challenge for researcher education is that early career researchers, including both doctoral students and post-PhD researchers, should learn to seek, use and provide social support in order to utilise this resource in their work (Durette, Fournier & Lafon 2016).

The availability of social support is a crucial, but not in itself sufficient, determinant of a positive doctoral and post-PhD experience. The fit between the needed and provided support, that is, *support fit*, is also a central ingredient in the positive doctoral and post-PhD researcher experience (Pyhältö et al 2015; Vekkaila et al 2016). To be functional, the provided support should promote coping with the particular problem being faced (Cohen & McKay 1984; Helgeson & Gottlieb 2000). This means that to be effective the support being offered should match the type of problem being faced. Accordingly, in order to be matched, the fitted support should fulfil at least two criteria: firstly, support should be available (accordingly, lack of support is mismatched support), and secondly, the type of support provided should be appropriate in terms of the support needed. The latter means that the type of support provided should be useful in terms of the task at hand, and also provided in the form that is usable for a doctoral student or a post-PhD researcher considering his/her current situation and competences. Moreover, sometimes, the source of support may affect the early career researcher's ability to utilise the support; for instance, some advice may be more easily taken from the supervisor than from a peer.

Also, the *support dynamics*, whether the support is received, given to another or reciprocal, the roles of the giver and receiver, and the reciprocity of interaction are important determinants for the experience of support, and related outcomes (Cohen & Syme 1985). There is, for instance, some evidence that early career researchers more often receive support than give it to the others (Vekkaila et al 2016; Pyhältö & Stubb 2012). This is partly natural, considering that doctoral students and post-PhD researchers are both still novices at their field. On the other hand, in the long term the role of the receiver might be problematic, since it does not provide optimal opportunity for rehearsal, and hence to learn how to give support or build reciprocal professional relationships with other researchers at the different career stages. This may further provide a hindrance in building sufficient researcher networks. Accordingly, in order to understand the function of social support in doctoral and post-PhD experience, one needs to consider at least four interrelated elements of the support (see Figure 13.1).

CHAPTER 13 • FUNCTION OF SUPERVISORY AND RESEARCHER COMMUNITY SUPPORT IN PHD AND POST-PHD TRAJECTORIES

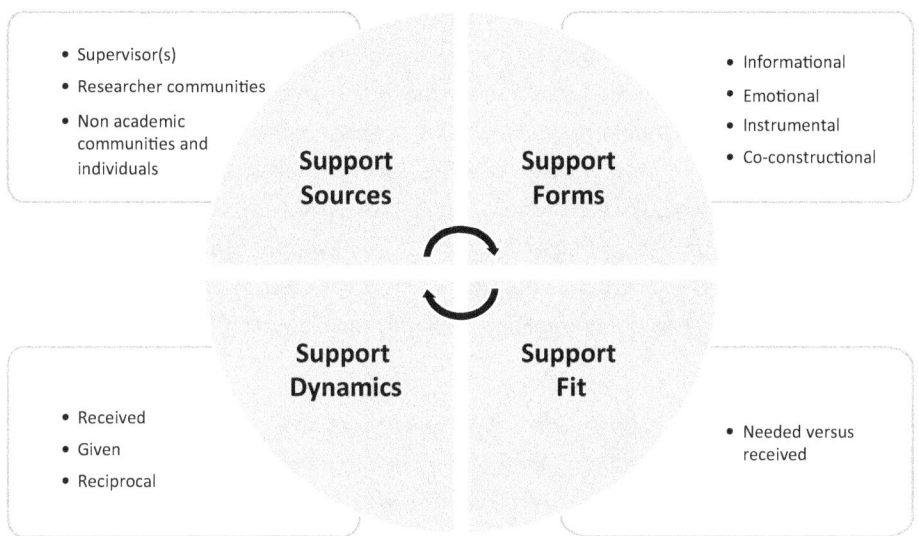

FIGURE 13.1 Anatomy of the Researcher Community and Supervisory Support Model

Firstly, different sources of support should be considered. Prior research implies that distinction, at least between supervisor(s), other researchers, researcher communities and non-academic communities and individuals from these communities can be made. However, an even more finely graded distinction is often useful in trying to understand functions of social support for early career researcher experience and related outcomes. Secondly, the different forms of support need to be regarded. It is proposed here that distinction at least between informational, emotional, instrumental, and co-construction support can be made. Thirdly, the support fit referring to match or mismatch between the support needed and received is a central ingredient in understanding socially embedded early career researcher experience. Fourthly, the support dynamics need to be taken into account, whether the support is received, given or reciprocal. Hence, the proposed Researcher Community and Supervisory Support Model developed to understand the function of social interaction in early career researcher experience comprises four dynamic, complementary and interrelated dimensions: 1) support sources, 2) support forms, 3) support fit, and 4) support dynamics (see Figure 13.1).

IMPACT OF RESEARCHER COMMUNITY AND SUPERVISORY SUPPORT ON DOCTORAL AND POST-PHD EXPERIENCE AND TRAJECTORIES

Previous research has identified both similarities and differences in experienced researcher community and supervisory support and related outcomes between the doctoral students and post-PhD researchers. In general, high quality researcher community and supervisory support has been identified as a key determinant of optimal doctoral and post-PhD researcher experience, and related outcomes such as productivity in terms of number of publications, reduced risk of attrition, employment, increased satisfaction, and resilience while facing challenges (Castello, Pardo, Sala-Bubaré & Suñe 2017; Gardner 2007; Ives & Rowley 2005; Horta 2009; Jackson & Michelson 2015; Puljak & Sharif 2009; Pyhältö, Stubb & Lonka 2009; 2016; Åkerlind 2009; Scaffidi & Berman, 2011; Vekkaila et al 2016). In turn, a lack of such support has been identified as highly problematic (Virtanen et al 2016; Pyhältö et al 2017).

For doctoral students, supervisors and their immediate researcher community, typically comprising research, project or seminar group members, provide the primary source of the support (Pyhältö, et al 2009; 2012). Compared to post-PhD researchers, doctoral students less frequently emphasise the professional communities outside academia, significant others or other sources of support such as social media networks, as central sources of support. Our results have shown that doctoral students emphasised their supervisor(s) and other senior researchers as the primary sources of both informational and instrumental support (Pyhältö et al 2015; Corner, Pyhältö, Peltonen & Bengtsen submitted; Virtanen et al 2016). Though the students less often emphasised instrumental support from the supervisor(s) than informational support, their supervisors recognised the issue to a great extent (Pyhältö, Vekkaila & Keskinen 2012; 2015). Interestingly, supervisory support was also associated with fit between the supervisors' and doctoral students' perceptions of frequency of supervision, main task of the supervisor, and resources and challenges of the doctoral journey (Pyhältö et al 2012; 2015).

Moreover, there is evidence that the researcher community, particularly peers, provides a central source of emotional support for doctoral students (Virtanen et al 2016; see also Hadjioannou, Shelton, Fu & Dhanarattigannon 2007; Maher, Seaton, McMullen, Fitzgerald, Otsuji & Lee 2008; Noonan, Ballinger, & Black 2007). Emotional support from the researcher community, particularly in terms of a sense of belonging, has been found to promote a positive doctoral experience, whereas the lack of such support has been shown to increase the risk of drop-out among them (see Gardner 2010; Pyhältö & Stubb 2012). For instance, those doctoral students who perceived themselves as members of their researcher community and experienced these relationships as empowering suffered less from distress and lack of interest in their studies than their less fortunate counterparts (Pyhältö et al 2009; Stubb, Pyhältö & Lonka 2011). Yet, our results on support dynamics among doctoral students imply that doctoral students more often receive support than give it to others (Pyhältö & Stubb 2012). For instance, we found that they rarely took active initiative in their researcher communities, but once they did, it was associated with experiencing less negative emotions, suffering less lack of interest in their studies and reduced risk for study abandonment.

Overall, experiencing researcher community and supervisory support has been found to be associated also with more engaging post-PhD research experience, whereas a lack of support, and diminishing feedback have been found to be related to reduced engagement in research activities, maladaptive writing perceptions and decreased research productivity (Castello et al 2017; Pyhältö et al 2017; Vekkaila et al 2016). Yet, evidence on the function of supervisory support among post-PhD researchers is less consistent. A number of qualitative studies suggest that supervisory support can have an influence on post-PhD researcher experience (see Chen et al 2015; Scaffidi & Bergman 2011); particularly instrumental support, such as writing recommendations and providing access to institutional resources, including infrastructure or opportunities to gain teaching experience, has been found to have a positive impact (Chen et al 2015; Rybarczyk, Lerea, Lund, Whittington & Dykstra 2011; Åkerlind 2009). However, in some quantitative studies no such association has been found (Jackson & Michelson 2015) or the association is quite small (see, for example, Eby, Allen, Evans, Ng & DuBois 2008). A reason for the less consistent findings in terms of supervisory support and positive post-PhD researcher attributes may be that the effect of the supervisory support may be mediated via expansion of researcher networks rather than directly. While supervisors can be a central resource for enculturation into a new researcher community and introduce newcomers into their own professional networks, as advanced early career researchers, post-PhD researchers also have their own researcher networks that they can utilise as sources of support. Yet, interestingly, reciprocal support, and particularly giving support to others, was rarely reported by post-PhD researchers (Vekkaila et al 2016).

We have also detected individual variation in experienced researcher community and supervisory support among both doctoral students and post-PhD researchers (Peltonen, Vekkaila, Haverinen, Rautio & Pyhältö 2017; Pyhältö et al 2016). Our recent study on Finnish doctoral students (Peltonen et al 2016) showed that the majority of the students had a sufficient researcher community and supervisory support profile whereas the minority of studies employed an insufficient support profile. Those students with an insufficient support profile suffered more from exhaustion and cynicism, were less satisfied with their supervision, and were more likely to consider dropping out than students with sufficient support profiles. The results confirm the findings of previous studies by showing that social support is a central determinant for successful doctoral studies (Ali & Kohun 2007; Gardner 2008; Martinsuo & Turkulainen 2011; Zhao, Golde & McCormick 2007). The results also show that the lack of experienced social support was associated with study abandonment intentions and experienced burnout (Peltonen et al 2016). Consequently, our results extended Jairam and Kahl's (2012) findings on the interrelation between social support and experienced stress during doctoral studies by showing that social support from the supervisor also decreases experienced exhaustion and cynicism, reduces the risk for drop-out, and increases satisfaction with supervision. Accordingly, receiving sufficient support both from the researcher community and from the supervisor(s), combined with reduced levels of reported friction, promoted doctoral studies, and advanced the odds for successful PhD completion.

Similarly, our study on UK and Spanish post-PhD researchers (Pyhältö et al 2016) showed that the majority of the researchers displayed an adequate researcher community and supervisory support profile whereas a minority displayed a reduced support profile. Those post-PhD researchers with an adequate support profile experienced more research engagement and were more satisfied with their post-PhD work. They were less likely to consider career abandonment and suffered less cynicism than their counterparts within the reduced support profile. Results also showed that post-PhD researchers in the social sciences were more likely to fall within the adequate support profile than their counterparts in the natural sciences. This finding is striking since prior studies of doctoral researchers in STEM disciplines suggest they are more satisfied with their supervision and researcher community support, and entertain higher PhD completion rates and shorter completion time than their counterparts in the social sciences or in humanities (Gardner 2009, 2010; Visser et al 2007; Wright & Cochrane 2000). So, perhaps, since post-PhD researchers are often mobile, also internationally (McAlpine et al 2016), they will find themselves in new institutions and not yet with developed local support. The finding also contradicts the common assumption that being a scientist, whether PhD or post-PhD, includes working in a supportive team environment (Cumming 2009). In other words, we cannot assume that being in a group automatically provides support.

Currently, research involving cross-country comparisons on researcher community and supervisory support is almost non-existent. So far we have conducted five cross-cultural comparisons showing that both similarities and differences occur in support experiences and related outcomes across the cultural contexts. Our comparisons on UK and Spanish post-PhD researchers' researcher community and supervisory support experiences showed no differences between the UK and Spanish post-PhDs in experienced support, though Spanish post-PhDs experienced more research engagement than their UK counterparts (Castello *et al* 2017; Pyhältö *et al* 2017). Our most recent comparison on Danish and Finnish humanities and social science doctoral students' support experiences showed that both Danish and Finnish doctoral students emphasised research community support over supervisory support (Corner *et al* submitted). The Danish students, however, reported higher levels of research community support and experienced lower levels of friction than their Finnish colleagues. The results also indicated that the only form of support in which the students expressed more matched than mismatched support was informational support. Further investigation showed that the Danish students reported a higher level of mismatch in emotional support than their Finnish counterparts, whereas the Finnish students perceived lower levels of instrumental support than the Danish students.

SOME IMPLICATIONS FOR FURTHER RESEARCH AND DEVELOPING EARLY CAREER RESEARCHER TRAJECTORIES

This chapter proposed an integrative conceptual model for building more comprehensive understanding of the anatomy and dynamics of researcher community and supervisory interaction. The *Researcher Community and Supervisory Support Model* distinguishes between four complementary elements of the support: 1) support source, 2) support form, 3) support fit, and 4) support dynamics. Each of the elements comprises several dimensions (see Figure 13.1). Based on tentative empirical evidence, the Researcher Community and Supervisory Support Model can provide both a conceptual instrument for building a more comprehensive picture about the socially embedded early career researcher's experience, and an empirical tool for breaking down the complex dynamics of researcher community and supervisory interaction. Even though model development is still at the early stages, and more empirical research is needed to test the model and develop it further, our experimentation in applying the model, both with doctoral students and post-PhD researchers, with difference disciplinary backgrounds and across countries, implies that the model can be used in exploring the complexity of researcher community and supervisory support. The model has been also tested in both qualitative and quantitative studies.

According to my understanding, the proposed model has potentially five core benefits. Firstly, the Researcher Community and Supervisory Support Model is integrative; it involves and combines the core determinants of researcher community and supervisory interaction, identified in the literature, drawing from different theoretical frameworks. Hence, it considers the complexity of such phenomena. Secondly, the model is specific enough to be applied to the elements in empirical designs either focusing on certain elements or combining all of them, depending on the focus of the study. Thirdly, though so far tested only with early career researchers, the model can be utilised in exploring, for instance, tenure track researchers, full professors or even PhD degree holders in non-academic careers, of course with some modifications in sub-dimensions of the support elements. Fourthly, the model is not method or context specific, and can hence be applied with different methods and across countries. Finally, it provides supervisors with a tool for analysing and reflecting on their journeys of supervision. Accordingly, the model can be utilised in facilitating supervisory development, for instance, in supervisory courses.

To test and develop the model, but more importantly to gain a better understanding of socially embedded researcher development and careers, further studies are needed, particularly exploring researcher community and supervisory support as complex composites focusing on interrelations between the sources, forms, fit and support dynamics. Also longitudinal studies looking at the development of various support trajectories and related outcomes of these trajectories, and studies examining support in different (both micro and macro) cultural settings are called for. Moreover, exploring the function of support outside academia and mediated forms of support, such as social media networks, would be highly beneficial for building further understanding.

Finally, in terms of developing more supporting learning and working environments for early career researchers, our studies and the proposed model have some implications. Firstly, our findings strongly indicate that researcher community and supervisory support play a central role in doctoral and post-PhD experience and related outcomes. Hence, support matters. Accordingly, recognising the importance of such support is useful in developing learning and working environments for early career researchers that enable them to flourish. At the same time, it is important to keep in mind that to be effective support needs to be matched to each person's individual needs, that is, one size does not fit all. This calls for dialogue with the doctoral students and post-PhD researchers, combined with systematic identification of the potential sources of support available in the institution, and skilfully using them. Secondly, although it seems that the majority of doctoral students and post-PhD researchers experienced sufficient researcher community and supervisory support, a number of them also suffered from insufficient support. This implies that it would be beneficial, from both the individual and the institutional point of view, to identify early career researchers at risk as early as possible, to be able to respond to their support needs, hence to avoid negative consequences resulting from insufficient support. Moreover, early career researchers can be assisted in learning sufficient support strategies, for instance, by creating opportunities for networking and researcher collaboration such as co-authoring and consortium building. They can also learn strategies for asking and providing support for each other, and learn how to cope and solve conflicts more independently within their communities, if encouraged and given the required opportunities and models. It seems that particularly arenas to learn when and how to provide and ask for reciprocal support are needed.

REFERENCES

Åkerlind G. 2009. Postdoctoral research positions as preparation for an academic career. *International Journal of Research*, 1(1):84-97. https://doi.org/10.1108/1759751X201100006

Ali A & Kohun F. 2007. Dealing with social isolation to minimize doctoral drop-out – A four stage framework. *International Journal of Doctoral Studies*, 2:33-49. https://doi.org/10.28945/56

Brailsford I. 2010. Motives and aspirations for doctoral study: Career, personal, and interpersonal factors in the decision to embark on history PhD. *International Journal of Doctoral Studies*, 5:15-27. https://doi.org/10.28945/710

Castello M, McAlpine L & Pyhältö K. 2017. Spanish and UK post-PhD researchers: Writing perceptions, well-being and productivity. *Higher Education Research and Development*, 36(6):1108-1122. https://doi.org/10.1080/07294360.2017.1296412

Castello M, Pardo M, Sala-Bubaré A & Suñe N. 2017. Why do students consider to drop out of doctoral degrees? Institutional and personal factors. *Higher Education*, 74(6):1-16. https://doi.org/10.1007/s10734-016-0106-9

Chen S, McAlpine L & Amundsen C. 2015. Postdoctoral positions as preparation for desired careers: A narrative approach to understanding postdoctoral experience. *Higher Education Research & Development*, 34(6):1083-1096. https://doi.org/10.1080/07294360.2015.1024633

Cobb S. 1976. Social support as a moderator of life stress. *Psychosomatic Medicine*, 38(5):300-314. https://doi.org/10.1097/00006842-197609000-00003

Cohen S & McKay TA. 1984. Stress, social support, and the buffering hypothesis: A theoretical analysis. In: A Baum, SE Taylor & JE Singer (eds). *Handbook of psychology and health*. Hillsdale: Lawrence Erlbaum. 253-267.

Cohen S & Syme L. 1985. Issues in the study and application of social support. In S Cohen & L Syme (eds). *Social support and health*. San Francisco: Academic Press. 3-22.

Cornér S, Pyhältö K, Peltonen J & Bengtsen S. 2018. Similar or different? Research community and Supervisory support experiences among Danish and Finnish Social Sciences and Humanities PhD students. (Submitted).

Cumming J. 2009. The doctoral experience in science: Challenging the current orthodoxy. *British Educational Research Journal*, 35:877-890. https://doi.org/10.1080/01411920902834191

Delamont S & Atkinson P. 2001. Doctoring uncertainty: Mastering craft knowledge. *Social Studies of Science*, 31(1):87-107.https://doi.org/10.1177/030631201031001005

Durette B, Fournier M, & Lafon M. 2016. The core competencies of PhDs. *Studies in Higher Education*, 41(8):1355-1370. https://doi.org/10.1080/03075079.2014.968540

Eby L, Allen T, Evans S, Ng T & DuBois D. 2008. Does mentoring matter? A multidisciplinary meta-analysis comparing mentored and non-mentored individuals. *Journal of Vocational Behavior*, 72(2):254-267. https://doi.org/10.1016/j.jvb.2007.04.005

Gardner S. 2007. "I heard it through the grapevine": Doctoral student socialization in chemistry and history. *Higher Education*, 54(5):723-740. https://doi.org/10.1007/s10734-006-9020-x

Gardner S. 2008. Fitting the mold of graduate school: A qualitative study of socialization in doctoral education. *Innovations in Higher Education*, 33(1):125-138. https://doi.org/10.1007/s10755-008-9068-x

Gardner S. 2009. Student and faculty attributions of attrition in high and low completing doctoral programs in the United States. *Higher Education*, 58(1):97-112. https://doi.org/10.1007/s10734-008-9184-7

Gardner S. 2010. Contrasting the socialization experiences of doctoral students in high- and low- completing departments: A qualitative analysis of disciplinary contexts at one institution. *Journal of Higher Education*, 81(1):61-81. https://doi.org/10.1080/00221546.2010.11778970

Hadjioannou X, Shelton NR, Fu D & Dhanarattigannon J. 2007. The road to a doctoral degree: Co-travelers through a perilous passage. *College Student Journal*, 41(1):160-177.

Helgeson V & Gottlieb B. 2000. Social support measurement and intervention: A guide for health and social scientists. In: S Cohen, L Underwood & B Gottlieb. *Support groups*. New York: Oxford University Press. 221-245.

Holland J. 1985. *Making vocational choices: A theory of vocational personalities and work environments*. 2nd Edition. Englewood Cliffs NJ: Prentice-Hall.

Horta H. 2009. Holding a post-doctoral position before becoming a faculty member: Does it bring benefits for the scholarly enterprise? *Higher Education*, 58(5):689-721. https://doi.org/10.1007/s10734-009-9221-1

House J. 1981. *Work stress and social support*. London: Addison-Wesley Educational Publishers Inc.

Ives G & Rowley G. 2005. Supervisor selection or allocation and continuity of supervision: PhD students' progress and outcomes. *Studies in Higher Education*, 30(5):535-555. https://doi.org/10.1080/03075070500249161

Jackson D & Michelson G. 2015. Factors influencing the employment of Australian PhD graduates. *Studies in Higher Education*, 40(9):1660-1678. https://doi.org/10.1080/03075079.2014.899344

Jairam D & Kahl Jr DH. 2012. Navigating the doctoral experience: The role of social support in successful degree completion. *International Journal of Doctoral Studies*, 7:311-329.

Maher D, Seaton L, McMullen C, Fitzgerald T, Otsuji E & Lee A. 2008. Becoming and being writers: The experiences of doctoral students in writing groups. *Studies in Continuing Education*, 30(3):263-275. https://doi.org/10.1080/01580370802439870

Martinsuo M & Turkulainen V. 2011. Personal commitment, support and progress in doctoral studies. *Studies in Higher Education*, 36(1):103-120. https://doi.org/10.1080/03075070903469598

McAlpine L & Amundsen C. 2015. Early Career Researcher Challenges: Substantive and Methods-Based Insights. *Studies in Continuing Education*, 37(1): 1-17. https://doi.org/10.1080/0158037X.2014.967344

McAlpine L & Amundsen C. 2016. *Post-PhD career trajectories: Intentions, decision-making and life aspirations*. Basingstoke: Palgrave Pivot.

McAlpine L, Turner G, Saunders S & Wilson N. 2016. Becoming a PI: Agency, persistence, and some luck! *International Journal for Researcher Development*, 7(2):106-122.

Meyer JHF, Shanahan MP & Laugksch RC. 2005. Students' conceptions of research. I: A qualitative and quantitative analysis. *Scandinavian Journal of Educational Research*, 49(3):225-244. https://doi.org/10.1080/00313830500109535

Noonan MJ, Ballinger R & Black R. 2007. Peer and faculty mentoring in doctoral education: Definitions, experiences, and expectations. *International Journal of Teaching and Learning in Higher Education*, 19(3):251-262.

Peltonen J, Veikkaila J, Haverinen K, Rautio P & Pyhältö K. 2017. Interrelations between supervisory researcher community support experiences and risk factors among doctoral students. *International Journal of Doctoral Studies, 12(1): 157-173*. ijds.org/Volume12/IJDSv12p157-173Peltonen3241.pdf

Puljak L & Sharif W. 2009. Postdocs' perceptions of work environment and career prospects at a US academic institution. *Research Evaluation*, 18(5):411-415. https://doi.org/10.3152/095820209X483064

Pyhältö K & Keskinen J. 2012. Doctoral students' sense of relational agency in their scholarly communities. *International Journal of Higher Education*, 1(2):136-149. https://doi.org/10.5430/ijhe.v1n2p136

Pyhältö K, McAlpine L, Peltonen J & Castello M. 2017. How does social support contribute to engaging post-PhD experience? *European Journal of Higher Education*, 7(4):1-15. https://doi.org/10.1080/21568235.2017.1348239

Pyhältö KM, Peltonen J, Rautio P, Haverinen K, Laatikainen M & Veikkaila JE. 2016. *Summary report on doctoral experience in UniOGS graduate school at the University of Oulu*. Acta Universitatis Ouluensis

Pyhältö K, Stubb J & Lonka K. 2009. Developing scholarly communities as learning environments for doctoral students. *International Journal for Academic Development*, 14(3):221-232. https://doi.org/10.1080/13601440903106551

Pyhältö K, Vekkaila J & Keskinen J. 2012. Exploring the fit between doctoral students' and supervisors' perceptions of resources and challenges vis-à-vis the doctoral journey. *International Journal of Doctoral Studies*, 7:395-414. https://doi.org/10.28945/1745

Pyhältö K, Vekkaila J & Keskinen J. 2015. Fit matters in the supervisory relationship: Doctoral students' and supervisors' perceptions of supervisory activities. *Innovations in Education and Teaching International*, 52(1):4-16. https://doi.org/10.1080/14703297.2014.981836

Rybarczyk B, Lerea L, Lund PK, Whittington D & Dykstra L. 2011. Postdoctoral training aligned with the academic professoriate. *Professional Biologist*, 61(9):699-705. https://doi.org/10.1525/bio.2011.61.9.8

Scaffidi AK & Berman JE. 2011. A positive postdoctoral experience is related to quality supervision and career mentoring, collaborations, networking and a nurturing research environment. *Higher Education*, 62:685-698. https://doi.org/10.1007/s10734-011-9407-1

Sfard A. 1998. On two metaphors for learning and the dangers of choosing just one. *Educational Researcher*, 27(2):4-13. https://doi.org/10.3102/0013189X027002004

Stubb J, Pyhältö K & Lonka K. 2011. Balancing between inspiration and exhaustion: PhD students' experienced socio-psychological well-being. *Studies in Continuing Education*, 33(1):33-50. https://doi.org/10.1080/0158037X.2010.515572

Väisänen S, Pietarinen J, Pyhältö K, Toom A & Soini T. 2016. Social support as a contributor to student teachers' experienced well-being. *Research Papers in Education*, 32(1):1-15. https://doi.org/10.1080/02671522.2015.1129643

Vekkaila J, Virtanen V, Taina J & Pyhältö K. 2016. The function of social support in engaging and disengaging experiences among post PhD researchers in STEM disciplines. *Studies in Higher Education*, 5:222-235. https://doi.org/10.5430/ijhe.v5n2p222

Virtanen V, Taina J & Pyhältö K. 2016. What disengages doctoral students in the biological and environmental sciences from their doctoral studies? *Studies in Continuing Education*, 39(1):1-16. https://doi.org/10.1080/0158037X.2016.1250737

Visser SM, Luwel M & Moed FH. 2007. The Attainment of doctoral degrees at Flemish universities: A survival analysis. *Higher Education*, 54(5):741-757. https://doi.org/10.1007/s10734-006-9021-9

Wright T & Cochrane R. 2000. Factors influencing successful submission of PhD theses. *Studies in Higher Education*, 25(2):181-195. https://doi.org/10.1080/713696139

Zhao C-M, Golde CM & McCormick AC. 2007. More than a signature: How advisor choice and advisor behavior affect doctoral student satisfaction. *Journal of Further and Higher Education*, 31(3):263-281. https://doi.org/10.1080/03098770701424983

"I HAVE LEARNT BUT AM STILL DEVELOPING": MASTER'S STUDENTS' EVOLVING CONCEPTS OF RESEARCH

Peter Rule & Jaqueline Naidoo

INTRODUCTION

Over the last decade there has been a shift in emphasis on research in social science postgraduate qualifications (Kawulich, Garner & Wagner 2009). In South Africa this shift has been from research as an independent, stand-alone study supervised by an individual supervisor, to a range of structured and supported research programmes, including research modules, cohort programmes (Motshoane 2016; Samuel & Vithal 2011), group research projects (Grant 2014) and collective supervision (Rule & Land 2017), which are meant to complement the supervisor – student relationship. This has not only resulted in a shift in the teaching of postgraduate research, but also in how postgraduate students are supervised. The importance of understanding research is a key concern of postgraduate studies in higher education institutions (NDP, National Qualifications Framework Act 67 of 2008). Internationally, there is a move to increase enrolment targets of postgraduate students, in particular, doctoral students. This trend is evident in South Africa as well and is highlighted in the National Development Plan which outlines a drastic increase in enrolment targets for postgraduate enrolments at South African higher education institutions.

However, although there have been changes in how postgraduate supervision is prioritised and organised, few studies have explored conceptions of research of postgraduate students, and particularly how these conceptions change over the course of a qualification (Pitcher 2011; Kawulich *et al* 2009; Meyer *et al* 2007; McCormack 2004). Such conceptions, and the nature of their evolution, are crucial to the quality of students' research journeys. Thus, the study on which this chapter draws was aimed at addressing the dearth of research on students' conceptions of research at a master's level and in a South African context. The focus was particularly on how students' conceptions of research change during a course of study.

LITERATURE REVIEW

An initial study by Brew (2001) examined conceptions of research methodology, focusing on experienced researchers' notions of qualitative research. McCormack expanded this study and explored the disparity between institutional assumptions and postgraduates' experiences. Meyer *et al* (2007) undertook a longitudinal study on postgraduate students' and supervisors' contrasting conceptions of research, which draws attention to qualitative dimensions of variance. In addition, Pitcher (2011) conducted a metaphor analysis of doctoral students' conceptions of research. Kawulich *et al* (2009) highlight the implications of knowledge of students' conceptions of social research for pedagogy.

One conceptual array that has particular relevance to students' conceptions of research is that of 'threshold concepts'. These are powerful concepts or conceptual portals which, once grasped, can transform the way in which a student understands and interprets a subject. Meyer and Land (2006), drawing on Turner's notion of liminality, introduce the notion of threshold concepts and suggest that learners undergo some form of transformation before crossing the threshold of understanding.

According to Meyer and Land (2006:7-8), threshold concepts have five features:

- *transformative*, where the students' views of what they learned, and sometimes students themselves, are transformed;
- *integrative*, in that students possibly make sense of different aspects of learning, the 'Oh, that's what it all means' moment when 'it' makes sense;
- *irreversible*, as once concepts are understood it is probable that they cannot be 'ununderstood';
- *bounded*, in that each concept does not explain the 'whole' of the discipline but specific and related aspects of that whole; and
- *troublesome*, that is challenging, difficult to come to terms with, even counter-intuitive.

This view of threshold concepts accords with Barnacle's (2005) understanding of knowledge in the process of 'doctoral becoming': that it is ephemeral, difficult and partial, but also potentially transformative of the researcher.

CHAPTER 14 • "I HAVE LEARNT BUT AM STILL DEVELOPING": MASTER'S STUDENTS' EVOLVING CONCEPTS OF RESEARCH

Kiley (2009) adopts the notion of threshold concepts as an analytical framework for understand the learning and development of doctoral students. She argues that threshold concepts are crucial to examining how doctoral students learn and represent critical concepts for a student's advanced understanding of a discipline and in her particular study, to be a researcher. She draws attention to the significance of a research culture as well as belonging to a "scholarly community for research learning" (Kiley 2009:294). She further asserts that understanding threshold concepts could assist students in crossing such thresholds and enhance their doctoral learning experience, lower attrition rates and improve completion times.

Furthermore, Kiley and Wisker (2009) examine research learning and teaching of doctoral students. They contend that

> a threshold concept is seen as something distinct within what would typically be described as 'core concepts'; that is, more than a building block. A threshold concept is one that, once grasped, leads to a qualitatively different view of the subject matter and/or learning experience and of oneself as a learner (Kiley & Wisker 2009:432).

Their findings present six possible generic research threshold concepts, which evidence themselves in the quality and level of the students' work at different stages in that work: argument, theorising, framework, knowledge creation, analysis and interpretation, and paradigm (Kiley & Wisker 2009:431). These generic research concepts were of particular interest in this study, which looked at students conceptions of research.

BACKGROUND TO THE STUDY

This study was conducted with postgraduate students enrolled on the Master of Education programme studying the core module Research Discourses and Methodology. This module is aimed at developing a critical understanding of and proficiency in the language and practice of educational research. A further aim is to develop students' understanding of a range of research designs, methodologies, and methods of data production with a view to making appropriate selection decisions of research design from an argumentative perspective. Additionally, it provides opportunities to participate in educational research discourse and debate. It is anticipated that students will achieve the following learning outcomes:

- Define and distinguish educational research from other forms of activities and writings.

- Recognise the characteristics of research paradigms or traditions (for example, positivist, interpretive, critical and post-structural paradigms) and key concepts in educational research methodologies.
- Discuss the research, theory, policy, practice and knowledge production community relationships.
- Understand the philosophical underpinnings of different research designs, data generation techniques, analysis and interpretation.
- Read and critique educational research texts.

RESEARCH METHODOLOGY

The main purpose of this study was to explore master's students' developing conceptions of research as a result of studying the core module Research Discourses and Methodology. This study was located within the interpretive paradigm since it set out to understand and make meaning of master's students' conceptions of research. It adopted a qualitative approach to study participants in their natural settings and generated textual data or narratives. The research design was a longitudinal case study that examined master's students' conceptions of research at the beginning and end of a semester.

According to Yin (2003), case study is an approach that is used to examine an event or incident in its context and it may comprise many variables of interest thus requiring multiple sources of evidence. Creswell (2002:61) contends that "[a] case study is a problem to be studied, which will reveal an in-depth understanding of a 'case' or bounded system, which involves understanding an event, activity, process, or one or more individuals". Creswell's definition appears to call for the researcher to start with a dilemma that will invoke layers of understanding about the system in which the problem resides. The system becomes the case, and the researcher chooses an event, activity, or process within this system to illuminate it. Merriam (2009:81) describes a case as "a single unit, a bounded system" and suggests that a case may refer to an event or activity or a group of individuals bounded in time and place. Van Wynsberghe and Khan (2007:80) maintain that a "case study is a trans-paradigmatic and transdisciplinary heuristic that involves the careful delineation of the phenomena for which evidence is being collected (event, concept, program, process, etc)". Furthermore, they contend that the constraint of the unit of analysis is accomplished by "(a) providing detailed descriptions obtained from immersion in the context of the case, (b) bounding the case temporally and spatially, and (c) frequent engagement between the case itself and the unit of analysis" (Van Wynsberghe & Khan 2007:90)

CHAPTER 14 • "I HAVE LEARNT BUT AM STILL DEVELOPING": MASTER'S STUDENTS' EVOLVING CONCEPTS OF RESEARCH

The aim of this study was to explore MEd students' conceptions of research at the beginning and end of a semester. Here the case was the cohort of Master of Education students who completed the module and the focus of the case was their conceptions of research. Given that this study examined the same individuals or sample over time, namely at the beginning and at the end of the semester, this research could be described as a longitudinal or diachronic case study (Thomas 2011). In such a study, data are captured at two or more points and the researcher is interested in the changes that occur at these two or more data collection points. Data were collected from the population of 34 master's students enrolled for the course. An open-ended questionnaire was used to collect data. Students were required to elaborate on their understanding of the term 'research' and describe themselves as a researcher. We acknowledge that a limitation of this longitudinal case study is that it employed one method of data collection (albeit at two moments), namely open-ended questionnaires, and did not employ multiple methods. This student questionnaire comprised the following research questions:

1. What is your understanding of the term 'research'?
2. How would you describe yourself as a researcher? What kind of researcher are you?
3. How has your conception of 'research' developed as a result of studying this module?

This study adopted a thematic content analysis approach to interpret and make sense of the data and comprised three levels of analysis:

- Within cohort analysis at two moments in time – at beginning and end of module
- Across cohort analysis – difference in trends at beginning and end of module – comparison
- Individual analysis – focused on individual responses – to what extent these exemplify general trends

RESULTS

A comparison of students' definitions of 'research' at the beginning and at the end of the course showed significant shifts. Below we present a sample to indicate some of the typical patterns of change.

SECTION B • SUPERVISORY JOURNEYS

Into the discourse of research

The first shift concerns students' tentative movement into the 'discourse' of research, often from a lay orientation derived from everyday life and/or a practitioner orientation from their studies and practice in education. In Table 14.1 two students' initial and final responses to the question 'What is research?' are presented (our emphases in bold).

TABLE 14.1 Students' responses to the question 'What is research?'

Research is an **investigation** of trying to find how and what happens in the real world. It is also about exploring **how people make sense of the world** they live in. Research is a **step by step approach** where the researcher tries to answer certain questions.	Research is a **scientific enquiry** where the researcher tries to find out the experiences and the lives of people in the **real life context**. Each research study is **underpinned by a particular paradigm**. (Simon)
Research is a **systematic way of finding facts** about something … you come to a … **conclusion,** you engage yourself in activities which will describe the **methods** you are going to use.	Research is a **systematic way** of **collecting data**. It can be **qualitative, quantitative or mixed method** approach. Its purpose is to get … an **in-depth understanding** of the problem. It has a **scientific** way of engaging in it. (Lihle)

Here Simon moves from describing research as an "investigation" to a "scientific enquiry". This locates research within the broader parameters of science, with its connotations of rigour, method, scholarship and systematic analysis. He also shifts in his understanding of the purpose of research from "trying to find out how and what happens in the real world" to "trying to find out the experiences and the lives of people in the real world context". The term 'context' implies a more complex understanding of the research situation. Interestingly, Simon brings in the notion of 'paradigm', one of the 'threshold concepts', in his second definition. His use of terms such as "scientific enquiry", "context" and "paradigm" indicate a shift from a lay or common-sense understanding of research towards a more specialised discourse as he begins to make these terms his own.

Lihle's responses are fascinating in the way that they indicate her movement into discourse of educational research. Her first sentences begin identically: "Research is a systematic way of…" Here she suggests, perhaps from her exposure to research in her honours course, an understanding of research as both rigorous ("systematic") and method-based ("way of"). Then she replaces the phrase "finding facts about something" (in the initial response) with "collecting data" (in the final response). While these phrases might be considered semantically equivalent, they indicate through the use of research-oriented vocabulary a discursive shift from lay ("finding facts") to more specialised discourse ("collecting data"). While her initial response shows some confusion or lack of clarity about the relation between "activities" and "methods", her second response shows a stronger grasp of the range of possible approaches. She is not yet at the stage where she can differentiate among the nuances of terms such as "qualitative" (arguably describing kinds of data and their analysis rather than the more nebulous "approach"), but she is able to indicate a purpose of research, which was missing from her first definition.

On the threshold of 'paradigm'

The students' responses also show the 'discovery' and appropriation of the concept 'paradigm' which Kiley and Wisker (2009) identify as one of the 'threshold concepts' in research. While it is missing from their initial responses, the concept appears, implicitly or explicitly, in their later responses (see Table 14.2).

TABLE 14.2 Students' evolving conceptions of 'approach' and 'paradigm'

I am probably more comfortable with **quantitative methods**.	I tend to favour a **post-positivist approach** … however, I also appreciate an **interpretivist approach** since this could be used to explain certain behaviours and dilemmas. (Jane)
I am an **action researcher** … trying to find solutions to **improve my practice**.	I see myself as a researcher who **is changing things or transformation**. I fall under the **critical paradigm**. I want to **improve my practice**. (Phindi)

Here Jane shifts from describing her preferences in term of "methods" to beginning to locate herself paradigmatically, although she calls post-positivism and interpretivism "approaches" rather than paradigms. She also indicates that the paradigmatic choice might depend on the research purpose, for example "to explain certain behaviours". This indicates the beginning of a move to create coherence by aligning paradigms with research focus ("certain behaviours") and research purpose ("to explain") rather than seeing these elements as discrete and unrelated.

Phindi retains the motivation for her research as improving her practice but is also now able to link this emphasis to "transformation" and "the critical paradigm". Here she is similar to Jane in positioning *herself* through the use of first person pronouns ("*I* want to", "*my* practice") within the discourse and beginning to stake out discursive territory.

ON THE PATH TO COHERENCE

One of the key shifts evident in the students' second set of responses was in developing coherence in relating paradigm and research methodology. Simon indicates this by linking "experiences", "interpretive paradigm" and "qualitative":

> I am interested in knowing more about peoples' experiences ... I am located within the **interpretive paradigm** ... adopts a **qualitative approach**. (Simon)

Carol shows that she grasps interpretivism as concerned with understanding, and that a "mixed methods approach" might fit with this:

> **Interpretivist** ... try to interpret and understand ... the **mixed methods approach** would be more suitable. (Carol)

Mary shows that the course has enhanced her awareness of creating coherence within a research design:

- I am more aware of the **different approaches** ... how these are **linked to paradigms**. (Mary)

Again, these responses show students beginning to develop a coherent approach to design in their attempts to link research approaches and paradigms. They do not include mention of methods of data collection and analysis that align with the research paradigm, questions and approach, which would be required in the research proposal, but they do indicate steps towards an appropriately linked-up understanding.

Shifting notions of 'truth'

Another interesting shift was in students' notions of truth. A number of responses indicated a transition from naïve realism (truth as 'facts representing reality') to more nuanced and multi-perspectival understanding which showed awareness of the researcher's agentive and constructivist roles (see Table 14.3).

TABLE 14.3 Students' evolving conceptions of 'truth'

Research is...undertaken to **find new facts** ... always concerned about **truth** ... discovering new knowledge to **find out what is true**.	I now understand research as **dynamic** ... there are **different perspectives of reality**. (Bheki)
... use approved methods to **find the truth or important facts**.	I believe that **reality is socially constructed** and that **subjective meaning** is important. (Simon)

Here the students' implicit shift from 'truth as facts' to 'truth as multi-perspectival and constructed' suggests that 'truth' is also a threshold concept in educational research since notions such as 'knowledge', 'analysis', 'interpretation' and 'findings' are pivotally informed by it. This resonates with Meyer, Shanahan and Laugksch's (2007) study which found that 'discovering the truth' was one of five dimensions of variation in the research conceptions of doctoral students.

Becoming a researcher

The students also conveyed shifts in notions of 'being a researcher' (Barnacle 2005). The two examples in Table 14.4 below indicate a movement from a more practical understanding of research as 'doing' to one which includes research as thinking and positioning oneself:

TABLE 14.4 Students' evolving conceptions of being a researcher

I am a researcher that **investigates social issues** that affects people's lives.	I am a researcher that is influenced and **attracted towards the Interpretivist and Critical paradigms** ... encourages me to **challenge those in power** ... bringing about **change**. (Thanda)
I would describe myself as an **action researcher** ... I like my research to be **hands-on and usable** ... like to **experiment practically**.	I am a **qualitative researcher** ... **find meaning** and purpose ... **think critically** ... make **change** where necessary. (Mary)

Mary's initial stance here is similar to that of many students who have a strong practitioner identity related to 'being an educator'. She sees her research as extending this practitioner identity: being "hands-on", "usable", "experimenting practically". As mid-career educators returning to study, students have developed strong practitioner orientations informed by the communities of educational practice of which they are a part. They bring this practice orientation to their initial understandings of research, often with some diffidence about, or even suspicion of, 'theory'. Mary's second response shows a shift from "action researcher" to "qualitative researcher" which she links to making meaning and purpose. However, she retains the action researcher's emphasis on criticality and change. This perhaps indicates an 'in-between-ness' in her positioning as she explores her research identity and what it might become.

MID-CONCEPTIONS

We introduce the notion of 'mid-conceptions' to capture the shifts in students' research conceptions in the process of becoming researchers. These mid-conceptions show development from their initial conceptions but are not yet as developed as they would be on students' completion of their theses. Students show an awareness in their responses that their conceptions are still in process:

> I have learnt **but I am still developing** ... (Sam)

> Most of the discourse ... in research was not clear before doing this module but now there is ... understanding of such concepts **although I need to read more about them.** (Lungi)

> ... exposed to different paradigms of which I am still confused ... **I still have to grasp them.** (Cedric)

> I fully understand research ... **although I need to go back to my notes** and get more about validity, trustworthiness and credibility. (Dora)

In these responses, the disjunctions ("although", "but") indicate liminal space in which students are negotiating thresholds of key concepts such as "discourse" (Sam), "paradigm" (Cedric) and "research" and its associated concepts (Dora). This resonates with Clarence's (2016:135) experiences as a doctoral student of the research journey as "a series of thresholds you can cross", which involves recognising oneself as a "becoming-researcher ... pushing you through your own liminal spaces and across uncertain thresholds".

The notion of mid-conceptions recognises the importance of the process of students 'becoming' researchers: on the way but not there yet. This process may involve struggle, confusion, a questioning of prior assumptions, sudden insights as well as feelings of inadequacy. Mid-conceptions suggest that you cannot get 'across' the liminal space of learning without generating 'midway' ideas – they are not 'wrong' but part of the apparatus of crossing over, such as ladders, bridges and boats which are essential for the journey but may not be useful once you have reached the other side.

SOME IMPLICATIONS OF MID-CONCEPTIONS FOR SUPERVISION

The main argument of this chapter is that the process master's students' developing conceptions and mid-conceptions of research is ongoing and evolving. As such, they have implications for the teaching and supervision of postgraduate students. Here we explore five of these implications.

One implication of 'mid-conceptions' is the importance of the supervisor recognising the process of transition among postgraduate education students (and possibly postgraduate students in other professions) from a practice orientation to a research orientation. This process could involve some necessary 'mid-conceptions' which allow students to link their practice and theory orientations. Supervisors should challenge students to examine their practitioner-oriented assumptions about research but also support them in exploring other conceptions.

A related implication concerns 'threshold concepts' within educational research and providing students with opportunities to negotiate these. Students' mid-conceptions could be around these pivotal concepts, for example 'paradigm', 'approach', 'method', 'evidence', 'truth' – as our data suggest. Students should be given the opportunity to explore these concepts, reflect on their own assumptions about them and begin to appropriate them with their own 'becoming-researcher' voices. Our research suggests that their understandings of these concepts will change at different stages of the research journey, and that this is part of their development as researchers. It might not be useful for supervisors to impose conceptions of research on students without their having an opportunity to reflect on their own assumptions about and experiences of research.

A third implication is affective in import. Mid-conceptions involve uncertainty and possible confusion, which is uncomfortable for students, but our data indicate that these mid-conceptions are a necessary part of their learning. The supervisor needs to take into account the affective side of transitioning towards more mature conceptions: anxiety, confusion, excitement, frustration, sense of failure. Being aware of this dimension might enable supervisors to employ a pedagogy of care (Noddings 1984; Zembylas 2010) which acknowledges the students' feelings and the power of these feelings in shaping their learning, and to avoid dismissing or belittling affective factors in the research journey.

A fifth implication concerns identity. Research is not just an 'objective' technical exercise but also about people, their identity formation and ontological becoming (Barnacle 2005). For students, the research journey might involve changes in identity ("I am an action researcher", "I am a qualitative researcher") as students take up and explore personal positions within research discourse. These changes might be transformative – many postgraduate students have acknowledged the transformational aspects of their research journeys (Clarence 2016; Motshoane 2016). Illeris (2014) argues that transformative learning involves not only cognitive changes in 'meaning perspectives' but also changes in elements of identity, which have not only cognitive but also social and emotional dimensions. Supervisors should recognise the identity dynamics of the research journey and give students the opportunity to articulate and explore these.

CONCLUSION

Based on master's students' responses to questions about the nature of research and their identities as researchers at the beginning and end of a research methodology module, this chapter has argued for the importance of students' 'mid-conceptions' of research. These mid-conceptions are students' ideas about research that have developed from their initial conceptions but are still evolving in their journeys as 'becoming-researchers'. They often concern threshold concepts in educational research such as 'paradigm', 'method', 'approach', 'evidence' and 'truth'. Recognising and valuing students' mid-conceptions of research can help supervisors to contribute to students' learning and identities in the research journey.

REFERENCES

Barnacle R. 2005. Research education ontologies: Exploring doctoral becoming. *Higher Education Research & Development*, 24(2):179-188. https://doi.org/10.1080/07294360500062995

Brew A. 2001. Conceptions of research: A phenomenographic study. *Studies in Higher Education*, 26:271-285. https://doi.org/10.1080/03075070120076255

Clarence S. 2016. Seeing yourself in a new light: Crossing thresholds in becoming a researcher. In: L Frick, P Motshoane, C McMaster & C Murphy (eds). *Postgraduate study in South Africa: Surviving and succeeding*. Stellenbosch: AFRICAN SUN MeDIA. 127-136.

Creswell J. 2002. *Research design: Qualitative, quantitative and mixed method approaches*. London: SAGE.

Grant C. 2014. Postgraduate research learning communities and their contribution to the field of educational leadership and management. *International Studies in Educational Administration*, 42(1):89-100.

Illeris K. 2014. Transformative learning re-defined: As changes in elements of the identity. *International Journal of Lifelong Education*, 33(5):573-586. https://doi.org/10.1080/02601370.2014.917128

Kawulich B, Garner M & Wagner C. 2009. Students' conceptions – and misconceptions – of social research. *Qualitative Sociology Review*, 3:5-25.

Kiley M. 2009. Identifying threshold concepts and proposing strategies to support doctoral candidates. *Innovations in Education and Teaching International*, 46(3):293-304. https://doi.org/10.1080/14703290903069001

Kiley M & Wisker G. 2009. Threshold concepts in research education and evidence of threshold crossing. *Higher Education Research & Development*, 28(4):431-441. https://doi.org/10.1080/07294360903067930

McCormack C. 2004. Tensions between student and institutional conceptions of postgraduate research. *Studies in Higher Education*, 29(3):1-17. https://doi.org/10.1080/03075070410001682600

Merriam SB. 2009. *Qualitative research: A guide to design and implementation*. San Francisco: Jossey Bass.

Meyer J & Land R. (eds). 2006. *Overcoming barriers to student understanding: Threshold concepts and troublesome knowledge.* Abingdon: Routledge.

Meyer J, Shanahan M & Laugksch R. 2007. Students' conceptions of research 2: An exploration of contrasting patterns of variation. *Scandinavian Journal of Educational Research,* 51(4):415-433. https://doi.org/10.1080/00313830701485627

Motshoane P. 2016. The benefits of being part of a project team: A postgraduate student perspective. In: L Frick, P Motshoane, C McMaster & C Murphy (eds). *Postgraduate study in South Africa.* Stellenbosch: AFRICAN SUN MeDIA. 183-190.

Noddings N. 1984. *Caring, a feminine approach to ethics & moral education.* Berkeley: University of California Press.

Pitcher R. 2011. Doctoral students' conceptions of research. *The Qualitative Report,* 16(4):971-983.

Rule P & Land S. 2017. Finding the plot in South African reading education. *Reading & Writing,* 8(1), a121. https://doi.org/10.4102/ rw.v8i1.121

Samuel M & Vithal R. 2011. Emergent frameworks of research teaching and learning in a cohort-based doctoral programme. *Perspectives in Education,* 29(3):76-87.

Thomas G. 2011. A typology for the case study in Social Science following a review of definition, discourse, and structure. *Qualitative Inquiry,* 17(6):511-521. https://doi.org/10.1177/1077800411409884

Van Wynsberghe R & Khan S. 2007. Redefining case study. *International Journal of Qualitative Methods,* 6(2):80-94. https://doi.org/10.1177/160940690700600208

Yin RK. 2003. *Case study research: Design and methods.* Thousand Oaks: SAGE.

Zembylas M. 2010. The ethic of care in globalized societies: Implications for citizenship education. *Ethics and Education,* 5(3):233-245. https://doi.org/10.1080/17449642.2010.516636

EMPLOYABILITY AND GRADUATE ATTRIBUTES OF DOCTORAL GRADUATES

Rachel Spronken-Smith, Kim Brown & Romain Mirosa

INTRODUCTION

> Although there is now a plethora of development programmes and research studies on what are generally called 'transferable skills', they are almost entirely at undergraduate level.
>
> (Cryer 1998:207)

One would hope that nearly 20 years on since Cryer's (1998) article we would now have a good understanding of transferable skills development in postgraduate students. However, in the intervening years the focus of research on graduate outcomes has remained firmly focused on undergraduate programmes, with a continuing paucity of studies on PhD graduates. The lack of knowledge is not just limited to the graduate attributes of PhD graduates, but also to their employment pathways after graduation. The sparse research that has been conducted, which is discussed below, is mainly from Europe, North America and Australia; little has been conducted in New Zealand. Therefore, in this chapter we discuss a study that was aimed at ascertaining initial employment destinations for New Zealand PhD graduates as part of their study and career journeys and soon after completing their PhD. We also indicate how their doctoral study helped prepared them for these jobs.

EMPLOYMENT PATHWAYS FOR DOCTORAL GRADUATES

Historically, the doctorate was used to prepare graduates for academia. However, studies in the last decade have revealed a declining proportion of doctoral graduates entering academia (see, for example, ACOLA 2016). Most published studies on employment destinations for PhD graduates are conducted about 3-12 months after graduation, so they do not yield any information on medium- or long-term careers. Regarding employment in the short term, data gathered largely through post-graduation surveys reveal that doctoral graduates are being employed in a range of careers. Studies from Australia (see, for example, ACOLA 2016; Guthrie & Bryant 2015; Neumann & Tan 2011), Canada (see, for example, King, Eisl-Culkin & Desjardins 2008), the USA (see, for example, Nerad 2007), and the UK (see, for example, Haynes, Metcalf & Videler 2009), have shown that about 50% of doctoral graduates work in the higher education sector. Thus a growing proportion of doctoral graduates are entering careers in governmental and non-governmental organisations, business and industry.

In New Zealand, there is a lack of published data on the initial destinations of doctoral graduates. However, the Graduate Longitudinal Study, which began in 2011, is tracking graduates from New Zealand universities at approximately two, five and 10 years after graduation to determine their career trajectories. Although the first follow-up report has been released (Tustin et al 2016), it reports on the entire dataset, with no specific data for doctoral graduates.

PREPAREDNESS OF DOCTORAL GRADUATES FOR EMPLOYMENT

Since doctoral graduates are entering a range of careers, a key question is: 'How well is doctoral education preparing them for these career options?' Traditionally, doctoral training was seen as an apprenticeship for academia, so is it now meeting the needs of training for careers beyond academia? Across the globe there has been a concern that universities are not necessarily preparing PhD candidates sufficiently well for careers beyond academia (see, for example, ACOLA 2016; Cuthbert & Molla 2014; Enders 2004; Roberts Report 2002; Wendler et al 2010). Implicit in the argument of many researchers is an assumption that universities are at least preparing PhD candidates well for academia. However, researchers of early career academics in South Africa and Sweden (Frick et al 2016) and New Zealand (Sutherland 2018), have found that doctoral education had not necessarily prepared graduates well for the academic environment. Apart from a few studies, what is lacking from the research on preparedness for employment is empirical evidence about the graduate attributes that doctoral graduates attain from their study, and how well these match expectations in the workplace – in academia and beyond.

Some researchers have explored the development of skills in doctoral graduates. Taking a qualitative approach, Mowbray and Halse (2010) interviewed 25 final-year PhD candidates at an Australian university to determine the skills the candidates believed they had developed during doctoral study and how these had contributed to their personal and professional growth. They theorised the PhD as the "acquisition of intellectual virtues", including personal resourcefulness, developing cognition, and developing research and other skills (Mowbray & Halse 2010:662). They proposed that the focus of a PhD on intellectual virtues countered the more instrumental focus on employability skills, and positioned the PhD as preparing graduates to face an unknown future. Durette, Fournier and Lafon (2016) used a survey method to identify the core competencies (akin to graduate attributes) of 2 794 PhD graduates across a range of disciplines in France. The six core competencies they found were knowledge and technical skills, transferable competencies that can be formalised (such as communication, innovation and project management), transferable competencies that cannot be formalised (such as cognitive abilities and ability to work in a team), dispositions including rigour, creativity and autonomy, behaviours such as perseverance, and meta-competencies such as capacity for adaptation (Durette *et al* 2016). The authors point out that although the doctoral experience should not be reduced to an atomistic list of competencies this approach is helpful in providing a "common vocabulary between doctoral holders and employers" (Durette *et al* 2016:1 368).

Neumann and Tan (2011) observed that the consistently high level of employment of doctoral graduates in a range of careers indicates that these graduates are competitive and successful in gaining jobs. They suggest that the employment statistics counter arguments regarding a lack of employability skills in doctoral graduates. However, although doctoral graduates are obtaining jobs, the question is whether they feel that their doctoral education has prepared them sufficiently well for this. Several Australian studies have provided some insight into this question. For example, in a study comparing research training of science PhD candidates in Australian cooperative research centres and university schools, Manathunga, Pitt and Critchley (2009) surveyed 115 recent graduates and asked them about the development of graduate attributes during their study and their perceived importance for industry and academia. In terms of graduate attributes developed during their PhD, participants gave the highest ratings to in-depth knowledge, critical judgement and analytical skills, understanding of intellectual property issues, and effective communication. The attributes perceived as being most important for academia were in-depth knowledge, effective communication, independence and creativity, and critical judgement and analytical skills. For industry, the most important were teamwork, an understanding of intellectual property issues, commercialisation, and leadership. The authors reported that although graduates from the cooperative research centres were better prepared for industry jobs than those trained in a university school, there was still a need for additional support to prepare graduates for employment more effectively.

In New Zealand, the PhD is a three to -four year research-only degree and, unlike the UK and Australia, there has not been a shift to formal research training in centres. Doctoral candidates can take optional courses, but these tend to be in discipline-specific areas or research methods courses (Sutherland 2018). Although most universities do provide extracurricular opportunities for doctoral candidates to develop transferable skills through engagement in workshops, short courses and, for a minority of candidates, internships, the effectiveness of these in terms of graduate outcomes is unknown. In a qualitative case study of a PhD programme in English in a New Zealand university, Sutherland and Corballis (2006) found a lack of structured and systematic opportunities to develop important transferable skills, and questioned whether the PhD was fit for purpose. Because little is known about how such ad hoc training approaches assist doctoral candidates in acquiring graduate attributes and preparing them for employment, the aims of this research were the following:

- Ascertain employment pathways for doctoral graduates soon after completing their degree.
- Explore the perceptions of doctoral graduates in terms of the development of graduate attributes during their doctoral study, and the application of these attributes in the workplace.

RESEARCH METHODS

To address the research aims a case study approach was used with a survey method. First we provide details of the case and then we discuss the survey method used.

CASE STUDY SETTING

The case was the University of Otago, a research-intensive university in New Zealand with approximately 21 000 students, including 1 300 doctoral students. The PhD programme at Otago is a three to -four year research-only degree, although optional papers can be taken in the first year of study. The university has a commendable PhD completion rate with 83% of candidates submitting their thesis for examination (thus a low comparative attrition rate), and a median time to submission for full-timers of 3.4 years (Spronken-Smith, Cameron & Quigg 2018). In 2015, the University of Otago adopted a graduate profile for PhDs (see the profile list below), which includes both affective attributes, such as global perspective and lifelong learning, and attributes highly relevant for the workplace such as communication, ethics and teamwork. As well as acquiring graduate attributes through their research activities, there are opportunities for generic skills development through a university-wide workshop programme (for example written and oral communication and research ethics), and short courses (for example commercialising research and preparing for academic careers). A few PhD candidates also undertake internships during their candidature.

University of Otago graduate profile for PhDs (http://www.otago.ac.nz/otago122601.pdf)

Description

A graduate who has qualified for the degree of Doctor of Philosophy (PhD) will demonstrate highly developed and independent skills in the definition, management and communication of original research in a specialist area. A PhD graduate will have made a significant contribution to knowledge in the particular field. On completion of their studies, PhD graduates will be able to:

i. undertake further advanced research of the highest quality that contributes to knowledge and exhibits authoritative international standing in their own subject field;
ii. continue developing personally and professionally in their careers; and
iii. make potentially innovative and important contributions to the communities and societies in which they reside.

Graduate attributes

- SPECIALIST KNOWLEDGE: Capacity to assimilate information at depth in a field of study, and to impart to others a clear understanding of it. Appreciation of the relevance and value of his or her original contribution to facts, theories and practices of the national and international knowledge community.
- GLOBAL PERSPECTIVE: Highly developed appreciation of global perspectives in the chosen discipline(s) and the nature of global citizenship
- INTERDISCIPLINARY PERSPECTIVE: Commitment to intellectual openness and curiosity, and the awareness of the limits of current knowledge and of the links amongst disciplines
- LIFELONG LEARNING: Commitment to the on-going acquisition of new knowledge and new skills, and a highly developed ability to apply these to an ever-changing environment

- SCHOLARSHIP: Commitment to the fundamental importance of the acquisition and development of knowledge and understanding
- COMMUNICATION: Highly developed ability to communicate information, arguments and analyses effectively, both orally and in writing
- CRITICAL THINKING: Highly developed ability to analyse issues logically, to challenge conventional assumptions, to consider different options and viewpoints, make informed decisions and act with flexibility, adaptability and creativity
- CULTURAL UNDERSTANDING: Knowledge and appreciation of biculturalism within the framework of the Treaty of Waitangi; knowledge and appreciation of multiculturalism; and an ability to apply such knowledge in a culturally appropriate manner
- ETHICS: Knowledge of ethics and ethical standards and a highly developed ability to apply these with a sense of responsibility within the workplace and community
- ENVIRONMENTAL LITERACY: Understanding of the principles that govern natural systems, the effects of human activity on these systems, and the cultures and economies that interact with those systems
- INFORMATION LITERACY: Highly developed ability to apply specific skills in acquiring, organising, analysing, evaluating and presenting information, in particular recognising the increasing prominence of digital-based activity
- RESEARCH: Highly developed ability to initiate, design, conduct and report independent and original research, a willingness to seek continuous improvement in research skills and quality of research, and an awareness of the application of knowledge
- SELF-MOTIVATION: Highly developed ability for self-directed activity and working independently
- TEAMWORK: Ability to work effectively as both a team leader and a team member
- LEADERSHIP: Demonstrates leadership within the discipline and within a workplace

SURVEY METHOD

Data were collected using an online Graduate Opinion Survey in 2015. This survey is adapted from the Postgraduate Research Experience Survey that the Higher Education Academy in the UK developed (https://www.heacademy.ac.uk/institutions/surveys/postgraduate-research-experience-survey). Some additional locally relevant items were added, particularly those concerning graduate attributes. The questions regarding employment and graduate attributes were:

- Are you currently employed? (No/Yes, Full-time, Part-time). If so, please provide your job title and employer (open-ended).
- What type of career did you have in mind when you completed your research degree? Options included:
  - Academic career in higher education (either research and teaching, or teaching only)
  - Research career in higher education
  - Research career outside higher education (for example in a private research organisation, a charity or in an industrial environment)
  - Teaching (at a level below higher education)
  - Any other professional career
  - Self-employment
  - Returning to or remaining with employer who is sponsoring your degree
  - Other (including not planning to enter employment – please specify)
- To what extent do you feel that the PhD encouraged DEVELOPMENT of each of the following attributes DURING your course of study?
- To what extent do you feel you have APPLIED each of the following attributes in your POST-UNIVERSITY experiences?

In the online survey, participants were able to access further information about each attribute. The list of attributes was wider than those in the profile, since the survey has been running for over 20 years, asking about these attributes. Participants were also able to provide freeform comments in relation to the questions on graduate attributes.

The survey was sent to all PhD graduates for whom the university had contact details (n=247 in 2015) approximately 18 months after they graduated. In 2015, 136 responses were received (yielding a response rate of 55%). However, not all respondents answered all the questions, resulting in varying sample sizes per question. The characteristics of the survey respondents are given in Table 15.1.

TABLE 15.1 Characteristics of survey respondents (n=136)

Characteristic		Response (2015)
Gender	Female	69 (51%)
	Male	64 (47%)
Citizenship	New Zealand	84 (63%)
	International	50 (37%)
Ethnicity	European	72 (55%)
	NZ Māori	7 (5%)
	Pacific island	3 (2%)
	Asian	28 (21%)
	Other	29 (22%)
First language English	Yes	84 (63%)
	No	50 (37%)
Disciplinary area (Divisions)	Commerce	13 (10%)
	Health Sciences	53 (39%)
	Humanities	28 (21%)
	Sciences	42 (31%)
Enrolment status	Full-time internal	114 (84%)
	Part-time internal	17 (13%)
	Full-time distance	8 (6%)
	Part-time distance	8 (6%)

DATA ANALYSES

Following quality checking of data, survey responses were tabulated and graphed, with descriptive statistics produced where appropriate. The open-ended responses regarding current employment were coded by the second author to allow a thematic analysis. The degree of development and application of the graduate attributes was graphed using radar charts. It was assumed that if there was a close match between the development and application of graduate attributes, this would indicate that graduates were well prepared for employment. Comparisons of the development and application of graduate attributes were first generated for graduates in the broad disciplinary groupings, or Divisions, as they are known at the University of Otago, and then a second analysis made comparisons according to the job the graduate was in at the time of the survey.

RESULTS

In this section, we first present the findings for employment 18 months after graduation and then consider the development of graduate attributes during doctoral study and application of these attributes by doctoral graduates in their post-university experiences, which we assume are mainly job-related.

Employment following graduation

The majority of graduates (73%) were employed full-time at the time of the survey, with 17% employed part-time and 10% unemployed. Some were continuing their studies (5% full-time and 3% part-time). Of those employed, 93% reported their work was related to their field of PhD study.

Figure 15.1 shows the career graduates had in mind when they completed their doctorate, together with the job they were in at the time of the survey. Approximately 55% of the graduates who responded hoped to obtain a career in academia, but only 29% managed to do so. However, 41% did gain a job in research in higher education, which was much higher than the 15% who had this career in mind. Only 4% gained a position in research outside of higher education, compared to 10% having this in mind upon graduation. More graduates than expected ended up in other professional careers (25% versus 11%).

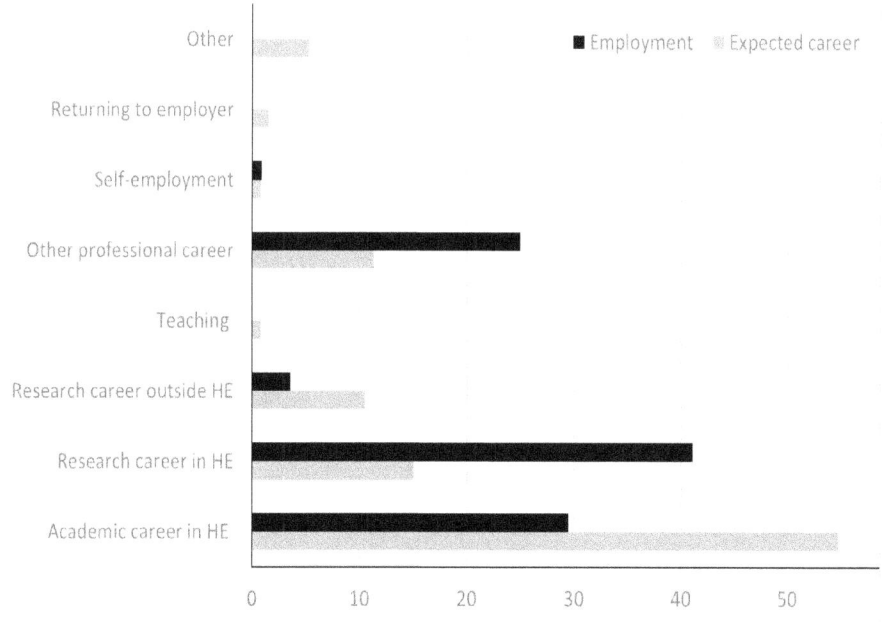

FIGURE 15.1 Employment outcomes (n=133) vs expectations (n=112)

DEVELOPMENT AND APPLICATION OF GRADUATE ATTRIBUTES

The perception of the development and application of graduate attributes for all PhD graduates is shown in Figure 15.2. The highest ratings for development of graduate attributes were for research and written communication skills, followed by academic rigour, the skills to plan work, problem-solving, independent judgement, and flexibility and adaptability. As shown in Figures 15.1 and 15.2, a very good match (< 5% difference) was noted between development and application of research skills, written communication skills and analytical skills. A good match (510% difference) was found for environmental literacy, academic rigour, information literacy, a multi-disciplinary approach, an awareness of ethical issues, and a global perspective. There were several attributes that graduates perceived were not well developed for their life after university, including teamwork skills (28% difference), self-confidence (19%), willingness to learn (18%), and the skills to implement change (17%).

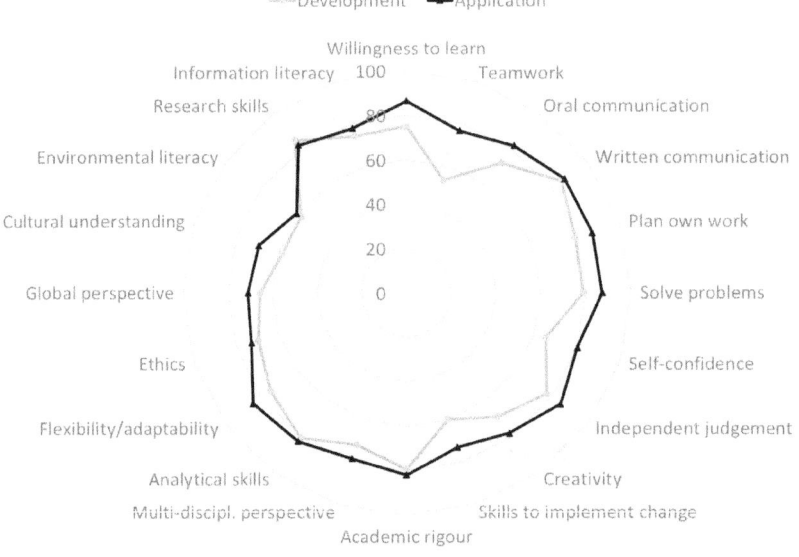

FIGURE 15.2 Development and application of graduate attributes – all doctoral graduates (n=108 to 133; the number varies because of differing response rates to the questions)

There were marked differences in the development and application of graduate attributes according to the broad disciplinary groups (commerce, humanities, science and health science) (Figures 15.4-15.7). The small sample of PhD graduates from commerce (Figure 15.4) reported much lower levels of graduate attribute development. Moreover, they perceived very high levels of application of many graduate attributes in the workplace, leading to a significant gap for attributes such as teamwork (57% difference), awareness of ethical issues (23%) and cultural understanding (22%). In contrast, PhD graduates from the humanities (Figure 15.5) had a very close alignment between the development and application of awareness of ethical issues and cultural understanding. However, like commerce graduates, the humanities graduates also had a significant gap for teamwork (31%), but there were also gaps for the skills to implement change (22%), oral communication (20%), problem-solving (19%), and flexibility and adaptability (17%).

Generally, there was a much better match between the development and application of graduate attributes for PhD graduates from the science and health science disciplines. In health science PhD graduates, the ability to work in teams was the major difference between development and application (22%), with self-confidence another significant gap (16%), and willingness to learn, and skills to implement change both at 13%. Science graduates reported the best match for development and application of graduate attributes, with teamwork and self-confidence the only two attributes perceived with > 10% differences.

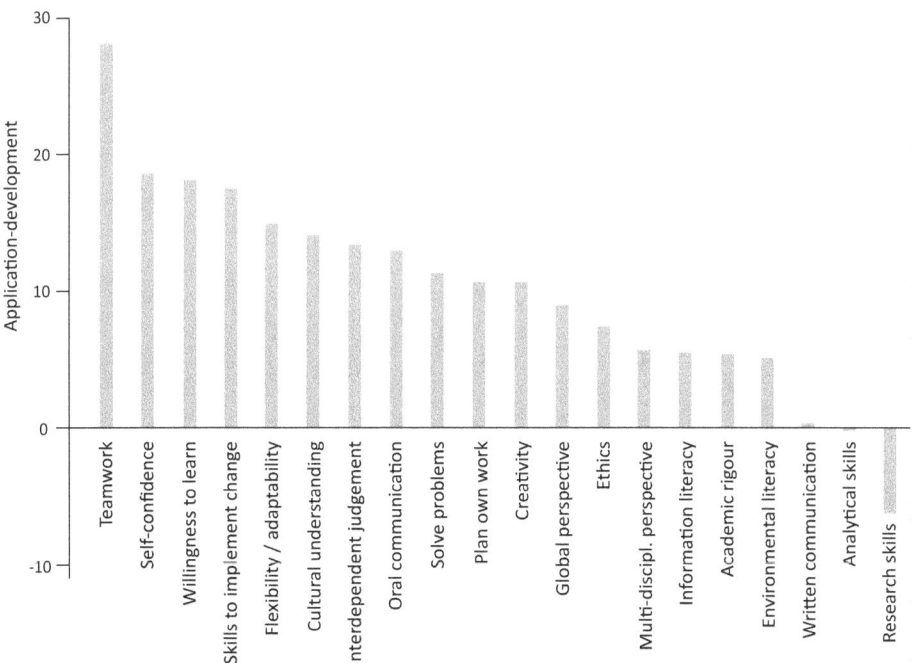

FIGURE 15.3   Difference between application and development of graduate attributes for all PhD respondents (n=108 to 133)

SECTION B • SUPERVISORY JOURNEYS

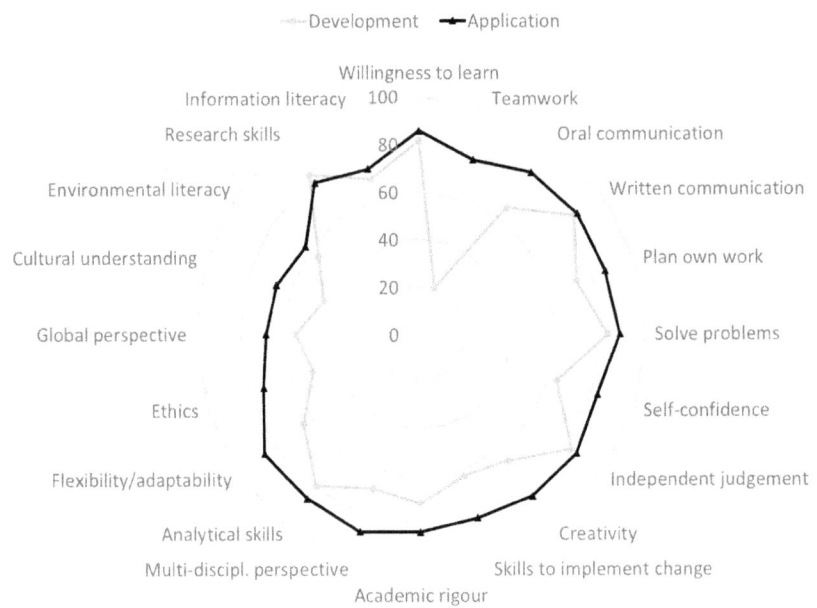

FIGURE 15.4 Development and application of graduate attributes in commerce graduates (n=10 to 13)

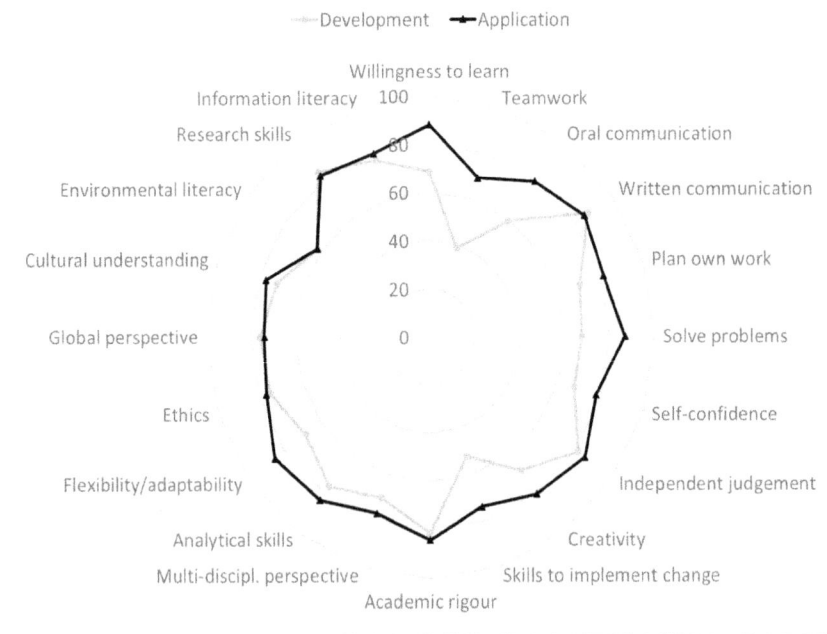

FIGURE 15.5 Development and application of graduate attributes in the humanities graduates (n=20 to 27)

CHAPTER 15 • EMPLOYABILITY AND GRADUATE ATTRIBUTES OF DOCTORAL GRADUATES

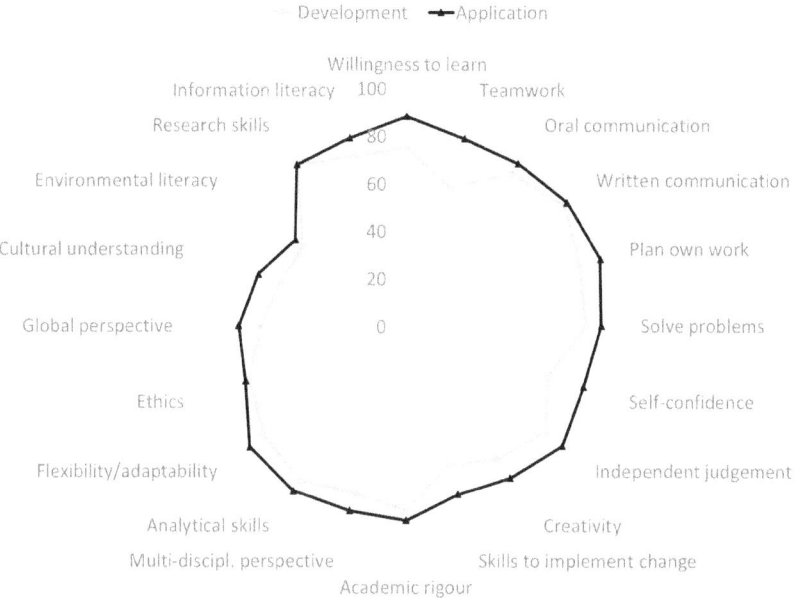

FIGURE 15.6 Development and application of graduate attributes in health science graduates (n=48 to 52)

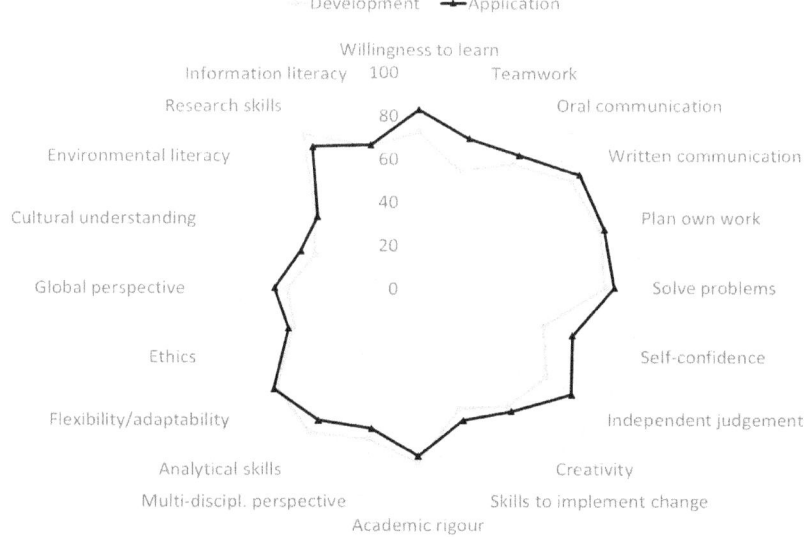

FIGURE 15.7 Development and application of graduate attributes in science graduates (n=31 to 41)

As well as rating their perceptions of the development and application of graduate attributes, PhD graduates were asked for freeform comments about their ratings; 49 respondents replied. There were several recurring themes relating to existing skill sets, developing skills via means other than direct research experience, and employment. A final theme reflected development of attributes enabling independent working.

The first theme was a view that students had developed a range of attributes prior to PhD study. For example, one respondent commented: "I entered 'does not apply' for skill development, as I had these when starting the PhD." Two respondents specifically mentioned previous employment: "Completing a higher degree was the culmination of years of planning, and builds on my business and public service experience," and "I had a reasonably strong skill set having taught at the university." The average age of PhD students at Otago is now about 32 years, so a proportion of PhD students may embark on doctoral study having amassed a diverse skill set from previous employment. A different respondent contemplated commencing a PhD without graduate attributes: "… it is my belief that you wouldn't be able to undertake PhD level study without first having these skills. There was a refinement of some of these skills." The university only developed a graduate profile for PhD students in 2015, so the respondents would not have been aware of this profile, nor of the expectation that such skills should be highly developed in PhD graduates, compared to lower levels of skill development in undergraduates.

The second theme recognised the difficulties of entering an academic and research career. Five respondents lamented the challenges of securing academic employment after their graduation. Despite feeling that they had achieved the necessary requirements for an academic position, one respondent commented that "[h]aving a PhD and great publications was not enough to get a job in research". One respondent who was employed in an academic career thought they were "lucky" to get their job, while others praised the preparation they had received for an academic career.

The third theme that emerged from freeform comments concerned how respondents developed skills outside of their direct research experience. Teaching opportunities proved useful for three respondents, as one noted: "The teaching experience that I undertook during my PhD is more valuable than the research experience." Two respondents reflected positively on training offered by the university: "The training and development workshops run by the HEDC [Higher Education Development Centre] were good avenues for PhD candidates to develop the skills required for subsequent career and life experience." On the other hand, seven respondents suggested that

CHAPTER 15 • EMPLOYABILITY AND GRADUATE ATTRIBUTES OF DOCTORAL GRADUATES

the university could do more to prepare students for transitions into careers other than academia: "I would like some more career focus from the research degree as many of my friends have struggled to find appropriate work."

The fourth theme concerned developing skills related to independent working. One respondent noted, "I think the way the PhD degree is structured actually actively discourages teamwork." Other respondents appeared to agree, as summarised by this comment: "The only things the PhD taught me in reality was endurance, persistence and coping with working in isolation." Respondents' freeform comments offer some explanation of the gap in developing and subsequently applying skills related to teamwork.

The final analysis compared the development (Figure 15.8) and application (Figure 15.9) of graduate attributes according to the three main employment categories. Note that academic careers include positions that combine teaching and research, as well as teaching-only positions.

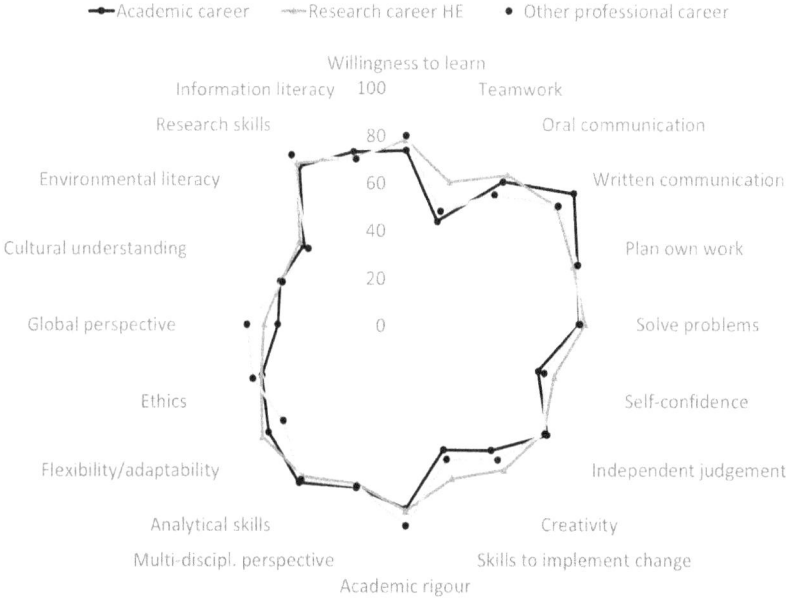

FIGURE 15.8 Perceived development of graduate attributes by career type (n=89 to 104)

SECTION B • SUPERVISORY JOURNEYS

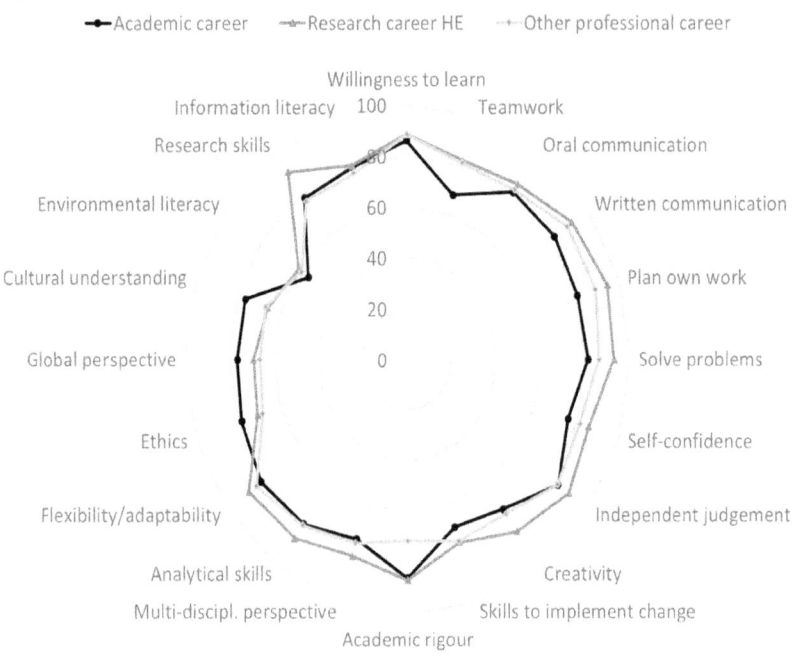

FIGURE 15.9 Perceived application of graduate attributes by career type (n=89 to 104)

Overall, there were similar perceptions of the development of most graduate attributes, irrespective of the end career (Figure 15.8). However, there was notable variation in the perceptions of the development of teamwork, the skills to implement change, global perspective and flexibility and adaptability. In terms of application (Figure 15.9), teamwork was perceived to be less important in academia, while an awareness of ethics, a global perspective and cultural understanding were perceived to be more important compared to research and professional careers, and academic rigour was perceived to be less important in a professional career.

DISCUSSION

Many assumptions are made about how well universities are (or are not) preparing PhD graduates for the workplace. Although only one case study with 136 survey respondents, our research provides some insights into employment outcomes for PhD graduates, as well as perceptions of preparedness for the workplace. Ninety per cent of respondents were employed with 73% in full-time employment, and 90% in careers at least somewhat related to their field of study. Regarding employment outcomes, we found that 71% of our respondents had gained a job in higher education 18 months after graduation. In our introduction, we cited many studies that have found only about 50% of PhD graduates work in the higher education sector. While our percentage is higher than these other studies, it should be noted that our response rate was 55%, and it is possible the non-responders may have a higher rate of employment outside higher education. It was notable that many of our graduates missed out on their desired mainstream faculty position, but instead ended up in a research position. This is likely due to the postdoctoral effect, and indeed postdoctoral positions are often stepping stones into tenure-track faculty positions (Chen 2015).

In terms of the development and application of graduate attributes, our study shows that overall there is a reasonable match between these for PhD graduates. Not surprisingly, some of the core abilities we associate with PhD graduates, such as research skills, written communication, academic rigour, the skills to plan work, problem-solving, and independent judgement were indeed perceived to be highly developed. While there are some similarities with the attributes reported to be highly developed by Manathunga *et al* (2009), direct comparisons are difficult due to the use of different attributes (for example effective communication vs oral and written communication). In our study, there were some skills that ideally should be highly developed, but were not. In particular, teamwork came up as the attribute most consistently perceived as being poorly developed compared to application after university. Given the isolated nature of many PhD projects, this is perhaps not surprising (McCallin & Nayer 2012). Other attributes that were perceived to be less well developed were the skills to implement change, self-confidence, and oral communication. Regarding skills to implement change, this perception is curious, since doctoral study will often involve necessary shifts in research as obstacles become apparent – such as difficulty with recruiting participants or experiments failing. Less curious is the finding that PhD graduates perceived low levels of self-confidence. This perception is likely due to the 'impostor syndrome' (Wisker 2016), often used to describe the anxiety people experience when they feel out of place or doubt the worthiness of their work, and which is common in high-achievers.

Our findings showed clear disciplinary differences in perceptions of the development and application of graduate attributes. These differences likely reflect disciplinary variations in research training, as well as opportunities to engage in activities outside the PhD. For example, in our science disciplines, PhD candidates will often undertake research in a team environment, many will be employed as tutors or demonstrators, most will present at several conferences, some will have opportunities to engage in a range of science outreach activities, and some will have research internships or visit research laboratories overseas. This range of activities can lead to a more holistic development of graduate attributes. In contrast, in the humanities and commerce disciplines at the University of Otago, the opportunities for teamwork and teaching are much less, candidates typically only obtain funding for one international conference, and there tends to be less extracurricular research opportunities. So it is perhaps not surprising that there are some deficits in skill development for PhD graduates from these disciplines at our University.

Although there were similar perceptions of the development of most graduate attributes, irrespective of the end career, there were differences for teamwork, the skills to implement change, global perspective, and flexibility and adaptability. Differences were also apparent for application of graduate attributes. For example, teamwork was perceived to be less important in academia. Although academic work is often individually focused, arguably more teamwork is being required for both teaching and research collaborations.

Our findings have implications for doctoral education at the University of Otago, and may be transferable to other institutions. Firstly, because some disciplines provide less opportunity through their research programmes for transferable skill development, it is important to find other mechanisms to assist students in further developing transferable skills. Such mechanisms can include providing workshops or short courses targeting specific skills. Departments in the commerce and humanities disciplines in particular should be encouraged to provide teaching opportunities for their PhD candidates, and also mobilise them for outreach activities – after all, they can be ambassadors for the disciplines. Sutherland (2018:76) noted that of the New Zealand early career academics she surveyed, less than half gained teaching experience during their doctorate, compared to nearly three quarters of those who did their doctorate overseas. Like Sutherland, we feel that more opportunities should be available for PhD students to teach. A range of activities to help humanities PhD students become aware of career options and to broaden their skill set has been identified by research on the 'Next Generation Humanities PhD' (McCarthy 2017). Secondly, it is apparent that PhD graduates are not always securing their desired career – at least in the first 18 months after graduation. This means that doctoral training should include career planning so that candidates are more aware of the likelihood of particular careers and can plan accordingly (see Sinche 2016 for an excellent guide for PhD students wanting to learn about, and plan for, career paths in science). As part of this planning, appropriate professional development opportunities should be identified to help broaden and enhance the skill set of the candidate, so they are well positioned for applying for desired positions (see, for example, Sinche 2016; Sinclair *et al* 2014; Sutherland 2018; Von der Lehr 2017).

Individual development plans are becoming much more commonplace in doctoral training and their value has been recognised (see, for example, McAlpine 2016).

Our research has some limitations. As the findings have been drawn from responses to one survey in one institution, they should be treated with caution. It is important to reiterate that we assumed that respondents to the survey were thinking of application of attributes in the workplace, rather than to their life more generally (the survey question asked for perceptions of application after university). We did not ask PhD graduates about the relative importance of bringing a skill set to a position, versus learning on the job. As Tomlinson (2012:425) suggests, "graduates' successful integration in the labour market may rest less on the skills they possess before entering it, and more on the extent to which these are utilised and enriched through their actual participation in work settings". Future research should explore this assertion, from both employer and employee perspectives.

CONCLUSION

The aims of this study were to ascertain employment pathways of PhD graduates from one university soon after completing their degree and to explore perceptions of doctoral graduates in terms of the development of graduate attributes during their doctoral study, and the application of these attributes after university. Regarding employment, 71% secured a job in higher education, but most were in postdoctoral or teaching-only positions rather than mainstream faculty positions that many desired. Overall, there was a reasonably close match between the development of graduate attributes and their application after university. The attributes that were perceived to be very well developed were research, written communication, analytical skills, academic rigour, the skills to plan work, problem-solving, and independent judgement. In contrast, the attributes that were less well developed, yet perceived as important in application post-university, were teamwork, self-confidence, and the skills to implement change. There were notable disciplinary differences in the development of graduate attributes that likely reflected the different approaches to doctoral training. In the science and health science disciplines, graduates perceived better development of a more holistic set of graduate attributes. In contrast, the humanities, and particularly commerce graduates reported some significant deficits in the development of attributes such as teamwork, the skills to implement change, and flexibility and adaptability – all important attributes for the workplace. Also, there was notable variation in the perceptions of the application of teamwork, the skills to implement change, global perspective, and flexibility and adaptability according to career type. Although this was a case study in a New Zealand context, we suspect our findings are transferable to other institutional settings – particularly where there are no coursework requirements for PhD study. Our findings have implications for the design of doctoral education programmes and point to the need to provide support for career planning and the purposeful development of transferable skills to prepare PhD graduates for the workplace more effectively.

REFERENCES

ACOLA (Australian Council of Learned Academies). 2016. *Review of Australia's research training system*. Melbourne: ACOLA.

Chen S. 2015. Postdoctoral positions as preparation for desired careers: A narrative approach to understanding postdoctoral experience. *Higher Education Research & Development*, 34(6):1085-1096. https://doi.org/10.1080/07294360.2015.1024633

Cryer P. 1998. Transferable skills, marketability and lifelong learning: The particular case of postgraduate research students. *Studies in Higher Education*, 23(2):207-216. https://doi.org/10.1080/03075079812331380394

Cuthbert D & Molla T. 2015. PhD crisis discourse: A critical approach to the framing of the problem and some Australian 'solutions'. *Higher Education*, 69:33-53. https://doi.org/10.1007/s10734-014-9760-y

Durette B, Fournier M & Lafon M. 2016. The core competencies of PhDs. *Studies in Higher Education*, 41(8): 1355-1370. https://doi.org/10.1080/03075079.2014.968540

Enders J. 2004. Research training and careers in transition: A European perspective on the many faces of the PhD. *Studies in Continuing Education*, 26(3):419-429. https://doi.org/10.1080/0158037042000265935

Frick BL, Albertyn RM, Brodin EM, Claesson S & McKenna S. 2016. The role of doctoral education in early career academic development. In: M Fourie-Malherbe, EM Bitzer, RM Albertyn & C Aitchison (eds). *The future of postgraduate supervision in the knowledge society*. Stellenbosch: African SUN MeDIA. https://doi.org/10.18820/9781928357223/12

Haynes K, Metcalfe J & Videler T. 2009. *What do researchers do? First destinations of doctoral graduates by subject*. Careers Research & Advisory Centre.

Guthrie B & Bryant G. 2015. *Postgraduate destinations 2014: A report on the work and study outcomes of recent higher education postgraduates*. Melbourne VIC: Graduate Careers Australia.

King D, Eisl-Culkin J & Desjardins L. 2008. *Doctoral graduates in Canada: Findings from the survey of earned doctorates, 2004/2005*. Statistics Canada, Culture, Tourism and the Centre for Education Statistics Division.

Manathunga C, Pitt R & Critchley C. 2009. Graduate attribute development and employment outcomes: Tracking PhD graduates. *Assessment & Evaluation in Higher Education*, 34(1):91-103. https://doi.org/10.1080/02602930801955945

McAlpine L. 2016. Post-PhD non-academic careers: Intentions during and after degree. *International Journal for Researcher Development*, 7(1):2-14. https://doi.org/10.1108/IJRD-04-2015-0010

McCallin A & Nayer S. 2012. Postgraduate research supervision: A critical review of practice. *Teaching in Higher Education*, 17(1):63-74. https://doi.org/10.1080/13562517.2011.590979

McCarthy M. 2017. *Promising practices in humanities PhD professional development*. Washington DC: Council of Graduate Schools.

Mowbray S & Halse C. 2010. The purpose of the PhD: Theorising the skills acquired by students. *Higher Education Research & Development*, 29(6):653-664. https://doi.org/10.1080/07294360.2010.487199

Nerad M. 2007. *Social science PhDs, five+ years out: A national survey of PhDs in six fields: Highlights report*. Washington DC: Center for Innovation and Research in Graduate Education, College of Education, University of Washington.

Neumann R & Tan KK. 2011. From PhD to initial employment: The doctorate in a knowledge economy. *Studies in Higher Education*, 36(5):601-614. https://doi.org/10.1080/03075079.2011.594596

Sinche M. 2016. *Next gen PhD: A guide to career paths in science*. Cambridge MA: Harvard University Press. https://doi.org/10.4159/9780674974791

Sinclair J, Cuthbert D & Barnacle R. 2014. The entrepreneurial subjectivity of successful researchers. *Higher Education Research and Development*, 33(5):1007-1019. https://doi.org/10.1080/07294360.2014.890574

Spronken-Smith R, Cameron C & Quigg R. 2017. Factors contributing to high PhD completion rates: A case study in a research-intensive university in New Zealand. *Assessment & Evaluation in Higher Education*, 43(1):94-109. https://doi.org/10.1080/02602938.2017.1298717

Sutherland K, 2018. *Early Career Academics in New Zealand: Challenges and Prospects in Comparative Perspective*. London: Springer.

Sutherland K & Corballis R. 2006. Reconceptualising the New Zealand PhD in English – Fit for what and whose purpose? *New Zealand Journal of Educational Studies,* 41(1):85-111. https://doi.org/10.1007/978-3-319-61830-2

Tomlinson M. 2012. Graduate employability: A review of conceptual and empirical themes. *Higher Education Policy*, 25:407-431. https://doi.org/10.1057/hep.2011.26

Tustin K, Gollop C, Theodore R, Taumoepeau M, Taylor, Hunter J, Chapple S, Chee KS & Poulton R (eds). 2016. *First follow-up descriptive report, graduate longitudinal study New Zealand 2016*. Dunedin NZ: University of Otago.

Von der Lehr N. 2017. *Where do the doctors go?* https://www.tidningencurie.se/en/nyheter/2017/10/23/where-do-the-doctors-go/?utm_campaign=unspecified&utm_content=unspecified&utm_medium=email&utm_source=apsis-anp3&utm_campaign=unspecified&utm_content=unspecified&utm_medium=email&utm_source=apsis-anp-3 [Retrieved 12 January 2018].

Wendler C, Bridgeman B, Cline F, Millett C, Rock J, Bell N & McAllister P. 2010. *The path forward: The future of graduate education in the United States.* NJ: Educational Testing Service.

Wisker G. 2016. Toil and trouble: Professional and personal expectations and identities in academic writing for publication. In: J Smith, J Rattray, T Peseta & D Loads (eds). *Identity work in the contemporary university: Exploring an uneasy profession.* Rotterdam: Sense Publishers. 143-154. https://doi.org/10.1007/978-94-6300-310-0_11

SECTION C
NEW HORIZONS FOR POSTGRADUATE SUPERVISION

16

DOCTORAL EDUCATION FOR SUCCESSFUL EXAMINATION IN THE EDUCATION DISCIPLINE

AN ANALYSIS OF EXAMINERS' CRITIQUES

Petro du Preez & Shan Simmonds

INTRODUCTION

A national survey involving 19 universities that offer a doctoral degree in the field of education found that doctoral programmes provide formal training for proposal writing, but not for the examination process (Du Preez & Simmonds 2016:353). This accords with the priorities of national doctoral initiatives such as the National Research Foundation's PhD project (NRF 2017), international partnerships such as the SANPAD-SANTRUST doctoral programmes (Smit, Williamson & Padayachee 2013), and institutional community and cohort programmes (Lotz-Sisitka et al 2010; Samuel & Vithal 2011) that offer guidance in the proposal and doctoral writing processes, but not necessarily in what the examination demands.

The need for capacity building and development programmes that focus on proposal writing and collaborative supervision have taken centre stage in light of the demand for more doctoral graduates in South Africa. A complicating factor is that only 34% of academic staff members at South African universities are qualified to provide supervision at this level (ASSAf 2010; South Africa 2011). At present the dropout rate is high among doctoral candidates; only an estimated 50% of them complete the degree (Cloete, Mouton & Sheppard 2015:22). Reasons for the low rate of completion include career/employment commitments, lack of financial support, family responsibilities, inappropriate project choices, and the inability of candidates to conceptualise their research and to present it clearly in academic writing (Cloete et al 2015). It could also be argued that being a doctoral candidate is a journey towards becoming part of the academic community. This involves what Wisker (2010:226) describes as gaining the capacity to engage at a sufficiently conceptual, critical and creative level of scholarship for successful doctoral study. Along the journey the candidate is confronted by "troublesome knowledge; movements on from 'stuck' places; movement through liminal spaces into new understanding; transformations; ontological change – seeing the self and the world differently, and epistemological contribution – making new contributions to understanding and meaning". These are the challenges that a candidate has to meet squarely.

Acknowledging that the examination process is subjective and often inconsistent (Lessing 2009), we explore ways in which supervisors and candidates can improve the chances of success in the doctoral examination process. The starting point must be an awareness of the expectations of examiners because ultimately "it is the thesis examiners who set the standard of what is acceptable as a thesis (or dissertation), and consequently set the standard for the award of a PhD" (Bourke 2007:1042).

Research done on written examination reports in Australia has shed some light on the expectations of examiners across disciplines (Bourke et al 2004; Bourke 2007; Bourke & Holbrook 2011; Holbrook et al 2004a; Holbrook et al 2004b; Holbrook et al 2007; Holbrook et al 2008). This chapter draws on examination reports of doctoral theses in education at selected South African universities to reveal what examiners expect. From a critical review of the examination report documents that these selected SA universities provide to examiners it was evident that most weight is placed on asking examiners to comment on where candidates have failed to meet expectations. Very little emphasis is placed on asking for their inputs on where candidates have met or exceeded expectations. As such, when analysing the examiners reports we found mostly their critiques of the thesis being examined. We deem these critiques valuable to assist supervisors and candidates to meet the expectations of doctoral examination. The aim is to assist supervisors and candidates in meeting these expectations. It is should be noted that how examiners should compile examination reports lay beyond the scope of the study on which this chapter draws.

Our findings revealed that candidates often fail to demonstrate that they have the ability to contribute new knowledge to the existing body of scholarship, mainly because they have not developed sound conceptual frameworks. Our aim was to offer a theory that supervisors and candidates could use during the journey towards the examining process, with particular attention given to critical questions that should be used to interrogate theses before they are submitted. We acknowledge that the examination process is extremely complex and riddled with power relations between examiners, supervisors and candidates. However, our findings indicate that there are several aspects that supervisors and candidates should take into account to meet the examiners' expectations.

RESEARCH DESIGN

As part of an NRF project entitled *Education research for quality PhD study curriculum-making: A South African meta-study 2014-2016* (Du Preez 2014), research was conducted involving the faculties/departments of education at four public South African universities. The aim was to explore the examination process by analysing the examiners' reports on doctoral theses between 2012 and 2014. At two of these universities the doctoral degree offered is a DEd, while the other two offer a PhD.[1]

There were N=91 candidates during this period whose theses by monograph were examined, of which n=30 candidates' examination reports were analysed. We deemed a 30% sample from the population sufficient to obtain data saturation in accordance with the theoretical sampling employed. Of the 30 concerned, 53% (16 candidates) were supervised by one supervisor, 43% (13 candidates) by two supervisors and 3% (1 candidate) by three supervisors. On average, these institutions appointed three examiners per candidate. Our sample comprised all the examination reports: 16 internal[2] (an average of 0.5 per candidate), 51 national external (an average of 1,7 per candidate) and 27 international external (an average of 1 per candidate), bringing the total number of examination reports analysed in this study to 94. At these universities, 23 of the theses analysed were placed in category B, indicating that revisions, often minor, were required rather than resubmission. Six of the theses analysed were placed in category C (major changes and resubmission for examination) and one thesis was failed (a category D was awarded).

We used grounded theory (Glaser & Strauss 1967) as the methodology for engaging with the examination reports as it enabled us to generate new theory instead of merely testing existing theories (Charmaz 2014). This methodology offers researchers guidance on working with datasets that are systematic, yet flexible and iterative (Birks & Mills 2015). Our work on the existing datasets soon confirmed that this methodology was an appropriate choice.

---

[1] This is in part because two of the universities are classified as universities of technology (with a more vocational and professional focus in the doctorate) so they offer a DEd and the other two universities are classified as traditional universities (with the focus more on a theoretical and philosophical doctorate) so they offer a PhD.

[2] At one of the universities the promoter is appointed as one of the internal examiners.

Four variables that might have had an impact on the findings were taken into account. Firstly, the fact that we did not have access to the version of the thesis that was submitted for examination presented certain problems. For instance, it was difficult to interpret the examiners' comments when they referred to particular elements or pages of the thesis. Secondly, we were not in the position to make any judgements on the theses as some of them fell outside our fields of expertise. Thirdly, universities often have structured examination guidelines for examiners to use when compiling the reports, and these guidelines influence the aspects highlighted by examiners. Fourthly, the examination reports that were analysed all came from the faculties of education at four South African universities. Aspects that examiners frequently highlight would vary should different disciplines be included in the sample.

To ensure trustworthiness of the data analysis, both of us analysed the reports and recorded decisions made so there would be a detailed and accurate audit trail. In addition, we were actively involved in the data generation process, we attempted to be as transparent about the interpretation processes as possible, we considered discrepancies between the reports, we obtained ethical clearance for the research, and we took every precaution necessary to protect the confidentiality and anonymity of the examiners, their reports and the candidates examined.

DATA ANALYSIS AND FINDINGS

In the first stage of data analysis, the complete examination reports of each candidate were analysed to generate initial codes for what examiners saw as the shortcomings in the theses. Stage two involved categorising those codes into themes and sub-themes. The themes that emerged revealed that examiners most frequently identified shortcomings with regard to background, scholarly review, research design, validity, reliability and trustworthiness, ethical considerations, technical aspects, and the claimed contribution made by the thesis. The sub-themes identify the specific concerns and critiques raised by examiners. We focused only on the negative comments (or critiques) on the assumption that we would be able to use these to provide guidelines for candidates and supervisors.

Tables 16.1-16.7 illustrate the 529 comments made by examiners across the 94 examination reports. Tables 16.1-16.3 list the number of comments made per theme: research design (151 comments), technical aspects (144 comments) and scholarly review (136 comments). These reveal that in the 94 examination reports, examiners commented, on average, more than once on these three themes. The three sub-themes commented on most frequently are next discussed in more detail.

TABLE 16.1 Shortcomings identified by examiners in terms of the research design

Research design	Total comments: 151
Shortcomings in the accuracy, scope and clarity of the data analysis and presentation of results	31
Sample size too small or too big; lack of clarity with regard to the choice of sample (participants and research environment)	20
Shortcomings in terms of the choice of methodology and its execution	18
Findings not aligned with the literature in the body of scholarship of the study	16
Justification of the execution of the data generation method(s) weak or not provided	14
Shortcomings with regard to the clarity, depth and rigour of the presentation and discussion of data findings	10
Detailed theoretical explanation given without a clear justification of the research design in the specific research study	9
The choice of data analysis methods not applicable to this research	6
Description and explanation of the links between research design elements weak or not given	6
Research design not linked to the larger research focus, research questions/hypotheses and/or aims/objectives	6
The depth and integration of a philosophy/paradigm/worldview insufficient/lacking altogether	4
Overall research design lacks rigour, critique and/or originality	4
Inconsistent or incorrect use of methodological concepts	3
Literature outdated, misquoted, overused and/or not relevant to the research design of the study	2
Research design not systematically presented or justified	2

The concerns that examiners raised most often, in order of frequency, were firstly that the analysis and presentation of the data did not accurately represent the results; the scope, in terms of what the study included and what it excluded, was either too wide or too limited; and the details provided were ambiguous or thin, requiring clarity or more information (31 of the 151 comments, 21%). One examiner stated that "a number of vague and unsubstantiated claims" were made in the analysis and presentation of the data brought the accuracy of the results into question. A second examiner noted that "[t]he study is seriously weakened by inadequate analysis of the data and synthesis of the findings". Secondly, the examiners drew attention to shortcomings related to the sample. Twenty of the 151 comments (13%) focused on this aspect. These shortcomings mainly concerned the size of the sample and inadequate information on the choice of sample and the research environment. Thirdly, 18 of the 151 comments (12%) emphasised that candidates failed to explain their choice of methodology, and while they referred to the literature on the methodology, they did not describe how they applied the methodology in their research study. Twelve other shortcomings with regard to the research design are listed in Table 16.1.

TABLE 16.2 Shortcomings identified by examiners in terms of the technical aspects

Technical aspects	Total comments: 144
Incorrect language use in terms of spelling and grammar	45
References inconsistent in style, omitted from the text and/or reference list or not an accurate representation of the source (in terms of author, date, etc.)	37
Writing style: Information often repeated (11) Inadequate or no links between paragraphs (8) Incoherent paragraphs and/or sections so restructuring recommended (13) Contradictions in raising concerns of validity, reliability and trustworthiness (1) Overuse of numbering and bulleted lists not in keeping with academic writing (1) Inappropriate use of passive and the third person (1)	35
Lack of technical accuracy in terms of typography	11
Tables or figures too vague, incorrect and/or inconsistent in technical layout	9
Chapter headings or section headings do not reflect the contents	5
Overall length of the thesis too long or too short	2

Another shortcoming frequently identified by examiners was related to the technical aspects of the thesis (144 comments). Three main sub-themes emerged from the critiques of the examiners. The first was incorrect language use, particularly spelling and grammar (45 of the 144 comments or 31%). Referencing was the second (37 of the 144 comments or 26%): inconsistent application of the referencing; references omitted from the text and/or the reference list; and incorrect representation of sources. The examiners were also critical of the candidates' style of writing (35 of the 144 comments or 24%), more specifically, repetition of information, lack of links between paragraphs, incoherence, inconsistency in the arguments, overuse of numbering or bullets, and inappropriate use of the passive voice. Four other technical shortcomings were raised by examiners (see Table 16.2).

TABLE 16.3 Shortcomings identified by examiners in terms of the scholarly review

Scholarly review	Total comments: 136
Literature only described No synthesis, depth, critique and/or rigour	39
Sources: Not recent, overemphasis on one or a few sources, and/or little or no reference to prominent scholars or seminal sources (21) Heavy reliance on Internet, non-primary and/or textbook sources (6)	27
Literature not justified, misrepresented, incorrectly quoted, no account taken of underlying assumptions, sweeping statements and/or over-generalisations made	18
Scope of literature too limited or too wide	13
Key concepts identified not appropriate, overemphasis on obvious concepts in the discipline, theoretically diverse concepts used synonymously and/or poorly clarified	11
The voice of the candidate not reflected	9
Relevance of literature to topic of study not highlighted	7
Gaps in the literature not identified	4
Context not taken into account (lacking in either national or international perspectives)	4
No theoretical framework	2
Lack of original engagement with the literature	1
Sections in scholarly review misplaced or irrelevant	1

The examiners' greatest concern was that the scholarly overview lacked synthesis, critical engagement, depth and rigour (39 of the 136 comments, 29%). For example, one of the examiners stated that the scholarly overview "lacks a good discussion and infusion of theoretical framework". They also identified shortcomings in the sources cited in the scholarly review (27 of the 136 comments, 20%). These included the use of dated sources, overemphasis on one source, grand theorists or essential theories not consulted, and dependence on sources that lacked the necessary rigour such as the Internet, and secondary or textbook sources. Eighteen of the 136 comments (13%) focused on the way the literature was interpreted and presented. Examiners noted that candidates failed to justify their choice of sources or misrepresented them, quoted them incorrectly, presented them as assumptions, and failed to acknowledge their sources or referenced them incorrectly. The result was that candidates made sweeping statements or overgeneralisations. Examiners mentioned nine other shortcomings with regard to the scholarly review (see Table 16.3).

Tables 16.4-16.7 illustrate the other four themes and their sub-themes. These shortcomings can be regarded as less significant because examiners referred to them only once or placed less emphasis on them.

TABLE 16.4 Shortcomings identified by examiners in terms of the contributions claimed

Contributions claimed	Total comments: 43
Not within the scope, research questions/hypotheses or aims/objectives of the study	9
No contribution to the discipline	
Too descriptive and a lack of normative conceptualisations	9
Inadequate level of significance and originality	8
Contribution merely implied	7
Over-generalisations and sweeping statements made	3
No reference to scholarly literature explored in the study to support the contribution claimed	3
Lack of applicability to the context studied	3
No mention of possible further research	1

TABLE 16.5 Shortcomings identified by examiners in terms of the background

Background	Total comments: 34
Research questions/hypotheses: ambiguous, unrelated to topic	10
Inconsistencies or weak links between the alignment of the title, research questions/hypotheses, aims/objectives and/or topic	9
Title: ambiguous, unrelated to topic	5
Problem statement: ambiguous, unrelated to scope, not current or novel	5
Aims/objectives: omitted, ambiguous, unrelated to topic	2
Focus/topic: scope too wide or too narrow, not related to discipline	3

TABLE 16.6 Shortcomings identified by examiners in terms of the validity, reliability and trustworthiness

Validity, reliability and trustworthiness	Total comments: 14
Too vague, not discussed in enough detail	5
Weaknesses in the design and application of the collection instruments as well as data analysis	3
Essential strategies omitted	3
Research does not reflect the theory on which it was supposedly based	2
Concepts inconsistent with methodology	1

TABLE 16.7 Shortcomings identified by examiners in terms of the ethical considerations

Ethical considerations	Total comments: 7
Incorrect reporting of data results	1
Technical approach: explained theoretically but no information on how it was applied in the research study	1
The need to keep the identity of the research environments and participants confidential and anonymous not respected	1
Detailed descriptions provided in the body of the thesis, instead of in an appendix	1
Description of ethical considerations and how they were met inconsistent	1
No information on how data would be stored and destroyed	1
No evidence given of obtaining permission from all stakeholders	1

Tables 16.4-16.7 reveal that ethical considerations received the fewest comments (7 comments) and that there were 14 comments related to strategies pertaining to validity, reliability and trustworthiness. There were more comments on shortcomings related to the contributions claimed (43) and the background (34).

REFLECTIONS ON THE FINDINGS

Reflecting on the findings, there are many reasons for concern. Firstly, one would assume that doctoral candidates have the ability to present their work in a scientifically acceptable manner. It seems that this is not the case. This finding accords with the work of Holbrook, Bourke, Lovat and Dally (2004a, 2004b) in Australian universities. They found that 80% of the examiners commented on the candidates' lack of basic communicative competence. Secondly, although commented on least, the lack of attention to ethical considerations is a matter of concern. Holbrook et al (2004a:136) found that "[t]he ethics of the research are barely mentioned which, given the attention paid to the issue in Australian universities, is quite surprising". The same comment applies to this South African study. One would expect that given the heightened awareness of the importance of research ethics, doctoral students would give scrupulous attention to ethical aspects. Candidates' failure to do so may well be another indication of their inability to conduct rigorous ethical research.

There are three further concerns with regard to the findings on the other main themes. These are the background of the study (Table 16.5), the scholarly review (Table 16.3) and the overall research design and execution (Tables 16.1 and 16.6). Comments on these aspects, especially the lack of coherence between them, are directly related to the scholarly contribution made by the candidate in the thesis. A comment such as, "The thesis does not make major new knowledge claims – a number of its broad conclusions have been argued elsewhere" is an indictment of a candidate, given the time and energy expended during the doctoral journey. It suggests that the candidate failed to examine the existing body of scholarship. Another examiner stated that "there is no demonstration of substantial contribution to knowledge ... this study has [not] produced new discoveries in the field". This suggests that the conceptual framework did not take account of current knowledge. Leshem and Trafford (2007:103) argue that a "conceptual framework is ... the means through which doctoral candidates provide their examiners with answers to such questions as: What was the wider theoretical significance of that reading? Why has the research been designed in that way? What is the conceptual significance of the evidence? Why does the thesis make a contribution to knowledge?" The theory we wish to put forward focuses on the fundamental importance of developing a coherent conceptual framework that could enable candidates to arrive at and justify their conceptual contributions. This should prevent candidates from receiving comments such as the following:

What is missing at the end of each section/chapter is an integrated perspective on what new knowledge was created, how it addressed the research question with its sub-questions and how this newly gained body of knowledge can enhance our understanding of the research topic.

A THEORY FOR PREPARING FOR THE EXAMINATION PROCESS

We suggest that one way in which a supervisor and candidate could prepare for the examination process is to interrogate the soundness of the conceptual framework and then to test the thesis against this framework, posing questions such as the ones Leshem and Trafford (2007:103) suggest. If we accept Leshem and Trafford's (2007) questions as legitimate, in the sense that they are the kind of questions that examiners tend to ask, the central importance of the conceptual framework cannot be doubted. The conceptual framework should orientate both the author and the reader, frame the arguments, direct the theoretical and empirical conclusions, provide methodological direction, and make it possible for the reciprocity between theory and data to be seen. In addition, we propose that the conceptual framework enables candidates to position their studies in terms of theoretical and empirical significance and in explaining the contribution they make to new knowledge.

What would a theory or a conceptual framework that enables supervisors and candidates to prepare for the examination process look like? In what follows we suggest the main elements of such a theory; acknowledging fully that there are many peripheral elements to the development of a conceptual framework that are not explicitly included. What we aim to do is to construct a theory that takes account of the main critiques presented by examiners.

Candidates should be able to correct any basic technical and grammatical errors in the thesis relatively easily. However, addressing criticisms that the conceptual framework is inadequate would pose a serious challenge. In light of our reflections on the findings, we propose a theory that addresses the criticisms related to the background of the study (we refer to this as the research questions, hypotheses and aims), the scholarly overview and the overall research design and execution.

The common criticisms of the scholarly overview by examiners that are listed in the sub-themes (Table 16.3) will not be repeated here. In our view, these criticisms reflect the candidates' inability to develop theoretical frameworks that uniquely take account of their research foci. To develop a theoretical framework, a candidate needs to select focused theories or models based on the work of leading theorists that relate to the research. They also need to be aware of what has been done in the field. This enables them to narrow the scope of their research and to explore the seminal literature in depth, and not fall into the trap of exploring the literature too widely. An in-depth, focused review of the literature creates the opportunity for candidates to engage more critically and rigorously with the body of scholarship, aggregating and collating related theories, models and works of different theorists. For candidates to engage critically with the theories, models and works of different theorists, they need a sound understanding of their philosophical underpinnings. This would enable them to weigh different theories, models and works of different theorists and to justify the scholarly choices made in constructing the unique theoretical framework of the thesis.

In Table 16.5 the shortcomings identified by examiners related to the background of the study (research questions, hypotheses and aims) are listed. These include the ambiguity of the research questions, hypotheses and aims or their unrelatedness to the topic or discipline, and too wide or too narrow in scope. Inconsistencies or weak links between the title, research questions/hypotheses, aims/objectives and/or topic are also frequently mentioned. Candidates need to formulate their research questions and hypotheses, whether they emanate from the body of scholarship or from lived experiences, in ways that allow them to generate theory and contribute to new knowledge, and not merely to describe existing problems or to provide answers to 'how to' questions. This is what we term the development of research questions and hypotheses that transcend the descriptive realm to enter the normative realm (see Simmonds & Du Preez 2014).

The research design attracted most comments by examiners, in particular, the failure to justify the selection of a methodology and to link it to the philosophy or paradigm that underpins it. The sampling, data collection and methods of analysis were also critiqued, not only in terms of their execution, but also in terms of their relationship to the selected methodology (see Punch, 2007 for more on this dimension). Figure 16.1 below illustrates these three dimensions.

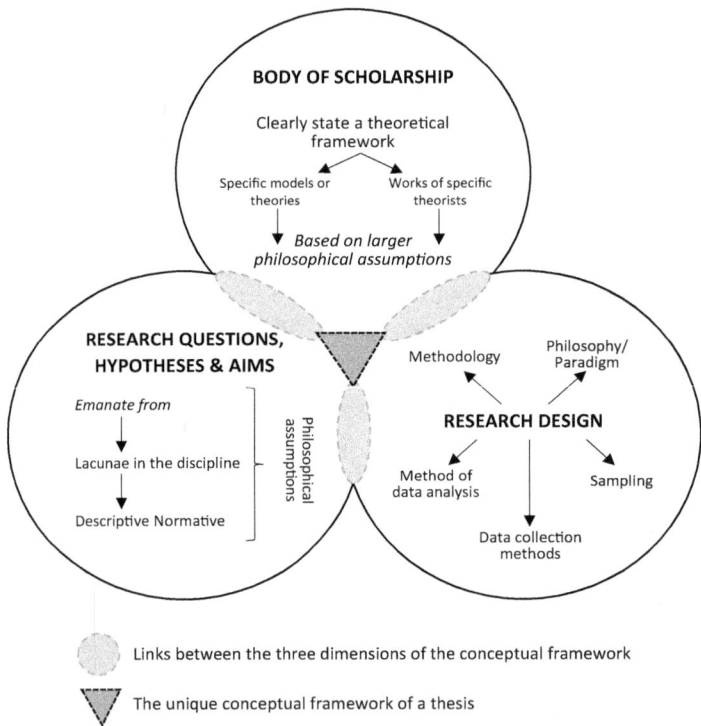

FIGURE 16.1 An illustration of the development of a conceptual framework

It is important to note that the development of a conceptual framework is not a linear process. Sometimes the research questions and hypotheses come first, sometimes the data or research design comes first (as is the case with this chapter), and at other times the framework emanates from the identification of the gaps in the scholarly overview. This theory should not be viewed as a recipe, but rather as a guideline to developing a unique conceptual framework. This process – which is flexible, iterative and open to change – begins in the proposal writing phase and runs throughout the study.

Candidates must be able to make conceptual links between the elements of the framework of the thesis and justify what is included at every point of their study. For example, the research design should be selected and justified in the light of the research questions or hypotheses and the scholarly overview. More importantly, candidates need to be philosophically and paradigmatically consistent to achieve overall coherence. Clearly explaining the links throughout the thesis increases the likelihood of creating a unique and sound conceptual framework and thus contributing to new knowledge. The significance of the research should emerge clearly. In preparation for the examination process, candidates and supervisors should interrogate the thesis to ensure that the conceptual links between the three dimensions are clearly stated and that the unique conceptual elements of the framework are highlighted.

CONCLUSION

We acknowledge that the examination process is subjective and inconsistent (Lessing 2009). Nevertheless, there are predictable requirements. We hope our work will contribute to theory on the construction of a sound conceptual framework that takes critical account of previous studies in the field, identifying the gaps or deficiencies in research and theory and showing how the current study makes an original contribution to knowledge. This should assist supervisors and candidates to have a greater awareness of how to meet the demands of the examination process – especially in education and perhaps in other disciplines in the humanities and social sciences. In particular, we focus on critical questions that could be asked to interrogate theses, from the first draft to the final version presented for examination. We recognise also that whereas the empirical findings of this chapter highlight weaknesses in doctoral theses, they may also expose weaknesses in doctoral examining *per se*. This is an avenue we deem worth exploring in our further research.

REFERENCES

ASSAf (Academy of Science for South Africa). 2010. *The PhD study: An evidence based study on how to meet the demands for high level skills in an emerging economy, Consensus Report.* Pretoria: ASSAF.

Birks M & Mills J. 2015. *Grounded theory: A practical guide.* London: SAGE.

Bourke S. 2007. PhD thesis quality: The views of examiners. *South African Journal of Higher Education,* 8:1042-1053.

Bourke S, Hattie J & Anderson L. 2004. Predicting examiner recommendations on PhD theses. *International Journal of Educational Research,* 41:178-194. https://doi.org/10.1016/j.ijer.2005.04.012

Bourke S & Holbrook, AP. 2011. Examining PhD and research masters theses. *Assessment & Evaluation in Higher Education,* 38(4):407-416. https://doi.org/10.1080/02602938.2011.638738

Charmaz K. 2014. *Constructing grounded theory: A practical guide through qualitative analysis.* London: SAGE.

Cloete N, Mouton J & Sheppard C. 2015. *Doctoral education in South Africa: Policy, discourse and data.* Cape Town: African Minds.

Du Preez P. 2014. Education research for quality PhD study curriculum-making: A South African meta-study. 2014-2016. Research proposal submitted and approved by the National Research Foundation (NRF).

Du Preez P & Simmonds S. 2016. Higher degree committee members' perceptions of quality assurance of doctoral education: A South African perspective. *International Journal of Doctoral Studies,* 11:341-365. https://doi.org/10.28945/3586

Glaser B & Strauss A. 1967. *The discovery of grounded theory.* Hawthorne, NY: Aldine Publishing Company.

Holbrook A, Bourke S, Fairbairn H & Lovat T. 2007. Examiner comment on the literature review in PhD theses. *Studies in Higher Education,* 32(3):337-356. https://doi.org/10.1080/03075070701346899

Holbrook A, Bourke S, Lovat T & Dally K. 2004a. Qualities and characteristics in the written reports of doctoral thesis examiners. *Australian Journal of Educational & Developmental Psychology,* 4:126-145.

Holbrook A, Bourke S, Lovat T & Dally K. 2004b. Investigating PhD thesis examination reports. *International Journal of Educational Research,* 41:98-120.Holbrook A, Bourke S, Lovat T & Fairbairn H. 2008. Consistency and inconsistency in PhD thesis examination. *Australian Journal of Education,* 52(1):36-48. https://doi.org/10.1177/000494410805200103

Leshem S & Trafford V. 2007. Overlooking the conceptual framework. *Innovations in Education and Teaching International,* 44(1):93-105. https://doi.org/10.1080/14703290601081407

Lessing A. 2009. The examination of research for dissertations and theses. *Acta Academia,* 41(1): 255-272.

Lotz-Sisitka H, Ellery K, Olvitt L, Schudel I & O'Donoghue R. 2010. Cultivating a scholarly community of practice. *Acta Academia,* 1:130-150.

Punch KF. 2006. *Developing effective research proposals*. Los Angeles & London: SAGE.

Samuel M & Vithal R. 2011. Emergent frameworks of research teaching and learning in a cohort-based doctoral programme. *Perspective in Education*, 3(29):76-87.

Simmonds S & Du Preez P. 2014. The centrality of the research question for locating PhD studies in the global knowledge society. *South African Journal of Higher Education*, 28(5):1606-1623.

Smit B, Williamson C & Padayachee A. 2013. PhD capacity-building, from aid to innovation: The SANPAD-SANTRUST experience. *Studies in Higher Education*, 38(3):441-455. https://doi.org/10.1080/03075079.2013.773218

South Africa. 2011. *National Development Plan: Vision for 2030*. http://policyresearch.limpopo.gov.za/bitstream/handle/123456789/941/NDP%20Vision%202030.pdf?sequence=1 [Retrieved 4 April 2016].

Wisker G. 2010. The 'good enough' doctorate: Doctoral learning journeys. *Acta Academia*, 1:223-242.

THE ORIGINAL CONTRIBUTION: MYTH OR REALITY IN DOCTORAL WORK?

Liezel Frick

BACKGROUND

> Graduate students are frequently exhorted to make an 'original' or 'significant contribution' to knowledge. Indeed, this is the most commonly, and often the only, explicitly stated criterion for the award of the PhD ... But what 'original' and 'significant' mean do not appear to have ever been operationalized or objectively defined for graduate students
>
> (Lovitts 2007:3).

The original contribution lies at the heart of what it means to be doctorate, as the work is expected to extend the horizons – the knowledge boundaries – of a particular discipline (or disciplines in the case of inter- or trans-disciplinary work). But how such originality manifests or what it looks like in a doctoral thesis has – as Lovitts (2007) rightly argues – not received much scholarly attention. Often indeterminate qualities are cited, such as inspiration, responsibility, cognitive excitement, personal synthesis, "wrestling", or "being adventurous" (Winter, Griffiths & Green 2000:35). Anecdotally, examiners and more experienced supervisors often describe originality as the "I'll know it when I see it" element of the doctoral thesis. Alternatively, neoliberal, performative and regulatory standards within higher education have tried to reduce doctoral knowledge work and originality to measurable outcome metrics and economic indicators (Bansel 2011). Neither of these approaches to originality – whether they be vague and subjective, or supposedly concrete and measurable – are really useful to a doctoral candidate wishing to make sense of what is expected of them to become doctorate, or for (novice) supervisors who want to help their students work towards scholarly success in and beyond the doctorate.

Lovitts's (2007:21-34) work distinguishes between a significant and an original contribution in doctoral work. The comparison between the two terms as described by Lovitts (2007) shows much overlap, although originality is most often cited in policy directives on the doctorate. A few authors have explicitly explored the notion of originality in doctoral work from various perspectives, including:

- how originality may be conceptualised (Frick 2010, 2011); defined (Phillips & Pugh 2010); and can be demonstrated (Gill & Dolan 2015);
- what the relationships between originality, creativity and innovation within doctoral work are (Baptista, Frick, Holley, Remmik, Tesch & Åkerlind 2015);
- how ethics governance processes may curb originality in doctoral work (Snowden 2014);
- a student perspective (Bansel 2011; Edwards 2014);
- how originality may manifest during oral examinations of doctoral students (Trafford & Leshem 2008); and
- how it can be broadly described across disciplines (Lovitts 2007); or how it can be made visible in a practice-based PhD (Winter *et al* 2000); nursing (Gelling & Rodriquez Borrego 2014); or in the humanities and the social sciences (Guetzkow, Lamont & Mallard 2004).

Originality at the doctoral level is multifaceted, which makes it difficult to pinpoint (Gill & Dolan 2015). Lovitts (2007:31) captures this varied nature of the concept as the reporting of a research endeavour that

> ... has not been done, found, known, proved, said, or seen before that results from

- asking or identifying new questions, topics, or areas of exploration
- applying new ideas, methods, approaches, or analysis to an old question, problem, issue, idea, source, thinker, or text
- developing or applying new theories, theorems, theoretical descriptions, or theoretical frameworks
- inventing, developing, or applying new methods, approaches, computations, techniques or technologies
- creating, finding or using new data, datasets, archives, information, materials, or sources
- developing or applying new analysis, analytic approaches, frameworks, techniques, models, or statistical procedures

- coming up with new ideas, connections, inferences, insights, interpretations, observations, perspectives
- producing new conclusions, answers, findings or proofs
- combining or synthesizing things (experiments, facts, knowledge, models of inquiry, problems, sources, technologies, theoretical constructs) from other fields or disciplines
- is publishable
- changes the way people think
- moves the field forward/advances the state of the art
- adds to knowledge.

Originality may be found in any one or multiple areas as highlighted above, but will rarely if ever constitute all these possible facets. Phillips and Pugh (2010:62) take a similar view, and add that originality often builds on existing work, including that of the supervisor(s), and can be nestled within or across disciplines. However, Gill and Dolan (2015:13) warn that the candidate still needs to take ownership of the work, and be explicit as "simply doing something original is not in itself necessarily enough to obtain a PhD; students also have to demonstrate, in a scholarly manner, how their research adds to the extant body of knowledge and what the potential wider implications of this new knowledge are for the subject, discipline and related research".

Despite these advances in our understanding of originality in doctoral work, Gill and Dolan (2015:12) argue that doctoral work often shows candidates' limited understanding of the concept of originality, as such work does not "critically demonstrate how, and in what way, the study meaningfully adds to the existing body of knowledge". In addition, there has been no concerted scholarly effort to investigate how originality manifests in the actual theses produced by doctoral candidates, which makes this chapter a useful addition to this section on new horizons for supervision. This chapter therefore explores the following questions:

- Do doctoral students account for originality in their theses?
- What, if anything, do theses constructions tell us about where and how originality features in doctoral work?

METHODOLOGY

The findings reported here are based on an analysis of theses across faculties produced at one South African research-intensive university over a nine-year period (2008-2016)[1], which were analysed to determine how students explicitly account for originality in the written output of their doctoral work. A total of 1566 PhD theses were included in the analysis. These theses were produced across nine faculties (constituting 75 distinct academic departments), thus include doctoral work across disciplines.

All full text doctoral theses were uploaded from the university online repository into a *Zotero* library in .pdf file format using the web browser integration and online syncing functions. Items were organized through a drag-and-drop interface, which was then used in subsequent searches as discussed below. *Zotero* (see www.zotero.org) is a free and open-source reference management software system, specifically developed to manage bibliographic data and related materials (such as .pdf files as was the case here). Since *Zotero* could accommodate the large dataset used in this analysis, it was a user-friendly analytical interface for the particular study.

Text analysis was done on two levels. The first level of analysis entailed a basic search for specific keywords related to the identified research issue. Keywords included in this search were:

- originality/original (*oorspronklike/oorspronklik*);
- contribution (*bydrae*);
- significance/significant (*beduidend/e*); and
- impact (*impak*).

Both English and Afrikaans terminology was used in the search, as some theses were written in Afrikaans. There were a small number of theses (n=7) that were written in languages other than English or Afrikaans (for instance French or German), and these were excluded from the study even though they contained English abstracts.

Since the first level of analysis only highlighted if, and (if so), where keywords occurred in the dataset of theses, a second level of analysis was conducted within the theses where the above-mentioned keywords were found to account for specificity and structure. For example, the use of the word 'significance' could relate to either a statistically significant finding (in which case the use did not necessarily mean that the work overall was significant or, for that matter, original), or the significance of the contribution as described by Lovitts (2007) above (in which case it was included for further analysis). In addition, 'contribution' could refer to another scholar's work other than the candidate's own. Each of the keywords included could have multiple possible meanings and applications within a thesis, and therefore a second level of analysis was necessary. The second level of analysis thus enabled a further delimitation of the actual theses to be included for further analysis, as well as a more accurate and richer descriptive analysis of the theses identified in the first level of analysis which were included in the second level of analysis.

RESULTS AND DISCUSSION

Even though further analysis was necessary in the second level of analysis (as described above), the initial first level of analysis was useful to provide a broad overview of the dataset. An indication of the prevalence of the selected keywords as an indication of doctoral thesis originality is shown in Figure 17.1 below.

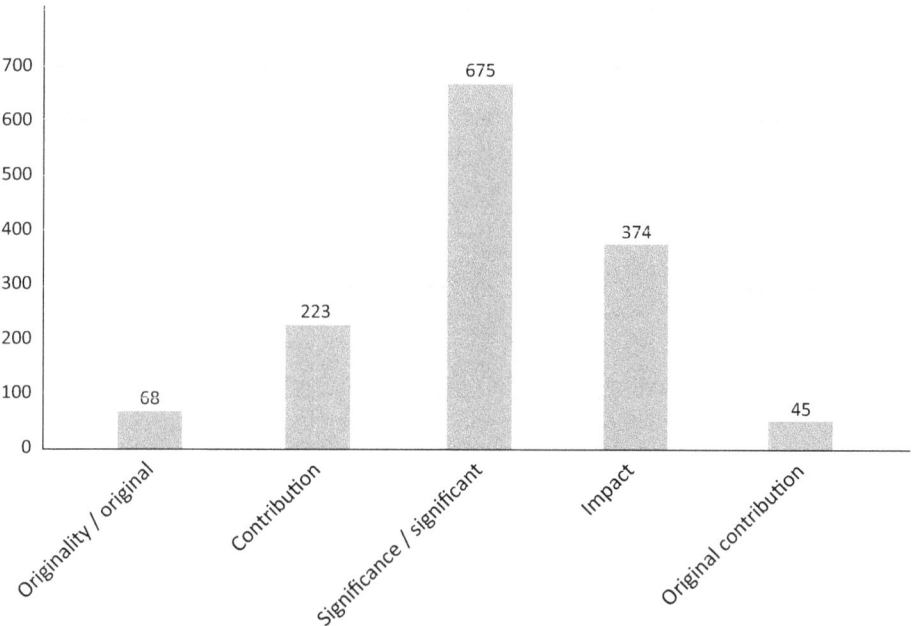

FIGURE 17.1 Overview of the data (Level 1 analysis)

As can be seen from Figure 17.1 above, the notions of originality and making an original contribution are not explicit features in the studied dataset that spans across disciplines. Only 4.3% (n=68) of the analysed theses contained the words 'originality'/'original' (or *oorspronklike/oorspronklik*), whilst 14.2% (n=223) made reference to a contribution (or *bydrae*). Given that these key terms may be used in various ways, 'original contribution' (*oorspronklike bydrae*) was employed as a separate search category. Only 2.9% (n=45) of the analysed theses contained this term, of which less than 1% of the analysed theses (n=15) contained an explicit reference to the original contribution of the actual thesis. Since the number of theses that explicitly addressed the issue of making an original contribution to the field of study was so limited, it did not warrant further statistical analysis. However, it was interesting to see that these 15 theses were distributed across disciplinary boundaries, including Business Management (n=2), Social Work (n=1), Medicine (n=1), Philosophy (n=1), Polymer Science (n=1), Biochemistry (n=2), History (n=1), and the majority being Engineering (n=6). In the case of Engineering, the theses were distributed across different engineering specialisation areas, and all were supervised by different supervisors. Thus the occurrence cannot be attributed only to the practices of one specific field or supervisor. This initial analysis seems to confirm Lovitts's (2007) claim that originality is more an implicit than an explicit feature of doctoral written work.

Since the work of Lovitts (2007) shows a notable overlap between the conceptualisation of originality and significance in doctoral work, the keywords 'significance' or 'significant' (*beduidend/e*) and 'impact' (*impak*) were also used in the first level of analysis. This search yielded notably more hits in both these searches, with 43% of the theses using the words 'significance' or 'significant' (*beduidend/e*) (n=675), and 23.9% of these analysed theses referring to 'impact' (*impak*) (n=374). However, as in the previous searches, these results need to be interpreted with some caution as the keywords could have a variety of applications not necessarily related to the so-called original contribution of the thesis itself. Further interrogation of these documents during the second level of analysis showed that this was indeed the case: in most instances it was found that these keywords were not related to the notion of an original contribution. These keywords were subsequently discarded in the second level of analysis.

Specificity and structure were important features within the subsequent analysis, as it is not only important to explain whether theses explicitly address the issue of originality (or not), but also where and how it is done (if at all). The second level of analysis focused on document analysis to account for specificity on *how* originality was established (as indicated in the less than 1% of the theses that specifically indicated the original contribution made by the doctoral research as highlighted above). This was then used in further analysis to account for structure in terms of *where* originality featured in the work. Structure provides an indication of the 'where', as it positions the issue as either central or peripheral to the doctoral work presented.

CHAPTER 17 • THE ORIGINAL CONTRIBUTION: MYTH OR REALITY IN DOCTORAL WORK?

Structure furthermore provides an indication of how readers (in the case of theses, most notably the examiners) are alerted to the notion of an original contribution.

The 15 identified theses in the second level of analysis showed that doctoral authors used different structures and strategies to highlight their original contributions to their readers. The examples below show that originality may be addressed in various parts of the thesis, ranging from the abstract, introduction and/or conclusions, to a separate statement by the author, or a specific sub-heading within the first chapter highlighting the 'significance of the study'.

The following examples show how originality may be addressed as part of the abstract of a thesis. Emphasis is added in underlined text to the original text to highlight the specific strategies the author used to emphasise originality.

> This study has been positioned as a contribution to the emerging literature relating to issues of transformation in South African sport by exploring historical change in the demographics of professional football in South Africa at an institutional level. … The original contribution of this study to the scholarship pertaining to South African football spans multiple dimensions. In addition to arguing that new elements need to be considered in the debate regarding the NFL's demise in the late 1970s, it also contains the first in-depth analysis of the relationship between the National Party's multinational sports policy and South African football historically. Consequently it contributes to the broader literature exploring the nexus between sport, politics and race in South African sport generally. It further analyses the trajectory of former NFL clubs – and their disappearance over time – in the period subsequent to the white league's disbandment. This constitutes a new axis of analysis within the historiography of South African football. By the time football unity arrived in 1991 only two former (white) NFL clubs remained within the top tier of South African professional football – this after the NFL had experienced notable popularity during the 1960s and early 1970s. The analysis of this drastic historical shift relating to institutional white football represents an important marker regarding the complex and multifaceted range of historical variables that impacted the game locally during the period 1959-90. As a result this study offers historical perspective to current debates on sporting transformation. It is argued that despite the fact that football itself has largely been positioned outside these debates, the study thereof still serves as a crucial lens through which to consider the demographic fluidity that has been present within South African sport historically. (History, Venter 2016:ii)

The contribution in this example is based on a non-empirical analytical thesis that is presented within the discipline of History, although the candidate argues that the existing debates on the topic have not been positioned from this disciplinary perspective. In addition, it positions the original contribution within the discipline itself as well.

In the following two examples from abstracts of doctoral theses, the originality of the work highlighted is focused on the methodological and empirical contributions made:

> Thermodynamic considerations provide a rigorous framework for the interpretation of chemical reactions, however little experimental data are openly available for the associated solution species in acidic iron sulfate systems. A key contribution of this work, and critical for the development of the overall model, is the direct measurement of speciation in iron sulfate solutions. Raman and UV-vis spectroscopy were utilised to make direct speciation measurements in the various subsystems of the $Fe_2(SO_4)_3$-$FeSO_4$-H_2SO_4-H_2O system that were previously unavailable in the open literature. The $FeSO_4^+$ and $Fe(SO_4)_2^-$ species were explicitly identified and measurements were supported and rationalised by static computational quantum mechanical calculations and ultimately permit the calibration of a robust, ion-interaction solution model with the explicit recognition of the important solution species up to 1.6 mol/kg $Fe_2(SO_4)_3$, 0.8 mol/kg H_2SO_4 over 25-90 _C.
>
> The specific original contributions of this work are
>
> - The direct measurement of aqueous speciation in the $Fe_2(SO_4)_3$-H_2SO_4-H_2O system by Raman and UV-vis spectroscopy
> - The development of a modelling framework to characterise speciation, activity coefficients and solubility in the mixed $Fe_2(SO_4)_3$-$FeSO_4$-H_2SO_4-H_2O system.
> - The measurement of Fe(III) reduction kinetics using SO_2 in concentrated sulfate solutions as a function of initial composition and temperature.
> - The development of a solution reaction model of Fe(III) reduction with SO_2 that accurately predicts the solution speciation and reaction rate with time as a function of composition and temperature.

Lastly, the vast complexity of industrial systems will nearly always result in a lack of specific experimental data that are required for the development of phenomenological models. This work emphasises the crucial role that engineering studies hold in the generation of such data to derive maximum practical value for industrial process development and optimisation. (Engineering, Biley 2015:iii-iv)

A contribution is presented towards this ongoing endeavor via original methodologies for measurements of cycling kinematics using wireless inertial and magnetic measurement systems (IMMSs) and technique analysis of expert rugby union goal kicking using stereophotogrammetry.

> Three studies are presented detailing the design and validation of sensor fusion algorithms for IMMS tracking of cycling kinematics … A novel optical motion capture method for tracking the crank angle was also developed using a two-segment definition.
>
> Three more studies present a novel technique analysis of fifteen professional goal kickers using stereophotogrammetry … The most important finding in all three studies was high inter-individual variability and low intra-individual variability, which highlights the nonlinear, athlete-specific dynamics of motor control in sports.
>
> In short, this work contributes towards understanding and overcoming challenges to cycling analysis using IMMSs. The tracking algorithms are resistant to errors caused by magnetic interference, centripetal accelerations and sensor-to-segment calibration. Similarly, the technique analysis of rugby goal kicking contributes towards evidence-based coaching by providing novel methodologies and data for understanding performance. (Engineering, Cockroft 2015:ii-iii)

Structurally, these three examples show the importance of making originality explicit from the start, at the entry point into the thesis – the abstract. In terms of specificity, the three examples serve to show that originality can manifest in multiple areas – be it epistemological, methodological, and/or empirical (Frick 2010, 2011).

One of the examples (Dlamini 2016) included references to originality in both the abstract and conclusions, as seen below. In the abstract, the candidate stated the following:

> The original contributions presented in this thesis are in the field of flight dynamics and robust control … A novel approach of analysing disturbance rejection capabilities of an aircraft with available actuators through a more robust combination of feedback states is discussed. From this analysis a new FBW control law is developed and its robustness evaluated. Through a comparison with an ideal system the limiting factors to improving the robustness of the B747 class of aircraft are identified. (Engineering, Dlamini 2016:iii)

The conclusion section of the thesis contained a section called 'Original contributions to the field', which made this aspect explicit to the reader. The candidate proceeds point-wise in this section to highlight exactly what he believes these original contributions are:

Original contributions to the field from this study are:

- The change in flight dynamics due to tail damage was presented and a clear analysis provided for the resulting behaviour. Whilst similar past studies show the change in aerodynamic coefficients and stability margins, this research presents a detailed analysis of the change in static and dynamic behaviour as well as trim qualities of the damaged aircraft.
- An evaluation of the robustness of a generic FBW system against tail damage of a large transport aircraft. Results of the robustness analysis are published in the Aeronautical Journal [34].
- A presentation of degradation in the aircraft's handling qualities due to tail damage. This provides a more informative idea concerning the pilot's capability to successfully complete their mission task. (Dlamini 2016:113)

This is an interesting structural example, as it addresses originality at both the start and the end of the thesis, providing an explicit wrap-around approach to dealing with the issue of originality. In terms of specificity, it shows a strong cognizance of the existing knowledge in the field, against which the new work is projected and shown to be original. In addition, in motivating its originality it refers explicitly to the publishability of the reported thesis work, which is an aspect highlighted by most authors as an important facet of determining originality (Gill & Dolan 2015; Lovitts 2007; Phillips & Pugh 2010).

The following example used the introduction to explicate the original contribution (but not the abstract, nor does the author explicitly return to this aspect in the conclusions). A specific sub-heading called 'Contribution of the study' is used in the first chapter to alert the reader.

> This study is to be seen as a pioneering study in the South African business environment and it contributes to the field of country of origin studies in a novel way, firstly by measuring the consumer ethnocentrism of (two) different racial groups in a mature developing country (South Africa) and secondly by investigating the potential impact of ethnocentricity on the buying intentions of these two different racial groups of South African consumers, specifically regarding items of clothing imported from China.
>
> The results of this investigation and subsequent recommendations are hoped to be useful in the development of suitable marketing strategies, especially communication strategies, not only for products exported to South Africa – in this case from the People's Republic of China – but also for products produced in South Africa. (Business Management, Pentz 2011:11)

In terms of specificity, this example seems to follow a more tentative phrasing than the previous examples, but that is probably realistic given the scope and reach of a doctorate – as advised by Gill and Dolan (2015). The particular example furthermore highlights context as an original feature of the work.

The following example also used the introductory chapter of the thesis to highlight the contribution. Here a section named 'Significance of the study' stated:

> The contribution of this dissertation is embedded in explaining why corruption is a systematic and complex problem situation that is connected with development. This dissertation questions the traditional approaches to manage and control corruption, i.e. from only an ethical and moral, or economic, or political perspective. This dissertation explains why the systems approach is suitable for containing systemic corruption; and how the approach can be applied to manage and control systemic corruption. The description provided of the obstructions to the five dimensions of development (co-producers of systemic corruption) has not been done before at the same length as in this dissertation. The impact of systemic corruption emphasises why and how corruption is so destructive for development. An aspirational taxonomy developed from comparative best practice case studies of USA and UK, Hong Kong and Singapore respectively is the author's interpretation of why reforms in these countries were systemic, compared to other international best and worst practices. The development of systemic and operational guidelines from best practice cases, provide insight for containing corruption. A key contribution is a discussion of developing countries' corruption problem situations. Key drivers, key uncertainties, and key strategies demonstrate how systemic corruption can be contained and dissolved. (Business Management, Coetzee 2012:27)

It is interesting that here significance is used rather than originality, but given that these two concepts seem to be closely related (as seen in Lovitts 2007), this is not surprising. The author furthermore takes strong ownership of the work, positioning originality as a critique on and extension of past work, as well as a novel application of new insights. In both the examples where originality is structurally positioned within the introductory section of the thesis, the work is introduced as original, but the authors do not explicitly return to this aspect later in the thesis to affirm their claims.

The final example used only the conclusions chapter to highlight the contributions made:
> In summary, the virtue ethics based approach or practice model developed in this dissertation offers the following contributions to the field of public health ethics. This approach:
> - Is holistic and multidimensional as it focuses public health policy development on several dimensions of human well-being rather than an exclusively biological perspective of health.

- Is context sensitive and "promotes a dialectic interaction between universal norms and practical 'on-the- ground' knowledge and understanding". (P130)
- Acknowledges the importance of 'the public' as moral agent and that moral choice and responsibility, viewed from the broader perspective of -- How should I live? and What constitutes 'the good life' for me and those with whom I interact? – impacts significantly on many matters falling under the broad umbrella of public health.
- Avoids casting public health issues as a contest between individual rights and interests and the 'common good' or public best interest and thus avoids the archetypical public health ethics tension between utilitarianism and rights based approaches to these issues.
- Identifies desired programme or policy outcomes that are both measurable and quantifiable and those that are difficult to measure or quantify but equally important for the overall success of the programme.
- Asserts that public health practitioners require both skills and certain character traits or virtues that can be taught or developed to some degree, in order to ensure they are able to fulfil their rolls in the 'practice' of public health adequately. (Philosophy, Horn 2010:231)

This example brings the reader to the original contribution at the closure of the thesis, first reporting the work that was done before staking a claim on originality. Originality is positioned within the new model that is presented as an outcome of the doctoral work, after which specific claims are made to substantiate why this model may be seen as original. In this way it conforms to the view of Gill and Dolan (2015:13) that "the original aspects of most PhDs are likely to be relatively narrow, focused and precise, and usually depend on the research and the candidate".

CONCLUSION

This analysis does not claim that the theses that did not explicitly claim to make original contributions did not contain original work (indeed the doctoral degrees would not otherwise have been awarded), but rather that these texts left the reader to judge where and how such originality manifested. When thinking about whether or not doctoral students account for originality in their written theses work (the first level of analysis in this study), it becomes clear that originality is more often an implied than explicit feature of doctoral written outputs, despite the prominence given to this aspect of doctoral work in national and international policy rhetoric on the doctorate. A decade since Lovitts (2007) called for making originality an explicit feature of doctoral work it remains a nebulous aspect of the doctoral thesis in the majority of studied theses.

When we consider what thesis constructions that do explicitly address originality tell us about this aspect in doctoral work (the second level of analysis in this study), the analysis shows that there is no golden rule for making originality explicit in thesis construction. But by making the contribution of the work explicit (possibly at the onset and closure of the overall argument), it may offer readers (including examiners) a better basis for judging the original merit of the work – as was shown in the various examples cited here. The analysis furthermore provides concrete evidence of the multi-faceted nature of originality in doctoral work, as no two examples had exactly the same permutation or combinations of aspects indicating how they claimed to be original.

Given the importance attributed to knowledge production and advances doctorates are expected to make – both in academe and beyond – a more explicit promotion of originality in doctoral work is proposed here as a new horizon for supervisors to explore within their different disciplinary contexts. The examples provided show a variety of ways in which this can be achieved.

REFERENCES

Bansel P. 2011. Becoming academic: A reflection on doctoral candidacy. *Studies in Higher Education*, 36(5): 543-556. https://doi.org/10.1080/03075079.2011.594592

Baptista A, Frick L, Holley K, Remmik M, Tesch J & Åkerlind G. 2015. The doctorate as an original contribution to knowledge: Considering relationships between originality, creativity, and innovation. *Frontline Learning Research*, 3(3):51-63.

Biley C. 2015. Thermodynamic and Kinetic Modelling of Iron(III) Reduction with Sulfur Dioxide Gas. PhD thesis. Stellenbosch: Stellenbosch University.

Cockroft SJ. 2015. Novel Motion Capture Methods for Sports Analysis: Case Studies of Cycling and Rugby Goal Kicking. PhD thesis. Stellenbosch: Stellenbosch University.

Coetzee JJ. 2012. Systemic Corruption and Corrective Change Management Strategies: A Study of The Co-producers of Systemic Corruption and its Negative Impact on Socio-economic Development. PhD thesis. Stellenbosch: Stellenbosch University.

Dlamini Z. 2016. Robust Fly-by-Wire under Horizontal Tail Damage. PhD thesis. Stellenbosch: Stellenbosch University.

Edwards M. 2014. What does it mean to be original in a PhD? A research student's perspective. *Nurse Researcher,* 21(6):8-11. https://doi.org/10.7748/nr.21.6.8.e1254

Frick BL. 2010. Creativity in doctoral education: Conceptualising the original contribution. In: C Nygaard, N Courtney & CW Holtham (eds). *Teaching creativity – Creativity in teaching*. Oxfordshire: Libri Publishing.

Frick BL. 2011. Demystifying the original contribution: Supervisors' conceptualisations of creativity in doctoral education. *Pertanika Journal of Social Sciences,* 19(2):495-507.

Gelling L & Rodriguez Borrego MA. 2014. Originality in doctoral research. *Nurse Researcher,* 21(6):6-7. https://doi.org/10.7748/nr.21.6.6.s2

Gill P & Dolan G. 2015. Originality and the PhD: What is it and how can it be demonstrated? *Nurse Researcher,* 22(6):11-15. https://doi.org/10.7748/nr.22.6.11.e1335

Guetzkow J, Lamont M & Mallard G. 2004. What is originality in the humanities and the social sciences? *American Sociological Review,* 69(2):190-212. https://doi.org/10.1177/000312240406900203

Horn LM. 2010. Virtue Ethics in the Development of a Framework for Public Health Policymaking. PhD thesis. Stellenbosch: Stellenbosch University.

Lovitts BE. 2007. *Making the implicit explicit. Creating performance expectations for the dissertation.* Sterling: Stylus.

Pentz CD. 2011. Consumer Ethnocentrism and Attitudes towards Domestic and Foreign Products: A South African Study. PhD thesis. Stellenbosch: Stellenbosch University.

Phillips EM & Pugh DS. 2010. *How to get a PhD.* 5th Edition. Maidenhead: Open University Press.

Snowden A. 2014. Ethics and originality in doctoral research in the UK. *Nurse Researcher,* 21(6):12-15. https://doi.org/10.7748/nr.21.6.12.e1244

Trafford V & Leshem S. 2008. *Stepping stones to achieving your doctorate by focusing on your viva from the start.* London: McGraw-Hill Education.

Venter GB. 2016. Gone and Almost Forgotten? The Dynamics of Professional White Football in South Africa: 1959-1990. PhD thesis. Stellenbosch: Stellenbosch University.

Von Backström WT. 2012. From Turbo-Machines to Solar Chimneys. PhD thesis. Stellenbosch: Stellenbosch University.

Winter R, Griffiths M & Green K. 2000. The 'academic' qualities of practice: What are the criteria for a practice-based PhD? *Studies in Higher Education,* 25(1):25-37. https://doi.org/10.1080/030750700115993

COHORT-WIDE RESEARCH EDUCATION

Wendy Bastalich

INTRODUCTION

A significant feature of the changing climate in research degrees in the past 20 or so years has been the expansion of structured, cohort-level research training, a novel development in the thesis-only doctoral education context where supervision has for the most part been the focus of research education. Most of the higher education literature on the doctorate focuses on students and supervisors and the impact of the changing policy climate on existing practices in doctoral education, or with curriculum development within the disciplines. There is a stream of current literature which takes up questions pertinent in the cohort-wide or extra-supervision, extra-discipline modes of supervision. This chapter analyses the conceptual origins and practical applications of some of this literature to widen the conceptual understanding of cohort-wide research education.

The chapter opens with a broad outline of cognitive learning theory which, I argue, broadly informs three salient foci identified within the higher education literature and within cohort-level research training. The three foci are referred to as 'cognitive processing', 'situated learning' and 'research writing', and are described in summary form first in a table, followed by a more detailed elaboration in the chapter.

The discussion is not intended to offer an exhaustive mapping of contributions in the area of cohort-level research training, or a point of view on which focus is 'better'. It is hoped that a description of research training approaches at the whole of cohort level will contribute to the discussion on emerging educational practice in the doctorate by bringing attention to an important but often neglected area, and support further dialogue among researchers and practitioners. At the same time, the discussion observes a number of important contributions that thinking and practice in the area has brought, including the promotion of cross-discipline networks and collaborative or networked research learning opportunities, a more inclusive rethinking of the space within which research learning takes place, and of the critical role of specialised writing support in research education.

EDUCATIONAL THEORY

The research and practice described below appears to be informed broadly by cognitive education or self-regulated learner theories. In the early 1980s, educational theorists working in the area of cognition and learning began to problematise what they saw as too great a focus on taught factual and conceptual knowledge at the expense of knowledge that could be applied (Cope 2005). The problem for these thinkers was that academic success in content learning was not a good predictor of performance outside schooling. As an antidote to an educational focus on abstract content, they emphasised the importance of learning within real-life activities and contexts, and, later on, the development of the cognitive structures students would need to develop to enable them to transfer their learning to new and diverse contexts, necessary in rapidly changing advanced economies (Cope 2005).

This emphasis upon the qualities needed for employment within a changing world (Hager & Holland 2006), different to a focus on transferring knowledge to be applied later in specific contexts, led many to emphasise the need for higher education to transform the person at an 'authentic' level (Barnett 2006). The focus is on the abilities and qualities students need, and upon real-world activities and relational contexts within which learners transform as persons, thereby preparing them for lifelong learning. The understanding is that competencies are not discrete, acquired and transferred apart from other competencies, but are embedded in cultural, ethical and social circumstances and relations of various kinds, often implicit, not easily described in language, or separated out neatly into different 'skills' or 'attributes' (Hager 2006). A competent person, in the widest sense of the term, is a person who is familiar with, can access, negotiate, and speak the language of the context, involving the development of identity as well as personal empowerment. These underpinning ideas are evident within doctoral practice and research at the whole of cohort level, albeit with slightly different emphases as outlined in Table 18.1 below.

CHAPTER 18 • COHORT-WIDE RESEARCH EDUCATION

TABLE 18.1 Foci in cohort-wide research education

Approach	Cognitive processing	Situated learning	Writing
Discipline, theoretical influence	Educational psychology (cognitive, behaviourist and constructivist)	Educational psychology (cognitive, constructivist, situated learning, communities of practice, sociocultural learning theory)	Educational psychology (sociocultural, communities of practice) and applied linguistics or academic literacies and critical literacies
Theoretical assumptions	Learning is a cognitive process involving learning management and monitoring, problem solving, and other thinking skills. Learning happens within real-world activity or experience and contexts. Learning transforms the person and identity.		
	Focus on cognitive learning processes – generalisable learning abilities are understood to be transferable to diverse settings. Learning itself becomes a skill; learners ultimately learn how to learn. Learning constitutes a transformation of being.	Focus on learning within context – individuals are understood to learn within and about specific social situations; they make meaning together, learn tacit or implicit knowledge crucial to success within social interactions. Competencies are not only acquired by individual minds; learners become part of communities, they come to belong to those communities, and they become different kinds of selves in doing so. Learning doesn't occur only at the individual level; organisations also learn.	Focus on language patterns and text – knowledge is understood to be socially and linguistically constructed. Competency involves becoming familiar with new text types and their cultural context and practices. Critical literacies – Focus on how education delivers to learners, or how language and 'discourse communities' (people engaged in similar discursive practices) operate (not so much a theory about how learning happens) (Cope 2005). Education supports stratified society. Culture determines how texts are produced and received, advantaging insiders and excluding outsiders of the culture.

TABLE 18.1 Foci in cohort-wide research education (...continued)

Approach	Cognitive processing	Situated learning	Writing
Understands the problem in doctoral education in terms of ...	Employability – Research students may be too specialised in a discipline, or insufficiently prepared for the workplace. Need more flexible workers ready to adjust to ever changing economic demands in a super-complex world. Learning – Research students may have behavioural (self-management) or metacognitive (for example threshold concepts, critical thinking, problem solving) learning needs.	Understanding of research education context – Focus on university/supervision and skill deficiencies overlooks multiple learning settings and players, the blending of industry/university learning at doctoral level, and lack of exploratory learning culture and access to research culture critical to becoming successful researchers. (Some are more excluded than others, such as those in Northern contexts, part-timers, internationals, social science and humanities.)	Access to textual/linguistic research genres and conventions – Research students are not taught how to read and write in unfamiliar research genres and contexts impeding their progress and the development of research identity, as well as underscoring existing cultural advantages.
Practical training application	Emphasis on development of transferable employment skills, abilities and dispositions, and individual metacognitive processes and behavioural aptitudes; emphasise reflection on experience of the research process.	Emphasis on ensuring recognition of and access to diversity of spaces, players, material resources involved in doctoral learning, and on building more collaborative, exploratory research culture.	Emphasis on teaching students how to reproduce specific text types, language features, and make research and discipline norms and rhetorical strategies in the students' target writing context explicit. Uses instructor-led pedagogy (either supervisor or language specialists alone or in collaboration with discipline experts), often involving scaffolded steps (analysis of discipline-specific target text/sub-text, co-construction, independent construction).
Objective	Meet employer/economic and discipline needs by producing self-disciplined, self-regulating, self-reflective and autonomous learners/researchers who proactively take charge of their own learning and research, and transfer a readiness to learn/research independently to future contexts.	Foster learning in communities of practice, create collaborative knowledge-sharing opportunities. Transform the research culture, including discipline, institutional and physical spaces, bring students into the centre of academic culture, and build researcher identity.	Support acquisition of language tools needed to learn and transform discipline knowledge for target audiences, and transform student identity through text work. Induct students into implicit and specific linguistic and contextual traditions and conventions that determine how texts are produced and interpreted. Empower students to succeed thereby challenging exclusivity of Western educational systems and social stratification it supports.

COGNITIVE PROCESSING

The 'cognitive processing' approach described in the first column of the table is separated out here because of its focus on transformations of cognition and of the person, as opposed to the learning context as for the other two foci. At the research level, in thesis-only contexts where no formalised subject learning takes place, the formulation of 'generic research skills' has prompted the development of centralised structured 'transferable skills' training. This has taken a number of forms in doctoral education, but all focus on the doctoral learner and their personality, experience, and the development of cognitive and behavioural processes and self-regulation or self-direction. The focus on developing the individual researcher may also be underpinned by creativity thinking which sees creativity as, at least partly, a personality trait, linked to independence of judgement, drive, self-confidence, openness to ideas and flexibility; or perhaps as a behavioural process, linked to specific stages such as preparation, incubation, illumination, and verification (see an overview by Walsh et al 2013:21-22). Within thinking about creativity there is often the idea that it involves active control (rather than subconscious processes or context-driven factors), such that there can be a purposeful generation of ideas for anyone who follows the creative process (Walsh et al 2013:21).

Research training examples of this approach are workshops on creativity, critical thinking and problem solving, or on behavioural aspects of learning, such as overcoming writer's block and procrastination. In the doctoral research literature, 'generic research threshold concepts' have been identified at both the cross-discipline level (Kiley & Wisker 2008) and the discipline level (Wisker & Robinson 2009). At the cross-discipline level these include questioning accepted concepts, and using literature and data to develop arguments, models and frameworks that contribute original insights to established knowledge (Kiley & Wisker 2008). While these insights may be operationalised within supervisor development, many transferable skills programmes are offered to students across disciplines or within discipline streams, such as science, technology, engineering and mathematics (STEM) or social sciences and humanities disciplines, and often take in 'generic skills' or 'employability skills' such as communication, team working and networking, career management and project management skills.

Miller and Brimicombe (2004) provide one of few descriptions of how policy has been interpreted at the university-wide level. The university-wide, cross-discipline programme they describe is based on student reflection on experience of the 'research journey', 'mapped' according to common research stages (defining the topic, writing the proposal, research planning, ethics, 'writing up', publication, examination, oral defence, and the 'wilderness years' in the middle). Training is inclusive of weekly meetings drawing on individual reflective journaling in which participants share and reflect upon both academic and emotional aspects of their research experience. Miller and Brimicombe (2004) observe that although bringing different disciplines together causes a kind of culture shock as a result of different epistemologies, reflection on experience of a common research journey ultimately gives the group coherence, and opens borders of encounter among multiple perspectives, stimulating discipline self-awareness and generativity.

An evaluation of a transferable skills programme in STEM disciplines at a research-intensive university in the UK (Walsh et al 2010) shows that the programme is valued by students who say it has a positive impact on their development as well as reducing a sense of isolation and improving confidence to succeed. The study found the programme is particularly appreciated by women and internationals who are also more career focused, with internationals more likely to be older and with clear research career aspirations. The authors note that these groups are also more likely to be excluded from local area cultures, and possibly particularly important for retaining women in STEM disciplines. Finally Walsh et al (2010:238-239) note that supervisors, and some students, at first perceive the programmes to be time wasting and they often have little knowledge of them, but ultimately they realise their value. They conclude that institutional support, including, critically, supervisor support is an important factor in student attendance.

More research is needed on transferable skills training to understand how these programmes support students or why students value them, and what they achieve in terms of outcomes. Even without this kind of reporting however, it can be observed that cohort-wide training of this kind radically alters the research environment simply by bringing students together who would previously be unlikely to cross paths, and who may be isolated within their local areas, and by supporting facilitated processes of self-reflection on both learning and emotional experience within the research process. It seems there may be positive implications of such programmes for equity and access, as well as student well-being, upon which research success ultimately depends.

SITUATED LEARNING

'Situated learning' is different from the transferable or cognitive processing focus because it is concerned with understanding the research learning context and how learning happens within it. There is also a stronger emphasis upon identity within learning. Doctoral research that analyses the contexts that doctoral students inhabit is more prolific than research on the other two foci, at least within the higher education literature. Research here has taken a variety of forms, giving rise to a number of important insights. Research has offered comprehensive depictions of the entirety of the research context in which doctoral students learn, including explicit and implicit, or hidden learning that takes place; the changes that would need to happen within research culture to support research learning and innovation; as well as the blended relationship between employment and academic contexts at doctoral research level.

Cumming (2010a, 2010b) argues for the need to move beyond attempts to define, list or classify skills, an approach that reflects a student deficiency model, and take in the multiple work, professional, industry and academic contexts and players students encounter in their learning beyond the academic/university context. The focus on the space within which learning occurs has highlighted not only social or interpersonal learning, but also how doctoral students enact their PhD identity within the physical or material dimension of space. Barnacle and Mewburn (2010) are critical of the ability of supervisor development and PhD generic skills programmes, seen to be de-contextualised from research practice, to support identity work, which they say has less to do with something innate about the candidate, and more to do with the research environment or "how both knowledge and the candidate are situated within research contexts and practices" that influence "what counts as knowledge, and the ways that being a researcher can be performed" (Barnacle & Mewburn 2010:442-443).

Although the implications of how context might shape knowledge and subjectivity remain largely unexplored within the higher education literature, a paper by Walsh *et al* (2013) provides one useful exemplification highlighting how culture affects the perception and production of creative science. Walsh *et al* (2013) note that STEM researchers, both students and their supervisors, often express 'aversion' to 'creativity' within science because of its historical association with mysticism, romanticism, expansiveness and unpredictability since the Enlightenment, and its opposition to scientific values of rationality, critical thinking, discipline and constraint. Walsh *et al* (2003:27) also document commentary by experienced scientists who say that creativity is riskier and not encouraged, or could be detrimental to research careers because of "the drive to get publications", and to "write boring papers, kick them out faster". Finally, they observe that both students and supervisors feel that the research context is critical to research creativity, listing specifically the importance of a positive research culture (providing a balance of support and freedom), constructive communication (which is informal with minimum hierarchy), and time and space to work creatively (including encouraging intellectual adventurousness and normative acceptance of mistakes).

Malfroy's (2005) study of doctoral programmes in environmental health, tourism and management, and in nursing and midwifery documents the close ties between academics and industry in these programmes which involve collaborative knowledge sharing in which work-based issues are central. In the programmes studied, students were frequently themselves professionals, sometimes leaders in their profession, and of a similar age and work background as their academic supervisors. This kind of observation, reflected elsewhere (Barnacle & Usher 2003), disrupts the assumption that research students are young with undeveloped careers, or that work and research learning and skills develop in separated spheres. Rather, blended or overlapping relations often exist between the disciplines and professional work; the two domains learning from one another, with students learning skills and knowledge from both domains, and applying them across both domains (Barnacle & Usher 2003).

A situated learning approach also brings concerns about access to networks and *habitus*, or socialisation into the discipline, and may emphasise the need to build and ensure equal access to discipline and local academic area research cultures. This reflects the view among educational theorists that learners need to understand shared symbols, values, beliefs, and organisational ways of doing things, and have access to support networks. This manifests in emphasis on the importance of bringing research students into the discipline by devising interactive research education activities that are inclusive of, but not limited to supervision, enabling students to learn about the rules, routines and practices operative in the discipline; theoretical perspectives; methodological questions; and practical know-how of the craft of research, from both peers and supervisors (Dysthe *et al* 2006). Enabling access to research culture also means attending to differences among students, particularly international and part-time students, who may find it more difficult to become part of research cultures (Deem & Brehony 2000). An emphasis upon situated learning therefore involves creating new research education practices, and transforming the research culture.

Researchers conclude there is also a need for change in the institutional culture to raise awareness among academics and administrators about the need and desire of research students for greater access to research cultures, including structured research training (Deem & Brehony 2000). Students, supervisors and others need to know how structured training and less individualised, more inclusive working environments benefit them (Deem & Brehony 2000). Academic socialisation, perhaps especially in the social sciences and humanities, which resists attempts to make the acquisition of research knowledge more systematised or visible, needs to be challenged (Deem & Brehony 2000).

The understanding of Lave and Wenger (1991:92-94) that "mastery resides not in the master but in the community of practice of which the master is part", entailing "a decentered view of master-apprentice relations", is reflected in a concern with power relations within research education and the possible detrimental impact of this view on learning. Hence, the emphasis upon collaborative work between academics and students, and a more exploratory and processual focus than an evaluative and output oriented focus, as well as upon collective models of supervision which can facilitate a sense of a community of researchers (Malfroy 2005). Rather than a focus on critiquing near-finished work, the focus of activities could be to present progress, ask for feedback, work on difficult problems or conundrums, allow for an 'intuitive' exploration of ideas related to the research process, and learn about new research methodologies and directions (Malfroy 2005). Boud and Lee (2005) remind us that, although peer learning offers pedagogic advantages, and is at the centre of research practices, it is important to question idealised assumptions that barriers of power and difference are removed in peer settings, and that the provision of opportunities for peer engagement will necessarily bring about learning and engagement. Boud and Lee (2005) caution that peers do not learn as a natural outcome of their being peers: there is a need to attend to aspects of pedagogy that actively develop a rich environment for peer learning.

Overall, a focus on the context of learning has led to a reconceptualisation of the research education space as more than supervision and the discipline, taking in employment and professional contexts, involving a range of players and settings. This enables recognition of the knowledge students already possess and the research they contribute, as well as what they need to be able to participate in as full members of discipline cultures. A focus on context has enabled transformations not only of how 'research education' and its context is understood, practised or performed, but of the institutional spaces and culture within which learning and innovation occur. This type of research and practice has implications not only for local and discipline areas, but institutional relations, practices and culture, as well as government policy.

WRITING

A third focus in research and practice around research training is writing, influenced by constructivist and situated learning theories, as well as the discipline of applied linguistics. Applied linguistics has interpreted education theory through a lens that questions how best to approach language teaching and learning. Literacies approaches agree that competency involves becoming familiar with research context, but emphasise enculturation into specific discipline practices via text work. The understanding that learning is situated leads to a departure from the simplistic view that writing proceeds from an 'ability to write', or that clear thinking leads to clear writing, requiring only an underpinning technical facility with English grammar, spelling, punctuation, citation rules or vocabulary. Instead, the understanding is that good writing emerges from often implicit agreements within communities of writers about what constitutes appropriate genres, writing patterns and language choices within them. It is not that we think in order to write (such that critical thinkers necessarily write well), but that writing requires knowledge of the target text and the expectations that surround it within the discourse community. The focus is on language use, text types and 'move' patterns, and 'discourse communities', or the expectations and conventions of research audiences; social practices which may be contested, multiple and changing.

Research writing perspectives also understand that learning how to reproduce research writing genres, patterns and language conventions involves the formation of research identity, as well as content learning and generativity (Kamler & Thomson 2004, 2006). As Kamler and Thomson (2004:196) assert, "writing is not just a way of 'telling' but a method of analysis, inquiry, discovery"; "writing is researching".

Critical literacies brings a more radical inflection to academic literacies, focusing not simply upon teaching students to conform to written research conventions, but for the need to recognise their cultural specificity, and, arising from this aspect, to adopt educational approaches that recognise the diversity of students' written and communicative contexts. This provides the understanding that research writing in the English international context is a specific genre involving specific patterns and presumptions, and that international writers are not 'language deficient', but are learning to recognise and become proficient in multiple discourse communities. Without text-based support, students can find it difficult to access specific writing practices in international research English, impeding discipline learning and communication, as well as the ability to contribute to global knowledge. And some are more marginalised and disempowered than others (writers outside Northern contexts, those from lower socio-economic groups, or those who, for whatever reasons, are not possessed of requisite 'cultural capital').

Unless students are enabled and empowered, existing educational and social values and advantages are underscored. For these contributors, research literacy is not a universal cognitive capacity, and expectations about research writing and communication are not necessarily made explicit or readily learned within interactive discipline contexts. They argue that a more targeted focus on writing is needed. In practice, both academic and critical literacies use processes of modelling the master, coaching from the master, followed by fading or independent construction, evident in Vygotskian scaffolding and, more broadly, constructivist approaches to learning (Cope 2005:54). The tendency for applied linguistics and education to operate in separate discipline forums means that the higher education field has relatively few contributions from applied linguists, although many applied linguists work in central units or faculty offices in universities and are involved in researcher and supervisor development. Carter (2011:731) argues that learning advisors with backgrounds in applied linguistics can complement supervision by bringing attention to the shared moves within research writing, bringing awareness of possibilities for creativity or deviation from generic moves, while ensuring work conforms to recognisable conventions.

Writing groups are also promoted by educators without literacies backgrounds. Some find that the strength of multi-disciplinary doctoral writing groups is that they encourage a focus on writing to balance against the supervisory and discipline focus on content expertise, thereby facilitating publication outcomes, as well as a non-competitive, supportive environment (Cuthbert *et al* 2009). Others (Mayer *et al* 2008) have found that facilitated writing groups give students greater confidence and authority in writing, support perseverance with the dissertation writing process, reduce isolation, give a sense of community, provide critical feedback, and promote skills in giving and receiving critical feedback. Here the cognitive theory focus on situated learning within a community of practice is seen in the emphasis on the transformation of self or identity. As Mayer *et al* (2008:266, 269) report, writing groups provide a "scaffold … to cross from being students to being scholars"; students learn to "appreciate how the language used, and the way our work was constructed, positioned us in different ways in relation to our readers and our research". This work suggests that one-off writing workshops that do not provide students with opportunities to engage in critiquing and supporting their own and others' writing on an ongoing basis, need to be supplemented by ongoing facilitated writing groups.

The literacies focus contributes by highlighting the importance of text work in research education, to enhance not only the quality and productivity of research writing, but also discipline learning and knowledge production, socialisation into the discipline, and equity and empowerment. Writing work can be facilitated within cross-discipline or discipline contexts, by discipline or writing experts, as well as within supervision with supervision development guided by writing expertise.

CONCLUSIONS

Educational theory and academic literacies are notable contributors to research and practice about pedagogy and curriculum in the whole of cohort research education space. They have contributed a number of important insights about learning beyond the supervision space, and have brought insights that genuinely offer radical and progressive transformations in research education. Cognitive approaches have contributed by providing generic skills or competencies training at scale, focusing on commonalities in cognitive processes or in research experience within research learning, facilitating reflection on experience and cross-discipline encounters.

Situated approaches have contributed by emphasising the multiple contexts within which research students learn, and the contributions of a wide range of players in research education. They contribute to doctoral education by bringing questions of student access to institutional, discipline and employment contexts and networks. They also suggest the need to change not simply our candidates, but institutions, to facilitate more collaborative forms of research learning and greater acceptance of this among academics and students. Research education in this situated frame considers where students actually are, whether in the discipline, working at home, in professional occupations, leadership roles, businesses, research labs, discipline communities, or departmental spaces, suggesting enhancements to access at every level and taking in equipment, resourcing, space, as well as access to networks and events. More research is needed in this area to understand how innovations or creativity in knowledge are defined or made meaningful by various contextual factors, including economic, disciplinary, philosophical and political, and what implications this may have for research education. Sociology would seem to be a rich hunting ground for this kind of analysis. As yet, it seems few higher education commentators on doctoral education have wandered far from educational psychology in their attempts to understand 'innovation' and the implications of its peculiar emphasis within doctoral education.

Research and practice around writing highlights students' need for systematic, practical support and advice about different research texts, and the patterns and language features within them, as well as how these practices reflect the Western research context. An implication of this is that interpersonal socialisation in the discipline and learning for generalist skills may not be enough to facilitate effective research writing, especially for students for whom the writing context is foreign. The other implication is that facilitating research writing is an effective way of supporting not only the transformation of identity from student to scholar or researcher, but also the learning and transformation of subject knowledge. Writing support is therefore central to equity and access, as well as student empowerment; and it also supports innovation by facilitating the entry of diverse perspectives into the elite Western research context.

All approaches work to support supervision, but when put into practice they suggest a transformation of the research culture from one often experienced by students as isolating, particularly for marginalised groups, to one in which students feel welcomed and supported by community, and full participants in the community. Cohort-wide research and practice also brings the role of 'outsiders' of various kinds into the research education frame, and it highlights the importance of institutional and policy change.

REFERENCES

Barnacle R & Mewburn I. 2010. Learning networks and the journey of 'becoming doctor'. *Studies in Higher Education*, 35(4):433-444. https://doi.org/10.1080/03075070903131214

Barnacle R & Usher R. 2003. Assessing the quality of research training: The case of part-time candidates in full-time professional work. *Higher Education Research & Development*, 22(3):345-358. https://doi.org/10.1080/0729436032000145185

Barnett R. 2006. Graduate attributes in an age of uncertainty. In: P Hager & S Holland (eds). *Graduate attributes, learning and employability*. Netherlands: Springer.

Boud D & Lee A. 2005. 'Peer learning' as pedagogic discourse for research education. *Studies in Higher Education*, 30(5):501-516. https://doi.org/10.1080/03075070500249138

Carter S. 2011. Doctorate as genre: Supporting thesis writing across campus. *Higher Education Research and Development,* 30(6):725-736. https://doi.org/10.1080/07294360.2011.554388

Cope N. 2005. Apprenticeship reinvented: Cognition, discourse and implications for academic literacy. *Prospect*, 20(3):42-62.

Cumming J. 2010a. Doctoral enterprise: A holistic conception of evolving practices and arrangements. *Studies in Higher Education*, 35(1):25-39. https://doi.org/10.1080/03075070902825899

Cumming J. 2010b. Contextualised performance: Reframing the skills debate in research education. *Studies in Higher Education*, 35(4):405-419. https://doi.org/10.1080/03075070903082342

Cuthbert D, Spark C & Burke E. 2009. Discipline writing: The case for multi-disciplinary writing groups to support writing for publication by higher degree by research candidates in the humanities, arts and social sciences. *Higher Education Research and Development*, 28(2):37-149. https://doi.org/10.1080/07294360902725025

Deem R & Brehony K. 2000. Doctoral students' access to research cultures – Are some more unequal than others? *Studies in Higher Education*, 25(2):149-165. https://doi.org/10.1080/713696138

Dysthe O, Samara A & Westrheim K. 2006. Multivoiced supervision of master's students: A case study of alternative supervision practices in higher education. *Studies in Higher Education*, 31(3):299-318. https://doi.org/10.1080/03075070600680562

Hager P. 2006. Nature and development of generic attributes. In: P Hager & S Holland (eds). *Graduate attributes, learning and employability*. Netherlands: Springer.

Hager P & Holland S. 2006. *Graduate attributes, learning and employability*. Netherlands: Springer.

Kamler B & Thomson P. 2004. Driven to abstraction: Doctoral supervision and writing pedagogies. *Teaching in Higher Education*, 9(2):195-209. https://doi.org/10.1080/1356251042000195358

Kamler B & Thomson P. 2006. *Helping doctoral students write: Pedagogies for supervision*. Routledge: London.

Kiley M & Wisker G. 2008. Threshold concepts in research education and evidence of threshold crossing. *Higher Education Research and Development*, 28(4):431-441. https://doi.org/10.1080/07294360903067930

Lave G & Wenger E. 1991. *Situated learning: Legitimate peripheral participation*. Cambridge: Cambridge University Press. https://doi.org/10.1017/CBO9780511815355

Maher D, Seaton L, McMullen C, Fitzgerald T, Otsuji E & Lee A. 2008. Becoming and being writers: The experiences of doctoral students in writing groups. *Studies in Continuing Education*, 30(3):263-275. https://doi.org/10.1080/01580370802439870

Malfroy J. 2005. Doctoral supervision, workplace research and changing pedagogic practices. *Higher Education Research and Development*, 24(2):165-178. https://doi.org//10.1080/07294360500062961

Miller N & Brimicombe A. 2004. Mapping research journeys across complex terrain with heavy baggage. *Studies in Continuing Education*, 26(3):405-417. https://doi.org/10.1080/0158037042000265962

Walsh E, Anders K & Hancock S. 2013. Understanding, attitude and environment: The essentials for developing creativity in STEM researchers. *International Journal for Researcher Development*, 4(1):19-38. https://doi.org/10.1108/IJRD-09-2012-0028

Walsh E, Seldon PM, Hargreaves CE, Alpay E & Morley BJ. 2010. Evaluation of a programme of transferable skills development within the PhD: Views of late stage students. *International Journal for Researcher Development*, 1(3):223-247. https://doi.org/10.1108/1759751X201100015

Wisker G & Robinson G. 2009. Encouraging postgraduate students of literature and art to cross conceptual thresholds. *Innovations in Education and Teaching International*, 46(3):317-330. https://doi.org/10.1080/14703290903069035

IN SICKNESS AND HEALTH, AND A 'DUTY OF CARE'

PHD STUDENT HEALTH, STRESS AND WELLBEING ISSUES AND SUPERVISORY EXPERIENCES

Gina Wisker & Gillian Robinson

INTRODUCTION

> Clearly, you can't budget for empathy. Today, I say that we should not accept this.
>
> (Anonymous Academic 2014)

Ill health, mental and physical, during PhD study, is now becoming more widely recognised, but is still under-researched. For doctoral students, health, stress and wellbeing are fundamentally linked with intellectual development, conceptual threshold crossings (Kiley & Wisker 2009) and achievement at doctoral level. Our established and recent research indicates a close connection between success in the intellectual, doctoral learning journey and sensitive, informed management of and support for physical and mental health issues experienced by doctoral students, whether they are ongoing, or appear as time-limited crises. The role of supervisors in supporting students with health issues is also under-researched, and is sparked latterly by recent concerns specifically with doctoral student health (Wisker & Gordon in *THE* 2016). Our focus here arises from recent work on wellbeing for both students and supervisors, where supervisor empathy and engagement at personal, institutional and learning levels is seen as fundamental in effective supervisory relationships with students. Postgraduate student learning journeys involve the whole person, over time, and both postgraduates and supervisors need to be aware of and develop strategies to minimise the damage done by ill health, and emotional and psychological upset, which can hamper general health and affect timely (or any) completion.

LITERATURE REVIEW

Reports on doctoral student ill health and stress are now widespread, with one study by Exeter's Students' Guild revealing 40% of PhDs at Exeter suffer ill health (Else 2015). This survey prompted the opening of a doctoral college to combat isolation and depression.

At Berkeley a similar study found high levels of depression among 790 graduate students, 47% of PhD students, and 37% of master's students, with 64% reporting depression in the arts and humanities fields, 43-46% in the biological or physical sciences and engineering, and 34% in the social sciences (Jaschik 2015). Factors reported include isolation; academic progress and preparation (or, rather, lack of these); academic engagement; career prospects; overall health; sleep (or lack of it); social support; living conditions; financial situation; confidence; feeling valued and included (or rather not feeling valued and included); and the adviser relationship more generally.

One article suggests that mental health issues may be the biggest barriers to graduate student success (Turley 2013) and another notes, "Almost half of graduate student respondents reported having had an emotional or stress-related problem over the past year, and over half reported knowing a colleague who had had an emotional or stress-related problem over the past year" (Hyun, Quinn, Madon & Lustig 2006). Still another article asks why graduate students quit: 'Why do so many Graduate students quit?' (Patterson 2016), although the stress, health and isolation issues reported elsewhere offer a good answer to that. Highly capable students are becoming stressed and ill, burn out and leave. Other literature (Neumann 1990; Morgan & De Bruin 2010; Ladner, Mihailescu, Kern & Romo 2016) suggests that universities are contributing to that 'burnout', which, we argue, first needs to be openly acknowledged. Well-planned, consistent support should accompany attitudinal change to prevent and mitigate against the causes, treat the symptoms and support the students. The role of supervisors and relationships with supervisors or advisors is mentioned in some of the literature as far back as identifying "benign neglect" (Gurr 2001: 85). This notion seems to suggest that beliefs about the necessity of autonomy and independence can lead to some supervisors leaving their students to get on with their research without the support the doctoral students and others (including other supervisors) consider essential. This suggests there could be quite a gulf between essential, sensitive and constructive support aimed at enabling autonomy and independence at the rate that is useful for the students and their work. It also suggests that there is an assumption that since independence is a final goal, students should be left to do all the work for themselves right from the start, unguided and unsupported. Focusing on academics' lack of response to the stress and despair that lack of progress and clarity about the doctoral learning journey can lead to, an article in the *Guardian* argues that "[i]t is not OK for academics to wash their hands of the situation" (Anonymous Academic 2014). However, in many cases supervisors are also stressed (Wisker & Robinson 2014), unsure of appropriate support, untrained, and themselves unsupported for the emotional and personal work needed. They are not the only form of support of course, and online communities are advocated in addition to supervisor support: "[L]urking on a forum where others express their academic worries can be cathartic" (Boyle 2014).

Postgraduate student learning journeys involve the whole person, over time. Both postgraduates and supervisors need to be aware of and develop strategies, including engagement with the wider community, and offering support to minimise the damage done by ill health, and emotional and psychological upset that can hamper general health and affect timely (or any) completion.

Historically, our engagement with the Doctoral Learning Journeys project highlighted the interrelation between dimensions of personal, emotional, health and wellbeing, with those of intellectual development (Wisker *et al* 2010), as shown diagrammatically in Figure 19.1.

FIGURE 19.1 Interrelation between dimensions of personal, emotional, health and wellbeing, with those of intellectual development (Source: Wisker *et al* 2010)

One of our arguments stemming from this discovered interrelationship is that those experiencing a range of concerns in the personal/emotional dimension or the professional dimension could find that it impacted on the doctoral students' work. And our work, when used with supervisors, advises them to consider taking this interactivity into account when supporting students' doctoral learning journeys. We have been involved with a variety of work on identifying doctoral student stress, ill health and supportive strategies for wellbeing and success, and these are shared here. Earlier work on doctoral orphans and breakdowns in supervisory relationships (Wisker & Robinson 2012, 2014), on postgraduate student wellbeing (Johansson, Wisker, Claesson, Strandler & Saalman 2013; Strandler *et al* 2013) offers insight into a range of potential contributing factors to ill health and stress, information on student experiences, and some supervisory and institutional, as well as personal strategies to manage, limit or sometimes solve these where possible. The 'Troublesome Encounters' project produced a toolkit for postgraduates and supervisors concerning wellbeing and resilience (Morris & Wisker 2011) and work on supervisors' wellbeing (Wisker & Robinson 2016) offers support for those supervising students who are affected by either their own or student issues of health and wellbeing.

METHODOLOGY AND METHODS

Case studies illustrating examples of doctoral student health issues and supervisor responses

Building on our own historical work with doctoral students on their learning journeys and with wellbeing and resilience in the doctoral journey, our recent research involved narrative interviews with current and ex-doctoral students in the UK, Israel, Sweden, and South Africa, 2015-17 (20). Research findings and suggestions for good practice derive from both our established work, and this new research data. We were granted ethical approval for this new interview-based work (2015-17) and have produced case studies from a mixture of the data analysis of student responses from the established work and the new work. We produced the case studies for several reasons. The confidentiality of the quotations and their specificity were so intertwined that we chose not to turn the interviews we carried out into thematically analysed sections with quotations as evidence. Instead we believe that for confidentiality, for sharing and development purposes it is better to amalgamate the individual situations and responses into narrative cases. Each case is given a pseudonym.

CHAPTER 19 • IN SICKNESS AND HEALTH, AND A 'DUTY OF CARE'

Cases

We developed anonymised composite cases (7) focusing on doctoral student physical health and supervisor and other (community) support for wellbeing, and resilience, in relation to the intellectual journey. The data have been amalgamated and developed into anonymised case studies with pseudonyms, to offer insights into problems identified from the student responses and thematised in the data, and some ways of addressing them, suggested by the experiences felt to be useful, also from the data. Cases are presented in narrative and descriptive style. The suggestions for good practice that follow the discussion of these cases come from (1) interview data from the same participants, (2) suggestions from the literature, and (3) our earlier work (Wisker et al 2010; Wisker & Robinson 2012, 2014), and the 'Troublesome Encounters' toolkit (Morris & Wisker 2011). The good practice considerations that emerged from each of these research projects are drawn here, below, into specific suggestions so that supervisors and students themselves might consider ways forward out of the difficulties of physical and mental health issues on the doctoral learning journey.

We have focused largely on the doctoral students and their mental and physical health and wellbeing with the intention that insights can feed into supervisor awareness and training.

Case studies illustrating examples of doctoral student health issues and supervisor responses

Case study 1 Dana – Cancer and researching close to home

Dana, a part-time mid-career woman student, was researching support work through workshops for women who were cancer sufferers. She herself was also suffering from cancer.

She and her supervisor invested in both the intellectual quality of her work, which was good, and in the emotional support that carrying out the workshops she ran for others, as well as the research, clearly offered her. Their interactions also offered some space for emotional meltdowns that always returned to a focus on the research work. Space was given in the supervision for these discussions about health and stress, and for the meltdowns (Dana usually cried), before returning to considering the work in progress. Some of the questions and issues considered from this case were whether it is beneficial or harmful or something in between if one researches the sufferers of an illness one has oneself; and how to mitigate against any ethical issues that could cause her or others psychological and emotional harm. Dana and her supervisor reported awareness of the ethical issues, some stress in sharing, and empowerment in working with others to support workshop participants in their own management of health and stress. Another issue was the way of respecting the student's own emotional response, supporting without marginalising the intellectual work, and then returning to the support of the intellectual work which Dana reported was helping her deal with her own issues, since it was progressing slowly, but well and she was achieving.

Case study 2 Anya – Physical issues; developed cancer quite early in the process

For Anya the studies and the research were a positive factor in her life as she was very ambitious to get her PhD. With the encouragement and support of other members of the cohort, she worked on her PhD in spite of sessions of chemotherapy.

Her supervisors were supportive but didn't push in order to avoid adding to the strain. She attended her PhD viva in between chemotherapy sessions. Examiners were empathetic and although rigorous, tempered the amendments to the situation (that is, long amendments were unlikely to be achieved). At the awards ceremony, a friend went to receive the award on her behalf. Anya attended in a wheelchair. She died shortly afterwards.

Case study 3 Brian – Complex physical and mental health issues

Brian had to deal with a number of health problems, operations and complex family situations, including very sick children, throughout his PhD studies. He also had some ongoing stress issues resulting from flashbacks to events during a war in which he had been a conscripted combatant.

Brian preferred to manage these issues mainly on his own and without significantly interrupting his studies. However, recognising the importance of the student's wellbeing, the supervisor respected that sometimes the lines of communication went quiet, and so they considered carefully when to gently enquire or to prompt. In supervisory meetings a pattern evolved where the issues were mentioned and briefly discussed at the start of the session. Having received empathy and support the student was then able to focus on the work. The research progressed in blocks between the periods of physical illness.

Case study 4 Vera – Suffered from lack of confidence

She said, "I was just a pre-school teacher, not an academic", "I haven't done enough", "I haven't progressed". There was no lack of ability as indicated by the proposal and early written work.

The first supervisor had a dominant personality and often upset the student with her harsh comments. The second supervisor was empathetic, recognising that the role of the supervisor is wider than managing the production of a thesis. It is also about managing the student's wellbeing and sometimes managing the system on behalf of the student: "The system pays little attention to caring for the student, it is all about the PhD process but we follow the system whether the system serves the student or not" (supervisor for Vera).

The student did not achieve her PhD. Retrospectively the second supervisor had a sense of failure, feeling that if she had been more in tune with the student's sensitivity Vera might have succeeded.

Case study 5 Athena – Had health and stress problems

During her second year of study, after she had collected the data and analysed it, the student, who at the time had a four year old child and suffered from anaemia, collapsed physically from burn-out.

She was hospitalised for a week and then took two terms out from her study, a decision supported by the supervisor and allowed by the system. The supervisor suggested she leave the thesis aside during this time to remove the pressure and advised her to concentrate instead on jointly publishing three small papers, which kept the student in touch with the supervisor.

Unfortunately, when she came to writing up the thesis her lung collapsed. At this point she had the choice whether to give up or complete. The supervisor at this point enabled the student to find her own solution. She decided to send her son to be with family in Greece and sat down and successfully completed her thesis.

Case study 6 Hanna – Homesick, distracted, untheorised

Hanna is from a Middle-Eastern country. She conducted master's work in the UK previously and then came to the UK in January in the snow when the university was shut, to start her PhD. She found accommodation difficult and moved four times. During the early part of her study, she finalised her marriage with her husband who was from another Middle-Eastern country, and flew there and then home to experience two or three ceremonies. She was homesick, away a great deal and unable to sort out bringing her husband to live with her (difficulties with visas).

Much of her time was spent on the phone sorting these problems out, and her work suffered. It was considered to be untheorised and simplistic, and however much extra support was put in place, it did not seem to progress. Ultimately she did not progress and returned home. However, perhaps because she had received strong local departmental support and thoughtful comments face to face from her supervisory team, she said she was not resentful and would be re-starting at a university close to her home town, and living in her new flat with her husband and her family nearby. It is just possible that the main supervisor felt more stress over this case than the student.

Case Study 7 Malik – Emotional and physical issues

Malik did his MA in the UK. Returning to study in the UK on a PhD and reuniting with his family should have been a positive experience and indeed it seemed so at first. Unfortunately, his family was 150 miles away, the student community support from his previous study location 100 miles away, the weather was very cold and wet, and the PhD journey was intellectually challenging and isolating. His marriage broke down, and he went into a period of silence and absence. His supervisors supported him by structuring regular meetings and setting agreed milestones. They invited him to events where he could meet other students, scholars and experts and introduced him to help set up networks. The transfer was approved and the doctoral journey seemed in progress.

Returning home to carry out field work, he fell ill immediately with typhoid. He recovered, returned to the UK and continued to progress slowly. He reported that regular supervision helped keep him on track. Then he ran out of time, his employer called him back to work and he was given a full workload, which slowed down his productivity.

At this point two of his three supervisors took voluntary severance and left the university. This is an ongoing issue and his hand-in date is in four months' time.

DISCUSSION AND SUGGESTING WAYS FORWARD

These students presented with a range of issues in their doctoral learning journeys. No single student in our study had just one issue – there were always intertwined issues. For some there was also the stress of the level of conceptual work together with that of working in a second or third language. This was often combined with a series of domestic crises and a range of serious, some ongoing, some short-lived, medical issues, all of which hampered their strength, their mobility, their concentration and their access to the facilities of the university as well as their networks within it. We did not formally interview the supervisors (although we had informal discussions with several), so all formal reports about activities are from the student responses.

Both established and new research report widespread issues of health and wellbeing affecting the PhD journey. Our research results reveal a range of physical and mental health issues which impede progress, although in some cases students reported that continuing with the PhD aided their health because it enabled intellectual growth and continuity of achievement and also supported their wellbeing. In the cases presented above, several students reported benefiting from the calm support of supervisors, which normalised the slow progress and emotional responses, since they refused to harass the student when such health issues impeded progress, rather offering supportive informative responses. Informal discussions with supervisors revealed some who are surprised, stressed and confused, untrained and conflicted in their experiences with students who present with such health issues. Some others mentioned in the student responses and who discussed their experiences informally with us were clearly more naturally attuned to ways of engaging in constructive and positive ways of working with the many issues and with the students. In some instances, institutional processes added stress to student experiences (time running out, deadlines for staged work), and in some other instances helped manage situations. The latter included the need for writing up time when a student had run out of real time, or the opportunity to gain a second opinion on student work which backed up the supervisor's sense that it was proceeding well, or not proceeding well.

Our case studies, developed from interviews, are evidence of experience of a range of issues. These can usefully be seen in the light of our earlier work, which has offered some suggestions on ways of identifying and tackling issues of ill health and problems with wellbeing with which PhD students present, and as seen in Figure 19.1 (above) clearly affect their doctoral learning journeys. Here we revisit the toolkit produced from the 'Troublesome Encounters' project (Wisker & Morris 2011), which suggests ways of addressing some of the issues, in practice, for supervisors and doctoral students.

DOCTORAL STUDENT, SUPERVISOR AND INSTITUTIONAL WELLBEING AND RESILIENCE SUGGESTIONS

Doctoral students undergo the full range of psychological, emotional, mental/physical health issues, yet sometimes this is treated as a surprise if either we (supervisors) or the institution is seeing doctoral students as a number, an income stream or (more generously) producers of a time-limited project. As supervisors, some of us did not expect health issues to arise; we would rather concentrate on the development and completion of the research project.

Perhaps because we work with doctoral students over a long period of time (longer than undergraduates or master's students) we will have more experience of accompanying them in their illness and health.

Some of us have never had experience of such issues ourselves (or would rather not engage with them); perhaps we feel it is not our role to be involved, and are not sure of the best routes to follow to resolve the issues as far as possible.

Supportive practices can be identified in terms of three dimensions: personal, learning and institutional, all of which map onto the 'doctoral learning journey' (see Figure 19.1 above):

Personal

Students' needs should be accommodated in different ways by different people:

- Family – by helping students balance life and work;
- Friends – communities of learning and close friends can support in a myriad of ways: psychological, social, physical;
- Supervisor – recognition and understanding of the nature and severity of an illness/disability; awareness of psychological and emotional issues; awareness of different needs/levels of resilience; empathy, listening skills; referral (with the student's permission and agreement) to trained counsellors and others who have ability and position to help.

Learning

- Supportive workshops; and
- Sharing, exchanging ideas within communities/cohorts/critical friends.

Institutional

- Efficient administrative systems;
- Flexibility within graduate schools to respond to and cope with issues of shortened/extended time, and demands stemming from illness, or mobility and domestic problems, among other things.

These practices are all highlighted in our interviews and discussions as being useful in supporting the students.

CHAPTER 19 • **IN SICKNESS AND HEALTH, AND A 'DUTY OF CARE'**

THE TOOLKIT INTRODUCED

The doctoral learning journeys research (Wisker *et al* 2011) showed links between all aspects of student research and life. Further work considered some of the stressful moments and issues that cause emotional and sometimes physical issues – supervisor neglect, procrastination, isolation, over-working, poor work-life balance habits (Wisker & Robinson 2012, 2014; Johansson *et al* 2013; Strandler *et al* 2014). These earlier research projects and the current project, reported here, have produced information about occupational (research student) illnesses associated with the research and the full range of other mental and physical health issues. Moving on from the early work of the doctoral learning journeys, in the 'Troublesome Encounters' research in 2011 one of the authors and a colleague focused on master's and EdD education postgraduates, their illnesses, wellbeing and resilience, and what supervisors did to support the students. This was expressed in a wellbeing and resilience toolkit from which we extract here as further illustration of research-based suggestions on what supervisors might do to support students and what the students might do to support themselves.

Table 19.1 is an extract from 'Safeguarding and Enhancing Research Students' Academic Wellbeing: A Toolkit for Supervisors and Departments in Education (& Humanities and Social Sciences)'. The full toolkit is available at http://escalate.ac.uk/6828. The headings have been added for this chapter.

TABLE 19.1 Advice themes and data/evidence from our research with specific comments for supervisors

		Supervisors
1. Ensure research students are aware of what support is available and what they are entitled to. 2. Ensure any problems are properly dealt with/supported as early on as possible. Enhanced retention and completion rates	1. "Your living circumstances are quite important. Last year I didn't feel well in the area and house where I lived, I felt that caused a lot of extra stress and I'm really happy that that's settled now." 2. "From my perspective when I'm not well and depression is bad then I just find learning really difficult. I find that I don't want to learn new things – it just seems like I've got enough whizzing around my head already and it can feel like an assault sometimes." 3. "A marriage breakdown is not an easy thing for me to face in a strange country but then because of the support from my supervisor, from my coordinator, from the faculty, from the university, my doctor and mental health team – it's enhanced my wellbeing." 4. "If I don't take good care of myself, I will be unable to do everything. I experienced three months of severe depression; I couldn't do anything. After that it is important for me to look after myself, to be healthy mentally, physically, emotionally. So that's important – I need to try even though it's not easy."	1. Be aware what support is available for students at the university and have the contact details and relevant literature to hand in order to refer, enable self-referral. 2. Ensure you know which members of staff to contact for advice and possibly support for yourself. Awareness of relevant disability, equality and diversity legislation so you know what students are entitled to 3. Ensure you are aware of any additional needs the student may have. Gain at least a basic understanding of observing signs of stress or other mental health issues. Encourage support seeking from within the university and/or an appropriate professional such as a GP. Establish trust with students so they are more likely to disclose any problems. Maintain professional boundaries and ensure students access the most appropriate form of support for them. 4. Encourage students to maintain basic personal wellbeing strategies such as good diet, exercise and sleeping pattern, particularly at times of stress to aid recovery. Department / Institution Target awareness of support available explicitly towards research as well as undergraduate students.

CONCLUSIONS

"The misery of PhD students seems to be pretty universal. I get fan mail from every continent. I should say I think the misery is mostly existential" (Cham in Powles 2014).

Health issues need to be recognised as part of the doctoral learning journey, and the supervisor's role in relation to this matter needs clarification and support. Supervisors and doctoral students can benefit from further consideration of recognising, and managing such issues of health and wellbeing.

Supervisors have a duty of care to engage as far as they can appropriately with the wellbeing of their doctoral students as it affects their learning. Such engagement will enable the students to make use of published research of successful practices, toolkits suggesting such good practice, and the wider community, including those practitioners offering professional support.

REFERENCES

Anonymous Academic. 2014. *There is a culture of acceptance around mental health issues in academia.* https://www.theguardian.com/higher-education-network/blog/2014/mar/01/mental-health-issue-phd-research-university [Retrieved 1 March 2017].

Boyle G. 2014. *PhD supervisor: The perfect one doesn't exist, so where else can you find help?* https://www.theguardian.com/higher-education-network/blog/2014/mar/27/phd-supervisor-university-seek-help-online-communities [Retrieved 27 March 2017].

Cham J. http://www.wired.co.uk/article/jorge-cham-phd

Else H. 2015. *Forty per cent of PhDs at Exeter suffer ill health, study reveals.* https://www.timeshighereducation.com/news/forty-per-cent-of-phds-at-exeter-suffer-ill-health-study-reveals/2019540.article [Retrieved 9 April 2017].

Gurr G. 2001. Negotiating the 'rackety bridge' – A dynamic model for aligning supervisory style with research student development. *Higher Education and Development*, 20(1):81-92. https://doi.org/10.1080/07924360120043882

Hyun JK, Quinn BC, Madon T & Lustig S. 2006. Graduate student mental health: Needs assessment and utilization of counselling services. *Journal of College Student Development*, 47(3):247-266. https://muse.jhu.edu/article/197830/summary. [Retrieved 23 April 2017]. https://doi.org/10.1353/csd.2006.0030

Jaschik S. 2015. *The other mental health crisis.* https://www.insidehighered.com/news/2015/04/22/berkeley-study-finds-high-levels-depression-among-graduate-students. [Retrieved 22 April 2017].

Johansson T, Wisker G, Claesson S, Strandler O & Saalman E. 2013. PhD supervision as an emotional process – Critical situations and emotional boundary work. Pertanika: *Journal of Social Science and Humanities*, 22 (2):605-662.

Kiley M & Wisker G. 2009. Threshold concepts in research education and evidence of threshold crossing. *Higher Education Research and Development*, 28(4):431-441. https://doi.org/10.1080/07294360903067930

Ladner J, Mihailescu SD, Kern L, Romo L. 2016. Burn out in university students: Time now for implementing new public health approaches. *European Journal of Public Health*, 26(1):132-144. https://doi.org/10.1093/eurpub/ckw172.042

Morgan B & De Bruin K. 2010. The relationship between the big five personality traits and burnout in South African university students. *South African Journal of Psychology*, 40(2):182-191. https://doi.org/10.1177/008124631004000208

Morris C & Wisker G. 2011. *Troublesome encounters: Strategies for managing the wellbeing of postgraduate education students during their learning processes.* http://escalate.ac.uk/6828.

Neumann Y. 1990. *Determinants and consequences of students' burnout.* Columbus, OH: Ohio State University Press.

Patterson TE. 2016. *Why do so many graduate students quit?* http://www.theatlantic.com/education/archive/2016/07/why-do-so-many-graduate-students-quit/490094. [Retrieved 6 July 2017].

Powles, J. 2014. *PhD comics' Jorge Cham on misery, hope and academia. Wired.* http://www.wired.co.uk/article/jorge-cham-phd

Strandler O, Johansson T, Wisker G & Claesson S. 2014. Supervisor or counsellor? – Emotional boundary work in supervision. *International Journal of Researcher Development,* 5(2):45-57.https://doi.org/10.1108/IJRD-03-2014-0002

Turley N. 2013. *Mental health issues may be the biggest barriers to graduate student success.* https://www.insidehighered.com/blogs/gradhacker/mental-health-issues-among-graduate-students [Retrieved 7 October 2017].

Wisker G, Morris M, Cheng M, Masika M, Warnes M, Trafford V, Robinson G & Lilly J. 2010. *Doctoral learning journeys final report.* https://www.heacademy.ac.uk/resources/detail/ntfs/Projects/Doctoral_Learning_Journeys [Retrieved 12 April 2017].

Wisker G & Robinson G. 2013. Doctoral 'orphans': Nurturing and supporting the success of postgraduates who have lost their supervisors. *(HERD) Higher Education Research and Development Journal,* 32(2):300-313. https://doi.org/10.1080/07294360.2012.657160

Wisker G & Robinson G. 2014. Picking up the pieces: Supervisor and doctoral 'orphans'. *International Journal for Researcher Development,* 3(2).

Wisker G & Robinson G. 2016. Supervisor wellbeing and identity: Challenges and strategies. *International Journal of Researcher Development,* 7(2). www.emeraldinsight.com/2048-8696.htm [Retrieved 3 April 2017]. https://doi.org/10.1108/IJRD-03-2016-0006

RESEARCH AS TRANSFORMATION AND TRANSFORMATION AS RESEARCH

Anisa Vahed, Ashley Ross, Suzanne Francis, Bernie Millar, Oliver Mtapuri & Ruth Searle

INTRODUCTION AND BACKGROUND

Literature suggests that the processes of research engagement are profoundly transformative (Healey, Jenkins & Lea 2014; Healey, Jordan, Pell & Short 2010; Nulty, Kiley & Meyers 2009; Shephard, Trotman, Furnari & Löfström 2015; Spronken-Smith, Mirosa & Darrou 2013). Through personal engagement in the research process student researchers are understood to be remodelled in terms of their identity, thinking and agency. There are however, fundamental transformational processes comprising threshold concepts and troublesome knowledge that higher degree students have to work through before they are enabled to progress with their studies. Unless these thresholds of learning are crossed and the troublesome knowledge 'managed', students are not transformed nor empowered to move from a space of 'becoming' magisterial students to actually undergoing a shift in identity that moves them into a space of 'being' postgraduate students. Scaffolding of postgraduate development options also often ends in the initial stages after the proposal is approved (Francis 2016a, 2016b; Francis nd; Kyvik & Olsen 2014). Attrition rates are highest at the mid-point of a study where many students grapple with their identity and in defining their research contribution in university spaces, which are often sites of exclusion for students at the top of the student hierarchy as well as those at the bottom (Elgar 2003; Francis 2016a, 2016b; Francis nd; Golde 2005; Kyvik & Olsen 2014). To attain the new horizon of being authoritative and confident knowledge developers, students need to develop their own voice, recognise their ability to engage actively and contest conceptually, and impart this knowledge that heralds their new-found scholarship.

No less profoundly, supervisors are also challenged to stretch their own identity and experience according to the needs of those they supervise, and in relation to the emergent demands on them as academics. The newly emergent South African higher education system, where supervisors are being held accountable for throughput in terms of both numbers and within tight timeframes, where funding, promotion and reward are linked systemically with these has created a system in which supervisors have to exert their agency, making fundamental choices in relation to their own positions, as well as in the interest of their students. Schulze (2012:7) strongly challenges the "dated, power centred ways of providing supervision", yet the system seems to mitigate against resistance. These constraints are emphasised by Mouton, Boshoff and James (2015:21), who conclude that "doctoral supervisors in South Africa conduct their supervision under less than optimal conditions. Increasing numbers, demands for constant monitoring and accountability, the pressure of throughput rates and efficient completion, together with moderate to poor-quality students make for very challenging work".

This chapter explores whether supervisors can, in this constraining context, truly create environments that will allow their students to expand their horizons as indicated above, or indeed develop and enable supervisors to broaden their own supervisory horizons. We therefore sought to systematically examine what it means, respectively, to be a research student at undergraduate and postgraduate levels, a supervisor of research, and an academic in this transforming and transformative nexus of activities. This self-reflection is against the backdrop of a complex and uncertain South African higher education (HE) context that is itself undergoing fundamental and dramatic 'transformation' and review of its identity, purpose and operational assumptions. In reflecting upon these roles and identities, two key questions were in need of answers:

1. To what extent is the personally transformative objective of the research endeavour, suggested and aspired to by the literature, being realised ('Research as transformation')?
2. What effect does the current and ongoing transformation of the HE sector have on the key players *(the authors' research students, their colleagues and the authors themselves)* against the backdrop of seemingly ever-expanding notions of the university research agenda and the role of the academic ('Transformation as research')?

The Teaching Advancement Universities (TAU) Fellowship project was launched in June 2015 and sought to develop a cadre of academics, leaders and mentors across a range of disciplines at various Southern African HE institutions.

The 12-month programme was funded by the Department of Higher Education and Training (DHET) and endorsed by both the Higher Education Learning and Teaching Association of South Africa (HELTASA) and the Council on Higher Education (CHE). As participants in the TAU Fellowship project, we represented six disciplines within the humanities, health and social sciences, with an average engagement in HE teaching and research supervision of approximately 20 years. We sought to answer the key questions through data derived from their respective individual TAU research projects (Figure 20.1); their own critical self-reflection on their identities as academics, and their experiences as research supervisors and researchers within the broad academic role.

Over a number of 'think aloud' brainstorming reflections, we recognised that the link across the five individual projects lay in the interconnected triad of the student, the supervisor and the research process itself, and the rich and nuanced interplay of personal identity, agency, resources, and shifting notions of 'outcome' or goal. To answer key questions, we recognised that the rich and varied data gathered from the individual projects could be harnessed effectively by individual and collective reviews through the conceptual lens of Activity Theory (AT). This theory is briefly described in the next section.

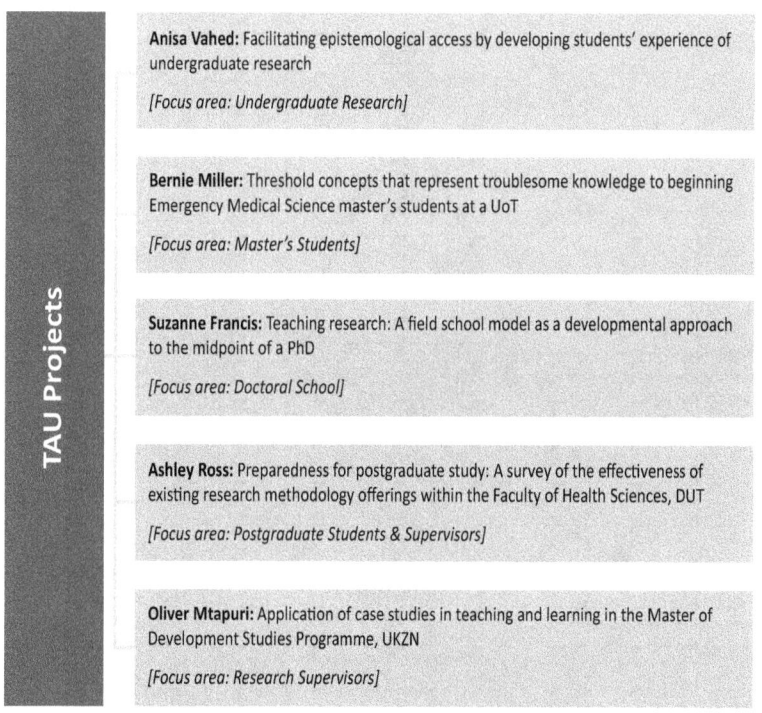

FIGURE 20.1 Individual projects

A BRIEF OVERVIEW OF THE ACTIVITY THEORY SYSTEM

Engestrom (2015) popularised AT using the concept of a collective *activity system*, as depicted by the familiar triangular model in Figure 20.2. The interactive elements of this third-generation activity system are the subject *(the person being studied)*; the object *(the intended activity)*; tools or mediating artefacts *(includes instruments, signs, language, machines and computers, among other things, by which the action is to be executed)*; rules *(sets of conditions that help to determine how and why individuals may act, and are a result of a social conditioning)*; division of labour *(which provides for the distribution of actions and operations among a community of workers)*; and community. Essentially, the relationship between the subject and the object of activity is mediated by a tool. Transforming the object into an outcome requires various tools such as computers, software, methods, ideas, procedures, the Internet, paper and pen. The relationship between the subject and the community is mediated by rules. Rules in this study consisted of university practices and policies, working hours, and working regulations, among other things. The relationship between the object and the community is mediated by the division of labour, that is, how the activity is distributed among the members of the community. Within the context of this study, this related to the power wielded by each TAU participant within the TAU community and the tasks for which they were responsible.

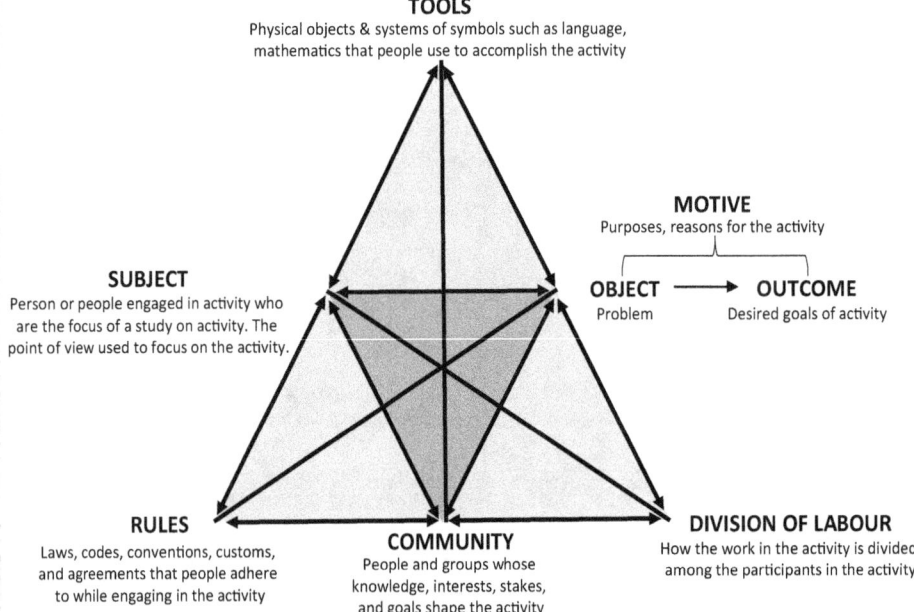

FIGURE 20.2 Activity Theory (Adapted from Engeström 2015)

The study on which this chapter draws was therefore aimed at analysing the rich data gathered and reports on what it means to be a research student at both undergraduate and postgraduate levels, as well as being a supervisor and an academic in a transforming academic environment.

RESEARCH DESIGN AND METHODOLOGY

An exploratory and descriptive qualitative approach was utilised and a case study research design was followed. As Creswell (2014:14) points out, case study research designs are used in many fields as they are particularly useful for developing an "in-depth analysis of a case, often a program, event, activity, process or one or more individuals". We obtained ethical clearance from our respective institutions. The rich data gathered from the individual TAU projects were analysed using Engeström's (2015) activity system as a heuristic device. The AT lens was used to analyse the *dialectic relationship between subject and object*, together with the systemic tensions that cannot be directly observed. The dynamic interrelated activities within the individual projects formed the system of activities. Consequently, the components of several activity system triangles emerged.

Trustworthiness of the qualitative results was enhanced by adhering to the principles of credibility, confirmability, transferability and dependability (Cohen, Manion & Morrison 2007). Credibility was maintained through frequent peer scrutiny. This meant that we, the authors, who are researchers and supervisors, were involved in reviewing and discussing the richness of the data gathered from our respective projects during TAU contact sessions and *ad hoc* meetings. Multiple methods such as individual interviews, focus groups, reflective reports and observations used to collect data across the individual projects further maintained the credibility of the findings. The aforementioned overlapping methods used to collect data, together with an in-depth description of all the data collection processes across individual projects enhanced the dependability, confirmability and transferability of the findings.

FINDINGS AND DISCUSSION

As illustrated in Figure 20.3, two AT systems emerged from the TAU projects where the main findings mapped the dialectic relationship between the subject and the object of activity mediated by tools (Figure 20.4). In Vahed's project (Figure 20.1), undergraduate students declared that the various teaching methods such as using EndNote, Turnitin, reading and writing workshops co-taught by academic development practitioners, role-playing exercises and playing educational games enabled them to gain access to and acquire the various research discourses. Significantly, students emphasised that having their research lecturers as well as academic development practitioners formatively assess their research through draft submissions of their proposals and reports increased their confidence and nurtured their writing skills. Arguably, the challenge of framing a research idea and the successive redrafting is truly new for undergraduate students, especially as they are expected to make the transition to an independent mode of study.

The research project at an undergraduate level is more likely to be the first time a student is expected to adopt an autonomous role as a researcher, which is different from their previous experiences where their work is driven mainly by their lecturer. Hence, introducing an academic development component into the teaching of undergraduate research, and conducting formative assessments on the various research tasks effectively facilitated undergraduate students' agency as they became more knowledgeable and focused. The more recent work conducted by Vahed and Cruickshank (2017) supports this observation. Essentially, their study addresses the issues of under-preparedness at undergraduate level.

CHAPTER 20 • RESEARCH AS TRANSFORMATION AND TRANSFORMATION AS RESEARCH

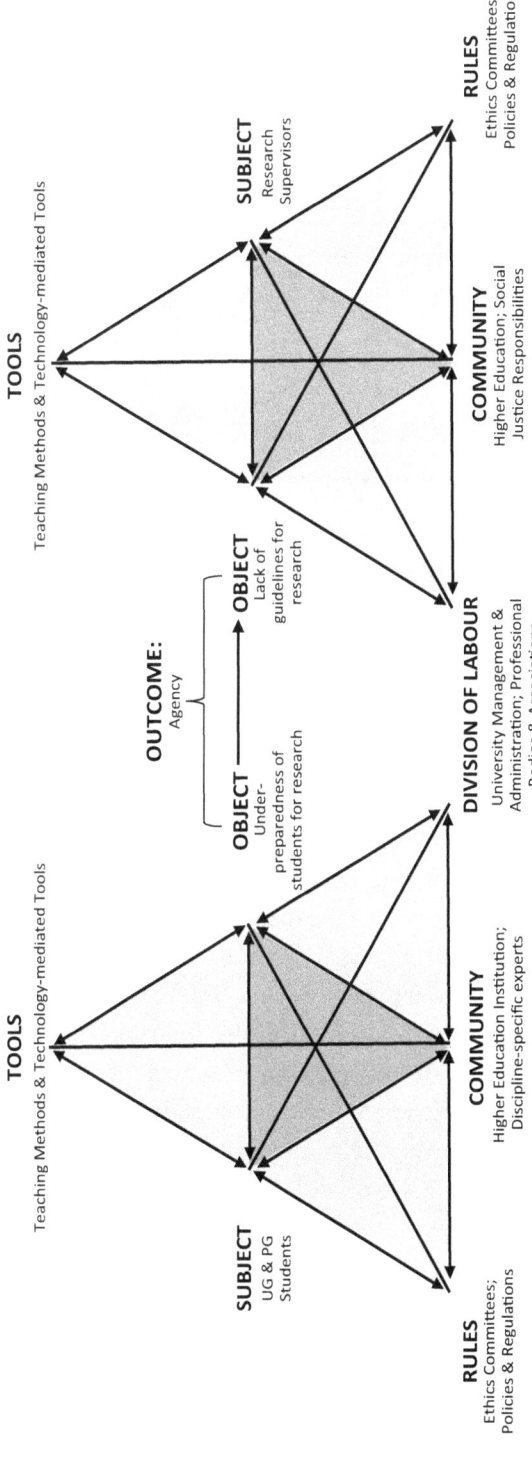

FIGURE 20.3 Activity systems of the TAU projects (Adapted from Engeström 2015)

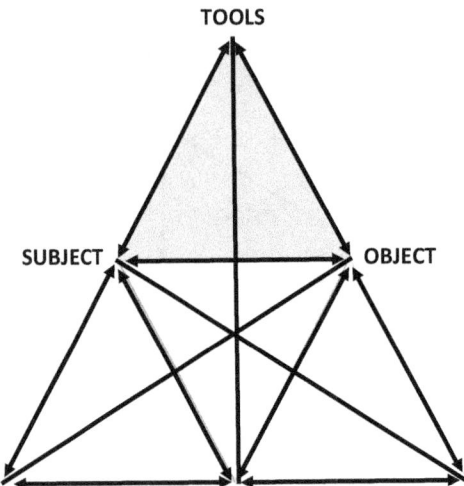

FIGURE 20.4 Sub-activity triangle of the dialectic relationship between the subject and object of activity mediated by tools

While the focus at undergraduate level is on curriculum and structured input, this is less evident in the South African postgraduate context. Some of the projects, however, included formal postgraduate teaching components and indicated that their mediating tool was teaching through case studies (Mtapuri's project in Figure 20.1), research methodology courses and workshops (Ross's project in Figure 20.1). Case studies present opportunities to analyse, interrogate, question and even disrupt preconceived notions through a dialogic peer conversation, while enriching and enabling the sharing of individual and group experiences through brainstorming. At universities, where knowledge production and co-production are foci of the academe, trans-disciplinarity, multi-disciplinarity, inter-disciplinarity and cross-disciplinarity require unpacking to enable research to produce outcomes, which is unlikely in a single disciplinary context. Case studies facilitate this multi-layered engagement. This aligns with the argument by Forsgren, Christensen and Hedemalm (2014) that case studies invoke reflection allowing for 'experiencing' reality and its complexity by bringing situations to life. Within the case studies, novel, unique and innovative vistas were provided, which empowered students to seek new knowledge and to shift their conceptual understanding.

In contrast, dis-embedded disciplinary methodology courses and workshops were sometimes felt to be less successful and needed to be aligned with faculty. Preliminary observations, regardless of the specific departmental preparatory offering, revealed that the period of exposure to new research concepts was brief; conceptually and informationally dense with insufficient time for exploration of meaning within the references of the specific discipline. Nevertheless, students emphasised the personal nature of the supervisor–student relationship and expressed high levels of personal satisfaction with their own learning and personal development under their supervision. The transformative impact of research engagement for both supervisor and student was identified as one of the most critical and rewarding aspects of the postgraduate research endeavour. For supervisors, case studies require them to step back, creating spaces for students to actively engage and develop their voice and confidence. Consequently, the traditional power and authority positions of supervisors are relinquished, while through reflection, supervisors may come to recognise new ways of engagement and a different view of themselves, opening new horizons for practice.

In addition, and as affirmed by Vahed's project (Figure 20.1), undergraduate students' active engagement with their individual research projects was significantly shaped and enhanced by their relationship with the research supervisors, who were passionate, dedicated, caring and effective communicators. These findings are consistent with Healey *et al* (2014), Azila-Gbettor, Mensah and Kwodjo (2015), Woolderink, Putnik, Van der Boom and Klabbers (2015) and Voelkel, Mello and Varga-Atkins (2016). Similarly, and as revealed in Millar's project (Figure 20.1), postgraduate students declared that their agency was enhanced by having supervisors who were available, approachable and supportive, and who maintained open lines of communication. Students therefore requested a more directive approach to be taken by the supervisor, while others requested a more dialogic interaction. In turning Archer's (2007) socialist realist lens on the student–supervisor relationship, the concepts of structure, culture and agency apply. By structure is meant social structures such as relationship, university and curriculum, where there is interplay between structure and agency. By culture is meant the ideas ("logical propositions that may be either contradictory or complementary") (Zeuner 1999), which individuals or groups hold, and which effect agency. 'Agency' may be regarded as the emergent power that individuals or groups possess which causes them to act. There is usually interplay between structure, culture and agency.

There is little doubt that the student–supervisor relationship is an example of the interplay between structure, culture and agency (Archer 2007), which is pivotal to the ontological aspects of learning, that is, to enable an actionable pathway to being a master's student. In other words, both the student and the supervisor bring their own agency and culture into the structure, that is, the supervision relationship, and it is in the interplay of these elements that transformation (for example transformation of student identity from undergraduate to postgraduate researcher) emerges or does not emerge, that is, the ontological aspects of being a master's student. This interplay between structure, culture and agency may or may not effect transformation in the supervisor too, depending on the supervisor's culture, that is, set of ideas held about what constitutes supervision and how this is affected by the interplay with structure, that is, the supervisory relationship, which leads to the emergence of agency. In this research project, the supervisors concerned experienced positive transformation as a result of this interplay.

Structure, culture and agency impact differently upon master's students because each brings his or her own subjective experiences and objective situation into the master's programme. The emergence of personal powers varied among students, which led to some being more enabled to make the transition into postgraduate studies than others. Importantly, the relationship between structure, culture and agency that each student experiences appears to link strongly to Meyer and Land's (2003) notion of threshold concepts. These concepts are a kind of gateway, or liminal space, to transformative understanding through which a student must pass in order to achieve understanding and learning within a formulated curriculum. A threshold concept is recognised as a key concept within a discipline or field, which students must grasp in order to move to deeper levels of learning. This leads to troublesome knowledge: knowledge that is conceptually difficult, counter-intuitive or 'alien' (Land, Meyer & Flanagan 2016). Engaging with the identified threshold concepts as tools of the research process leads to epistemological and ontological transformation and the transition into *becoming* and then *being* a master's student.

Notably, master's students seem to have a troubled identity because on the one hand they are confident and take pride in being research students, yet on the other hand many of them feel stressed and anxious. This indicates that their personal powers have emerged differently. While considering themselves as emerging scholars with feelings of being productive and confident, they also find it difficult to establish their own identity as scholars because they do not realise and/or accept how much reading there is to do, and how much clear thinking and writing is required. Thus a disconnection manifests between their identity and their ontological access into masters' studies. University of Technology students further expressed that there is a wide gap between the Bachelor of Technology (BTech), which is their only experience of prior research, and a master's research project. A critical point deserving of mention is that attempts have been initiated to reduce the aforementioned disjuncture, such as introducing research in the lower undergraduate programme, as further elaborated by Vahed and Cruickshank (2017).

The shift into PhD work requires a further identity and conceptual leap. The doctoral students in Francis's project spent two weeks in the southern Kalahari in a San (or First Nations) community. The field-school was structured around ten themed days that consisted of morning workshops, afternoon field work and evening problem-solving and writing sessions. Through this, two key mediating artefacts emerged. First, the environmental context was purposefully selected to be both a 'safe space' yet disarming for everyone, no matter the narrative that people brought with them. The San of the southern Kalahari is one of the most marginalised communities. The transformative power of the field-school is located in the ideological, historical and political context of a fluid and shifting fieldwork encounter.

As the field became the driver of what the students were to do and to achieve each day, the bigger purpose of an African research agenda for humanity emphasised the bigger reason for the PhD. As the social conditioning of the students (rules) began to change, the intended activity or object (students more invested in the PhD completion, greater research capacity) began to become more evident as the transformed subject became more invested in the community. In this case, this was represented through their realisation of their broader humanity and real life purpose (Figure 20.5). It was shown that problem solving in a socially, economically, developmentally, politically and ethically sensitive context builds real agency.

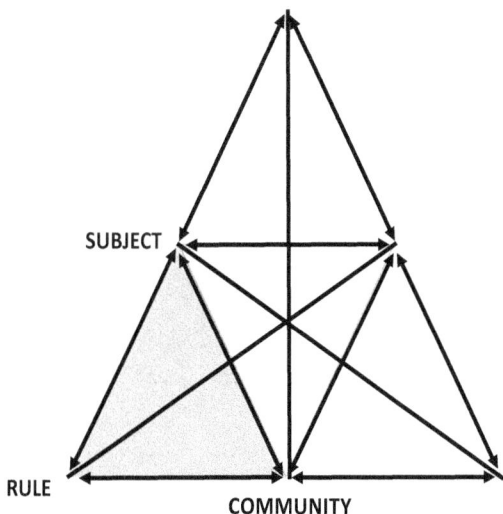

FIGURE 20.5 Sub-activity triangle of the dialectic relationship between the subject and community of activity mediated by rules

In attaining individual academic outcomes, the community and the division of labour faded in and out of focus within the evolving activity system. For example, in grappling with the issues that informed their projects, the TAU participants engaged with the challenges of developing as researchers, primarily as supervisors and as postgraduate teachers (agency). Their epistemic assumptions, or subject position, impacted on the type of tools they used to teach, which in turn influenced how they acted on the object of activity. Moreover, the authors had to deal with their broader identities of not just *being* academics but of engaging in a process of perpetual *becoming*, with conflicting responsibilities in the higher education arena (community) and whose influences bring to bear on the object. As researchers themselves, lecturers, administrators, as well as individuals with their own values and beliefs, they confronted the social and academic systems (division of labour) that not only constrained their choices but also offered them opportunities to assert their own agency (Figure 20.6). Ultimately, supervisors acknowledged that they became more equipped to defend their ontological position and to revise it in light of new knowledge and experiences. Consequently, there was a gradual transfer of agency to the students. After all, as is the case in this study: "The journey that we walk is better walked with others in order to harness the power to individually and collectively imagine and innovate unbounded; and with hindsight we know better" (Vahed, Ross, Millar, Mtapuri & Francis 2016).

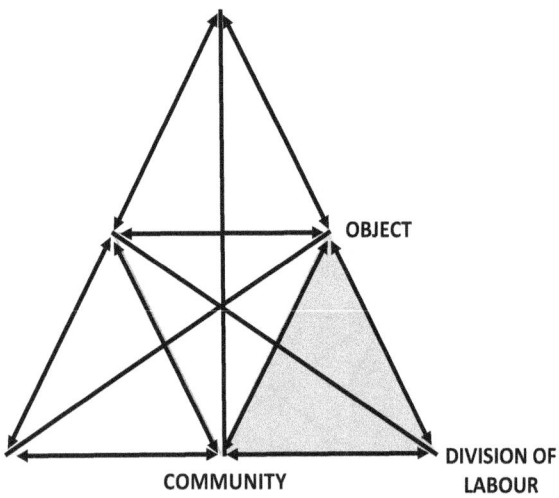

FIGURE 20.6 Sub-activity triangle of the dialectic relationship between the object and community of activity mediated by division of labour

As an embodiment of the key questions themselves, the journey of research as the subject of research and as transformative agent served as a catalyst for earnest self-reflection on our personal identities; our challenges and affirmations within our professional and academic contexts; and the meaning of the Fellowship process in our individual and collective journeys of growth and transformation. As a collective, we recognised that despite our different professional identities, the idiosyncrasies of our respective universities, and our respective roles as researchers and supervisors of research, our journeys and experiences within the higher education landscape had converged upon a shared point of identification: we were all 'schizodemics' (Figure 20.7).

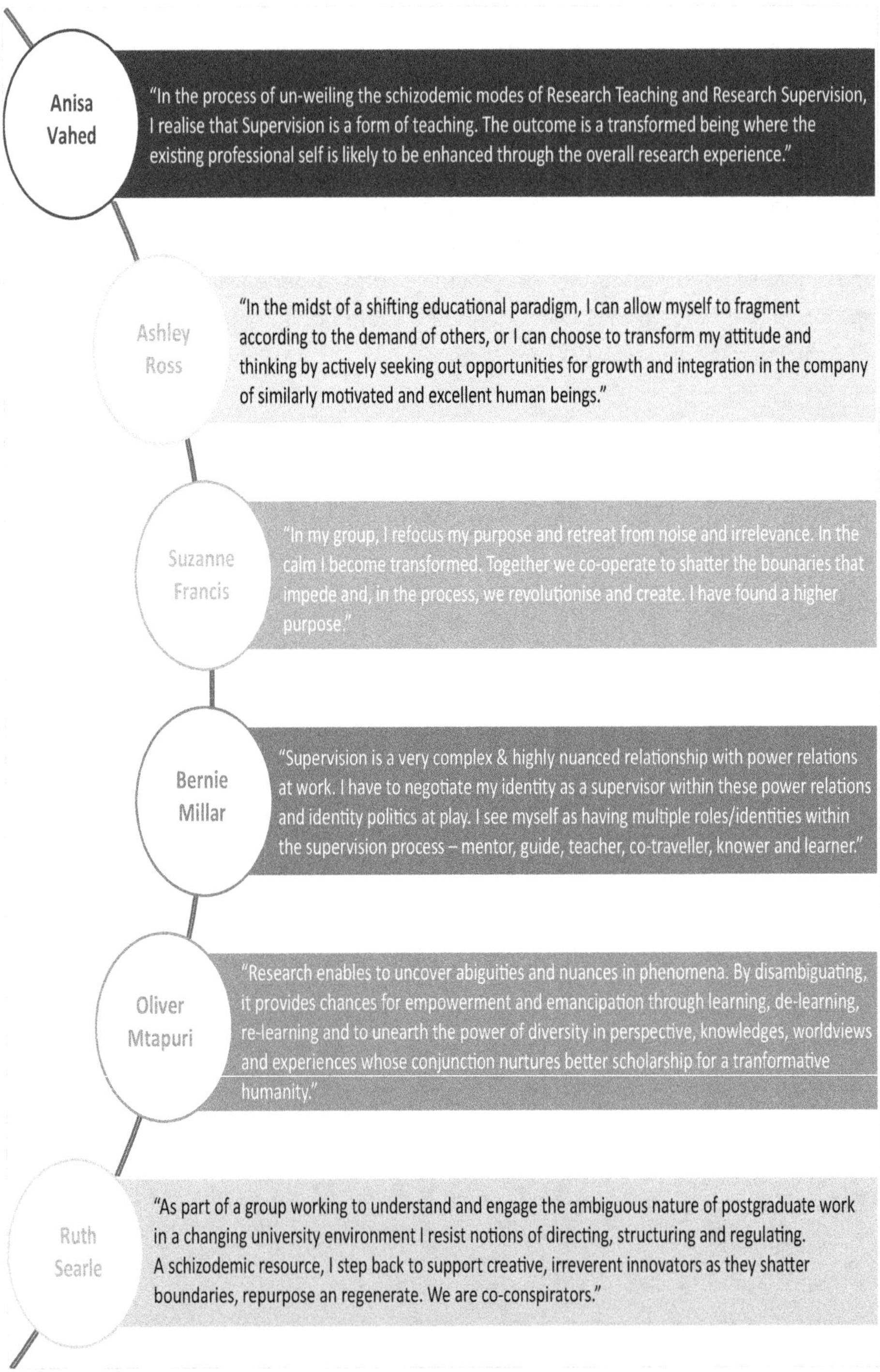

Anisa Vahed: "In the process of un-weiling the schizodemic modes of Research Teaching and Research Supervision, I realise that Supervision is a form of teaching. The outcome is a transformed being where the existing professional self is likely to be enhanced through the overall research experience."

Ashley Ross: "In the midst of a shifting educational paradigm, I can allow myself to fragment according to the demand of others, or I can choose to transform my attitude and thinking by actively seeking out opportunities for growth and integration in the company of similarly motivated and excellent human beings."

Suzanne Francis: "In my group, I refocus my purpose and retreat from noise and irrelevance. In the calm I become transformed. Together we co-operate to shatter the bounaries that impede and, in the process, we revolutionise and create. I have found a higher purpose."

Bernie Millar: "Supervision is a very complex & highly nuanced relationship with power relations at work. I have to negotiate my identity as a supervisor within these power relations and identity politics at play. I see myself as having multiple roles/identities within the supervision process – mentor, guide, teacher, co-traveller, knower and learner."

Oliver Mtapuri: "Research enables to uncover abiguities and nuances in phenomena. By disambiguating, it provides chances for empowerment and emancipation through learning, de-learning, re-learning and to unearth the power of diversity in perspective, knowledges, worldviews and experiences whose conjunction nurtures better scholarship for a tranformative humanity."

Ruth Searle: "As part of a group working to understand and engage the ambiguous nature of postgraduate work in a changing university environment I resist notions of directing, structuring and regulating. A schizodemic resource, I step back to support creative, irreverent innovators as they shatter boundaries, repurpose an regenerate. We are co-conspirators."

FIGURE 20.7 'Schizodemics' – the transformed beings

Schizodemics are passionate but confused, somewhat disillusioned and overburdened scholars, who are required by an increasing managerial and 'box-ticking' university system to pursue excellence in many and diverse academic roles. Each of these roles is complex and nuanced in its own right, and they are required to juggle these in an unending switching of hats: from independent researcher, to undergraduate teacher, to administrator, to research supervisor, to committee member, to academic leader, to self; and all that is important outside of the university. Within a 'model' in which there is an increasing number of 'rules' (university imperatives, review committees, administrative 'hoops'), and increasingly stretched and inaccessible 'tools' (methodological discord between supervisor and student researcher, pedagogical imperatives and an increasingly technological *zeitgeist*), schizodemics are burdened under an undue 'division of labour'. They are assumed to be competent as research supervisors through the mere completion of their own PhD, and are thrust into complex power relationships and identity politics in which research expert/ mentor/ guide is conflated with discipline expert, teacher extraordinaire, academic head and administration obsessive. The schizodemic seeks to 'offset' the systemic tension by attending supervision courses, and engages in frequent and (self-) critical self-reflection: WHO am I? How can I do all these things better? Do I have to do it ALL? What are the consequences if I do not do it ALL, or do it differently? Is THIS why I'm an academic?

As schizodemics and participants in the TAU Fellowship project, we also came to recognise that we are in fact both 'subject' and 'object' within the research supervision endeavour (Figure 20.3). The external 'tension' of the system may be reduced by the shared journey, by the exchange of passion and ideas and through the 'community' of equally rebellious, equally tired and stretched, and equally passionate schizodemics. The TAU fellowship programme brought together autonomous reflectors within a communal space whose projects reflected their individual concerns and interests as they found or created agency within their context (Archer 2007). Through the mists and shifting boundaries within HE emerged the transformed beings with new horizons: we are not required to know it all, or even to know more. We are not everything to everyone. We are partners, travellers a little further along the road than those we supervise. We need to develop the agency of those we supervise. We need to hold our passion within our grasp and to focus on what is really important and what feeds our souls. Why are we REALLY academics? While we retreat from the inanity and dispassionate box-ticking that the university has become, we feed ourselves on the enlightenment and transformation that comes from our unrestrained and sincere engagement with fellow schizodemics. We CAN be excellent teachers

AND excellent researchers. We CAN be passionate knowledge creators and good human beings. We just need to keep still and listen ...

CONCLUSION

Within the current context of flux, research emerged as both object and agent of transformation of personal and collective identity, agency and access (both epistemologically and ontologically). It has long been acknowledged that engaging in research and PhD studies in particular engenders substantive changes in students. This being a highly transformative process is obvious, and highlighted in particular by Millar's work on conceptual thresholds. Moving into the research space substantively changes the learning process, requiring different ways of thinking and placing the individual in greater control of the activity, of the knowledge and of the writing. It requires that researchers be prepared to have their ideas, knowledge and perspectives challenged, to try and take on new visions in relation to situations. Shifts in epistemology and recognising the multifaceted ways of 'coming to know' challenges identities and values, thereby constantly creating transformations. Beginning this at undergraduate level, as Vahed explores, and Ross extends in his interrogation of preparedness, ensures that better prepared students move into the postgraduate sector with different mind-sets. In dealing with postgraduates, and allowing them the space to develop new understandings and challenge assumptions, the work of Francis, Millar and Mtapuri show the need to create spaces for development.

As the supervisors grappled with preparedness through exploring the interface between undergraduate and postgraduate study, they had to ensure that as supervisors they understood the stumbling blocks and liminal spaces in order to devise ways to assist. Through working to develop understandings and skills at the undergraduate level; by assisting conceptual development and epistemological engagement in coursework; or by disturbing the taken-for-granted assumptions through engaging with unfamiliar contexts and understanding ourselves, each grappled with their own threshold moments. It is clear that they, too, undergo substantive changes with each engagement, confronting different challenges that each student presents. The more invested the supervisor, the greater the change. Out of the mist of engagement emerges the transformed being.

REFERENCES

Archer MS. 2007. *Making our way through the world. Human reflexivity and social mobility.* Cambridge: Cambridge University Press. https://doi.org/10.1017/CBO9780511618932

Azila-Gbettor EM, Mensah C & Kwodjo SM. 2015. Challenges of writing dissertations: Perceptual differences between students and supervisors in a Ghanian polytechnic. *International Journal of Education and Practice,* 3(4):182-198. https://doi.org/10.18488/journal.61/2015.3.4/61.4.182.198

Cohen L, Manion L & Morrison K. 2007. *Research methods in education.* London & New York: Routledge Taylor & Francis Group.

Creswell JW. 2014. *Research design: Qualitative, quantitative and mixed methods approaches.* Los Angeles: SAGE.

Elgar FJ. 2003. *PhD completion in Canadian universities: Final report.* Halifax, Nova Scotia, Canada: Dalhousie University.

Engestrom Y. 2015. *Learning by expanding: An activity-theoretical approach to development research.* New York: Cambridge University Press.

Forsgren S, Christensen T & Hedemalm A. 2014. Evaluation of the case method in nursing education. *Nurse Educ Pract,* 14(2):164-9.

Francis S. 2016a. *Teaching research scholarship: A field-school model as a developmental approach to the mid-point of the PhD project report.* Durban, South Africa: HELTASA/CHE.

Francis S. 2016b. Teaching for PhD retention. Teaching and Learning Conference. Chester: University of Chester:

Francis S. (n.d). Pedagogies of the PhD: Transforming the mid-point through the principles of space, access and critical consciousness. (Article under review.)

Golde CM. 2005. The role of the department and discipline in doctoral student attrition: Lessons from four departments. *The Journal of Higher Education,* 76(6):669-700. https://doi.org/10.1353/jhe.2005.0039

Healey M, Jenkins A & Lea J (eds). 2014. *Developing research-based curricula in college-based higher education.* York, UK: The Higher Education Academy.

Healey M, Jordan F, Pell B & Short C. 2010. The research-teaching nexus: A case study of students' awareness, experiences and perceptions of research. *Innovations in Education and Teaching International,* 47(2):235-246. https://doi.org/10.1080/14703291003718968

Kyvik S & Olsen TB. 2014. Increasing completion rates in Norwegian doctoral training: Multiple causes for efficiency improvements. *Studies in Higher Education,* 39(9):1668-1682. https://doi.org/10.1080/03075079.2013.801427

Land R, Meyer JHF & Flanagan MT. 2016. *Threshold concepts in practice.* MA Peters (ed).: Rotterdam: Sense Publishers. https://doi.org/10.1007/978-94-6300-512-8

Meyer J & Land R. 2003. *Threshold concepts and troublesome knowledge: Linkage to ways of thinking and practising within the disciplines.* Edinburgh: University of Edinburgh.

Mouton J, Boshoff N & James M. 2015. A survey of doctoral supervisors in South Africa: Leading article. *South African Journal of Higher Education,* 29(2):1-22.

Nulty D, Kiley M & Meyers N. 2009. Promoting and recognising excellence in the supervision of research students: An evidence-based framework. *Assessment & Evaluation in Higher Education*, 34(6):693-707. https://doi.org/10.1080/02602930802474193

Schulze S. 2012. Empowering and disempowering students in student-supervisor relationships. *Koers – Bulletin for Christian Scholarship*, 8: 18-32.

Shephard K, Trotman T, Furnari M & Löfström E. 2015. Teaching research integrity in higher education: Policy and strategy. *Journal of Higher Education Policy and Management*, 37(6):615-632. https://doi.org/10.1080/1360080X.2015.1102823

Spronken-Smith R, Mirosa R & Darrou M. 2013. 'Learning is an endless journey for anyone': Undergraduate awareness, experiences and perceptions of the research culture in a research-intensive university. *Higher Education Research & Development*, 33(2):355-371. https://doi.org/10.1080/07294360.2013.832169

Vahed A & Cruickshank G. 2017. Integrating academic support to develop undergraduate research in dental technology: A case study in a South African University of Technology. *Innovations in Education and Teaching International*, 1-9.

Vahed A, Ross A, Millar B, Mtapuri O & Francis S. 2016. Research as Transformation and Transformation as Research: TAU PosterTeaching Advancement at University (TAU) 2015/2016: Durban, South Africa: HELTASA/CHE. https://doi.org/10.1080/14703297.2017.1279068

Voelkel S, Mello LV & Varga-Atkins T. 2016. Supporting students during their undergraduate research projects using audio recordings. *Innovations in Education and Teaching International*, 1-8. https://doi.org/10.1080/14703297.2016.1263233

Woolderink M, Putnik K, Van der Boom H & Klabbers G. 2015. The voice of PhD candidates and PhD supervisors. A qualitative exploratory study amongst PhD candidates and supervisors to evaluate the relational aspects of PhD supervision in the Netherlands. *International Journal of Doctoral Studies*, 10: 215-235. http://ijds.org/Volume10/IJDSv10p217-235Woolderink0852.pdf https://doi.org/10.28945/2276

Zeuner L. 1999. Review essay: Margaret Archer on structural and cultural morphogenesis. *Acta Sociologica*, 42(1):79-86. https://doi.org/10.1080/00016999950079961

SPACES, JOURNEYS, NEW HORIZONS — WHERE ARE WE NOW AND WHERE DO WE WANT TO GO?

Cally Guerin

Research supervision and researcher education continue to evolve as universities and governments influence and respond to changing social, political and economic conditions. These changes mean that research agendas are made possible by factors outside the disciplines in which they sit, just as much as new knowledge is born out of the current state of each discipline. Research supervision operates within this context, answering the demands of the institutions in which they are located, as well as the current needs of disciplinary directions. Those disciplines also interact with each other and with the world beyond, especially if they are to remain vibrant and relevant. In thinking about the spaces, journeys and new horizons of research supervision, this book has explored some of the current concerns preoccupying our research community, and opened up conversations about where we might want to go in future.

Academic research thrives on interactions across disciplines and with the world outside the academy. While we are right to be wwary of the audit culture and 'impact agenda' that drives the measurement of research in ways that may also impact negatively on academic freedom and the advancement of blue-sky or theoretical research, university research does need to engage with the world beyond academia. I firmly believe that doctoral research has an important role in contributing to the public good and making the world a better place. Keeping an eye on being useful while allowing space for creativity is one way of doing just that. Universities, perhaps especially those that are publicly funded, are not an end in themselves; rather, they are at the service of the wider societies in which they sit. In countries like South Africa, where universities have a mandate to build research capacity, the research agenda must necessarily focus on the public good; university research is expected to play a pivotal role in developing and facilitating the social, economic and cultural vision of the nation and its people.

The boundaries surrounding universities need to be permeable, making space for new ideas and ways of doing research to move into and out of the academic world. Innovative forms of funding and data collection are successfully crowdsourcing the resources for academic research from outside the university system (Osimo, Priego & Vuorikari, 2017; Silberzahn & Uhlmann 2015), and citizen science is advancing knowledge in conjunction with university projects (Cooper, 2017). Rigorous, ethical research is working across the boundaries between the academic world and wider society. Research into postgraduate supervision needs to ask: What is the relationship between university research and research that happens in spaces outside universities – in industry, in government, in non-government organisations – that is, the places in which the vast majority of our graduates find employment? The importance of this relationship plays out in the chapters here by Ortega & Kent, and by Goneos-Malka. The radar charts provided by Spronken-Smith, Brown and Mirosa provide further insights into the graduate attributes that doctoral graduates use in their work both inside and outside universities.

As researchers into this sector of higher education, we need to keep asking questions about what we are doing, why we are doing it that way, and whether there are more effective ways of doing research supervision. Research supervision today is performed against a background of ever-increasing demands and diminishing resources. Wherever we are situated – in South Africa, in Australia, in the northern hemisphere – supervisors are expected to do more with less: supervising more students and of greater diversity, producing more publications with higher impact, and creating more output that engages with the world beyond the university, but supported with fewer staff, smaller budgets and less time in which to deliver high-quality research. The collection of essays in this book demonstrate that there is a thriving community of researchers reflecting on the issues facing supervisors and candidates, critiquing current practices and behaviours, and offering viable alternatives for understanding research supervision. Our research at this meta-level is designed to influence how researchers are educated, and the results then filter down to how research is conducted in all disciplines.

This book has provided an enticing array of ways into thinking about the pressing issues we face in this space of research supervision and researcher education. Of particular interest is the range of theoretical approaches adopted – these give us new ways to think about the issues, revealing blind spots and blank spots that can

CODA • SPACES, JOURNEYS, NEW HORIZONS – WHERE ARE WE NOW AND WHERE DO WE WANT TO GO?

help us ask new questions and create new practices leading to better outcomes. For example, cultural historical activity theory and relational theory are used to shed light on community research learning (Grant); activity theory is employed to highlight how identities are transformed through the experience of research (Vahed et al.) and to inform understanding of cohort supervision (Winberg & Winberg); and the social integration model and its context-specific modifications help us better understand how to achieve timely completions of dissertations (O'Neil and Dos Santos). After reminding us of the huge range of theories from Social Sciences, Humanities and Education used in doctoral education research, Hopwood adds the insights of practice theory to bring further insights to our attention.

Research supervision is always situated in an international space – I write from my desk at the University of Adelaide in South Australia, geographically isolated from my peers in South Africa, the UK, Europe, North America and elsewhere. Yet I feel thoroughly connected with researchers around the world who share my concerns and fascination with the questions facing research supervision in the 21st century. Of course our work is inflected by the situated specificities of local university and national policies and priorities, but at the same time we look to see where this research fits with what's happening in our disciplines around the globe. It makes sense for us to meet at conferences like Postgraduate Research Supervision and to publish research from around the world in a book like this one – our work is global and can't rest in isolation from what everyone else is doing. The chapters in this volume on originality (Frick), on thesis writing (Bitzer, Trafford & Leshem), on conception of research (Rule & Naidoo), and on examination (Du Preez & Simmonds) point to shared concerns that draw on data from specific locations but help us understand researcher education internationally. Smith and McGloin remind us that academic mobility is having a powerful impact on how research is conducted at doctoral level all around the globe.

Research supervision also – necessarily – occupies a digital space in today's universities. We still see hard copies of research materials and thesis drafts with comments hand-written by supervisors, but much of the work itself is conducted online: literature searches, statistical analyses, survey instruments, email and skype communication between supervisors, candidates and study participants, research writing, data storage, and the list goes on. Access to reliable, high-speed internet remains less ubiquitous, though, and feeds into inequalities in researcher education more generally. 'Power' (in the senses of both political and electrical) remains central to digital futures, and consequently the opportunities to build research capacity and lead research and innovation internationally.

Traversing this territory requires research literacies that include digital competency, and also critical awareness of the social and cultural implications of research. In the simplest form, research literacies include the ability to read and understand others' research methods and findings; to interpret the ways in which this information is presented in written and oral forms; to assess such information critically; and to undertake and write an account of such research in the forms appropriate to the particular context (Badenhorst & Guerin, 2016). But more than straight forward skills, a literacies approach includes understanding the social, cultural and political connotations of these activities, as Bastalich reminds us in this volume. It engages with questions such as: what questions can be asked in this context, and who is allowed to ask those questions? What knowledge will be valued, and what will be dismissed as irrelevant? And underlying this critical awareness are decisions about whether to conform, transform or resist dominant discourses.

Journeys of and through research supervision are often bumpy and convoluted for both supervisors and candidates. The transformative education that takes place during doctoral education has implications for the personal and public identities that emerge. As well as the mental health issues that Wisker and Robinson explore in this book, the tangled relationships with supervisors (Mansfield & Purcell) and the strength to be gained from a positive psychology approach (Henning), we need to manage the complex mix of desire, fantasy and faith that accompanies entry into and exit from the world of academic research. For supervisors, this includes an understanding of their own identities in this context (Botha), and the identity challenges for academic staff working across disciplines when they move into research degrees in teaching and learning (Leibowitz, Wisker & Lamberti). Pyhältö takes this further, reminding us that what happens during candidature has important implications for where our graduates work on completion of their degrees.

Many of our current questions about the most effective forms of research supervision in the current climate are still to be answered, and others will emerge as we continue our work. It is right that the doctorate and research supervision are constantly under interrogation – this facet of Higher Education hasn't stood still since its inception, and the creation of knowledge is never a static project. As we peer into the distance of the new horizons for our research while reading and reflecting on this collection of essays, many new questions will continue to emerge. This constant questioning is partly what makes research supervision such a dynamic and exciting field.

REFERENCES

Badenhorst, C., & Guerin, C. (Eds.). 2016. Research literacies and writing pedagogies for masters and doctoral writers. Leiden, Netherlands: Brill.

Cooper, C. 2017. Citizen science: How ordinary people are changing the face of discovery. London: Gerald Duckworth & Co.

Osimo, D., Priego, L.P., & Vuorikari, R. 2017. Alternative research funding mechanisims: Making funding fit for Science 2.0. In A. Esposito (ed.), Research 2.0 and the Impact of Digital Technologies on Scholarly Inquiry. Advances in Knowledge Acquisition, Transfer, and Management Book Series. IGI Global, Hershey, PA.

Silberzahn, R., & Uhlmann, E. L. 2015. Many hands make tight work: Crowdsourcing research can balance discussions, validate findings and better inform policy. Nature, 526(7572), 189-192. https://doi.org/10.1038/526189a

NOTES ON CONTRIBUTORS

Dr Wendy Bastalich is a research education lecturer in the Teaching Innovation Unit at the University of South Australia where she works with doctoral students and supervisors. She has written about doctoral programs and supervision, and the impact of policy and regulatory atmospheres on research education and the social sciences and humanities.

Eli Bitzer is Emeritus Professor of higher education at Stellenbosch University. His interests are in promoting postgraduate education, supporting research excellence, the training of novice supervisors and postgraduate student advising.

Nonnie (MM) Botha is Emeritus Professor in the Faculty of Education, Nelson Mandela University, South Africa. She served the academic community in various management positions and in several institutions, mainly in postgraduate education. Her masters' and doctoral research supervision and scholarly publications include topics such as higher education mergers, research trends, Africanising university curricula, inter-culturalism and postgraduate pedagogies, policies and practices. She facilitates workshops on these topics and does contract work for universities and other entities.

Kim Brown is a finishing PhD candidate at the University of Otago, whose doctoral research is investigating what collegiality looks like in a doctoral environment. Her research interests include doctoral education, sustainability education in a tertiary environment, and community-engaged learning and teaching.

Carla Dos Santos obtained her Master's degree in Industrial Psychology at the University of Pretoria. The focus of her research relates to time to completion of master's mini-dissertation students. Her master's study was awarded the 'Best master's dissertation' in 2017, and was presented at two national conferences. Her fields of interest are Human Resource Development and Organisational Behaviour.

Petro du Preez is an Associate Professor (North-West University) and Extraordinary Professor (TUMA University, Tanzania). Her research focuses on curriculum studies and higher education. She has supervised 13 masters and doctoral studies. Her forthcoming, co-edited book is '*A scholarship of doctoral education: On becoming a researcher*'. Petro is Editor-in-Chief of 'Transformation in Higher Education'.

Prof Suzanne Francis is a HELTASA TAU Fellow and Honorary Associate Professor (University of Kwa-Zulu Natal), twice awardee of the Vice-Chancellor's Distinguished Teaching Award, lecturer (University of Chester), and Fellow of the Higher Education Academy. She publishes on African Politics, Conflict and Peace Studies, pedagogies of the PhD, diagnostic assessment and transformational teaching.

Liezel Frick is Director of Centre for Higher and Adult Education and Associate Professor in Higher and Adult Education at Stellenbosch University. Her research focuses on creativity in doctoral education and doctoral pedagogy. She has successfully supervised masters and doctoral graduates, published various articles and book chapters related to this topic. She is also involved in various projects related to doctoral education and early career researcher development.

Dr Amaleya Goneos-Malka holds a PhD in Marketing Management, and is enrolled for a second PhD that addresses customer experience in e-commerce through artificial intelligence. She has been an integral part of the African marketing and communication industry, working with the world's leading marketers and brands; and has won several prestigious local and international awards.

Callie Grant is an Associate Professor and Head of Educational Leadership and Management at Rhodes University, South Africa. Her research interests include distributed leadership, teacher leadership and learner leadership as well as school resilience. She is also interested in higher education studies, particularly as it relates to teaching, learning and knowledge-building, doctoral education and post-graduate supervision practices. She also enjoys teaching courses on qualitative research methods.

Cally Guerin has worked as a lecturer in literary studies, cultural studies and gender studies, as an academic editor and as a teacher of English language. Since 2008 she has been employed at the University of Adelaide in the area of researcher education, delivering programs for doctoral candidates and their supervisors. Her interest in establishing collaborative research cultures is reflected in her co-authorship of research papers with students and colleagues on the topics of doctoral supervision, research writing and academic identities. Cally is a founding co-editor of the *DoctoralWriting* blog.

Sanchen Henning is a research psychologist and Associate Professor at UNISA Graduate School of Business Leadership. She researches the fields of leadership and organisational behaviour as well as research methodology. She is both passionate and curious about the psychodynamics of work and the conscious and unconscious forces that bind individuals, teams and organisations together. In her research she mainly favours system psychodynamic theory, positive psychology and complexity theory.

Nick Hopwood is Associate Professor at the School of Education, University of Technology Sydney. He is also Extraordinary Professor at Stellenbosch University, Department of Curriculum Studies. He has completed a number of projects relating to doctoral education, and coordinates Higher Degrees by Research in the School of Education at UTS. Nick has won several awards and special commendations for his work supporting research students within his home university, through direct engagement overseas, and via his blog and YouTube channels.

Julia D. Kent is Vice President of Best Practices and Strategic Initiatives at the Council of Graduate Schools. She has conducted research on a broad range of topics in graduate education, including PhD careers pathways; diversity and inclusion; international collaborations; and professional doctorates.

Pia Lamberti has worked for eighteen years in higher education development. In her current capacity as the Head of Research Capacity Development in the University of Johannesburg's Postgraduate School she oversees a programme that offers postgraduates and academic staff across the faculties opportunities to develop as researchers or supervisors.

Brenda Leibowitz was an NRF SARCHi Chair: Post School Education and Training (PSET) in the Faculty of Education at the University of Johannesburg. She was Professor and lead researcher (South Africa) for the ESRC-NRF Funded Research project Southern African Rurality in Higher Education (SARiHE). She was also convenor of the Southern African Universities Learning and Teaching (SAULT) Forum. She sadly passed away in 2018.

Shosh Leshem is Professor of Education at Oranim Academic College of Education and Kibbutzim Academic College, Israel. She was Head of Teacher Education for 8 years and senior lecturer at the Advanced Studies Faculty. She has been a visiting lecturer in many universities in Europe and South Africa conducting workshops for doctoral students, doctoral supervisors and examiners. She has published extensively on a wide range of topics in the field of education. Her current fields of interest are doctoral education, supervision, mentoring, language acquisition and teacher education.

Nick Mansfield is the Dean of Higher Degree Research at Macquarie University in Sydney. He has responsibility for the quality of the university's research training programs, both in terms of academic outcomes and student experience.

Dr Bernie Millar is a HELTASA TAU (Teaching Advancement at University) fellow and senior lecturer in the Curriculum Development Unit at the Cape Peninsula University of Technology (CPUT). Her research interests include Critical Realism, Multilingualism in Higher Education, Teaching and Learning in Higher Education. She has delivered numerous papers on these interests at conferences.

Romain Mirosa is Surveys Manager at the University of Otago and Chair of the Association for Tertiary Education Management (ATEM) in New Zealand. His research interests include graduate outcomes, institutional research and tertiary education management.

Prof Oliver Mtapuri is a HELTASA TAU Fellow and professor in Development Studies at the School of Built Environment and Development in College of Humanities at the University of Kwa-Zulu Natal, Durban, South Africa. His areas of research interest include poverty, redistribution and inequality, community-based tourism, public employment programmes, research methodologies, climate change and project management.

Dr Jaqueline Naidoo is a lecturer in the School of Education at the University of KwaZulu-Natal. Her postgraduate teaching focuses on research discourses and methodology, teacher identities and teacher development. She has published in the areas of teacher development, HIV & AIDS education, teacher emotions and narrative methodology.

Sumari O'Neil is a senior lecturer at University of Pretoria. She has completed a PhD in the field of Industrial and Organisational Psychology, focussing on postgraduate research supervision. Her research interests are within the fields of management education with specific focus on postgraduate research learning and the application of qualitative methodology.

Suzanne T. Ortega has been President of the Council of Graduate Schools, an organization of approximately 500 universities that grant master's and doctoral degrees in the US and Canada since 2014. She has served in a variety of senior academic roles at US universities.

Kirsi Pyhältö (PhD) is Professor of Educational Sciences in the Faculty of Educational Sciences at the University of Oulu, and research director in the Centre for University Teaching and Learning, at the University of Helsinki. Her research interests include doctoral education and researcher careers (see more https:// researchondoctoraleducation.wordpress.com/)

Sally Purcell is the Manager of the Higher Degree Research Professional Skills Development Program at Macquarie University. She has extensive experience in Human Resources and careers development at a number of Australian universities.

Gillian Robinson is an Emeritus Reader at Anglia Ruskin University, UK. She has publications in postgraduate students' learning, cross-cultural supervision and threshold concepts, based on research derived from running an international PhD programme for 12 years, and in Art and Design Education. Gillian is a practicing artist with exhibitions in the UK, Japan, Cyprus and Israel.

Prof Ashley Ross is a HELTASA TAU Fellow and the Deputy Dean, Faculty of Health Sciences at Durban University of Technology. He has been engaged in research supervision for 20 years, and has successfully supervised over 50 dissertations and theses in a range of health disciplines. Prof Ross has presented papers, workshops and seminars in a range of national and international settings.

Peter Rule is an Associate Professor in the Centre for Higher and Adult Education at Stellenbosch University. He has published in the areas of adult education, dialogue and learning, and case study methodology. His most recent book,' Dialogue and Boundary Learning' came out in 2015.

Dr Ruth Searle has worked in academic development and the area of higher education for many years. Her interests cover various areas of teaching, learning and curriculum with a special focus on the supervisor within the postgraduate arena. She was an advisor on the TAU programme

Shan Simmonds is Associate Professor of Curriculum Studies at the North-West University and a member of the Edu-HRight research unit (Education and Human Rights in Diversity). Shan's areas of research are higher education, curriculum studies, and human rights education. She is the associate-editor for the journal Transformation in Higher Education.

Dr Rebekah Smith McGloin is Director of the Doctoral College and Centre for Research Capability Development at Coventry University. Her current role focuses on the development of people and the implementation of systems and structures to support growth in research activity; from postgraduate researcher to professor.

Rachel Spronken-Smith is a Professor of Higher Education and Geography, and Dean of the Graduate Research School at the University of Otago, Dunedin, New Zealand. She is Chair of the New Zealand Deans and Directors of Graduate Studies. Her research interests include doctoral education and undergraduate research and inquiry.

Dr Anisa Vahed is a HELTASA TAU fellow and a senior lecturer/dental technologist in the Department of Dental Sciences, Faculty of Health Sciences at DUT. Her research interests include metallographic structure of newly developed dental materials, teaching and supervision of undergraduate and postgraduate research, and epistemological access through discipline-specific games.

Professor Christine (Chris) Winberg holds the South African National Research Foundation Chair in Work-integrated Learning and leads the Work-integrated Learning Research Unit in the Education Faculty of the Cape Peninsula University of Technology in Cape Town, South Africa. Chris' research area is professional and vocational education (with a particular focus on engineering education), the professional development of university teachers and technical communication.

Dr Simon Winberg is a lecturer in the Department of Electrical Engineering at the University of Cape Town, South Africa. He worked in the embedded systems industry in both South Africa and in the USA prior to becoming an academic staff member at UCT. His research interests are engineering education and high performance computer systems for the acceleration of scientific computing applications.

Gina Wisker is Professor of higher education and contemporary literature and Head: Centre for Learning and Teaching, University of Brighton, UK. She is also academically affiliated to the University of Johannesburg and Stellenbosch University, South Africa. Her research interests are in learning and teaching, and postgraduate study and supervision. She has published several books on postgraduate education and is chief editor of the SEDA journal *Innovations in Education and Teaching International,* a Principal Fellow of the Higher Education Academy, a senior fellow of SEDA and a National Teaching Fellow.

www.ingramcontent.com/pod-product-compliance
Lightning Source LLC
Chambersburg PA
CBHW080406230426
43662CB00016B/2335